MW00782931

Managing the Insider Threat

No Dark Corners

Managing the Insider Threat

No Dark Corners

Nick Catrantzos

CRC Press
Taylor & Francis Group
Boca Raton London New York

CRC Press is an imprint of the
Taylor & Francis Group, an **informa** business

CRC Press
Taylor & Francis Group
6000 Broken Sound Parkway NW, Suite 300
Boca Raton, FL 33487-2742

© 2012 by Taylor & Francis Group, LLC
CRC Press is an imprint of Taylor & Francis Group, an Informa business

No claim to original U.S. Government works

Printed in the United States of America on acid-free paper
Version Date: 20120123

International Standard Book Number: 978-1-4398-7292-5 (Hardback)

This book contains information obtained from authentic and highly regarded sources. Reasonable efforts have been made to publish reliable data and information, but the author and publisher cannot assume responsibility for the validity of all materials or the consequences of their use. The authors and publishers have attempted to trace the copyright holders of all material reproduced in this publication and apologize to copyright holders if permission to publish in this form has not been obtained. If any copyright material has not been acknowledged please write and let us know so we may rectify in any future reprint.

Except as permitted under U.S. Copyright Law, no part of this book may be reprinted, reproduced, transmitted, or utilized in any form by any electronic, mechanical, or other means, now known or hereafter invented, including photocopying, microfilming, and recording, or in any information storage or retrieval system, without written permission from the publishers.

For permission to photocopy or use material electronically from this work, please access www.copyright.com (http://www.copyright.com/) or contact the Copyright Clearance Center, Inc. (CCC), 222 Rosewood Drive, Danvers, MA 01923, 978-750-8400. CCC is a not-for-profit organization that provides licenses and registration for a variety of users. For organizations that have been granted a photocopy license by the CCC, a separate system of payment has been arranged.

Trademark Notice: Product or corporate names may be trademarks or registered trademarks, and are used only for identification and explanation without intent to infringe.

Library of Congress Cataloging-in-Publication Data

Catrantzos, Nick.
   Managing the insider threat : no dark corners / Nick Catrantzos.
       p. cm.
   Includes bibliographical references and index.
   ISBN 978-1-4398-7292-5 (hbk. : alk. paper)
   1. Corporations--Security measures. 2. Employee crimes--Prevention. 3. Sabotage in the workplace--Prevention. I. Title.

HD61.5.C37 2012
658.4'73--dc23   2012001242

Visit the Taylor & Francis Web site at
http://www.taylorandfrancis.com

and the CRC Press Web site at
http://www.crcpress.com

Contents

Foreword   xvii

Preface   xix

Author   xxi

PART I   DIAGNOSTICS

Chapter 1   The Problem and Limits of Accepted Wisdom   3
             Introduction   3
             The Problem   4
             Terms of Reference   4
             Historical Approaches   5
                 Types of Studies on Hostile Insiders   5
                 Studies Focusing on Motivations   6
                 Studies Focusing on Compilations and Cases   7
                 Studies Focusing on Cyber Insiders and More Controls   8
                 Losing Sight of Existential Threats by Aggregating Cases Too Liberally   8
                 Limits of Cyber-Centric Bias   9
             Implications   9
             Questions for Online or Classroom Discussion   10
             Exercises for Group Projects   10
             Endnotes   10
Chapter 2   New Research and Contrarian Findings   15
             Delphi Research on Insider Threat   15
                 Initial Research Findings Confirming Accepted Wisdom   17
             Alternative Analysis Takes Shape   18
                 Why Infiltrator vs. Disgruntled Careerist?   18
                 Infiltrator's Challenges vs. Defender's Capacity   20
                 Infiltrator Step 1: Get through Screening   21
                 Infiltrator Step 2: Gather Information   22
                 Infiltrator Step 3: Exploit Vulnerabilities   24

The Alternative   24

Balancing Trust and Transparency: The Copilot Model   26

    Contrast with Traditional Strategy   27

    New Insider Defenses   28

        Close Probation   28

        Transparency on the Job   28

        Team Self-Monitoring   29

Comparison with Other Security Strategies   29

Questions for Online or Classroom Discussion   32

Exercises for Group Projects   32

Endnotes   33

PART II   KEY PLAYERS

Chapter 3   Agents of Change—Corporate Sentinels   39

Key Activities   39

Corporate Sentinels   41

    Traditional Role   41

    Expertise and Alienation   41

    Sentinel Alienation   44

    Perfunctory Adaptation   44

    Imperial Overreach or Power Play   44

    Cronyism or Favor Exchange   45

    Transformational Role in a No Dark Corners Approach   45

    A Sentinel's Guide to People Security   46

    Human Relationships   46

    The Dishonest Employee   47

    Management Responsibility in Loss Prevention   47

    Procedural Controls   47

    Pre-Employment Screening   48

    Personal Safety and Self-Defense   48

    Workplace Violence   49

    Unfair Labor Practices   50

    Security and Civil Rights   51

    Conclusion   53

Questions for Online or Classroom Discussion   55

Exercises for Group Projects   55

Endnotes   56

Chapter 4   Agents of Change—Leaders and Copilots   57

            Leadership's Attitude to Sentinels and Insider Threat Defenses   58

            Where to Begin   59

                Know Your World   59

                Start Somewhere   61

                At Least Ask   61

            Why Leaders Falter   62

            The Issue–Attention Cycle Meets Insider Threats   63

                Phase 1: Pre-Problem   63

                Phase 2: Alarmed Discovery   64

                Phase 3: Awareness of Difficulties   64

                Phase 4: Gradual Decline of Public Interest   65

                Phase 5: Post-Problem   65

            Alternative Approach   67

                Another Opportunity: Rotational Assignments   69

            Questions for Online or Classroom Discussion   71

            Exercises for Group Projects   71

            Endnotes   71

PART III   MAKING A DIFFERENCE

Chapter 5   Rethinking Background Investigations   75

            Introduction   75

            Traditional Background Investigation Process   76

            Identity Verification   77

            What Gets Investigated and How   77

            Credentials and Credibility   78

            Where Blurred Accountability Comes with a Price   79

            Other Red Flags Often Unseen   80

            Adjudication of Adverse Findings   80

            Transformational Opportunities with a No Dark Corners Approach   81

                Making a Team Out of Warring Camps   81

                Alternative Process: Adjudication by Team vs. Fiat   82

                Resolving Differences   82

                Ramifications for the Entire Process   83

                Who Should Perform the Background Investigation?   83

            Case Study: A David Takes on Goliath in Pre-Employment Background
            Investigations   84

	The Setting	84
	All-Find's Approach	84
	Pro-Back's Approach	85
	Business Outcome	85
	Conclusion	86
	An Overlooked Problem: Investigating the Nonemployee	86
	Access the Real Issue	87
	Questions for Online or Classroom Discussion	91
	Exercises for Group Projects	91
	Endnotes	91
Chapter 6	**Deception and the Insider Threat**	**93**
	Introduction	93
	Deception's Role	93
	Inadequacy of Defenses	94
	Representative Methods for Detecting Deception	95
	What Do Polygraph Examiners Know about Deception?	95
	The Reid Technique	96
	Background	96
	Key Features	97
	Limitations	97
	The WZ Method	98
	Background	98
	Key Features	98
	Limitations	98
	Scientific Content Analysis	101
	Background	101
	Key Features	102
	Limitations	102
	Other Techniques for Detecting Deception	102
	Cross-Examination	103
	Background	103
	Key Features	103
	Limitations	103
	Behavioral Detection	104
	Background	104
	Key Features	105
	Limitations	106

Contents

ix

The Deceiver's Edge 106
What Makes a Good Liar 107
No Dark Corners Applications 107
   Interrogation 108
      Application 109
   Debriefing 109
      Application 109
   Interviewing 110
      Application 110
   Conversation 110
      Application 111
   Elicitation 111
      Application 111
Where to Expect Deception from Trust Betrayers 111
The Infiltrator's Deception 112
   Deceptions Possible in Screening Process 112
      Possible Indicators 112
   Deceptions Possible during Probation Period 114
      Possible Indicators 114
   Deceptions Possible after Probation While Seeking Vulnerabilities 115
      Possible Indicators 115
The Disgruntled Insider's Deception 116
   Deceptions Possible in Screening Process 116
      Possible Indicators 116
   Deceptions Possible during Probation Period 116
      Possible Indicators 116
   Deceptions Possible after Probation While Seeking Vulnerabilities 117
      Possible Indicators 117
The Detection Dilemma 118
Context-Based Anomaly Detection 119
At Least Ask 121
Know Your World 121
Start Somewhere 121
The What-If Discussion 122
Sample Scenarios 122
   Core Cast 122
   Scenario 1: A Bad Feeling Early On 122

	Questions to Explore	124
	Scenario 2: A Rising Tide of Concern	125
	Questions to Explore	127
	Deception's Role in Scenarios	128
	Questions for Online or Classroom Discussion	129
	Exercises for Group Projects	129
	Endnotes	129
Chapter 7	**Lawful Disruption of the Insider Threat**	**135**
	Introduction	135
	What Is Lawful Disruption?	135
	Defender Dilemmas	138
	Three Biases of Authorities That Risk Undermining the Institution	139
	Prosecutorial Bias	139
	Investigative Bias	141
	Intelligence or Need-to-Know Bias	141
	Deciding How Far to Go	143
	Risks in Failure Analysis and Problem Solving	144
	Representative Options: What Defenders Can Do Themselves	146
	Changes That Increase Perceived Effort for the Desired Attack	146
	Changes That Increase Perceived Risk for the Attacker	147
	Changes That Reduce the Anticipated Yield of the Attack	148
	Changes That Alter the Insider's Guilt or Justification for Attacking	148
	Techniques of Lawful Disruption by Employee Level	149
	Leader Disruptions	150
	Corporate Sentinel Disruptions	150
	Team Member Disruptions	151
	Techniques Based on Exploiting Disruptive Behaviors Already in the Workplace	152
	The Tank	153
	Description	153
	Disruption Value	153
	The Sniper	153
	Description	153
	Disruption Value	153
	The Grenade	154
	Description	154
	Disruption Value	154

The Know-It-All   154

   Description   154

   Disruption Value   154

The Think-They-Know-It-All   154

   Description   154

   Disruption Value   154

The Yes Person   155

   Description   155

   Disruption Value   155

The Maybe Person   155

   Description   155

   Disruptive Value   155

The Nothing Person   155

   Description   155

   Disruptive Value   155

The No Person   155

   Description   155

   Disruptive Value   155

The Whiner   156

   Description   156

   Disruptive Value   156

The Layered Offense   156

   Core Cast   156

   Scenario 1: Disrupting a Suspected Infiltrator   156

   Discussion   159

   Scenario 2: Disrupting an Insider Threat of Workplace Violence   160

   Discussion   162

   Scenario 3: Disruption Taking an Unexpected Turn   163

   Discussion   164

   Scenario 4: Disruption at the Top   165

   Discussion   167

Comparative Observations   167

Practice   168

A Distress Call and Unpredicted Turn of Events   169

   Problem   169

   Response   169

   Disruptions   170

Potential Outcomes   170

Sequence of Actual Outcomes   171

Lessons Learned   172

Questions for Online or Classroom Discussion   172

Exercises for Group Projects   172

Endnotes   173

Chapter 8   Existential Insider Threats   175

Introduction   175

First Things First   175

Protecting People and Property   176

Defender's Advantage in Dealing with Infiltrators   177

Spillover Effects from Defending against Existential Insiders   177

The Big Three Existential Insider Threats   178

Sabotage with Cascading Impacts   178

Decapitation Attacks through Assassination   182

Espionage Yielding Decisive Victory   183

Problems of Threshold and Accumulation   183

Aligning Existential Threat Defense with the DHS   186

What Makes It an Existential Threat?   187

Assistance with Evaluating Existential Magnitude   188

DHS Protective Security Advisors   188

Local Task Force Entities with a Protective Mandate   191

Red Teaming Defined   196

Where to Recruit Red Team Members   197

Red Teaming Value to Countering Existential Insider Threats   201

Red Team Members from Within   203

Drawing from the Risk or Vulnerability Assessment Team   203

Red Teaming More for Existential than Nonexistential Threats   204

Worse Case and Worst Case Scenarios   206

When Red Team or Special Resources Are Not an Option   206

Avoiding Warning Fatigue   207

Recommended: The Software Developer Approach   208

Conclusion   209

Questions for Online or Classroom Discussion   209

Exercises for Group Projects   210

Endnotes   210

Chapter 9   Other Insider Threats   215

Introduction   215

Cyber Attacks—Insider or Other Threats?   216

Threats of Violence   218

   Domestic or Intimate Violence   218

   Threats on the Job   218

Exploiting Employer Assets for Gain   219

   Financial Gain   219

   Self-Aggrandizement   224

Unifying Themes and Need for a Systematic Approach to Lesser Insider
Threats   226

The Threat Scale   227

Application of Threat Scale to Insider Threats by Category   230

   Scale for Cyber Attacks   230

     0: Nuisance Level   230

     1: Escalating Irritation   231

     2: Chronic, Active Disruption   231

     3: Unacceptable, Proximate Harm   232

   Scale for Threats of Violence   232

     0: Nuisance Level   232

     1: Escalating Irritation   233

     2: Chronic, Active Disruption   234

     3: Unacceptable, Proximate Harm   234

   Scale for Exploiting Assets for Gain   235

     0: Nuisance Level   235

     1: Escalating Irritation   235

     2: Chronic, Active Disruption   236

     3: Unacceptable, Proximate Harm   236

Special Cases   237

   Sympathizers   237

   Lynch Mobs, Flash Mobs, and Overwhelming Crowds   238

   Citizen Unrest and Uprising   240

   Sporting Event Mayhem   241

   Undermining Contemporaries   241

   Prodigal Kin   242

   Misguided Redeemers   243

Fleeting or Occasional Insider Threats—A Nebulous Category of Others 244

Extortion as Another Indirect Threat 246

Lessons of One-Off Cases 246

Implication of Changing Workplace Dynamics for Insider Threats 247

The Shamrock Organization as Incubator for No Dark Corners 247

A Final Caution: Instant Intimacy and Insider Threats 249

Conclusion 250

Questions for Online or Classroom Discussion 251

Exercises for Group Projects 251

Endnotes 252

Chapter 10   Consulting for No Dark Corners Implementation 257

Introduction 258

The Inside–Outside Dilemma 258

Recommended: Outside Diagnosis, Hybrid Prescriptions, Internal Implementation 261

Institutional Insertion Points for a No Dark Corners Program 262

Sudden Impact Response 262

Postmortem Redesign 263

Strategic Anticipation 265

Application Opportunities for No Dark Corners Consulting 266

Where to Begin 267

Consultant's Role 269

Objectives and Resources 270

Metrics 270

Value 271

Fees, Compensation, and Effectiveness 271

Making Change Happen 272

Pilot Programs 273

Exemplars 273

Engaging 101: Some Features of Starting a No Dark Corners Assignment 274

Delivering 101: Some Ways of Navigating a No Dark Corners Assignment 277

Findings 101: Common Findings to Expect in a No Dark Corners Consulting Engagement 280

Disengaging 101: Drawing the Assignment to a Close 281

The Laser and the Flashlight 283

Checking the Flashlight's Bulb and Battery 284

	Conclusion	285
	Questions for Online or Classroom Discussion	286
	Exercises for Group Projects	286
	Endnotes	287
Chapter 11	**Answer Guide**	**289**
	Chapter 1	289
	Chapter 2	291
	Chapter 3	294
	Chapter 4	298
	Chapter 5	301
	Chapter 6	303
	Chapter 7	305
	Chapter 8	307
	Chapter 9	310
	Chapter 10	313
	Endnote	315
Appendix A:	Three Rounds of Delphi Questions	317
	A. Delphi Round 1 Questions	317
	B. Delphi Round 2 Questions	317
	Part I: Ratings	317
	Part II: Questions for Your Reaction and Comment	318
	Part III: Scenarios and Related Questions	319
	C. Delphi Round 3 Questions	320
	Rating Question	321
	Countermeasures	321
Appendix B:	Summary of Delphi Round 1 Findings Accompanying Round 2 Questions	323
	Thoughts from Delphi Round 1	323
	Analysis	324
Appendix C:	Summary of Delphi Round 2 Findings Accompanying Round 3 Questions	327
	Highlights of Delphi Round 2	327
	Part I	327
	Part II	327
	Part III	327
	Overall	328

Appendix D: Delphi Expert Comments and Stories   329

             A. Transparency: Pushing Out Management Data   329

             B. Two-Person Rule   330

             C. A Business Decision to Favor Infiltrators   330

             D. Small World Insider Challenges   330

             E. Why No "Broken Windows" in Infrastructure Defense   330

Index   333

Foreword

When conflict is a question of force against force, options are simple. Victory goes to the side that has the bigger numbers, the better weapons, or superior maneuvering capability. But what happens when the real danger comes from within? Insider threats scare all of us because we can never be sure that we are so strong, so fast, or so powerful that one well-placed betrayer cannot cost us everything. This book examines precisely this challenge of our age, the insider threat, and how to defend against it.

Nick Catrantzos and I trace our collaboration to the 1990s, when Nick worked on one of my consulting engagements for a major information powerhouse. The latter came to me after spending tens of millions of dollars to anticipate an upcoming crisis situation. Somehow, though, corporate leaders had the nagging feeling that they may have missed something. Nick's job became to uncover what they had missed, while my job was to figure out how to do this on a limited budget, with an impending deadline, and on an uneven corporate landscape where not all departments involved in the project were on the same page. Between the two of us, Nick and I found that the Achilles' heel here was that various departments were not communicating with each other and were thus more likely to duplicate, collide, or fail when the actual crisis came. In a sense, the client had adequately defended against outsider threats without realizing how vulnerable the organization was from within. This, to me, offered a revealing insight into insider threats and how they crop up in the best of organizations. The story ended well, but we had our moment of truth in telling the bad news to the client. To the latter's credit, they eventually asked me to send Nick to visit their headquarters after they had taken our recommendations to heart and started bringing their various departments to work together in crisis simulations and regular drills. In short, they brought their talented people out of the dark corners into the light of shared purpose and collaboration. And they were proud of this—even to the point of showing off in front of us. In my mind, this little consulting engagement epitomizes what Nick's No Dark Corners approach is all about.

Since this consulting involvement, Nick went on to study the conventional wisdom on insider threats as a topic for a master's thesis. The findings from his social sciences research surprised him. Why is it that more controls do not work? Why does overreliance on specialized security functions—called corporate sentinels—frequently end up being counterproductive? Why don't some standard insider defenses like background investigations expose hostile trust betrayers? These are some of the questions answered in *Managing the Insider Threat: No Dark Corners*.

This book begins with a CliffsNotes version of Nick's insider threat research and ends with a thought-provoking examination of what it takes to advise an organization on how to institute the No Dark Corners approach to insider threat defense, whether by launching it internally or through outside, consulting resources. As I have learned in more than 25 years of international consulting, sometimes where an organization stands on an issue depends on where its advisers sit. Some entities accept, welcome, and insist on keeping certain engagements entirely in-house. Others have to go outside not only for objectivity but also to avoid the awkwardness of exposing certain doubts and vulnerabilities to underlings or rivals in the same organization that they have to work with on a routine basis. So this last chapter on consulting resonates particularly well with me.

In between the research findings and the last chapter, though, Nick presents some fascinating contrarian ideas about issues such as

- Why infiltrators are more likely to be the more serious danger to an organization than ordinary, disgruntled employees
- How deception plays a role in every kind of insider threat, from the most serious, existential threat to the kind of nuisance that just makes life more difficult on the job
- How the smart leader and resourceful organization have more options than most realize, particularly when it comes to using tactics of lawful disruption to thwart hostile trust betrayers

This is just a small sample of what awaits the reader of this book. The reader will find that this work taps a multitude of sources and the author's expertise in offering new insights into how to deal with the kind of threat every professional fears and, sooner or later, must face. This book demystifies the insider threat, making solutions accessible to any professional, not just to specialists. The No Dark Corners approach gives all of us a chance to take a hand in our own protection. Written intelligently, supported analytically, and filled with useful case studies and examples, this book is destined to become a classic in taking a holistic approach to solving a very vexing predicament. I hope you enjoy it as much as I did.

James E. Gordon
Managing Director
Navigant Consulting
Hong Kong, 2011

Preface

An enemy launching a frontal attack can be anticipated and repulsed. An adversary who attacks from within, however, is not so readily countered. This book began as a study seeking to identify defenses against trust betrayers who were targeting critical infrastructure. It then evolved into a thesis that earned top writing honors at the Naval Postgraduate School[1] and into a subsequent article in the peer-reviewed journal *Homeland Security Affairs*.[2] Bolstered by further research commissioned by a professional security industry association, the work next migrated into an industry research report, *Tackling the Insider Threat*,[3] samplings of which reappear in this book in Chapter 10 in edited form, with the permission of the ASIS Foundation. This book now synthesizes the findings of these preceding works, building upon them to explore the insider threat in some of its different dimensions and to present interpretive methods for applying No Dark Corners strategies to contend with real-world insider trust betrayal as an existential and non-existential threat.

Using a Delphi method, this work harvested insights of experts from mature arenas of defense against insider threats, such as workplace violence and counterespionage, in order to assist with defending against the insider threat to critical infrastructure. Findings uncovered flaws in institutional defenses that adversaries can exploit, with infiltrators posing a greater threat than disgruntled insiders. Resulting recommendations ran counter to accepted wisdom. These recommendations shaped the contours of a No Dark Corners approach that applies and extends seminal theories of Oscar Newman's *Defensible Space* and George Kelling's *Fixing Broken Windows*.

ORGANIZATION OF THE BOOK

The student or practitioner will find this book progressing through three sequential phases of exposition. Part I, Diagnostics, begins with problem definition (Chapter 1) and research findings (Chapter 2) that led to the No Dark Corners strategy for addressing insider threats. With these foundational underpinnings, Part II then shifts gears to examine agents of change, namely, key players in a position to implement or undermine the No Dark Corners strategy, including corporate sentinels (Chapter 3) as well as leaders affecting application of this approach (Chapter 4).

Next, in Part III, the book examines key areas where No Dark Corners–style engagement can make a difference in the way the institution counters insider threats: rethinking background investigations (Chapter 5), recognizing deception (Chapter 6), and lawful disruption (Chapter 7). Continuing a migration from the theoretical to the practical in applying the innovations of No Dark Corners within an organizational framework, succeeding chapters examine application challenges for existential threats and involvement with the Department of Homeland Security (Chapter 8) and for other institutions, such as businesses facing nonexistential insider threats (Chapter 9) that are nevertheless damaging to the enterprise, with both chapters noting particular challenges for representative work environments. The final chapter (Chapter 10) offers a consulting framework for introducing new insider defense insights into organizations and institutions seeking to reduce their exposure to malicious insiders.

Throughout the book, each chapter offers questions to stimulate online or classroom discussion as well as exercises or problems suitable for team projects. After the final chapter, an answer guide follows, although it would be more accurate to label this not so much a list of correct responses as propositions and thoughts to stimulate further inquiry on the part of observers or practitioners.

Appendices at the end of the book present details that some readers might find arcane while others might regard as too abbreviated. The first of these treats the Delphi questions and feedback material used in the original No Dark Corners research (Appendices A to C), so that those wishing to use a similar method of social sciences inquiry can build on and surpass work done to date in a field that has been previously visited but by no means trampled. Another appendix (Appendix D) captures some of the representative, unstructured insights that Delphi respondents offered during the period of inquiry.

No Dark Corners replaces a laser with a flashlight. The laser is the narrow beam of workplace monitoring only by corporate sentinels or security specialists. The flashlight is a broader beam of employee engagement and monitoring on the front lines at the team level. There are no easy answers. No Dark Corners represents one approach to filling the gaps in traditional insider defenses in order to deliver the victory of ownership over surprise.

ENDNOTES

1. N. Catrantzos, *No Dark Corners: Defending against Insider Threats to Critical Infrastructure*, MA thesis, Center for Homeland Defense and Security, Naval Postgraduate School, Monterey, CA, September 2009.
2. N. Catrantzos, "No Dark Corners: A Different Answer to Insider Threats," *Homeland Security Affairs*, Volume VI, Number 2, May 2010. Retrieved May 11, 2011 from http://www.hsaj.org/?fullarticle=6.2.5.
3. N. Catrantzos, "Tackling the Insider Threat," *Connecting Research in Security to Practice*, Alexandria, VA: ASIS Foundation, 2010. Content from *Tackling the Insider Threat* was used with the permission of the ASIS Foundation.

Author

Nick Catrantzos teaches homeland security and emergency management for the School of Management, University of Alaska, Fairbanks. Formerly a security director for a large public utility and critical infrastructure, he previously directed operations for two international security consultancies, Control Risks and Kroll Associates, and led public sector vulnerability assessments under ManTech Security Technologies. In late 2009, he graduated from the Naval Postgraduate School's Homeland Security Master's Program, where he won top writing honors for his thesis on insider threats. As an intelligence collector, he was awarded the Meritorious Service Medal for outstanding service to two government agencies. Subsequently, he safeguarded stealth technology in the defense industry.

Catrantzos first grew interested in insider threats while managing intelligence exploitation of defectors at an overseas location. Subsequently, in the corporate arena during the closing days of the Cold War, he handled the business aspects of defense against hostile intelligence collectors and potential traitors seeking to clandestinely acquire the benefit of advanced American technology. At Lockheed's headquarters he oversaw all background investigations of corporate employees and comanaged the institutional response to an international hostage situation involving staff trapped in a war zone. Later, he developed institutional policies and protocols for handling threats of workplace violence.

Catrantzos first began his involvement with infrastructure defense in 1996, when he briefed the newly formed President's Commission on Critical Infrastructure Protection. He subsequently moved into private-sector security and crisis management consulting, returning to concentrate on public sector vulnerabilities after the events of September 11, 2001.

The sole California representative to serve on three successive federal panels on drinking water infrastructure, Catrantzos was recognized in 2007 with the highest award of the Association of Metropolitan Water Agencies for dedication to security progress that "is a very significant contribution to water systems throughout the country."

Catrantzos has contributed to two industry guidelines, *Facility Physical Security Measures* and *Workplace Violence Prevention and Intervention*, via the American Society for Industrial Security (ASIS) International, and has contributed to ASIS *Security Business Practices Reference* Volumes 2, 3, 5, and 6.

Nick Catrantzos has been a Certified Protection Professional, a licensed investigator, and a certified incident commander. He graduated magna cum laude with a baccalaureate in linguistics and summa cum laude with a master's in security studies with an emphasis in homeland security. He spent many years managing adverse consequences. Now he concentrates on preventing them.

He may be reached via www.NoDarkCorners.com, which links to his blog, http://all-secure.blogspot.com, where he discusses issues of moment.

PART I

Diagnostics

CHAPTER 1

The Problem and Limits of Accepted Wisdom

> The greatest obstacle to discovering the shape of the earth, the continents and the ocean was not ignorance, but the illusion of knowledge.
>
> Daniel J. Boorstin

INTRODUCTION

A frontal attack can be countered through force or maneuver, but a hostile insider attack may do its worst before activating a single defense. All a malicious insider needs to carry out an attack are access to a worthy target, an open door, and a dark corner from which to study and strike. Frontal attacks can be anticipated or met with traditional fortifications whose effectiveness is limited only by resources and imagination. However, attackers operating from within can carry out attacks that are fatal to an organization without requiring an opposing army or sophisticated weaponry. Given sufficient access and license, trust betrayers can be devastating. This we know, because insider threats repeatedly surface as an abiding concern for defenders. Nevertheless, insider threats remain statistically rare, making them more difficult to analyze, defend against, or anticipate.

What do we do about insider threats? Prevailing wisdom recommends doing more: look harder, submit our fellows and ourselves to newer and more microscopic security audits and restrictions, the better to detect our adversaries. How well do such defenses work? At best, results are mixed. At worst, doing more of the same delivers results more promissory than substantive, while alienating the average employee.

This book looks at the insider threat from a multidisciplinary perspective. It reviews the literature on this subject and draws on Delphi research tapping seasoned professionals with broad career experiences. Ultimately, the book arrives at an alternative to prevailing wisdom. That alternative proposes taking institutional defense out of the arcane realm of specialists and distributing the role more widely at the work team level. The proposed approach deputizes coworkers to take a hand in their own protection, as a copilot must be ready to fly a plane if the pilot falters by mischief or misadventure. The resulting team-level engagement leaves fewer places for hostile insiders to elude scrutiny, hence fewer opportunities to prepare and carry out an insider attack.

THE PROBLEM

The insider threat is an Achilles heel for any enterprise or institution targeted for destruction by adversaries. Although risk and vulnerability assessments skyrocketed in the aftermath of 9/11, as reflected in the federal subsidies promoting them, the security focus centered largely on vulnerability to attack of large populations.[1] In this context, adversaries were characterized as traditional attackers working as outsiders who generally approach their targets head on with brute force—precisely in the manner of the 9/11 hijackers.

In this context, the insider threat has generally attained secondary status. One possible reason is that there is a dearth of statistically significant data on hostile insiders. As a review of the current literature indicates, trust betrayal—whether in espionage or other fields—remains statistically rare.[2,3] Where analyzed further, the insider threat has been subordinated to cyber security studies centering on hackers and disgruntled employees, ex-employees, or consultants.[4-6] Although such studies have supplied value and focused attention on the problem, they have offered few solutions other than to advise added scrutiny. Data compiled to date suggest that the vast majority of insider cyber attacks have been either fraud-driven or moderate in scope and impact. In other words, such attacks remain less than devastating to the targeted employer—the modern, electronic equivalent of embezzlement or vandalism.[7] Similarly, such studies preserve their narrow focus by intentionally excluding cases of espionage, while at the same time avowing that the threat remains real and advising ordinary, more-of-the-same solutions such as layered defense.[8] Consequently, it is difficult for security practitioners to derive new insights from cyber-centric insider threat investigations and their attending platitudes. The net result is that today's insider threat remains substantially as it did yesterday: frequently studied retroactively yet seldom yielding practical tools, tactics, or recommendations that would serve a defender in countering the threat.

The overall aim of this research was to identify countermeasures that defenders can use to prevent terrorist attacks via trust betrayers and thereby reduce the vulnerability of critical infrastructure and institutions. The journey to this destination involved applying lessons of experts from other, more mature arenas of defense from insider threats, such as workplace violence, line management, corporate security, and counterespionage. In the course of following this path, the inquiry also sought to answer, "If current indicators and countermeasures fall short, what should we do differently?"

TERMS OF REFERENCE

Throughout this book, the operational definition of *insider threat* is an individual and, more broadly, the danger posed by an individual who possesses legitimate access and occupies a position of trust in or with the infrastructure or institution being targeted. *Hostile* or *malicious insider* and *trust betrayer* also refer to the individual who represents an insider threat, although these two terms focus more attention on the individual than on the phenomenon. *Infiltrator* refers to a subset of hostile insider who sees himself or herself as an adversary before attaining insider status within the targeted infrastructure or institution. The infiltrator joins a targeted employer or group under false pretenses as a means of obtaining sufficient access to facilitate an attack. *Institutions* as used here refer to public and private sector enterprises, employers, entities, and organizations.

This book's focus is on the kind of hostile insider that poses an existential threat to the institution. Accordingly, the foundational research described focuses less on unbounded definitions of insider threat that include malingering or contentious employees or naysayers who may pose a nuisance or cause difficulties for the organization yet stop short of bringing it down to its knees.

HISTORICAL APPROACHES

The body of literature on the insider threat owes its existence to analysts of different areas of focus, as examined and sampled in the sections that follow. Psychological and sociological analyses of those who betray delve into motivations and enabling social contexts. Studies and historical documents related to espionage lean heavily on memoirs, historical compilations, and showcasing of flaws and pitfalls. More recently, emerging concerns over cyber security and susceptibility of critical networks to denial of service attacks have come to the fore in government-sponsored studies on insider threats.

Increasingly, government works appear to subordinate the insider threat to cyber security studies,[9] centering on hackers and disgruntled employees, ex-employees, or consultants who cause damage via computer networks. Although such studies have value, some have also limited their focus by concentrating exclusively on the specialized area of information technology.[10,11] Indeed, in one report to the President, infrastructure experts underscored this danger of focusing too intently on IT:

> Essentially, the threat lies in the potential that a trusted employee may betray their obligations and allegiances to their employer and conduct sabotage or espionage against them. Insider betrayals cover a broad range of actions, from secretive acts of theft or subtle forms of sabotage to more aggressive and overt forms of vengeance, sabotage, and even workplace violence. The threat posed by insiders is one most owner–operators neither understand nor appreciate, and it is a term that is commonly used to refer to IT network use violations. This often leads to further confusion about the nature and seriousness of the threat.[12]

Efforts to develop predictive models to detect and thwart malicious insiders have ranged from a quantitatively based yet unproven formula[13] to broad-based theoretical models designed mainly to predict the triggers that lead an assassin or radical group to take violent action.[14,15] Others focus exclusively on detecting anomalous behavior in hindsight, on the assumption that trust betrayers are disgruntled and detectable by mistakes rooted in character flaws—while standing mute about infiltrators disciplined enough to avoid such mistakes.[16] The literature contains much analysis on the psyches,[17,18] social climates,[19] and cyber vulnerabilities[20,21] associated with malicious insiders. Yet analysis appears more limited when it treats pragmatic lessons and inferential guidance that apply directly to practical countermeasures. However, research on threats from assassins to saboteurs suggests that applicable findings may be adaptable from indirectly related works and may offer more promise in charting a course to defending against the malicious insider who is more dangerous than a computer hacker.[22–24]

Types of Studies on Hostile Insiders

The literature elucidating the insider threat divides into three general categories: individual-centered studies focusing largely on psychological motivations or social context, case study

TABLE 1.1   Insider Threat Categories of Research and Comparative Attributes

	Individual Motivations and Psychosocial Context	Descriptive Compilations, Biographies	Government Cyber or Regulatory Focus
Focus	Insider as deviant Enabling social contexts	Sensational headlines Fatal flaws of defenders	Technology-driven controls Regulatory oversight
Countermeasures	Counseling, early intervention and rehabilitation, workplace hygiene factors	Inferential, i.e., reverse-engineered from finger-pointing at unseen vulnerabilities Awareness programs	Barriers to access, with emphasis on automation Process monitoring Compliance audits and quantitative models
Unaddressed Issues or Gaps	Accounting for why most others matching same profile do not become insider threats	Analytical examination of trends and patterns to contribute to prediction or mitigation	Pragmatic and pervasive solutions vs. narrow recommendations that focus mainly on imposing rules and monitoring compliance

compilations with cases that are anecdotal or biographical, and government-sponsored studies focusing largely on cyber threats. Table 1.1 arrays these various approaches in relation to one another.

Studies Focusing on Motivations

Those efforts that center around individual motivations and the psychological or socio-logical context of individual cases of insiders tend to dwell on underlying causes such as ideology, avarice, and social isolation, if not even appearing as apologists.[25] While expanding their focus to look at the more modern phenomenon of insider threats that apply to cyber attacks, others who view the insider through a behaviorist's lens predict-ably accord primary emphasis to stressors in the insider's life.[26] Even an analyst who has looked at individual cases in this framework and made historical compilations of numer-ous other cases of insider threats, notes that analysis of motivation and context alone provides unsatisfying answers.[27] Similarly, other analysts lament the extent to which the "trust literature is dominated by" sociological approaches that take issue with the lim-ited value of studies that attempt to illuminate trust betrayal purely through focus at the individual level.[28] Such studies fail to account for why the vast majority of people with similar pedigrees and circumstances neither betray trust nor violate loyalties to become malicious insiders.

One sociologist looks beyond traitors and saboteurs to consider prisoner informants, scabs crossing union picket lines, Nazi collaborators, and whistleblowers as insiders whose status as betrayers ultimately rests on whether there exists a support group to back their actions, since "one cannot gain a hero or martyr image by oneself."[29]

Studies Focusing on Compilations and Cases

Studies with more of a multidisciplinary approach show promise in shedding more light in this area.[30] Eoyang,[31] for example, notes that actions involving an insider's betrayal of trust are generally the result of calculation, not impulse. This note dovetails readily with the observations of Allen and Polmar,[32] whose study of more than 70 cases of insider betrayal left them characterizing the betrayers of the 1980s as motivated by "marketplace espionage" and otherwise appearing "faceless, unglamorous people" who were "seemingly ordinary." Others invest entire careers at examining multiple cases over time, such as American traitors studied for more than 20 years by the Defense Personnel Security Research Center.[33]

Descriptive compilations and biographical narratives shift the focus to dramatic, anecdotal elements of cases of insider betrayal. Media accounts number among these kinds of stories, such as a case involving an airport elevator mechanic who was allegedly abusing his access for 20 years to smuggle illegal aliens into Los Angeles.[34] Similarly, more sensational accounts of betrayal and capture, once ripped from newspaper headlines, lend themselves particularly well to timely compilation (as by Allen and Polmar), whereas analysis and application to countermeasures may lag.[35] A recurring theme in compilations is the showcasing of failures in detection of foul play. The level and accuracy of detail varies in such works, and their didactic value is principally in highlighting examples of breaches to defend against and security gaffes to avoid. Thus, a KGB memoir looking at notorious American traitors such as the FBI's Robert Hanssen and CIA's Aldrich Ames reflects this insight:

> Intelligence officers might think they're chiefly responsible for recruiting agents, but most of the work really consists of finding people who want to be recruited.[36]

Such memoirs occasionally reveal insights that only come after a long career in intelligence or counterintelligence, hence Wright's conclusion that there is only one way to uncover the malicious insider. "Put him through an extremely thorough vet," probing through the insider's entire life and career, "until his secret life begins to unravel."[37]

Even a short career as a case officer can yield complementary insights. A variation in the harvesting of lessons learned through memoirs comes from examining lessons designed for those whose job it is to seek out and exploit insiders. By inferring or reverse engineering guidance out of pitfalls, one case officer supplies this useful indicator: "Cover stories are what typically get agents into trouble."[38] He goes on to explain how cover stories must be credible yet uncomplicated. This links the foregoing perspective of Wright, a senior British MI5 executive at the end of his career, with Waters, a fledgling CIA case officer reaching the same epiphany from a different vantage.

Sobering advice from practitioners takes many forms. It may not necessarily be encouraging for those interested in countering or intercepting insiders, as another memoir reveals:

> The KGB usually only found out about moles within its ranks when a Western defector, such as Edward Lee Howard, fled to our side with information about Soviet traitors.[39]

A unique variation of this theme appears in Fishman's look at insider self-dealing and betrayal of nonprofit organizations, which leans heavily on compiling historical scandals. However, Fishman sees the promise of technology to enhance oversight by using web postings of audit trail data where the information becomes transparent and subject to scrutiny and action by "citizen–soldiers."[40]

Studies Focusing on Cyber Insiders and More Controls

Cyber security specialists, whose focus dominates current government studies on insider threats, observe that most insider cyber attacks to date have been either fraud-driven or reversible in scope and impact, that is, less than devastating to the target.[41,42] It is thus difficult to rely on lessons focusing exclusively on cyber-centric insider threat investigations, if the objective is to defeat the kind of insider whose unimpeded attack could be fatal to the institution or enterprise targeted. Finally, in the arena of government studies on insider threats, there are signs of a growing appreciation of the significance of the hostile insider as a potentially catastrophic vulnerability and some efforts to compare cyber and espionage cases, while still acknowledging that most cyber attacks by insiders appear to occur after termination of employment.[43]

What remains unstated but may yet contribute to the self-limiting nature of cyber-dominated insider threat research is the subtle, permeating influence of such cyber world fixtures as COBIT[44] (Control Objectives for Information and related Technology) standards on how information technology professionals handle security and compliance-related tasks. Consequently, it comes as little surprise that recommendations for addressing the insider threat arising from this camp invariably speak of "controls," emphasizing the use of automated monitoring tools and technology to track and restrict network access. They also lean in the direction of generating more rules as conditions of use—the equivalent of lengthening software license agreements that any computer user must acknowledge and accept before launching a given software application. The difficulty with these trademarks of the cyber security bias is not that they are valueless. It is that they are insufficient or counterproductive. Adding the controls does produce an audit trail. This audit trail demonstrates due diligence. The proper display of due diligence then helps defend against charges of negligence after a breach occurs, thereby fending off fault-finding and finger-pointing campaigns. But just because a suite of controls prevents casual intrusion or hacker attacks by outsiders does not mean the same controls will stop a knowledgeable insider threat.

Losing Sight of Existential Threats by Aggregating Cases Too Liberally

Another pitfall in overemphasizing the cyber component in the growing body of government-sponsored studies on hostile insiders is analogous to the problem that workplace violence research suffers when its purview is extended to armed robbery. At present, the National Institute for Occupational Safety and Health includes armed robberies in compilation and reporting of workplace violence statistics.[45] Thus, although practitioners in this field are most interested in understanding and preventing rampage killings of the kind associated with either disgruntled employees or spillover of domestic violence into the place of business, their efforts are diluted by skewed data. The person who comes to the office and kills a boss and several coworkers is quite different from the criminal who shoots a convenience store clerk or taxi driver while conducting a holdup at gunpoint. Yet, the distinctions are lost when the cases are aggregated too liberally. This kind of liberal aggregation is precisely what distorts the picture of the insider threat when cyber attacks by hackers and mischievous teenagers are combined with seriously destructive sabotage meticulously planned and executed by a hostile insider whose aims and capacity for destruction are much more focused and lethal.

Limits of Cyber-Centric Bias

Finally, the cyber-centric lens distorts as much as it magnifies. One international observer studying in the context of defenses dating to the President's Commission on Critical Infrastructure Protection in 1996 and extending to post-9/11, uncovered a case of hyper-reality as an outgrowth of overconcentration on the cyber threat.[46] Specifically, Cavelty noted that a senior critical infrastructure protection adviser expressed shock that the September 11 carnage did not originate from cyberspace, as that was widely believed to be the most likely source of the next attack. At present, predictions of imminent catastrophic cyber strikes continue to attract media attention as the next worst threat to come,[47] yet they are often based less on statistically valid analysis than on surveys of cyber security practitioners at best providing "a rough measure of executive opinion."[48]

IMPLICATIONS

Insider threat studies concentrating exclusively on hackers and cyber network attacks risk skewing analysis and recommendations in the direction of adverse events that seldom represent existential threats to the organization. Even though such cyber adversaries may attain the equivalent of insider access and privileges once they have breached firewalls and cyber access controls, they are seldom true insiders. By Ben-Yehuda's[49] construct, there is no treason if there is no corresponding betrayal of trust and violation of loyalty. So hackers and typical cyber attackers possess neither the trust nor loyalty that would qualify them as insiders. Nor do they possess the corresponding level of esoteric insider knowledge that would multiply the destructive power of their typical attack. Consequently, remotely based cyber attackers who are not insiders carry out actions akin to intrusion by stealth or outsider sabotage. What they may have in common with insiders is deception. But they are not fatal insider threats. Miscategorizing them distorts efforts to arrive at a common analytical core linking genuine insider threats to attack preconditions, their telltale signatures, targeting process, and susceptibility to detection and deception.

Similarly, overconcentration on the sensational aspects of insider threat cases or on the psychological motivations and societal contexts of the act of betrayal are equally self-limiting. Their emphasis on the root causes of betrayal or on the idiosyncratic experience of a given malefactor soon becomes the primary focus, leaving security practitioners to fend for themselves in trying to infer useful security countermeasures on their own.

The professional literature that covers this theme indicates that the insider threat is dangerous and often examined, only to be followed by calls for more study. The steady appearance of more studies and convening of groups such as Noonan and Archuleta's for their report to the President supports the argument that the insider threat to critical infrastructure continues to present a problem of national concern that is by no means solved or adequately addressed. Under the circumstances, what is absent in finding better ways to counter hostile insiders is a level of insight that goes beyond the limited fields of view that the three camps represent. What is needed is a level of insight that amplifies experience, which Leonard and Swap[50] have defined as "deep smarts," the lens through which we now look to a Delphi research effort for an alternative view.

QUESTIONS FOR ONLINE OR CLASSROOM DISCUSSION

1. If insider threats are indeed rare, and most people are not trust betrayers, how does this affect the ability to carry out research into hostile insiders? How do you account for the claim that hostile insider action is comparatively rare?
2. Why do you suppose that, as Band et al. assert, the majority of cyber insider attacks appear to be tracing to *former* insiders, that is, to employees or contractors who are no longer working at the targeted institution?
3. Identify three or more factors that affect the extent to which an act of trust betrayal may be more readily deterred or condoned based on ambient working conditions. What can a defender do about these conditions?
4. Taking into account the checkered trajectory of some IT ventures, ranging from Apple's failed Lisa handheld computer to Microsoft's problems with the Vista operating system and the much feared Y2K debacle that never quite unfolded at the turn of the last century, does the cyber community face unique challenges in credibility when casting the spotlight on the cyber-centric view of insider threats? Discuss.

EXERCISES FOR GROUP PROJECTS

1. Review popular literature from the 1980s and explain what made 1985 the Year of the Spy. Now, retrieve a copy of Herbig's study of treason over time and draw out the similarities and differences between then and now in the individuals who are willing to commit treason against the United States. What, if anything, has changed? Does this affect the capability to defend against today's traitor? If so, how? If not, why not? Does the motivation to commit espionage have any impact on the ability of counterespionage officers to detect traitors?
2. Contrasting the 1980s with the present day, once more, how have advances in technology or changes in cultural norms affected the ease or difficulty of detecting a trust betrayer and intervening before this individual has an opportunity to carry out an attack?
3. Identify a case of trust betrayal in your work environment, profession, or industry that led to significant changes in how one does business. Analyze this case individually and then as a group. To what extent were the changes beneficial? Did they meet their objective, or were they put in place as the result of overreaction? Were there any unintended consequences? Over time, is the affected institution better off for having instituted the changes? What alternatives might you propose as a team?

ENDNOTES

1. T. Masse, S. O'Neil, and J. Rollins, *The Department of Homeland Security's Risk Assessment Methodology: Evolution, Issues, and Options for Congress*, CRS Report for Congress RL 33858. Washington, DC: Congressional Research Service, 2007, pp. 5–9. Retrieved August 16, 2008 from https://www.hsdl.org/homesec/docs/crs/nps32-02070709.pdf&code=6a9f9433e059472a02fc2d35079cfc84.
2. See E. D. Shaw and L. F. Fischer, *Ten Tales of Betrayal: The Threat to Corporate Infrastructures by Information Technology Insiders*, Monterey, CA: Defense Personnel

Security Research Center, 2005, p. 34. Retrieved May 24, 2010 from https://hsdl.org/?view&doc=86525&coll=public. Shaw and Fischer, looking at espionage as a subset of trust betrayal, argued that such trust betrayal appeared relatively rare, while betrayals by cyber insiders might be poised to be more frequent, hence more amenable to profiling and categorizing by subtype.

3. J. P. Parker and M. F. Wiskoff, *Temperament Constructs Related to Betrayal of Trust*, Monterey, CA: Defense Personnel Security Research Center, 1991, p. 4.

4. R. C. Brackney and R. H. Anderson, *Understanding the Insider Threat*, Santa Monica, CA: RAND Corporation, 2004. Retrieved August 14, 2008 from http://www.rand.org/pubs/conf_proceedings/CF196/index.html.

5. D. M. Cappelli, A. M. Moore, R. Trzeciak, and T. J. Shimeall, *Common Sense Guide to Prevention and Detection of Insider Threats*, 3rd ed.—Version 3.1. Pittsburgh, PA: Software Engineering Institute, Carnegie Mellon University, 2009.

6. E. C. Leach, "Mitigating Insider Sabotage and Espionage: A Review of the United States Air Force's Current Posture." Master's thesis, Air Force Institute of Technology, Wright-Patterson Air Force Base, Ohio, 2009.

7. E. Kowalski, D. Cappelli, and A. Moore, *Insider Threat Study: Illicit Cyber Activity in the Information Technology and Telecommunications Sector.* Pittsburgh, PA: U.S. Secret Service and Carnegie Mellon Software Engineering Institute, January 2008, pp. 24–26.

8. Capelli, Moore, Trzeciak, and Shimeall, pp. 6–8.

9. Brackney and Anderson, p. 32.

10. Kowalski, Cappelli, and Moore, 2008.

11. "DoD Insider Threat Mitigation: Final Report of the Insider Threat Integrated Process Team," Department of Defense, April 24, 2000. Retrieved August 18, 2008 from https://acc.dau.mil/CommunityBrowser.aspx?id=37478.

12. T. Noonan and E. Archuleta, *The Insider Threat to Critical Infrastructures.* The National Infrastructure Advisory Council, April 6, 2008, p. 32.

13. A. J. Puleo, "Mitigating Insider Threat Using Human Behavior Influence Models." Master's thesis, Air Force Institute of Technology, Wright-Patterson AFB, Ohio, 2006.

14. R. B. Fein and B. Vossekuil, *Protective Intelligence and Threat Assessment Investigations.* Washington, DC: National Institute of Justice, 1998.

15. D. T. Olson, "The Path to Terrorist Violence: A Threat Assessment Model for Radical Groups at Risk of Escalation to Acts of Terrorism," Master's thesis, Naval Postgraduate School, Monterey, CA, 2005. Retrieved September 5, 2008 from https://www.hsdl.org/homesec/docs/theses/05Sep_Olson.pdf&code=08ed3b0e4d34e346e2dc3540cdc0e1f8.

16. Leach, p. 8.

17. J. Kaupla, "Are you hiring future champions or future saboteurs?" *ERE.net* (recruiters' network), May 25, 2008. Retrieved August 24, 2008 from http://www.ere.net/2008/03/25/are-you-hiring-future-champions-or-future-saboteurs/.

18. Shaw and Fischer, 2005.

19. N. Ben-Yehuda, *Betrayals and Treason: Violations of Trust and Loyalty*, Cambridge, MA: Westview, 2001.

20. Noonan and Archuleta.

21. Kowalski, Cappelli, and Moore.

22. Fein and Vossekuil.

23. Olson.

24. "Physical Vulnerability of Electric System to Natural Disasters and Sabotage," U.S. Congress Office of Technology Assessment, report OTA-E-453, Washington, DC: U.S. Government Printing Office, June 1990.

25. For example, J. Bulloch, in *Akin to Treason* (London: Arthur Barker, 1966; p. 151), dwells on the psychology of personal motivation to the point of characterizing traitors as sad individuals. M. Boveri, on the other hand, in *Treason in the Twentieth Century* (J. Steinberg, Trans., 1961) London: MacDonald, 1956, p. 13, focusing on social context, takes the view that treason is a necessary precursor to radical change in all organized societies.

26. Shaw and Fischer epitomize this approach in their analysis of insider cyber threats, with the result that they accord primacy to personal stress as a dispositive factor, on pp. 15–20, possibly reflecting Shaw's bias as a clinical psychologist.

27. Ben-Yehuda, p. 110.

28. Parker and Wiskoff, p. iii.

29. M. Akerstrom, *Betrayal and Betrayers: The Sociology of Treachery*, New Brunswick, NJ: Transaction Publishers, 1990, p. 50.

30. See Sarbin, Carney, and Eoyang who, like Ben-Yehuda, also focus attention on betrayal of trust and associated indicators that are relevant to arriving at a deeper understanding of malicious insiders.

31. Eoyang, C., "Models of Espionage," in *Citizen Espionage: Studies in Trust and Betrayal*, ed. Sarbin, T., R. Carney, and C. Eoyang (Westport, CT: Praeger, 1994), 69–91.

32. Allen, T. B., and N. Polmar, *Merchants of Treason: America's Secrets for Sale*, New York: Delacorte Press, 1988, pp. 3, 47.

33. K. L. Herbig, a historian who spent two decades studying traitors at the Defense Personnel Security Research Center, has written extensively on her findings, including in *Changes in Espionage by Americans: 1947–2007*, Technical Report 08-05, Monterey, CA: Defense Personnel Security Research Center, March 2008, p. v.

34. D. Weikel, "LAX tightens security measures after alleged smuggling," *Los Angeles Times*, September 5, 2008. Retrieved September 5, 2008 from http://mobile.latimes.com/detail.jsp?key=179165&full=1.

35. In the case of Allen and Polmar's book, for example, the cases mentioned answered the demand of a market created by *Time Magazine*'s label of 1985 as the Year of the Spy, which fueled other commercial successes in this genre. One of these was *Washington Post* reporter Pete Earley's *Family of Spies*, which told the story of John Walker's compromise of classified codes to the Soviets while Walker served in the U.S Navy and of Walker's subsequent recruitment of family and friends to continue providing a stream of classified material for Walker to sell long after Walker had retired from military service.

36. V. Cherkasin, *Spy Handler: The True Story of the Man who Recruited Robert Hanssen and Aldrich Ames*, New York: Basic Books, 2005, p. 27.

37. P. Wright, *Spycatcher: The Candid Autobiography of a Senior Intelligence Officer*, New York: Viking, 1987, p. 301.

38. T. J. Waters, *Class 11: Inside the CIA's First Post-9/11 Spy Class*, New York: Dutton, 2006, 81.

39. O. Kalugin and F. Montaigne, *The First Directorate: My 32 Years in Intelligence and Espionage against the West*, New York: St. Martin's Press, 1994, p. 202. Oleg Kalugin, former KGB general officer, was an impromptu stand-in for a scheduled FBI speaker at a 2000 security conference in Washington, DC. The FBI speaker was stuck in traffic while the former KGB general extemporized in fluent English on issues of the day. His wit and polish gave Kalugin the air of a Soviet version of William F. Buckley.

40. J. J. Fishman, *The Faithless Fiduciary and the Elusive Quest for Nonprofit Accountability*, Durham, NC: Carolina Academic Press, 2007, pp. 310–311.
41. Kowalski, Cappelli, and Moore, 2008.
42. DoD, 2000.
43. S. Band, D. Cappelli, L. Fischer, A. Moore, E. Shaw, and R. Trzeciak, *Comparing Insider IT Sabotage and Espionage: A Model-Based Analysis*, Carnegie Mellon University Software Engineering Institute, Pennsylvania: Carnegie Mellon University, pp. 40, 52. Retrieved March 20, 2010 from www.cert.org/archive/pdf/06tr026.pdf.
44. COBIT is an IT governance framework for addressing the combined requirements of controls, technology, and business risk. The IT Governance Institute first published COBIT in April 1996. Today COBIT emphasizes regulatory compliance in relation to IT governance. COBIT has become the standard for IT audits, particularly in rating compliance to the Sarbanes-Oxley Act of 2002. For more information, refer to http://www.isaca.org/Content/NavigationMenu/Members_and_Leaders/COBIT6/Obtain_COBIT/CobiT4.1_Brochure.pdf.
45. This is why handling cash, dealing with the public, and delivering people or goods rate as high risk factors according to NIOSH. See http://www.cdc.gov/niosh/violrisk.html for more details. Within this framework, a taxi driver who also works at a convenience store would rank among the most susceptible to workplace violence when, in reality, he would be most likely to encounter armed robbers and suffer injury in the interaction.
46. M. D. Cavelty, "Like a Phoenix from the Ashes," in *Securing the Homeland: Critical Infrastructure, Risk and Insecurity*, ed. M. D. Cavelty and K. S. Kristensen, London: Routledge, 2008.
47. See, for example, J. Stein, "The threat is real—Why aren't we worried? Book review: *Cyber War* by Richard Clark and Robert Knake," *Washington Post*, May 23, 2010. Retrieved May 23, 2010 from http://www.washingtonpost.com/wp-dyn/content/article/2010/05/21/AR2010052101860.html.
48. S. Baker, S. Waterman, and G. Ivanov, *In the Crossfire: Critical Infrastructure in the Age of Cyber War*, Santa Clara, CA: McAfee, Inc., 2010. Retrieved May 12, 2010 from http://resources.mcafee.com/content/NACIPReport.
49. Ben-Yehuda, pp. 307–308.
50. D. Leonard and W. Swap, "Deep Smarts," *Harvard Business Review*, September 2004. Retrieved July 29, 2008 from http://harvardbusinessonline.hbsp.harvard.edu/hbsp/hbr/articles/article.jsp?ml_action=getarticle&articleID=R0409F&pageNumber=1&ml_subscriber=true&uid=24509483&aid=R0409F&rid=24600531&eom=1.

CHAPTER 2

New Research and Contrarian Findings

It is not logic that we need. . . It is insight, the faculty of grasping at once the essential out of the irrelevant.

Will Durant

DELPHI RESEARCH ON INSIDER THREAT

The author's hostile insider studies began as a social sciences research effort carried out under the rigors and oversight of the Naval Postgraduate School, Monterey, California. The data gathering took place between January and April 2009, with subsequent analysis and academic review culminating in the author's published thesis on this subject in September. The research inquiry asked seasoned defenders, investigators, and line managers to answer questions and distill judgments through the iterative Delphi research process.[1] This project consisted of recruiting a dozen experts from different organizations and disciplines and then asking them three series of questions over time. Respondents operated independently, with guarantees of confidentiality, and without any knowledge of or interaction with each other. After the first round of questions, Delphi respondents saw a compilation of all their answers and then addressed a second round of questions that were suggested by the first. Similarly, for the third and final Delphi round, respondents received compilations of their aggregate responses to the second round of questions in addition to a final series of questions informed by preceding rounds. This approach also followed the counsel of analysts who advised, "We need multidisciplinary research teams (not just *geeks*) investigating what we should look for as indicators of possibly malevolent behavior."[2]

The group of experts in this study consisted of a dozen professionals representing different disciplines, with many having overlapping experience in fields such as

- Counterespionage
- Systems integration
- Operations management
- Fraud and threat investigations
- Critical infrastructure protection
- Prevention of workplace violence
- Local law enforcement investigations

- Human resources intelligence collection
- Workplace violence defense and response
- Defense against systemic institutional fraud
- Corporate response to handling reputational risk
- Federal law enforcement undercover assignments
- Crisis management and crisis information handling
- Management of public agency ombudsman functions
- Military service in combat and noncombat environments
- Behavioral analysis and post-traumatic-stress interventions

Each respondent was selected, in part, for availability and, in part, for possessing

- At least 20 years of professional experience
- First-hand exposure to managing or investigating insider threats
- Current and foundational professional experience outside of each other's organization and unconnected to the researcher's purview, employment, or sphere of influence

Each Delphi round involved transmitting questions by e-mail, and receiving responses via e-mail, with at least 2 weeks between rounds. All respondents agreed to participate in the study under strict confidentiality protections, and each signed an informed consent document as part of a rigorous internal review board's oversight consistent with all contemporary social sciences research efforts. Of the dozen experts who agreed to participate in three rounds of Delphi surveys, 100% saw the process through from start to finish, from January to April 2009.[3]

THE DELPHI METHODOLOGY FOR INSIDER THREAT STUDY

Note: In various professional symposia and interchanges, the author has repeatedly addressed questions about the application of Delphi method of social sciences research to the insider threat problem. Here follow answers to the most frequently raised questions.

WHY ONLY 12 RESPONDENTS INSTEAD OF, SAY, 2000?

The Delphi process is iterative yet anonymous, requiring a significant commitment on the part of respondents, including responses that took the form of explanatory narratives that were far more demanding than surveys. In order to obtain meaningful insights rather than just confirming the author's opinions as a more superficial inquiry could easily do, this Delphi study sought out practitioners who each have more than 20 years of experience of being in responsible charge in their respective fields and were willing to voluntarily participate in what would otherwise constitute billable hours. This undertaking required the fullest stretch of the author's network and demands of professional courtesy. Despite 31 years of industry experience and an address book with some 2024 entries, the author rated himself fortunate to be able to assemble a dozen professionals who contributed their career thoughts throughout the Delphi process.

WHAT ABOUT THE POTENTIAL EFFECTS OF GROUPTHINK OR ONE EXPERT INFLUENCING ANOTHER?

The Delphi method isolates respondents from each other, rather than gathering them together in a focus group. This technique not only defends against group-think but gives equal deference to the laconic and introverted whose voices might otherwise go unheard in the presence of more vocal and extroverted participants gathered together in the same room.

WOULD IT NOT BE BETTER TO SEEK OUT MORE RESPONDENTS?

To increase respondent numbers, the research would have risked a corresponding low-ering of the bar in experience and insight of Delphi experts. Neophytes are in greater supply, as are graduate students who would be more receptive to providing iterative responses. However, such a response pool would necessarily rob the process of the kind of wisdom and "deep smarts" that come only through broad, practical experi-ence over time.[4] In Delphi research, the smallest number of respondents should not be less than 10; hence, this study settling on 12—in case of any losses from one round of questions to the next. In practice, informed analysts have gone on record to state that "the sample size varies. . . from 4 to 171 'experts.' One quickly concludes that there is no 'typical' Delphi; rather that the method is modified to suit the circumstances and research question."[5] Other analysts, applying the Delphi method to policy issues, found useful sample sizes varying from 10 to 50 experts.[6]

Finally, since 12 jurors suffice to deny one of liberty or exonerate one of capital crimes, the Delphi dozen appeared to comprise a sufficiently diverse group to offer meaningful yet independent wisdom in this research effort.

DID THIS RESEARCH MEET ANY RIGORS OF ACADEMIC OVERSIGHT?

The Delphi research effort itself extended from January through April 2009 and consisted of three iterative rounds of questions and feedback. Recruitment of experts and gathering of their signed, informed consent forms, in satisfaction of the requirements of the institutional review board of the Naval Postgraduate School, took place between November 2008 and January 2009. Two PhD faculty advisers supplied functional guidance and critiques of the research process and scrutinized the gathering and presentation of its yield.

Initial Research Findings Confirming Accepted Wisdom

At the outset, Delphi experts suggested that traditional countermeasures, such as ran-dom audits, would offer high value in defending against a devastating attack. The Delphi experts independently converged on the accepted wisdom reflected in the foregoing litera-ture review and represented in Table 2.1.

The worst insider threat initially seemed likely to be a disgruntled employee with (1) the capacity to plan a devastating attack and (2) the arcane knowledge to make the most of the opportunity.[7] Upon further exploration, this assertion did not survive scru-tiny. Indicators of the disgruntled trust betrayer included unexplained anger and other

TABLE 2.1   Insider Countermeasures and Indicators First Suggested by Delphi Panel

Observable Indicators	Countermeasures
• Undue secrecy	• Random audits
• Decline in performance	• Frequent duty rotations
• Arrogance, displays of ego	• Background investigations and vetting
• Own disclosures or revelations	• Investigating reports of suspicious acts
• "Beat the system" talk, behavior	• Technological monitoring of employees
• Unexplained anger, behavior changes	

Note: These indicators and countermeasures have no special order or correlation to each other.

suspicious behaviors, such as undue secrecy and self-aggrandizement, potentially serving as red flags. Similarly, countermeasures such as random audits, monitoring of employees, and vetting investigations appeared likely to offer value as ways to thwart this kind of insider. By the end of the Delphi process, however, the same experts identified flaws in their own initial thinking. Their later judgments flew in the face of the accepted wisdom and ran counter to their own initial impressions of what constituted effective countermeasures.

ALTERNATIVE ANALYSIS TAKES SHAPE

Three shifts in perspective and conclusions of the Delphi experts moved them away from the accepted wisdom. The sea change came as a result of research questions that required the respondents to think like an *attacker rather than* a *defender*. This change made the respondents realize they could penetrate institutional defenses with relative ease. Out of this realization, Delphi experts determined that they could more usefully recruit, train, and direct an infiltrator rather than a disgruntled career employee. Finally, the Delphi experts arrived at recommended countermeasures involving a final change of perspective: reliance on work team members rather than exclusive reliance on corporate sentinels, that is, the institution's security, audit, and other specialists charged with watching for telltale signs of foul play.

Why Infiltrator vs. Disgruntled Careerist?

For the Delphi respondents, one seminal, game-changing realization was that an infiltrator poses the greater threat if the goal is to inflict damage fatal to the institution. What supported this conclusion was Delphi respondent convergence on the view that existing defenses do little to foil the prepared infiltrator.

Delphi expert observations, here, dovetailed with some findings in the published literature. Specifically, traditional insider defenses appeared to be readily advised and just as readily circumvented. In fact, analysts making career studies of traitors, now extending their reach to cyber insider threats, continue to recommend measures that have yet to eliminate treason. Their recommendations include more awareness training for the workforce, encouragement to snoop on and report "concerning" behavior of fellow employees, and even assigning individual risk values to these employees.[8] Some observers, basing their analysis on insular surveys of fellow specialists, also add their technology-intensive solution—automated invasive monitoring by multiplying sniffer programs and computerized audit trails to more closely follow every possible false step of every potential insider.[9]

With a mind-set recalling cyber aficionado shock at the low-technology nature of the 9/11 attacks,[10] such observers see employees constituting the weakest link, thereby missing their potential as the first and possibly only line of defense.[11] In the process of dispensing this standard advice to address vulnerabilities and downright failures by intensifying countermeasures that have already proven ineffective, these advisers alienate not only employees of the institution but their security staff as well. One cyber security analyst, however, swam against this tide. Examining the flawed assumptions and computing the adverse results of imposing too many security controls, Microsoft researcher Herley raised eyebrows at a new security paradigms workshop in Oxford by demonstrating that users often have sound, rational reasons for rejecting overbearing security prescriptions.[12]

Epiphanies surfaced when the Delphi experts independently admitted that the very countermeasures they had earlier recommended would present little impediment if they were the ones plotting the insider attack. The resulting Delphi consensus was that

- Infiltrators are the better choice for a terrorist seeking an insider for a devastating attack.
- Standard defenses in all but specialized environments (such as nuclear security) pose few insurmountable obstacles to an infiltrator.
- Underexploited resources available within the average organization can be optimized to provide better protection against insider threats than sole reliance on security and other corporate sentinels.

Research findings suggested that the terrorist attacking as an insider would be more likely to be an infiltrator than a disgruntled careerist already in place.[13] A career employee with long-term access and detailed knowledge of inner workings will necessarily know more about how to dismantle critical assets than an infiltrator new to the organization. The same careerist, given time and planning, is in the best position to develop and carry out a devastating attack that circumvents defenses. However, the disgruntled insider is potentially unstable and difficult to control. According to the Delphi experts, this employee is not a joiner and is likely to be too egoistic to accept direction. Volatility makes this person an operational risk likely to compromise an attack out of disagreement with the particulars or out of spite at not being consulted on every move.[14]

Additionally, targeting information for attackers remains highly accessible in the age of the Internet, particularly if the institution targeted historically operated openly without the defenses available outside the national security arena. The institution's critical assets may also be immobile. Thus, in contrast to advanced weapons classified for reasons of national security, critical infrastructure and other institutions cannot be relocated or concealed once locations and operating details have been compromised. In this context, the targeting information necessary for mounting an attack need not be so esoteric as to be available exclusively to a career insider with very detailed knowledge.

Instead, as the Delphi experts reasoned, an infiltrator who gets through the door, even at a relatively low level for a limited time, should be able to accumulate enough details to enable an attack without having to spend years masquerading as an innocuous employee. Additionally, as more than one Delphi expert noted, many infrastructures and institutions are desperate for talent and have aging workforces with little effective succession planning. Thus, as one expert noted, average employers are prone to welcome any skilled workers without criminal convictions who show an interest in accepting entry-level positions. The same employers make frequent use of contractors, who soon gain unfettered access to their systems. This situation gives an infiltrator two paths of entry:

as a direct employee or as a contractor. Infiltrators may even try the two approaches concurrently without fear of one rejection contributing to another. In this context, if the remaining defenses (as delineated below) are also flawed, the chances for a successful attack begin to tilt more in favor of an infiltrator than a disgruntled insider. Infiltrators may not have quite so much access, but they can definitely be better controlled, focused, and more disciplined about concealing telltale indicators of an impending attack to avoid compromising that attack.

Infiltrator's Challenges vs. Defender's Capacity

The weaknesses of traditional defenses against this insider threat appear more evident if depicted in the context of the mutual challenges of infiltrator and defender, as Figure 2.1 illustrates.[15]

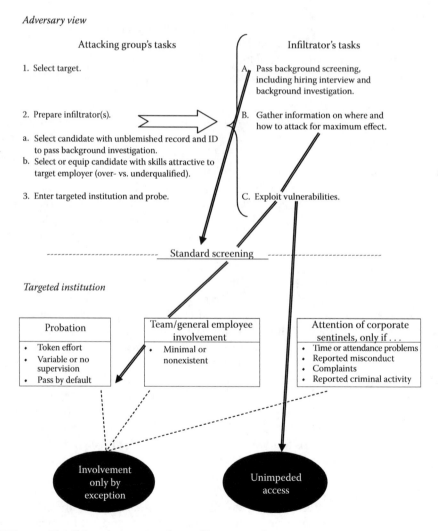

FIGURE 2.1   Traditional situation for infiltrator and target.

Figure 2.1 depicts the situation in which infiltrator and targeted employer find themselves when these countermeasures and their limitations impinge upon each other in the traditional scheme of penetration and defense. In this conceptualization, the adversary's job is to select a target, prepare an infiltrator, and gain entry into the target to the point of being able to probe and maneuver with unimpeded access. It falls to the infiltrator to pass the background check and then enter and pass a probationary period. The probation period itself affords sufficient freedom of maneuver to gather information unimpeded by close scrutiny or interference. The infiltrator eluding detection or interference is free to operate in the dark corners of insufficient oversight and supervision, as long as his behavior and work performance do not deviate so much from the norm as to invite attention.

Infiltrator Step 1: Get through Screening

The standard screening, or pre-employment, background investigation presents a low hurdle to the prepared. As long as the infiltrator does not have a record of criminal convictions or obvious disqualifications (e.g., inability to lift 25 lb in a job whose essential functions require some manual labor), he or she has little to fear from the third-party consumer reporting agency performing the background check.

The more invasive background and update investigations required for national security employment are not available for most employers, including entities operating the nation's critical infrastructure. Nor is it feasible to demand the same level of scrutiny for a maintenance mechanic as for an intelligence analyst. Besides, the telltale component of such investigations—the probe for financial irresponsibility—is only useful in cases where trust betrayal is primarily driven by money, exemplified in the so-called "marketplace espionage" most frequently observed in counterintelligence cases of the 1980s.[16] However, as Herbig[17] discovered in her study of trust betrayal in such cases over time, the trend in the past 10 years has changed: the most common driver for today's traitors is divided loyalties, that is, ideological rather than monetary motivation. Consequently, yesterday's focus on finances as an indicator of possible trust betrayal offers limited value in detecting today's traitors who will be living well within their means. Such trust betrayers will also be showing no signs of the kind of debt indicative of financial hardship that would make them targets for bribery or ostensible candidates for selling out their employers to relieve financial distress.

Similarly, an infiltrator sent into an organization to attack it will be unlikely to draw attention by amassing bad debts that set off financial responsibility alarms, assuming a credit report is even requested or studied as part of the background investigation. Nor will this individual invite negative scrutiny through drunk driving or criminal convictions that the average background investigation detects through a standard check of superior court records in counties of residence and of employment.[18] Insulating the infiltrator even more from what such background investigations uncover is that the infiltrator is already under the control and sponsorship of a primary, albeit undisclosed, employer: the attacker. Thus, the infiltrator is seeking employment not so much for monetary or professional reward as for access to an assigned target. Meanwhile, the attacker coaches the infiltrator to avoid actions that would raise eyebrows. The larger and more sophisticated the attacker's organization, the more candidates are available to choose from in qualifying an infiltrator, and the more likely that the ultimate selectee will arrive on the job with an unblemished record.

To complicate matters further for defenders, the legal constraints affecting employers in the United States severely limit a critical infrastructure steward's ability to expand the scope of a background investigation or to use its product in any way that is not demonstrably related to a given job vacancy.[19] The same applies to any program for performing update investigations on existing employees. As one industry guideline cautions, "The consideration of extraneous information that is not a valid predictor of job performance can create a source of liability."[20] In the context of employment laws prohibiting job discrimination yet defending privacy, it is the rare hiring manager who dares flaunt such guidance by rejecting any otherwise qualified applicant, even if subtle or stated antipathies against the United States surface during the hiring process. Fidelity to America is seldom called out as a hiring criterion for work at a utility that operates critical infrastructure or at any institution whose principal business does not involve national security. In the broader context of employment law, antidiscrimination protections, and limitations on the extent to which employers may practically scrutinize applicants for work, background investigations are unlikely to unmask any but the most unsophisticated of infiltrators.

Update investigations, if performed at all, typically come after 7 years because this is the standard limit that many states and the Fair Credit Reporting Act recognize as the maximum period for making criminal history available for retrieval for employment purposes.[21] Like pre-employment investigations, updates performed through a credit bureau or other agency falling under the rules of this Act must also be fully disclosed to the subject of the investigation. An infiltrator requiring more than 7 years to gather insider information to support an infrastructure attack would have aged enough to cast doubt on his or her motivational zeal and to be suspected of beginning to identify too closely with the target.

Infiltrator Step 2: Gather Information

As Figure 2.1 shows, once safely through the door the infiltrator now interacts primarily with fellow employees and a supervisor, who supplies the institution's direct oversight during the probationary period. Corporate sentinels, whether security staff, auditors, information systems guardians of the computer network, human resources recruiters, attorneys, or others with assigned responsibility for various monitoring functions, rarely interact with the new employee. They may participate in a new-hire orientation, but otherwise they deal with the newcomer only if the latter's actions or questions affect their various disciplines. The new employee benefits from a grace period during which minor transgressions committed in the course of gathering information are easily dismissed as a rookie's excusable faux pas. Unless the neophyte does something egregious to excite remark, he or she is unlikely to face a random audit or active monitoring of computer key strokes, or time and duration of access into a given work space. On the rare occasion when an infiltrator's actions invite challenge, all that are necessary to deflect focused attention of corporate sentinels are a ready apology and a profession of ignorance.

To further limit opportunities for detecting an infiltrator's suspicious gathering of insider information via random audit, Delphi experts in business and operational audit note that so-called random audits are seldom truly random. As one of the experts pointed out, the astute observer sees them coming. Moreover, many audits are perfunctory, particularly if auditors consider themselves overextended and disinclined to take on the extra work of sustaining a negative finding. As one analyst found in a longitudinal study of organizations susceptible to accountability failures, cases are "resource intensive and, as a result, enforcement is necessarily selective."[22] This explains why a resource-intensive audit will not be "wasted" on a neophyte who has still not even passed probation.

In many—if not most—organizations, audits are by definition adversarial. They are, therefore, regarded as a necessary evil perpetrated by individuals who are more tolerated than esteemed. To the extent that auditors are aloof, disdainful, or menacing, they struggle to obtain active cooperation. One Delphi expert has seen that coworkers are even more likely to defend than to report a trust betrayer who has managed to come across as "just one of the guys." The greater scrutiny is likely to focus on activities affecting financial performance or high-value losses. However, until the moment of attack, the infiltrator targeting critical infrastructure is unassociated with any loss-producing events that would invite such scrutiny. In such circumstances, it is the rare audit that will identify and focus sufficient attention on an infiltrator to elicit anything more than an oral warning or mild rebuke. Consequently, the traditional audit poses little threat to the infiltrator operating with a modicum of training and sophistication.

Technology exists to remotely monitor every keystroke an employee makes whether operating a desktop computer or a supervisory control and data acquisition (SCADA) system—the principal means of controlling valves and distribution of signals, power, or water when handling a critical infrastructure component. It is possible to configure control room access so that no one individual may enter a critical area alone. It is also possible to remotely monitor such areas through video surveillance. These capabilities can theoretically prevent all but the most astute from carrying out undetected acts of mischief. However, when applied to the challenge of detecting and thwarting an infiltrator bent on attacking critical infrastructure, technology alone falls short for several reasons.

For every device capable of tracking activity, there must exist somewhere in the institution a means of distinguishing suspicious activity from acceptable routine. A surveillance camera or automated log cannot by itself tell whether an operator laying hands on a SCADA panel is doing his job or interfering with another's. Such a determination requires human judgment. True, some automated tools can approximate a level of human judgment, if given precise details and parameters of what kind or number of transactions become suspect once they exceed a certain frequency in a given period or take up significantly more time than necessary. However, the effort needed to establish these boundaries and the resources necessary to automate associated triggers exceed the capacity of the average financially strapped employer. Nor is this investment in proportion to the expected benefit.

The same caution applies to the labor-intensive alternative to this technology-based solution: invasive snooping by a designated monitoring force. Delphi experts with career experience as line managers in critical infrastructures opined that such snooping negatively affects productivity and morale, while often leading to an unintended consequence. It sparks the creativity of aggrieved operators to find new ways to elude or defeat monitoring systems because they dislike being watched like wayward children.

Undermining such corporate sentinels, whether human overseers or automated devices, soon becomes part game, part badge of honor. Coworkers transfer this knowledge of how to bypass what they regard as invasive monitoring to peers and newcomers alike—including the potential infiltrator—because they know that if all the workers are defeating Big Brother, then management will be unable to single out any one employee for punishment.

Infiltrator Step 3: Exploit Vulnerabilities

At this point in the penetration effort, if the infiltrator has managed to survive the screening process and stay under the radar of corporate sentinels, inertia and initiative are on his side. The more he blends, the less he stands out, and the more likely he is to gain the unwitting support of coworkers and management alike, particularly if seen to be a competent team player who gets along well with others.

One contradiction in defensive strategy highlights how traditional measures can be self-undermining. The common thread that unravels the foregoing defenses when exploited by an infiltrator or any hostile insider is a lack of active involvement on the part of the workforce on one hand, tied with what infrastructure workers perceive as the offensiveness of too much oversight on the other hand. One career analyst of trust betrayers explained the latter phenomenon by stating that vigilance against disloyalty "threatens the ecology of trust and raises the likelihood of disloyalty because of a motivation to resist excessive oversight.[23]

In this framework, the institution comes to rely excessively on its corporate sentinels, viz. its designated watchers, such as security staff. Accordingly, the rest of the workforce remains indifferent to the defensive role that employees and managers have ceded to specialists. Meanwhile, the capacity of these sentinels to focus limited resources on discovering a needle-in-the-haystack level of visibility of an insider threat is constrained by average employee resistance to draconian security measures that are too costly and impede operations. Into the space between general employee indifference and constraints on corporate sentinels, the infiltrator and any insider threat can create a dark corner to carry out hostile activity with impunity, as Figure 2.1 illustrates.

THE ALTERNATIVE

One way to overcome the vulnerabilities shown in Figure 2.1 is to reexamine the infiltrator's penetration sequence in light of how a different strategy might apply the same institutional resources to better effect. Figure 2.2 shows such an alternative end-state.

What has changed? First, the screening process no longer relies excessively on a search for indicators that uncover neither infiltrator nor other hostile insider. As one executive who studied trust betrayal for an entire career pointed out, many experts find that personnel investigations do not prevent espionage or detect those who may commit such a crime.[24] Instead, the process now pays special attention to verifying identity. It takes advantage of government resources through a program that U.S. Immigrations and Customs Enforcement (ICE) makes available to companies and infrastructure institutions alike—ICE Mutual Agreement for Government and Employers (ICE/IMAGE). For a fraction of the resources necessary to conduct update investigations of utility employees every 7 years,[25] employers can instead devote more attention to verifying basic identity and right-to-work authorizations of new hires in order to defend against potential infiltrators. They improve their internal capacity for such detection by availing themselves of a federally funded program that trains human resources recruiters to check credentials and gives them access to Social Security and immigration databases to facilitate verification of employment eligibility.[26]

The new screening program will not necessarily catch all infiltrators any more than it will defeat individuals who enter the institution benevolently and only later develop hostility and a propensity to betray or destroy. However, the program will reduce the ability

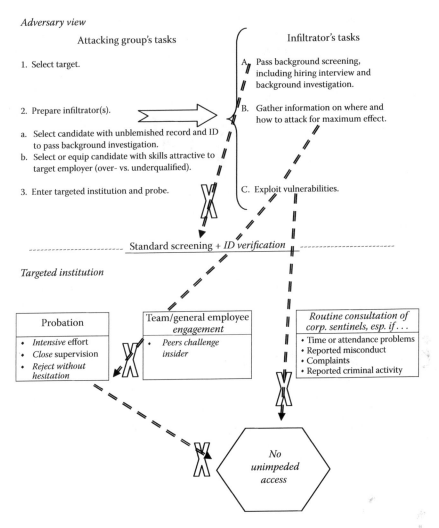

FIGURE 2.2   Desired end-state facing infiltrator.

of terrorist organizations to infiltrate their agents with falsified credentials, which, absent increased scrutiny, receive only token examination from the most junior clerk assigned to processing employment applications. This is why Figure 2.2 shows an X next to the arrow depicting the infiltrator's first task. The new screening program complicates the challenge for the infiltrator, but does not eliminate it altogether.

More importantly, however, the biggest change from the traditional (Figure 2.1) to the alternative approach (Figure 2.2) is the active engagement of the general employee population. Employees now support the screening process by at least verifying credentials through their own professional and trade networks. The immediate supervisor monitors the employee closely throughout the probationary period. During this interval, the new default expectation is not that all newcomers pass probation without egregious incidents, but that all are released from probation unless they demonstrate talent worth keeping. This demonstration must satisfy not only the supervisor but teammates as well, which forces close interaction on a daily basis. Moreover, during probation, new hires are treated like student pilots who are not ready for solo flight—never left alone in the cockpit. Only, in the case of critical infrastructure, the student is a new employee and the cockpit is any critical asset or control system. At the same time, this alternative approach requires a culture of constant team interaction and self-monitoring that reduces opportunities for clandestinely probing and undermining the institution. It eliminates the dark corners represented by the black ellipses in Figure 2.1, because in Figure 2.2 employee oversight means there are fewer places to hide. This is the No Dark Corners approach that reconfigures the job to reduce the chances of an individual to occupy a sensitive area undetected. It breathes life into this security prescription of management expert Tom Peters while exhorting security professionals not to see their contribution exclusively in the character of corporate sentinels:

> I don't want you to be security people for the organization, but to make everyone else in the organization a security person. You don't "do" security. You help all the employees do it. . . You win the game when I and my colleagues are the real security people in the place.[27]

At the heart of the cultural shift, this alternative approach also increases the opportunity to detect any insider threat because it spreads defensive responsibility pervasively, rather than relying exclusively on corporate sentinels.

BALANCING TRUST AND TRANSPARENCY: THE COPILOT MODEL

How can a cultural shift in the workplace create a team whose members constantly monitor each other without undermining the trust vital for group cohesion? On the surface, it would appear that such a team is merely relieving assigned corporate sentinels of their snooping duties. After all, as organizational consultant Stephen Covey has observed, suspicion can generate the behaviors that managers and leaders are defending against, thus fostering a collusive environment of distrust.[28] Extending the copilot and cockpit metaphor from the preceding discussion on probation, however, offers an answer to this apparent contradiction.

In line with the cultural shift to internal team monitoring, every team member becomes not an inquisitor but a copilot. Each member exemplifies the elements of the copilot definition of a "qualified pilot who assists or relieves the pilot but is not in command."[29] The copilot maintains a vested interest in maintaining safe altitude and air speed and in arriving on schedule at the right destination. Applied to the work team, this model makes every team member a copilot. Neither a copilot nor a team member need become a snoop or tattletale. Yet both should be in a position to fully monitor what is happening in the cockpit or control room, with aircraft gauges or with SCADA displays. In this context, a copilot level of engagement becomes cohesion producing because it demonstrates a shared sense of ownership in the team's work. As an added benefit, engaging employees in a more collaborative endeavor such as this offers a way to relieve what some management analysts characterize as the "deadening impact of routine."[30]

Although many parts of a given countermeasure carry forward into the new framework, the means of applying the countermeasure changes fundamentally. This approach now transforms invasive techniques into performance gauges for work teams. A video camera monitoring a critical process involving hazardous materials should now be welcome as a way for a fellow team member to be able to summon assistance if another team member in the area gets hurt—not as a spy camera for helping bosses catch subordinates in the act of violating established procedures. The same cultural shift should make team members appreciate having a backup control room operator or lineman within earshot or line of sight, rather than bristle at the thought of not being trusted to work alone. Embracing the copilot model should transform additional physical or electronic monitoring into a welcome means of summoning assistance. It should also limit opportunities for a hostile insider to act against the institution. Ultimately, greater transparency and work redesign should limit opportunities for clandestine and damaging activities by eliminating the dark corners that insider threats need to do their worst.

Contrast with Traditional Strategy

Applying the new strategy communicates to the would-be insider threat that someone may be watching. In a traditional approach, the watcher is a corporate sentinel, and there are seldom enough watchers to monitor every process or venue. By contrast, in a No Dark Corners setting, the one who may be watching is a coworker who has a proprietary interest in a job, a work team, and the institution, and will therefore act to defend them.

Key to this strategy are not only innovations but also what management authority Peter Drucker emphasized as a primary duty of all organizations: organized abandonment of processes and strategies that are no longer working.[31]

Measures that impede an infiltrator's ability to surveil or strike take precedence over measures that are easily bypassed and offer negligible value in defeating an insider threat. Organizing these measures to contrast them with the traditional defenses that accepted wisdom favors underscores even more the distinctions of the new approach. Figure 2.3 presents this contrast in the form of a strategy canvas where the status quo appears in bold, solid line and a breakaway challenge to this strategy appears in a gray, dashed line.

The strategy canvas is at once a gauge and a framework for revealing where traditional insider defenses have faltered and where innovations offer alternatives to reduce chronic vulnerabilities. The canvas visually communicates the current state of affairs

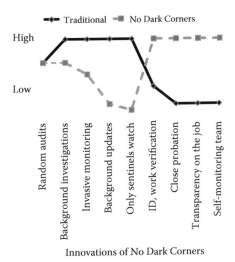

FIGURE 2.3 Strategy canvas: traditional vs. No Dark Corners.

in insider threat defense (solid line) while also showing the potential for breaking new ground (dashed line) to reduce susceptibility to infiltrators and, by extension, to any hostile insider.

New Insider Defenses

In addition to adjusting defensive measures already discussed at length throughout these pages, Figure 2.3 draws attention to three particular innovations that reflected insights both of Delphi experts and of published analysts of trust betrayers. These three are close probation, transparency on the job, and team self-monitoring. All three measures offer productivity as well as defensive benefits.

Close Probation

As one study shows in extolling the virtues of close probation, "organizations that systematically integrate new employees enjoy lower turnover, and the recruits report greater commitment and job satisfaction."[32] This and the other tools intend to defeat hostile insiders through the kind of scrutiny that corporate sentinels cannot match: the scrutiny of a coworker, or what one analyst calls a "citizen–sentry."[33]

For most organizations, probationary periods are a theoretical means of rejecting a new hire before work rules confer the equivalent of tenure or lifetime employment. Yet, Delphi respondents reported that the probation process is seldom fully exploited. Hiring managers hesitate to let probationary employees go, particularly if the hiring process was lengthy and demanding. To make matters worse, the longer a vacancy goes unfilled, the greater the chance of losing that position, as upper management can see work getting done despite the vacancy. Finally, where mentoring and monitoring of new hires are deficient, hiring managers keep the new hires past probation by default, to give them the benefit of the doubt. By contrast, No Dark Corners puts a premium on using probation as originally designed. The default shifts away from keeping the new hire absent flagrant misdeeds. Instead, the new default becomes termination at the first sign of misgivings and automatic release at the end of probation absent outstanding performance. The only way to keep a probationary hire becomes via the support of frontline supervisors and fellow members of a work team. The supervisor acts as the pilot, with the rest of the team as copilots—all having a vested interest in assuring that anyone joining their ranks can be trusted in their institution's equivalent of the cockpit.

Transparency on the Job

In keeping with the new strategy for maximizing the value of probationary periods, transparency on the job means that every task, operation, or action performed at a critical infrastructure site should be within the actual or virtual line-of-sight of a knowledgeable peer or supervisor. Similar to the two-person-integrity rules of working in some classified or nuclear environments,[34] every job and work space should be designed to maximize visibility to peers and minimize opportunities for clandestine, hostile action.[35] Although critical infrastructure employers seldom have the staffing to implement a forced buddy system like this under all circumstances, the selective use of surveillance cameras to monitor critical operations can at least reduce infiltrator assurance that clandestine activities will remain undetected. The deterrent value of this kind of system is analogous to that of having surveillance cameras and their associated video monitors openly placed near the cash register at retail convenience stores. This practice in retail security is thought to deter robbery because of the uncertainty it creates about who may be watching in the eyes of the potential robber.[36,37] Process-monitoring cameras, which assist with environmental watching of systems to ensure that they are operating within design tolerances and of hazardous areas in order to dispatch rescue crews, are already commonplace at infrastructure sites, as are security surveillance cameras and access control systems in public areas, particularly in Britain.[38] Designing new work sites, as they come online, to increase such visibility reduces the perception of concealment opportunities and increases the opportunity for fully engaged team members and other employees to spot untoward activity while routinely looking out for each other.

Team Self-Monitoring

Finally, the new alernative recognizes and seeks to exploit the difference between over-the-shoulder audits and self-policing out of work team cohesion and pride. As a Delphi expert observed, the most effective use of audits occurs when internalized at the work team level. Instead of shrinking from oversight as a form of witch hunt, team members focus on "how we can make things better" discussions. By including such discussions in regular team meetings and also encouraging informal one-on-one comments between employee and supervisor after each formal meeting, members should become their own most ardent diagnosticians. This self-monitoring presents an imposing threat of discovery for the infiltrator who may be adroit in hiding from corporate sentinels but cannot hide from the team.

As another Delphi expert noted, metrics by themselves may supply only an illusion that management can track all work and make necessary course corrections in time. As a senior executive in a large infrastructure organization, he found that he did not have time to read let alone check for discrepancies in employee performance based on all the timekeeping, output measures, budget variance, and failure analysis records available only to senior executives. So, this expert pushed out these data to frontline managers who could at least track themselves and their own teams. As a result, first the managers and soon the team members started gauging themselves and monitoring their own performance, improving effectiveness in the process. Some teams competed with each other in friendly rivalry. More teams and their managers, though, began competing with themselves, striving to beat last month's or last year's best record. An expert reasoned that this kind of self-monitoring, properly encouraged and applied to defense against insider threats, would present an almost insurmountable obstacle to infiltrators intent on an attack against critical infrastructure. Within a general management context, independent management studies on trustworthiness also confirm this expert view that few approaches rival the effectiveness of anomaly detection by peers in a social network[39] or even the value of management–employee communications in deterring sabotage in business settings.[40]

COMPARISON WITH OTHER SECURITY STRATEGIES

The new strategy of configuring work space for maximizing opportunities for teammates to exercise a proprietary interest in their work and for promoting transparency relies on employees—legitimate insiders—defending an institution and its infrastructure by taking ownership. No Dark Corners is to critical infrastructure what Defensible Space is to community housing and Fixing Broken Windows is to community policing: a defensive strategy relying on legitimate users of a given space to exercise a proprietary interest sufficient to defeat adversary encroachment. In his seminal work, *Defensible Space*, architect Oscar Newman examined data from housing projects in New York to make a case for reconfiguring residential areas to enhance the natural human tendency of territoriality. In his words, "defensible space is a model for residential environments which inhibits crime by creating the physical expression of a social fabric that defends itself."[41]

Although Newman made efforts to extend his work to nonresidential environments with government sponsorship, the latter appeared to make little progress in the course of 20 years, despite considerable investment.[42]

In a variation of Defensible Space applied to order maintenance in public spaces, James Q. Wilson and George Kelling offered the Broken Windows theory 10 years later.[43] Then, Kelling's follow-up research demonstrated multiple successes in crime reduction in major urban cities—all based on the premise that neighborhoods decay into crime and disorder if the little things, such as broken windows, remain untended.[44] Soon, vandals break all the remaining windows. Conversely, attention to the little things, such as fixing broken windows, sends a communal message of a sense of ownership. This demonstration of proprietary interest, in turn, deters offenders, driving them away from protected areas.[45]

No Dark Corners extends the foregoing theme of a sense of ownership to infrastructure and institutions, in a way that recalls the housing application of *Defensible Space* and the community order maintenance of *Fixing Broken Windows*. The difference is that although the other two models apply exclusively to public spaces, the new approach adds private space into the mix, as all critical infrastructures and most institutions have control rooms or physical assets that are not open to the public, hence, out of the public view. Invariably, however, some important assets remain exposed, such as transmission lines, reception areas, and aqueducts, which may be visible or accessible to members of the public.

Why has the new alternative not surfaced before? According to observers of organizational cultures under stress, whether induced by sabotage, terrorist attack, or workplace violence, "denial is a powerful feature of organizational culture; it prevents sense making when crises appear."[46] Moreover, many, if not most, organizations and institutions operate within the private sector. By extension, their critical assets must therefore be under private rather than public control, hence beyond the reach of the earlier models that rely on stimulating a sense of ownership exclusively in public areas, such as Defensible Space and Broken Windows. To complicate the protective challenge further, critical infrastructure and institutional assets may extend across both public and private spaces. Many of them are impossible to secure in the traditional sense. For example, transmission lines, aqueducts, and fiber-optic cables stretching across broad expanses of undefended territory hardly lend themselves to being kept under the control of locks and intrusion alarms. Moreover, in a world of increasing complexity, it may well be that modern society has come to over-rely on specialists, for fear of burdening the general workforce or risking errors. We perpetuate self-imposed limits by advising the average employee to leave it to the professionals. Thus, catching insiders, in this mind-set, becomes the work of specialists who fill the ranks of corporate sentinels. Meanwhile, this approach routinely characterizes nonspecialists—the average employees—as the weakest links,[47] thereby foreclosing the option to mobilize them as one's first line of defense. After all, as a recent British security guide has demonstrated, true stakeholders consist of anyone who has an interest in the operational security of the site, including security staff, occupants, and operators.[48] Involving the entire community of stakeholders in its own defense, then, significantly extends the protective reach of sentinels otherwise operating in isolation.

How does a security practitioner implement the new approach? Every manager and innovator must operate within the opportunities and constraints created by that individual's own management and organizational culture. Ideally, the practitioner operates in an environment receptive to innovation and to a business case that aligns the copilot approach of insider defense with improved productivity and teamwork. Recognizing that security practitioners seldom operate in ideal circumstances, one must look to take advantage of opportunities for pilot programs and even incremental change while identifying and cultivating an organizational champion. Management authority Peter Drucker routinely advised introducing new approaches via a low-risk pilot program to allow the institution an opportunity to get acquainted with changes while giving innovators the chance to fine tune the program to handle unexpected complications. Nevertheless, there may be circumstances where an organization is unreceptive to a pilot program or where the security practitioner is unable to obtain enterprise-wide support for those aspects of the program that fall beyond his or her authority, such as modification of the employee probation process. In such conditions, an incremental approach may still offer opportunities. One may not be able to change the entire probation process, yet still modify how one's own department takes advantage of that process. Buoyed by successes, one may then influence other departments with like-minded allies to pay closer attention to the probation process as a way of avoiding the eventual consequences of poor hiring decisions. Similarly, by making the most of the security department's organizational discretion and by using the strategy canvas (Figure 2.3) as a guide, one may gradually shift managerial emphasis to give greater priority to key features of the new approach without flying in the face of tradition. Finally, as with implementing any security program that is not the product of a regulatory mandate or executive edict, it is always helpful to identify an advocate or champion from top management who can see the value in the alternative approach and offer counsel and support in instituting necessary change without unduly animating organizational antibodies.

No Dark Corners reduces relatively unproductive but resource-intensive investment in countermeasures that an infiltrator can readily bypass. It shifts exclusive reliance of institutions on overly specialized monitors, the corporate sentinels, to the larger employee population, especially the work team closest to the infiltrator or other hostile insider. It also redirects some investment away from moderately useful pre-employment background investigations and unproductive update investigations, which may deter obvious criminals but will not defeat a hostile infiltrator.[49] Instead, the strategy shifts this investigative scrutiny to verifying identity and right-to-work documentation, which takes the form of supplemental identification, and which the ICE arm of the DHS is advancing through its ICE/IMAGE program of enhancing the capacity of all employers, including infrastructure stewards, to close the door to a major penetration vulnerability in the hiring process.[50]

At the same time, this new strategy brings to bear the tools of close probation, work redesign for transparency, and self-monitoring for greater engagement of the employee population and, in particular, the work team.

In a No Dark Corners workplace, standard screening will have new emphasis on identity and right-to-work verification. False credentials will be subject to discovery, making it particularly difficult for a foreign adversary to penetrate an American institution. Close probation means an infiltrator will face unabated scrutiny, supervision, and evaluation. Similarly, a fully engaged employee population and work flow design that eliminates hiding places while promoting transparency will reduce opportunities for the infiltrator gathering sensitive information and breaching protocols under the banners of ignorance or deficient supervision. Corporate sentinels previously mistrusted will be accessible to team members to follow up on their concerns and suspicions. In the process, the sentinels themselves will become part of the extended family seen as supporting the work team. Opportunities for unfettered, clandestine access will be severely constrained, subject to monitoring by people or devices, and too limited to exploit reliably.

QUESTIONS FOR ONLINE OR CLASSROOM DISCUSSION

1. Identify at least two other ways of performing research on the insider threat that would not involve the Delphi method. Are there any attractive or limiting factors with these approaches?
2. What are some of the strengths and limitations of using technology to detect and deter insider attack? How would such methods work in your organization?
3. Identify at least three limitations of the average pre-employment background investigation, recalling your own for your present position, if possible.
4. What makes an infiltrator a better choice for insertion into a target with the assignment to develop the means to carry out a fatal attack from within? Would a disgruntled career employee not be better suited to do this?
5. How well does your probation system work for new employees? Compare your system with at least one other. Which is better? Why? What is the percentage of new hires released from employment during probation compared to that of those retained after successfully completing the probationary period? Is either probation system actively used by hiring managers, or is its provision for release of underperforming new hires seldom exercised?
6. Does your organization operate under a situation where corporate sentinels may have power but lack status, whereas team members working on core business enjoy much greater status? If so, how does this affect the way that sentinels and team members get along with each other? Is there mutual respect or tension between the two camps? How can you tell?

EXERCISES FOR GROUP PROJECTS

1. Select an organization and then chart the process by which it recruits and hires new employees or otherwise grants liberal access to its facilities and operations. Examine that process and identify exploitable weaknesses. Using a red team approach, describe how you might exploit those weaknesses as an infiltrator and what defender actions or countermeasures would introduce obstacles to infiltration.
2. Using open sources, identify an employer considered good to work for and another employer considered exceptionally difficult. Now look at their grievance processes and, to the extent that you can, the kind of people problems they have. What can you infer about which organization would be more vulnerable to an insider threat? Why?
3. Identify a team environment for a pilot program and institute a No Dark Corners–style copilot approach to self-regulation as an alternative to invasive monitoring or overproliferation of rules. What kind of results would you expect? What did you experience?

ENDNOTES

1. For details on Delphi methods and utility, the reader may find an authoritative reference in G. J. Skulmoski, F. T. Harman, and J. Krahn, "The Delphi Method for Graduate Research," *Journal of Information Technology Education* 6, 2007, available at http://jite.org/documents/Vol6/JITEv6p001-021Skulmoski212.pdf. Readers unfamiliar with Delphi research and its particular application to this problem may question the legitimacy of the Delphi method, or even of all such qualitative methods in terms of their scientific validity. The textbox in this chapter answers these questions at length for readers with this interest, and appendices in this book supply a close look at the interative questions that the author used in soliciting input from the Delphi experts who contributed to the insider threat study.

2. R. C. Brackney and R. H. Anderson, *Understanding the Insider Threat*, Santa Monica, CA: RAND Corporation, 2004, p. 14. Retrieved August 14, 2008 from http://www.rand.org/pubs/conf_proceedings/CF196/index.html.

3. N. Catrantzos, "No Dark Corners: Defending Against the Insider Threat to Critical Infrastructure." Master's thesis, Center for Homeland Defense and Security, Naval Postgraduate School, Monterey, CA, 2009, pp. 6–10.

4. D. Leonard and W. Swap, "Deep Smarts," *Harvard Business Review*, September 2004. Retrieved July 29, 2008 from http://harvardbusinessonline.hbsp.harvard.edu/hbsp/hbr/articles/article.jsp?ml_action=getarticle&articleID=R0409F&pageNumber=1&ml_subscriber=true&uid=24509483&aid=R0409F&rid=24600531&eom=1.

5. Skulmoski et al., p. 5.

6. H. Linstone and M. Turoff, Eds., *The Delphi Method: Techniques and Applications.* Newark, NJ: New Jersey Institute of Technology, 2002, p. 82.

7. Catrantzos, pp. 5–38.

8. E. D. Shaw, L. F. Fischer, and A. E. Rose, *Insider Risk Evaluation and Audit*, Technical Report 09-02. Monterey, CA: Defense Personnel Security Research Center, 2009, pp. 30 and 40.

9. J. Garcia, "Mitigating Insider Sabotage," *SANS Institute InfoSec Reading Room*, September 21, 2009, pp. 2 and 13. Retrieved March 19, 2011 from http://www.sans.org/reading_room/whitepapers/casestudies/mitigating-insider-sabotage_33189.

10. M. D. Cavelty, "Like a Phoenix from the Ashes," in *Securing the Homeland: Critical Infrastructure, Risk and Insecurity*, ed. M. D. Cavelty and K. S. Kristensen, London: Routledge, 2008.

11. Garcia, p. 22.

12. C. Herley, "So Long, and No Thanks for the Externalities: The Rational Rejection of Security Advice by Users," *Proceedings of the New Security Paradigms Workshop*, Oxford, United Kingdom, September 8–11, 2009, pp. 1–12.

13. Catrantzos, pp. 11–41.

14. Catrantzos, p. 26.

15. Catrantzos, pp. 43–50.

16. T. B. Allen and N. Polmar, *Merchants of Treason: America's Secrets for Sale*, New York: Delacorte Press, 1988, pp. 3 and 47.

17. K. L. Herbig, *Changes in Espionage by Americans: 1947–2007*, Technical Report 08-05, Monterey, CA: Defense Personnel Security Research Center, March 2008.

18. In the United States, employment-related investigations can only legitimately use conviction records, not arrest records. Only law enforcement has access to the latter and is prohibited from sharing them with employers so that the latter do not

unfairly affect an applicant's livelihood by making adverse hiring decisions before the legal system has decided actual guilt. See pp. 20–24, *Pre-employment Background Screening Guideline* (Alexandria, VA: American Society for Industrial Security, International, 2006), http://www.asisonline.org/guidelines/guidelinespre-employ.pdf.

19. Equal Employment Opportunity Commission, *Employment Tests and Selection Procedures* (2009), 1–6, http://www.eeoc.gov/policy/docs/factemployment_proce dures.html.

20. *Pre-employment Background Screening Guideline*, p. 24.

21. Ibid., pp. 20 and 22.

22. J. J. Fishman, *The Faithless Fiduciary and the Elusive Quest for Nonprofit Accountability*, Durham, NC: Carolina Academic Press, 2007, p. 274.

23. R. M. Carney, "The Enemy Within," in *Citizen Espionage: Studies in Trust and Betrayal*, ed. T. Sarbin, R. Carney, and C. Eoyang, Westport, CT: Praeger, 1994, p. 21.

24. M. Anderson, "Introduction," in *Citizen Espionage: Studies in Trust and Betrayal*, ed. T. Sarbin, R. Carney, and C. Eoyang, Westport, CT: Praeger, 1994, pp. 1–17.

25. The seven-year number is based on the standard state limit for reporting of criminal convictions and that the Fair Credit Reporting Act uses for employment-related background screening (*Pre-employment Background Screening Guideline*, pp. 20, 22).

26. *ICE Mutual Agreement for Government and Employers*, U.S. Immigrations and Customs Enforcement, March 2, 2009. Retrieved May 20, 2010, from http://www .ice.gov/partners/opaimage/image_faq.htm.

27. T. Peters, Speech on emerging security trends. Keynote address presented at the 2007 seminar and exhibits, American Society for Industrial Security, Las Vegas, NV, September 25, 2007.

28. S. M. R. Covey and R. R. Merrill, *The Speed of Trust: The One Thing That Changes Everything*. New York: Free Press, 2008, p. 292.

29. Merriam-Webster, 2009.

30. F. Vermeulen, P. Puranam, and R. Gulata, "Change for Change's Sake," *Harvard Business Review*, June 2010, pp. 73.

31. P. Drucker, *Managing in the Next Society*, New York: Truman Talley Books, 2002, p. 295.

32. C. Fernandez-Araoz, B. Groysberg, and N. Nohria, "The Definitive Guide to Recruitment in Good Times and Bad," *Harvard Business Review*, May 2009, pp. 74–84.

33. Fishman, p. 311.

34. R. L. Honnellio and S. Rydell, "Sabotage Vulnerability of Nuclear Power Plants," *International Journal of Nuclear Governance, Economy and Ecology*, 1 (2007): 312–321.

35. This recommendation recalls an unrelated but complementary observation that the corporate security director of a retail fast-food corporation shared with the author in 2001, in Miami. Specifically, the director noted that his greatest value to his employer came as a result of close integration with the business, because he required each of his staff members to spend time in one of the stores. Consequently, when Security came to design the operating manual for opening and closing each retail establishment, the security director was able to integrate secure cash handling and loss prevention procedures into day-to-day operations instead of trying to add them as an appliqué. Losses from both internal theft and armed robbery declined as a result.

36. M. Nieto, K. Johnston-Dodds, and C. W. Simmons, *Public and Private Applications of Video Surveillance and Biometric Technologies*, California Research Bureau, Sacramento: California State Library Foundation, 2002, p. 34.
37. P. Murphy, "Surveillance," in *Security Business Practices Reference, Volume 2*, Alexandria, VA: American Society for Industrial Security, 1999. Note that Patrick Murphy, Loss Prevention Director for Marriott International, confirmed experiencing an 84% decline in losses from armed robberies as a result of Marriott's openly visible installation of surveillance cameras, which led him to publish his experience as a best industry practice in 1999 and which still held true 10 years later (personal communication, July 23, 2009).
38. See p. 16, Nieto, Johnston-Dodds, & Simmons, op. cit., and R. Day, "Remotely Monitored CCTV Reduces Theft by 80%," in *Secure Times*, Essex, UK: Sheen Publishing, Ltd., May, 2009, p. 19. Richard Day, a manager whose British firm had been experiencing high losses of construction equipment to burglars, credited remotely monitored surveillance cameras for reducing such losses by 80% as of June 2009.
39. S. M. Ho, "Trustworthiness in Virtual Organizations," *Proceedings of the Fifteenth Americas Conference on Information Systems*, San Francisco, California, August 6–9, 2009, p. 6.
40. J. Giesberg, "The Role of Communication in Preventing Workplace Sabotage," *Journal of Applied Social Psychology*, 31 (2009): 2439–2461.
41. O. Newman, *Defensible Space: Crime Prevention through Urban Design*, New York: Macmillan Publishing Company, 1972, p. 6.
42. O. Newman, personal communication, November 21, 2002. Newman's remarks came in an e-mail response to the researcher's inquiry regarding whether he was still teaching his principles or aware of any such program of instruction he would currently recommend for security practitioners.
43. J. Q. Wilson and G. L. Kelling, "Fixing Broken Windows," *The Atlantic Monthly*, March 1982.
44. G. L. Kelling and C. M. Coles, *Fixing Broken Windows: Restoring Order and Reducing Crime in Our Communities*, New York: Touchstone, 1996, p. xv.
45. Kelling's theory is not without its critics. However, much of the criticism is directed not at whether Fixing Broken Windows works to take back public spaces from offenders who otherwise scare away legitimate users, but at larger societal issues, such as the inevitable displacement of offender activity that occurs in neighboring communities that are not using the same strategy. Some find it objectionable that a winning strategy applied to one community ends up shifting the problem to a neighboring community. Similarly, other critics object that changing demographics may also account for crime. Since Kelling did not offer his theory as a panacea or as the sole explanation for decreases in crime, himself taking account of other factors, including Newman's work, it is more accurate to say his theory may have been challenged but not discredited. More recent criticisms focus on community policing aspects of the theory, which vary greatly depending on the police force. However, as researchers Braga and Bond highlighted, this point vindicated the theory in a recent study, which found that cleaning up the physical environment in Lowell, MA was very effective, while a corresponding increase in misdemeanor arrests was not (C. Y. Johnson, Breakthrough on "Broken Windows," *Boston Globe*, February 8, 2009. Retrieved July 5, 2009 from http://www.boston.com/news/local/massachusetts/articles/2009/02/08/breakthrough_on_broken_windows/?page=2).

46. J. Wang, H. M. Hutchins, and T. N. Garavan, "Exploring the Strategic Role of Human Resource Development in Organizational Crisis Management." *Human Resource Development Review*, 8 (2009): 22–53.

47. Garcia, op. cit.

48. Centre for the Protection of National Infrastructure, *Guide to Producing Operational Requirements for Security Measures*, London: CPNI, 2010, p. 10.

49. Basic pre-employment background investigations continue to offer value as a tool of due diligence that may detect or deter criminals and individuals with a history of misconduct. They do not pose a serious obstacle to a moderately prepared infiltrator whose selection will in some measure depend on having a history free of criminal convictions and otherwise free of easily identifiable discrepancies that background checks are designed to spot.

50. *ICE Mutual Agreement for Government and Employers*, op. cit.

PART II

Key Players

CHAPTER 3

Agents of Change—
Corporate Sentinels

Teams do not develop themselves. They require systematic hard work. To build a successful team, you don't start out with people—you start out with the job. You ask: What are we trying to do? Then, what are the key activities (to achieve our results)? ...Then, and only then, do you ask: What does each of the people at the top have by way of strength? How do the activities and skills match? ...You identify individual strengths, then you match the strengths with key activities. And position your players to take action.

Peter Drucker

Every play, campaign, or endeavor seeking widespread impact among a population of good size must have its protagonists and must be ready to face antagonists as well. So it is with the stage, the church, and the job. So, too, it is with considering a No Dark Corners innovation for the institution. Here, the protagonists' ranks begin with corporate sentinels, whose traditional purview inclines them to see insider threats as their problem. Then there are the leaders of the organization, whose support when granted or withheld decides whether a new approach will have a chance to take hold. Rounding out the protagonists, then, are the team members on whom it falls to make the transformation from weakest link to first line of defense. If mishandled or badly treated, any of these protagonists can turn into antagonists more virulent and unyielding than the most determined adversary. And there is always at least the possibility of an antagonist, not only in the form of a hostile insider but also in the form of an adversary organization that cultivates or exploits this individual. As we examine the protagonists and their roles in a No Dark Corners environment, however, we begin, as management icon Peter Drucker suggests, not with personalities but with what we are seeking to achieve, what strengths the various protagonists have to offer, and how these strengths and players match with key activities.[1]

KEY ACTIVITIES

As identified in the strategy canvas of the preceding chapter, the key activities for instituting a No Dark Corners innovation are the following:

1. Random audits
2. Background investigations
3. Invasive monitoring
4. Background updates

5. Assignment of insider defense to corporate sentinels exclusively, or not
6. Identity and employment verification
7. Close probation
8. Transparency on the job
9. Self-monitoring teams

Items 1–3 are basic due diligence functions that remain necessary at some level, regardless of whether the institution adopts a No Dark Corners strategy or continues to toe a more traditional line. These three items involve activities that require some degree of specialization and that seldom impinge upon either leaders or work teams in their daily routines. We can safely leave items 1–3 into the primary care of corporate sentinels whose job descriptions require conversance with such duties. Random audits, for example, fall smoothly within the mandate of an internal audit or business controls function, and can there safely remain. Invasive monitoring, similarly, will tend to involve the kind of remote diagnostics that are second nature to information technology staff tasked with monitoring system health and guarding against network intrusion and abuse. Alternatively, a security or safety function may also be responsible for some monitoring of operations and people, particularly where hazardous substances or high value assets are involved. These, too, are activities that continue to fall within sentinel purviews, and can safely remain in this province, subject to reasonable checks and balances.

Items 4–7, however, are where No Dark Corners diverges markedly from the traditional approach. Consequently, these will be areas open to greater involvement and oversight by engaged work teams. Indeed, only two of the activities, 4 (background updates) and 6 (ID and employment verification), would tend to be more specialized, and hence more likely to find their way to a corporate sentinel to administer. However, even if corporate sentinels contribute to carrying out these activities, it is important to leave the door open to broader contribution. Specifically, an immediate work team member may well be the first to recognize inconsistencies between an insider's avowed background and work history and the same individual's actual capabilities and knowledge as demonstrated on the job. If team members are barred from contributing their frontline observations when it comes time to look into items 4 and 6, then the institution unwisely denies itself an opportunity to detect and thwart a potential infiltrator with an imperfect legend or cover story. Moreover, for the remaining activities it is even more important that the employees best able to spot inconsistencies and suspicious maneuvers, that is, fellow team members, be not only empowered but expected to contribute in a process of ongoing, meaningful evaluation of new candidate team members.

Although top managers may not and should not involve themselves equally in such activities, it remains useful to preserve an option for their involvement, since executives can offer a different perspective and since the span of their own professional networks frequently means that they possess the capacity to reach out informally to more places and counterparts in the event there is a need to validate or refute suspicions about why a probationary employee here was really let go by a competitor in the same industry.

In this context, prudence would suggest that corporate sentinels retain the lead for performing the activities in 1–3 and probably also 4 and 6, while retaining at least secondary responsibility for the remainder, whereas team members take the lead for those remaining activities, with support from sentinels when necessary.

Let us now take a closer look at sentinels and team members, though, in order to better understand how they work and fit into the larger organization.

CORPORATE SENTINELS

Traditional Role

Corporate sentinels are hated sentinels. Increasingly specialized, insular, and removed from the core business or operations, they stand apart from the larger employee population. Often, this psychological distance is further amplified through physical segregation of their work space from the general population. The specialized skills necessary for becoming a corporate sentinel—whether an auditor, security practitioner, computer forensics technician, or even a corporate recruiter—are necessarily alien to the core business and to employees not immersed in the given discipline's argot and mantras. That the institution willingly assists the sentinel in wearing a prominent cloak of confidentiality may serve a useful business purpose. However, it also further stands the sentinel apart from coworkers. These conditions isolate the sentinel, giving rise to real or perceived elitism that inevitably fosters alienation and an us-vs.-them divide that soon permeates the workplace.[2] By their own self-definition, the sentinels are the watchers who must maintain a certain professional distance from the people they are watching. They must also guard against revealing their methods and information sources to the uninitiated or to the people against whom they may one day have to act. Meanwhile, to the rest of the workplace, secrecy makes the sentinels suspect. After all, the employees sustaining the core business or operations are the ones doing the productive work that ultimately pays for what many may regard as the luxury of compensating nonproductive, overhead employees to watch them. Add ego to the mix and the proud worker chafes at nosy sentinels looking over his shoulder just as much as the conscientious auditor feels obligated to uncover operator deficiencies in controls in order to earn her salary. Invariably, the two camps develop adversarial views of one another. At best, they carve out neutral corners to inhabit, each confining oneself to respective purview and staying out of the other's way.

Expertise and Alienation

As a professional watcher, the corporate sentinel is expected to accumulate and deploy some degree of specialized expertise otherwise unavailable to the meaner herd. Thus, the recruiter is expected to know more about screening applicants than the hiring manager. The auditor is supposed to be uniquely qualified to uncover fraud. The security practitioner should be able to detect breaches and threats. The computer forensics specialist is the one best able to determine if someone is abusing the institution's network or computer assets. To each of the different classes of sentinel, there attaches a given expertise and area of primary responsibility. Moreover, institutions being what they are, it is only natural for the various sentinels to carve out their own niche and, over time, to guard jealously their prerogatives. In this traditional environment, there is a single, universal message that reaches the general workforce whenever an issue arises that could be construed as belonging legitimately in the province of a corporate sentinel: Leave the matter to the expert. The corollary is that the designated expert is a sentinel who will not welcome participation or interference from the average employee, that is, the nonspecialist and nonsentinel. What results follow this approach?

First, average employees begin and end their involvement in a case with a referral to a sentinel. They know that to do otherwise would invite institutional scorn. Second,

because there are always times when there are more potential cases to probe than specialized sentinels to handle them, the sentinels must prioritize. Depending on the workload
and perceived significance or even subjectively dictated priorities, sentinels may well take
on cases that their internal clients perceive as frivolous while overlooking cases the uninitiated perceive as much more significant. What is the net result if this perceived disconnect continues? The general employee population gradually limits its reporting of cases to
the corporate sentinels. If the sentinels additionally develop a reputation for being high-
handed or for imposing burdens on the reporting organization, employees consult them
even less frequently—or only when directed by higher authority. Consequently, the very
employees who are in a position to be the first line of defense against an insider attack
become incentivized to do little if the matter falls within the purview of a corporate sentinel and to do nothing if it falls within the purview of a hated sentinel. These conditions
ultimately favor the hostile insider operating with the savvy to exploit systemic weakness.

What makes early detection of a hostile insider more difficult under the foregoing
circumstances is that the workforce at large cedes all defensive responsibility to corporate
sentinels. "Leave it to the experts" becomes a litany chanted in prelude to "It's not my
job." To the extent the corporate sentinels are hated sentinels, their efforts engender more
suspicion than support, and it is just as likely that the average employee will reveal what
he learns of a sentinel's interest in a hostile insider as that he will support that sentinel's
efforts to confirm or refute suspicions about the insider. Regardless of whether the compromise springs from naivete or a desire to settle scores with hated sentinels, the result for
the institution is the same: a lost opportunity to thwart an attacker.

CASE STUDY: COLLISION OF THE SINGLE-MINDED

Bob is an organizational security officer practicing at the journey level. He is edu-
cated, having a degree in the social sciences but not a level of specialization that
would make him immediately marketable based on his degree alone. He spent his
first few years after college trying his hand at a number of different occupations
until settling into a security role in his thirties. Now, entering his forties, Bob feels
he knows his business, does a good job for his employer, and tries to add value even
when others in the larger institution aver otherwise.

Sally is an up-and-coming engineer within the core business of Bob's employer.
Ten years his junior, she nevertheless earns a third more than Bob does and, in her 5
years working where Bob has been working for 12 years, she has already had three
promotions to his two. Sally has a bright future and growing reputation as a rising
star. She works on important projects, contributing materially to the bottom line
of the enterprise.

Bob, on the other hand, is seen not so much bright as steady. He is respected
because he is reliable, causes no trouble, and meets his obligations consistently.
Within the security hierarchy, Bob is seen as a solid performer whose advancement
hinges on the timing of retirements and vacancies for which he may qualify.

Sally and Bob are civil to each other, but hardly more than that. Sally sees Bob
as the personification of some arcane set of rules that no one publishes or explains
before fussing over their breach. To her, Bob is forever nagging Sally and other productive employees about security violations and the need to protect against unseen
threats with little regard for what such efforts represent in terms of lost productive

time. If Sally fails to secure a sensitive operating manual from a work team where everyone has equal access to it, because she has only 15 minutes for lunch before leading a technical meeting on a major project, Bob is sure to be the one to discover this infraction and add to the frustrations of Sally's already too-short business day.[3] Now, she gets called into her superior's office to explain a security violation, forcing compressed lunch plans aside and assuring that she will have another hour of explaining and other acts of contrition to perform after finishing the 2 extra hours of overtime the current project will consume this evening.

Bob, meanwhile, is incensed at Sally's chronic violation of security protocols to compensate for her headlong rushing throughout the enterprise, as though the future of the entire organization depended on her unimpeded ability to juggle feathers in a hurricane while the likes of Bob were casually tossing anvils at her. Bob feels it is a tribute to his unruffled calm that he has been able to restrain his temper in reporting this, the latest of Sally's serial security infractions. A lesser soul would be spewing epithets, calling the employee hotline or ombudsman, and loudly demanding some overt display of progressive discipline for Sally—just to prove that institutional leadership is serious about the rules and underlying policies that Sally appears to be flaunting on a daily basis. Instead, Bob feels he is being a calm professional by merely going to Sally's boss and his own with the latest incident, deferring to their good judgment while also taking careful note of how they will handle the matter.

What does this situation do for insider threats in the ambient environment?

Positive

- Draws some level of attention to security and operational problems, thereby increasing the likelihood that principals will discuss their differences and resolve them instead of ignoring them and aggravating the situation over time.

Negative

- Reinforces antipathies and negative stereotypes that two opposing camps within the institution have of each other, limiting likelihood of any cooperation that is not forced. Thus, neither camp is likely to approach the other to air concerns over a suspected infiltrator or other insider threat, for fear of derision or interdepartmental retribution.
- Fosters an environment where core business employees on whose efforts the health and growth of the institution relies will condone or seek out ways to bypass security rules and their enforcers, that is, corporate sentinels, because they regard them as obstructionist.

Insider Exploitation Opportunity

- Dana, the probationary assistant hired to relieve Sally of routine burdens so that Sally can assume the technical lead on a new project of vital importance to the employer, now finds at least two socially acceptable reasons for violating the same security rules confronting Sally. First, the boss, Sally, leaves no doubt that these rules are counterproductive, hence unrespected by persons of consequence within the main organization. Second, even if

Sally receives the equivalent of a wrist-slap for violating these rules, the larger organization communicates through its institutional reactions that the rules do not apply so seriously to employees intimately involved with the core business. If Dana is an infiltrator, Dana now has the opportunity to also flaunt the rules at least once without fear of serious repercussion. Indeed, even if Dana has no thoughts of sabotage or maleficent action, the visible tug-of-war between Sally and Bob makes it virtually impossible for Dana to align in any meaningful way other than with Sally, that is, against Bob and the hated sentinel function he epitomizes.

Sentinel Alienation

Being human, sentinels seek the same kinds of validation that any employee desires from an employer in the form not only of compensation but also of demonstrable acknowledgment of value or expertise. As sentinels are more likely to be part of a staff rather than line organization, they are likely to feel greater pressure to prove their value, since the core business probably started and could often continue without them. Consequently, as a function of ambient conditions and sentinel predisposition, it is the rare sentinel who does not inspire resentment by falling into one of these chronic behavior patterns, and Bob, in the case example, is no exception.

Perfunctory Adaptation

This is the short-sighted end of the spectrum along which corporate sentinels view how they fit into the larger organization. The sentinel who adopts this perspective sees his or her role strictly in terms of following a defined mandate and nothing more. Thus, any discussion of how the sentinel may provider greater value by doing something differently is likely to be a spark that falls on damp kindling. To the insouciant sentinel narrowly focused on performing a task strictly within defined parameters, it does no good to talk of higher responsibility or to seek advice to evaluate a threat. In the case of a hostile insider, a team member hesitates to discuss misgivings with a myopically insouciant sentinel because the latter refuses to serve as sounding board. Indeed, this sentinel's unreceptive response drives others away, which the sentinel embraces as a tactic for keeping focused on his or her narrowly defined role.

Imperial Overreach or Power Play

At the polar extreme of perfunctory adaptation comes imperial overreach. This kind of sentinel construes everything to be his or her business. Although this perspective may appear more inclusive and welcoming to the team member seeking consultation, it soon exhausts collaboration once the employee sees the imperial sentinel introducing opinions or mandates at the expense of productivity. To this kind of sentinel, everything is a big deal. Every matter is a nascent game-changer. Consequently, every case becomes labor-intensive and demanding, with no leavening to provide a sense of proportion. The busiest employees soon learn to avoid the sentinel afflicted with imperial overreach because they lack the time and energy to turn even a casual inquiry into a major production. Another variation of this kind of sentinel stance is the power play. The sentinel inclined to power play is typically one who has little or no positional authority to interpret rules or make exceptions but just enough power to say no. Exercising that limited power becomes, for this individual, one of the few opportunities that the organization gives to have an impact on the business of others who are more important to the larger organization. Thus, saying no makes the power play sentinel as close as he or she will ever be to a position of ascendancy over the team member seeking his or her assistance. Indeed, some observers could see in this sentinel–team member relationship the validation of a theory on how status and power form distinct means of differentiating oneself in a hierarchy. According to this theory, power relates to control over resources, whereas status relates to the respect one possesses in the eyes of others.[4] In this construct, it is the team member who is a rising star in the core business who has higher status, whereas the sentinel would appear to be compensating for a perceived deficit in status through the exercise of power.

Cronyism or Favor Exchange

The sentinel propelled by cronyism or favor exchange is a wheeler-dealer tailoring services not to business need but to ulterior agendas. This sentinel tells the employee either what the employee wants to hear or what will serve the employee's own ends, provided the employee is willing to reciprocate by exchanging favors with the sentinel. In practice, this approach ranges from weighing in favor of terminating someone because the employee is one's friend, master, or a political ally who is at the sentinel's door for help in removing someone disliked—or for bypassing normal checks and balances by getting the sentinel to expedite processing and approval of someone in good graces.

Transformational Role in a No Dark Corners Approach

In a No Dark Corners workplace, the corporate sentinel evolves from being the only designated defender and likely point of failure to a collaborator who exists to support the team that constitutes the first line of defense. Just as a kicker can save the football game with a field goal or an artillery strike can make the difference between frontline troops being overrun by enemy soldiers, so does the corporate sentinel go from being a hated obstacle to a specialized resource to call into play when in need of reinforcements. Yet, like the kicker or artillery barrage, the sentinel becomes an asset to be brought into play—not the only resource or excuse for losing the contest.

How does one promote this transformation? First, the institution adopts the strategic innovations of the No Dark Corners approach, in effect empowering team members to take an active hand in controlling who remain within their ranks. Second, however, it is necessary to eliminate artificial silos, ruefully recognized as cylinders of excellence,[5] by striking a delicate balance between empathy and objectivity. In practice, this objective is best met by embedding at least some sentinels into work spaces where the institution's primary operations take place. What then keeps the embedded sentinel from losing all objectivity and going native? One answer lies in what foreign ministries and state departments do to keep their diplomats from forgetting their loyalties: periodic consultations with peers (i.e., in this case, with other sentinels) and regular rotations. Another answer is in rotational assignments for employees from core business units into sentinel functions, thereby cross-pollinating each camp, demonstrating the value each has to offer to the employer, and fostering interpersonal relationships that extend throughout careers and beyond rotational assignments.

The purpose of these measures is to inculcate in sentinels a leadership lesson, once articulated by management innovator Robert Townsend, to throttle the sentinels' impulse to look down on those they serve, since:

> You can't direct people to trust you. It starts with consistent action, trusting the people below you, even though they meet only 50 percent of your expectations for what you wish you had below you. You've got to convince yourself that they're capable of growing the other 50 percent... You've got to start trusting down. And trust is earned by that. Eventually you'll be trusted if your actions are the same as your words.[6]

The transformational component of reversing the chronically adversarial stance that sentinels tend to adopt against other employees extends beyond a security role to one of institutional leadership. As Townsend pointed out, transforming the organization is about "cleaning up the system so it will embrace good leadership, not subvert it."[7]

A Sentinel's Guide to People Security

No asset is imperiled or in need of defense without the presence of people or other life forms coveting it. As corporate sentinels engage in the balancing act that involves an endless tug-of-war between productive operations and the protection of same, it is useful to review their larger responsibility to the institution and what value they should offer to serve it and fellow employees. Here follows one such refresher primarily for security but equally applicable to other corporate sentinels.

Human Relationships

The internal, human-to-human culture of a corporation is ironically and probably the most important asset vital to maintaining a resilient and secure environment. The response of the security team to catastrophic incidents is usually quite obvious and formulaic: assess damage, protect life and property from further damage, and support restoration of the enterprise. The human hazards that security must address require more subtlety and caution. Human assaults on security may include the obvious outsiders causing intentional harm, such as spies, vandals, thieves, and rioters who are impeded by physical and electronic countermeasures. But of equal concern are those who have permission to enter—with employees obviously in this group—but also the visitors, clients, customers, and contractors who flow through the organization on a daily basis and constitute the broader universe of insiders. The motivations for loss-causing human behavior carry any number of labels—drunkenness and substance abuse, emotional distress, financial straits, or simply a venal character and navigation through life.

Whether a workforce is enthusiastic and loyal to the mission and goals of an enterprise is something beyond the authority or power of any corporate sentinel. But, again and again, the first and most important tripwire in detecting a breach of security in an organization is a tip or observation passed on by a concerned employee troubled by the behavior of another. Although the security organization is not principally responsible for maintaining a cooperative and security-conscious environment, the security team can tap into these attitudes and loyalties to leverage its concern and connections across the enterprise landscape. A security-conscious workforce is a force multiplier that in many ways pays more dividends than a budget increase.

The Dishonest Employee

There are dishonest individuals in any human population, but the ability of a dishonest individual is certainly strengthened in a neglectful or outright hostile work environment where employees do not perceive their best interests to conform to the goals of the enterprise. It is not the burden of the security team to engage in moral training, but dishonest activity, from fraud to outright intentional and deceptive sabotage, can fall into the lap of the security team first. What is done with the information received depends on the organizational structure of the enterprise but in most cases is driven principally by the human resources team. It is very much, however, the job of security to first attempt to detect such negative behaviors in ways that do not violate human or employee rights, and it is certainly Security's job to conduct formal investigations to gather evidence and to measure the extent of damage caused by dishonest behavior or intentional harm.

Management Responsibility in Loss Prevention

Most senior management teams would rather focus on business expansion, increase in revenue, market share, or strategic missions. It is also their responsibility to detect and stem losses and, more fundamentally, to detect and cull from any workforce those who intentionally act in ways that damage or impede the essential operations of the enterprise. For these often reluctant tasks, senior management will turn to a dedicated and professional security team or other corporate sentinels. Management must set the tone in promoting a culture of accountability throughout the enterprise and support this effort through both positive example and business process transparency. This investment of management effort, over time, ultimately communicates the message that dishonesty or insider attack and undermining of the organization are unacceptable under any circumstances. The net result is the development of a culture that, ideally, stigmatizes dishonesty and sabotage or at least offers reduced support or tacit collusion in such undermining activities on the part of coworkers or fellow insiders.

Procedural Controls

The most vital procedural controls to stem and detect losses are quite often beyond the purview and design of the security team. For example, the system for the detection of fraud in a financial institution is most commonly the product of a team of auditing specialists and the IT organization. In this day of sophisticated computer assaults, these systems can be quite complex and elaborate, driven by developments in industry custom and practice, and become a matter for the security team only when the breach, and often when the breaching individual, are fully detected and identified. However, more conventional systems of barriers and physical identification used to control physical access to facilities and high-value assets remain principally a security team assignment. Planning the system of impediments used for access control monitoring their integrity, and detecting a breach are security team duties in almost every substantial organization.

Pre-Employment Screening

The best way to prevent losses is to avoid hiring someone likely to produce them in the first place. Thus, one of the principal duties of care that any organization owes its customers and employees is the screening of persons who would cause loss or harm before such individuals are admitted into the workforce as insiders. It often falls to the security team to assist or lead in gathering and analyzing lawfully obtained and relevant information about a job, promotion, or retention candidate. There are many and probably will be more rules and prescriptions about what can and cannot be done in checking and investigating the background of a potential hire to any organization. Use of information that may turn up in the course of an investigation, such as disabilities, ethnicity, sexual orientation, and even arrests as distinct from convictions, is highly proscribed and cannot be used in determining suitability for hire. The purpose of investigatory inquiries is to verify what statements have been made by a candidate in support of an application and to gather other relevant information that the candidate may not have provided but is relevant in making an informed determination of competence and suitability. A candidate can be required to provide legally obtainable information relevant to hiring, and the information must be accurate and truthful. In almost any enterprise, intentional falsification or omissions by a candidate are disqualifying events, but increasingly an organization may not reject a candidate categorically even in these circumstances unless they can show direct relevance to the job in question, hence the importance of a robust probationary period and a real—rather than an aspirational—capacity for hiring managers to readily dismiss new hires that raise red flags or prove unsuitable.

Personal Safety and Self-Defense

The principal emphasis of the security apparatus is to protect against the loss of assets or impediments to human or staff contributions caused by neglectful or intentionally hostile individuals or by catastrophes. It is also often the responsibility of security to monitor the workforce and protect individuals from harm that may range from random violence (such as parking lot assaults, rapes, and accidents caused by on-site traffic and movement). Patrol systems are ordinarily set up to move security teams in random, but organized patterns emerge through places such as storage facilities, parking structures, and avenues of ingress and egress where employees and other authorized visitors may be in peril. It is vital that such patrolling and monitoring systems be themselves the subject of audit and testing to measure and confirm their effectiveness. Security design enhancements, such as protective lighting, reduction of places for concealment, and surveillance systems, can also increase the effectiveness of security staff. Too often, elaborate identification and barrier systems are effectively maintained only to find that random thieves and rapists are able to assault employees in remote and unprotected parts of the employer's property. It is also worth deploying time and budget from the security team to assist in raising security consciousness and self-defense skills of workforce members who predictably find themselves put by their work patterns into dangerous or imperiled circumstances.

Workplace Violence

Providing a safe workplace is not only an obvious responsibility of any institution—it is also federal and often state law.

Workplace violence is one of the most recent and darkest chapters in America's social history. Today, homicide is the number one cause of death in the workplace for women and the number two cause for men. The most dangerous position is ironically sales and service where deranged or furious killers are likely to invade and perpetrate mayhem against an organization.[8]

Threat management focused on reducing this development is an increasingly critical part of the security team and one to which sentinels neglect or ignore at their career peril. A proper threat management program directed at workplace violence would extend from pre-employment screening to writing and maintaining guidelines and would also inform access control and physical security systems. It is increasingly part of responsible security management to both form and drill an incident management team that will deploy and respond to any claims of harassment, physical threat, assault, or homicide encountered in the workplace. A completely minimal incident team would include senior level managers from security, HR, the C-suite, and Legal with divisional correlates when an enterprise has more than one significant location. The team approach is always superior to reliance on one dedicated expert who finds himself or herself unable to mobilize sufficient resources in time to prevent the incident and attending casualties. Informal information paths are also very important in intercepting growing threats from disgruntled formal employees or disaffected spouses who may communicate their intentions days or weeks before actually committing their horrid actions.

There are forms of unacceptable behaviors, such as discrimination and harassment, which can foreshadow acts of violence. A threat management program should be particularly sensitive to escalating incidents of troubling behavior and be prepared for legal and quick interventions. If reasons for managing workplace protections against violence were not a moral imperative, then senior management should certainly be concerned about the liabilities that ensue after such actions take place. Losses in plaintiff judgments are in the many millions of dollars, and that does not even begin to include loss in productivity and reputation that may ensue in the general disruption accompanying a violent incident.

Unbalanced or exaggerated worries that attentive security may violate individual rights can disadvantage both employee and organization by denying obvious and escalating threats. Human behavior typically follows an identifiable scale with regard to those who commit workplace atrocities and homicides: first disgruntlement, then verbal intimidation and threats, property damage, actual violence against individuals without weapons, and finally dangerous violence with weapons. Much of this predictable escalation, however, happens outside the workplace, but that does not mean that people inside the walls are unaware of it. Most legal restrictions do not curtail the gathering of this type of information but rather restrict, understandably, its inappropriate use and application. An agile and fully legal response in managing and protecting employees against such people is almost always completely possible and security management should not shy away from its responsibilities to be vigilant and attentive to signs and sources of impending danger.

Early intervention, even offering a compassionate ear to someone who has acted in anger in a minor incident, can work effectively to deflect and defer something that may otherwise grow in intensity over time—derailed either because the individual is able to let off steam in a discussion or simply knows that their behavior is now known by watchful coworkers or security team members. Time and again, those who have studied troubled individuals in the context of a workplace have found that early intervention and providing individuals other options from treatment to counseling have averted much more disastrous options that typically come when such individuals feel that their back is against the wall and no one understands or cares about their grievance.

Unfair Labor Practices

A good grievance process supplies a path for diffusing tension, thereby reducing incipient insider hostilities and decreasing the availability of ready collaboration with more serious insider threats such as hostile infiltrators.

The interface of the security team with the workforce is both inevitable and yet fraught with sensitivities that can have enormous consequences for the institution if badly managed. In organizations that have formal contractual relationships with their workforce, such as union or association agreements, the security team must be aware, conversant with, and sensitive to the rules that such agreements and the broader federal and state laws that apply. Within the United States, the National Labor Relations Act is the foundational law in this area, and the National Labor Relations Board adjudicates unfair labor practices. Typical points of friction between security staff and union representatives arise from perceptions of interference with legitimate attempts to organize employees to initially seek representation by collective bargaining agents, the taking of protected labor actions such as strikes, and collective bargaining sessions at which security may be asked to maintain order. The most egregious examples of overreaching in the use of security teams, for example, in strike-busting and the dismissal or harassment of union organizers, are artifacts of the past. Inappropriate use of undercover investigations during periods of labor unrest or organizing, however, remains possible even today. Accordingly, there is a positive burden on security managers to sensitize their staff at every level to the procedural shop, plant, or workplace protections afforded to such activities as literature distribution, organizing meetings and discussions, and the use of signage and other means to encourage membership and union support. On the other hand, there are labor practices by those who would organize employees that are equally unfair and sometimes illegal, which can be reported, confronted, and challenged. Sometimes this work is delegated to the security team and must always be executed with the utmost sensitivity and in close partnership with the enterprise's Legal and HR specialists that can help Security navigate these dangerous waters. For an enterprise that operates one or more negotiated labor contracts, conflict typically centers on the processing of just-cause discharges. Establishing credible evidence of misconduct or unsuitability of an employee must typically, in such circumstances, be worked carefully through complex grievance machinery that may delay or derail resolution that would satisfy nonunion management. Also, behavior and interactions of guard force members with individuals who are members of labor organizations are subject to more intense scrutiny and can be unfairly interpreted in a different light given the expressed or assumed attitude of the enterprise toward its unionized membership. The arbitration of an employee's own grievances also must follow in unionized environments a careful set of impartial processes set by contract and by law.

The violation or avoidance of the set and formal procedural rules can result in a collapse of the process and harsh financial fines or liabilities for the enterprise. During legal labor actions, such as a strike, the guard force must be carefully monitored and restrained in the face of what may sometimes be provocative actions and even threats made by people "walking the line" near access gates to enterprise facilities. Surveillance during such periods is typically intensified to detect any affiliated or exploitive actions of sabotage or even theft, but security managers must be vigilant to be sure that increased security measures do not overstep the bounds of law, regulation, or behavior that would put the enterprise in a bad or unfavorable light. Policies that invade communication such as heightened scrutiny of e-mail and correspondence may be particularly scrutinized during such times as an unfair intimidation of legitimate rights to communicate and organize. Video surveillance, which is typically done anyway to assure the integrity of the enterprise's barrier and identification system, can prove particularly valuable as evidence when passion overrides judgment and employees commit damaging actions that may be intended to provoke harsh reactions or draw attention to labor issues. Under such circumstances, surveillance video may not only supply the documentation necessary for the enterprise in pursuing injunctive relief from harmful or dangerous protests but also serve as a damper to mischief on both sides of a conflict, as the parties involved come to realize that their misdeeds are likely to be captured and revealed in any judicial proceedings.

Security and Civil Rights

The rights and duties of the citizens of the United States are principally established by the federal and state constitutions, which are the controlling documents for American law. Each constitution may establish what is or is not a criminal action, and the legislative power granted by the constitutions gives state and federal legislatures authority to create criminal codes. Some statutory violations may be defined as outside the criminal code, particularly those involving traffic and vehicular activity, and in some states the use of drugs or alcohol. A minimal understanding of the defined criminal statutes is essential to effectively monitor institutional and employee behavior. Whether an individual has the right to use, possession, or even abuse of institutional property or assets is critical to which kind of protective action a security force may take. A security force of a large institution is commonly and frequently dealing with all sorts of offenses that may violate internal rules and codes but also constitute criminal violations. Certainly, destruction of property, threats of force or actual force against individuals, unauthorized entry, or theft fall into these categories.

Nothing is more urgent among the many assignments given to Security than protecting the safety and integrity of the human beings engaged in the institution's operations. Basic violations in this arena include actual intentional injury, intimidation, the use of force, or the threatening of force. Intent is a critical element in the criminal prosecution of such offenses and it often falls first to security professionals inside the institution to gather this and other evidence of what led up to and caused an individual to commit such prohibited actions. In some cases, the security team itself may find it is the target of criminal investigations—particularly when force is used to protect and defend either persons or property. The rules of permissible use of force are different from state to state and Security leadership must have an understanding of the constraints on force specified in local and state law. The most sensational criminal activities are often the least common. For example, bomb threats are a frequent occurrence in the United States but they are mostly hoaxes. Extortion is also a frequent theme in Hollywood but is somewhat rare inside the walls of most institutions. Kidnapping, which is a real and present threat in some regions of the world, particularly South America, rarely happens in the United States in cases that involve institutions or their employees. (The most frequent cases of kidnapping usually involve child custody disputes and touch corporate and institutional concerns only when an incident affects an aggrieved parent who may be an employee and must leave work to address the situation.)

If a security action or investigation uncovers evidence of criminal activity, local or federal police authorities should be immediately engaged and integrated in the institutional response. In some cases, law enforcement officials will actually take command of the response and some crimes may require law enforcement authorities to use warrants. An arrest warrant authorizes law enforcement personnel to take a person into custody. A search warrant authorizes the search of a place that may be owned and protected by a particular institution. In no case should institutional security teams execute such warrants, which are issued almost exclusively to judicial officers or law enforcement personnel for execution. Security people may be deputized as law enforcement officers in some asset protection situations, but they will seldom take the lead in arresting anyone under a government warrant. More typical security team responses in the early stages of an incident involving an unruly or misbehaving employee or visitor are to practice self-protection techniques and in certain, urgent cases, containment. Physical constraints on private persons, such as handcuffing or incapacitating of an individual, are best left to police authorities except in the most desperate of circumstances. Security personnel must also act prudently in any interrogation situation where an individual may be subject to the Miranda requirements, particularly if the security team is seen as acting in support of police officers or within earshot of them. (It is a common confusion, however, particularly when a security team includes former police officers, to assume that Miranda warnings are necessary for internal interviews. They are not. *Miranda* is a decision of the U.S. Supreme Court that essentially holds that suspects in a custodial environment may not be interrogated until they have been first warned of their rights to counsel, to funding if they cannot afford counsel, and to their right to make no statement at all if they so choose.) It is not infrequent that security officers or investigators are found to have acted as "police officers" in any situation that spills over into the criminal courts. A fundamental understanding of entrapment is also sometimes relevant. This is an inducement to entice a person not otherwise disposed to do so to commit a criminal offense when the principal purpose of the inducement is simply to prosecute that person criminally. The most important attitude for an institutional security team with regard to known criminal activity that falls within institutional activities and processes is to engage official law enforcement authorities at the earliest possible moment and to be sure that the institution's own legal counsel is available at all times for consultation and advice.

There are other aspects of work life within an institution that may involve violation of other rights and privileges protected by law. Equal opportunity, which is premised on using the force of law to encourage racial, gender, and religious parity, is perhaps the most active and conflict-ridden area in which institutional action may raise questions about statutory violations. In most institutions, the HR office is the principal monitor of what does and does not constitute conformity with equal employment opportunity rules and statutes. An institution is also commonly constrained by National Labor Relations rules involving employee rights to organize and form labor associations, certain state and federal contract-compliance rules monitoring fairness and the awarding of federal and state contracts, and any number of other rules and tripwires prohibiting institutional actions and decisions based on national origin, religion, color, gender, race, or disability. But institutional legal counsel is the best guide as to what is or is not acceptable in such circumstances, as other issues may include right to representation in proceedings likely to result in discipline. Searches are also problematic if they are not performed on a consensual basis. Searching desks and lockers, which are essentially the property of the institution, is generally permitted, particularly if the individual has consented.

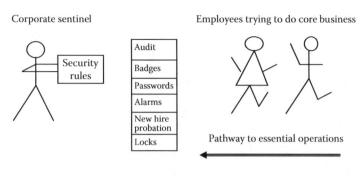

What is the sentinel doing?
- Erecting a wall?
- Tearing down a wall?

FIGURE 3.1   Corporate sentinel to other employees.

Conclusion

Corporate sentinels invariably find themselves in challenging circumstances. On the one hand, they are specialists who exist to perform at times tedious functions that line employees pursuing core business lack the time or expertise to tackle. On the other hand, they remain purveyors of a staff service, a support function whose demands cannot long overshadow those of core business without undermining essential operations. Figure 3.1 depicts where these sentinels stand in the view of the rest of the institution's employees, with a certain irreducible ambiguity regarding what role the sentinel shown is actually playing. Is he erecting barriers? Or is he removing them? Corporate sentinels succeed when they take on the character of artisans performing a useful function without forgetting the fundamental objectives of the masters they serve.

WHAT SHOULD A CORPORATE SENTINEL LOOK LIKE? AN ARTISAN, PARTICULARLY IF A SECURITY PRACTITIONER

SECURITY FOR ARTISANS

Security is receptive to scientific advance, but is no field for scientists to dominate.[9] The exigencies of protection are too fluid and the stakes too high for submitting one's livelihood, assets, or life to rigid metrics and laboratory-grade theories that fall apart on first contact with mortal hazard. On the other hand, security is no long-term home for artists, either. Not that the protective world needs be inhospitable to creativity or innovation—particularly if they produce desired protection on time and within ambient resource constraints. However, the artist's highest aspiration to be and do something unique will find a better home elsewhere. In the protection business, it is not only useful but necessary to be able to replicate and commoditize one's highest achievement, to spread it widely and often without taking credit for it. In this context, die-hard artists will surely look to greener pastures more befitting their egos and temperaments. Where does that leave us, then, if security is neither art nor science and if security welcomes visitors from both camps but offers neither a home?

Security at its best is a home for artisans. It is one of those hybrid disciplines whose highest expression derives from synthesis, from blending theory and innovation together and then applying the mixture with gusto and finesse to situations where success may occasionally surface but where failure is unmistakable and fatal to people, institutions, or careers. Security is no place for the faint of heart, for the indecisive, for the chronically risk-averse. It can be a natural fit, however, for defenders, pragmatic idealists, and masters of the calculated risk.

A first-rate security practitioner takes the pains of a fine craftsman (without giving the pains of a technical expert or temperamental artist) and applies skills that require not only knowledge but some level of apprenticeship. This practitioner takes enough pride in mastery of the discipline to keep honing skills that improve the way he or she practices the craft. Security professionals at the top of their game do for colleagues and neophytes what others did for them: teach, share, question, explain, and improve. They resist the temptation to hoard knowledge or mask ignorance. Some are blunt. Others are tactful. Some are didactic and prolix. Others are laconic, only answering questions rather than volunteering information. All the pros have successes under their belt, as well as misfires it pains them to remember. The good ones will tell you about both. The great ones will have one or more whoppers in the failure column. When they talk about those, they remember what they learned from their mistakes, how they did better next time.

Security professionals are as frustrated or stymied as anyone else. They learn to make peace with an imperfect world and navigate the uncertain waters that raise them high one day, only to submerge them to the depths the next day. Over time, security professionals learn to take vicissitudes in graceful stride. They learn to anticipate adverse consequences, and this knowledge carries over into organizational life. They see it coming. Ideally, they dodge the blow. When dodging is no option, at least they brace for the punch.

Security professionals put some distance between themselves and others. It keeps them objective and creates more room for maneuver, more reaction time. Most of the time, Security is no one's best friend. Often, though, Security is their only friend. Security people know they get paid to try where others run or hide. Part of their job is not just what they do under routine conditions, but what they are prepared to do when things go bad.

Security people may have ambitions, but they learn to keep them in check. Crime pays better. So do the kinds of jobs that require more ethical flexibility. Organizational dynamics can put security practitioners at odds with some employee populations more than others. Fortunately, the world keeps serving up just enough danger to remind most organizations why they have and keep Security on the payroll.

Security at its best keeps spectacular losses from happening. This makes it unspectacular and its consummate practitioners relatively unheralded. Only the professionals know among their ranks or just within themselves. And when they craft a worthy defense or foil an otherwise devastating attack, they know. They look up. They smile. And maybe that is enough.

QUESTIONS FOR ONLINE OR CLASSROOM DISCUSSION

1. Looking at Figure 3.1, adopt one of two positions and list actions on the part of corporate sentinels that would support your position.
   Position 1: The sentinel is erecting barriers to employees as they pursue core business.
   Position 2: The sentinel is removing these barriers to make employees more effective.
2. Now switch positions and make the opposite case.
   See notes above.
3. If the drawing in the figure is insufficient to illustrate either case adequately, then what indicators would you develop and monitor to determine whether a corporate sentinel is impeding or facilitating operations?
4. What is the proper role of management in guiding the way sentinel and average employee interact with one another?
5. How should good-faith differences between employee and sentinel be resolved? By whom?

EXERCISES FOR GROUP PROJECTS

1. Select an organization (it need not be your own) where there are at least two well-run corporate sentinel functions that are generally accepted by employees and supported by management. Assume that your group is taking over both functions and that your task is to completely undermine them to the point of eroding all user support and voluntary compliance. To this end, what are at least three things you could do? How long would it be before you attained the desired effects?
2. Select a corporate sentinel function that is generally maligned or not respected within your organization or another. Assuming a timeline of 6–12 months, develop a turnaround strategy, assigning different tasks to group members with the intent of improving that sentinel function's effectiveness over time. Based on what you learned in this chapter and what the preceding exercise told you about what it takes to undermine a working sentinel function, what do you need to do in this case? What should you do first? Is this turnaround possible by working solely within the sentinel function's confines, or do you also need to go across organizational lines to attain the desired result? Elaborate. Conclude by giving a timeline of actions for your first 6 months of sentinel rehabilitation.
3. Selecting an organization that appears to have too many sentinels concentrated at headquarters locations, can you develop an approach to embedding one corporate sentinel at each of multiple field sites where that one sentinel represents multiple sentinel functions and works in and with core business employees every day? Develop a pilot program to try this out. What dividends would you expect or be able to demonstrate to be able to make the case for trying this alternative approach? What resistance would you anticipate and from what organizations?

ENDNOTES

1. P. Drucker, *Managing the Non-Profit Organization*, New York: HarperBusiness, 1992, p. 152.
2. For a similar phenomenon detailed at length by a *Washington Post* reporter who was embedded with the U.S. Marines in a combat zone and then followed a class of Marine recruits through basic training to witness firsthand how their shared experiences bonded them together while alienating them from outsiders, see T. Ricks, *Making the Corps*, New York: Touchstone, 1997.
3. As farfetched as such an example may seem initially to those outside of draconian national security environments, such kinds of infractions and their policing are precisely what Chemical Facility Anti-Terrorism Standards (CFATS) proposed as a step in the direction of securing the chemical infrastructure. For insight into such proposals, consult early CFATS legislation, including 6 Code of Federal Regulations Part 27, 72 Federal Regulation 17688 (April 9, 2007), 65396 (Nov. 20, 2007), and the related congressional testimony of one rare dissenter, Clyde Miller, in Statement of Clyde D. Miller, Director, Corporate Security, BASF Corporation, before the United States House of Representatives' Committee on Homeland Security, Subcommittee on Transportation Security and Infrastructure Protection, "Chemical Security: The Implementation of the Chemical Facility Anti-Terrorism Standards and the Road Ahead," December 12, 2007. Miller highlights precisely this kind of contrived administrative burden created in an environment where security regulation takes no account of existing conditions and constraints.
4. For more discussion on this subject, see J. C. Magee and A. D. Galindky, "Social Hierarchy: The Self-Reinforcing Nature of Power and Status," *The Academy of Management Annals*, 2 (August 2008): 351–398.
5. The "cylinders of excellence" coinage traces to Christopher Bellavita, Director of Academic Programs, Center for Homeland Defense and Security, at the Naval Postgraduate School, where his coinage circulated widely over the course of classroom discussions between 2008 and 2009.
6. Robert Townsend and Warren Bennis, *Reinventing Leadership*, New York: HarperCollins, 1995, p. 62.
7. Townsend, op. cit., p. 46.
8. D. L. Ray, "Dealing with a Violent Employee," in *Issues in Security Management*, ed. R. R. Robinson, Boston: Butterworth-Heinemann, 1999, p. 106. In addition to a career with the Royal Canadian Mounted Police, Ray has spent considerable time in private security and, for a time, worked for the same international security and investigations consultancy as the author.
9. Reprinted by permission from N. Catrantzos, "Security for Artisans," May 16, 2010, on All Secure Blog, http://all-secure.blogspot.com/2010/05/security-for-artisans-security-is.html and subsequently reprinted as letter to editor, *Homeland Security Affairs Journal*, Volume 7, January 2011. Retrieved July 4, 2011 from http://www.hsaj.org/?article=7.1.8.

CHAPTER 4

Agents of Change—
Leaders and Copilots

When people feel they own an organization, they perform with greater care and devotion. They want to do things right the first time.

Captain D. M. Abrashoff

Setting an example is not the main means of influencing another, it is the only means.

Albert Einstein

When a copilot takes over to land a transport plane after the pilot's heart attack, he or she is assuming a leadership role. So, too, in daily organizational life does leadership spring forward to answer myriad questions and exigencies. Only a modest fraction of day-to-day leadership actions trace directly to officially designated executives. The rest come from team members who fill voids and slip into the copilot role whenever the situation calls for a steady hand otherwise absent from the controls.[1] Every team member has the capacity to lead, if only by positive example. There are formal leaders and informal leaders, some designated, others respected for reasons of skill, wisdom, or longevity. Ideally, one begins by combining with influential leaders who also legitimately occupy a position of authority in the institution. As leading icon of management, Peter Drucker, long ago noted,

> Character is not something one can fool people about. . . The spirit of an organization is created from the top. If an organization is great in spirit, it is because the spirit of its top people is great. If it decays, it does so because the top rots. . . No one should ever be appointed to a senior position unless top management is willing to have his character serve as the model for his subordinates.[2]

A CAUTIONARY TALE: HOW OVERCONFIDENCE MAKES BAD LEADERS

Unlike a trained and disciplined infiltrator, a self-dealing trust betrayer embedded in an organization is much more prone to self-exposure through overconfidence. And attaining executive rank offers little protection.

The New York governor's exposure as a client of an upscale prostitution ring in March 2008 afforded editorialists license to hold forth against the sins of hubris and hypocrisy.[3] Then psychologists could take their turn to use the tale to illustrate the contradictory sides of human nature. But to the security professional, Governor

Spitzer's folly in creating audit trails when sending a coin-operated bed mate across state lines and making arrangements via communications susceptible to federal wiretap illustrates a phenomenon also seen among spies and traitors: indiscretion borne of overconfidence.

Whence the association between an extramarital affair and treason? The requirement for deception is the same. As a tradecraft instructor once told my class of aspiring case officers many years ago, "Maintaining your cover takes the same talent you would use if cheating on your spouse." Thanks to Governor Spitzer, we can see that carrying out such illicit rendezvous indiscreetly is equally susceptible to breakdowns in basic tradecraft which, fundamentally, means breaches of security. After all, tradecraft amounts to nothing more than precautions taken to assure personal security and to safeguard a given operation.

So, setting aside the admittedly unsavory betrayals and hypocrisy permeating Spitzer's actions, let us examine his basic security failure. Here is a trained prosecutor with considerable expertise in the use of wiretaps and surveillance and forensic document examination. He should be an expert in conducting illicit activities without leaving traces, yet he leaves a trail for any rookie investigator to trip over while probing a prostitution ring. What is the fundamental failure? Tradecraft or, in other words, failure to follow routine, mundane, and elementary security precautions.

Although psychologists and pundits may speculate at the root cause and use this failure in operational security to underscore the governor's arrogance, there is another fundamental truth at the heart of the matter. It would have come into play even if Governor Spitzer were the most modest of men without any grandstanding proclivities. In reality, it comes equally into play in espionage cases and in cases where the most sophisticated traitors and case officers make the one fatal flaw that gives them away and compromises their operations or even their lives. What is the fundamental truth behind all these catastrophes?

Security is never convenient. And the corollary to this truth is that even the brightest participants in questionable activities will eventually surrender caution to convenience—hence their exposure. And it does not matter how smart they are, or how powerful, or how adroit in all other matters. All it takes is the calculated or chance exploitation of one fatal flaw in security, and exposure will result, with the attending ramifications of whatever represents catastrophe to those concerned. Ask the governor, after he added security malpractice to his growing list of fatal flaws.

LEADERSHIP'S ATTITUDE TO SENTINELS AND INSIDER THREAT DEFENSES

If we grant that leaders play a pivotal role, then the behavior and attitudes they display will serve as the model for other employees, including fellow team members and even the entire workforce. If leaders are attentive to those parts of the job that fall within the purview of corporate sentinels, treat the sentinels themselves with civility, and show that mitigating insider attacks and trust betrayal are important to them because they are important to the institution, it is still possible that other employees may not mirror this attitude. However, if leaders do the opposite, treating corporate sentinels and concerns over trust betrayal with scorn or ignoring them altogether, the support of the employee population for either sentinel or insider threat defense will seldom rise above widespread lip service.

Another shaper of leader attitudes is risk homeostasis, the tendency for taking higher risks in one area by taking lower risks in another.[4] Research supporting this theory indicates that once given a greater capability to reduce risk—whether in vehicle safety devices such as seatbelts and antilock brakes or enhanced corporate resources to attain desired objectives—many people will still fail to reduce accident rates or achieve business results because the new capabilities in essence provide a safety net that spurs taking more risks than they otherwise would. The lesson inferred by one student of this tendency is that once attaining a threshold resource level necessary to get started with an innovative idea, one should move forward without delay. Otherwise, as counterintuitive as it may seem, waiting longer for more resources increases the risk of failure.[5]

WHERE TO BEGIN

Leaders, particularly at the top of the institution, must balance conflicting demands on their time and attention. They neither can nor should be expected to command the same level of narrow expertise in specialized functions of their corporate sentinels nor anticipate every single ramification that each insider threat defense may produce for all team members in the core business. However, leaders should be able to establish guidelines and metrics to predispose their organizations to operating effectively and to measure when performance shortfalls are signaling a problem that demands managerial intervention. Even in the absence of additional resources or an externally imposed mandate that gives them the means or justification for getting involved in insider threat defense, leaders at any hierarchical or resource level always have these three options for improving institutional resistance to sabotage by trust betrayers:[6]

- Know your world.
- Start somewhere.
- At least ask.

The foregoing advice applies equally to the leader of a large organization struggling to mediate conflict between corporate sentinels and operations executives as well as to an individual stakeholder running a one-person operation while trying to determine just how much energy to devote to defense against real or potential trust betrayers. We begin by examining the recommendations individually.

Know Your World

Before allocating time or money to protecting anything, the wise leader first takes stock, engaging in the fundamental management task of ordering priorities. Put another way, leaders must demonstrate a penetrating understanding of their own institution and of how a variety of demands, conditions, and risks impinge upon them and affect their business. They must, in short, know their world, for as one management advisor has said, "To affect any organization, the best thing any manager can do is to run his or her area well."[7]

In this context, the leader must first ask what requires protection. Armed with a deep understanding of the operation and what the institution's stakeholders and customers consider as value, the leader should be able to identify which assets are critical to the institution's mission. Next comes the task of prioritizing critical assets. A good way to begin is with zeroing in on the irreplaceable, the assets whose loss or compromise would be fatal to the institution's business and reason for existence. Applying this kind of knowledge offers immediate value to both corporate sentinels and line employees who may not have the frequent experience of stepping back and looking at the big picture.

For example, in a business with 200 different work sites, perhaps only 18 contain production facilities responsible for 85% of the revenue of a given corporation. Of the 18 production facilities, say 6 are old and scheduled for decommissioning, whereas the other 12 are capable of sustaining production at present and projected future levels. To a corporate sentinel rightly concerned with protecting this production capacity, it may seem prudent to institute a rule that requires intensive vetting and rigid escort requirements for anyone working at company work sites, on the theory that more controls are better controls—a theory unsupported by No Dark Corners' fundamental research and other entrepreneurs.[8] To a non-sentinel work team member, however, having to provide escorts to contractors and vendors at all 200 facilities appears to be a cavalier imposition of lost productive time. In virtually no time, both camps may lock horns and enter into the equivalent of internal declarations of war, with each camp making a good argument with its strongest cases and examples. The leader, however, knowing the operating climate, can instantly recognize that the sentinel's rules make more business sense at the 12 critical production facilities than at the remaining 188 facilities where, perhaps, administrative or sales activities take place with few catastrophic consequences in the event of disruption. Applying this knowledge to resolve the conflict between the two opposing camps allows the leader to show recognition of the value of each camp's argument while also bringing them both into line with basing such decisions less by personal affront and more by what benefits the interests of the institution.

What has the leader just done in the foregoing example? The leader has carried out a risk assessment based on an informed understanding of exposure and impact of loss. Although there exist numerous methodologies for performing quantitative and qualitative risk assessments, such as the Risk Assessment Methodology of Sandia National Laboratories or the Analytical Risk Methodology of Booz, Allen, and Hamilton, they all depend on evaluating vulnerability and impact of loss which, in turn, require an informed understanding of the various assets of the organization and how they interrelate to each other.

What can individuals who do not possess this deep understanding nevertheless contribute to informing leaders' decisions on risk? They can remain alert to surroundings, the better to detect what is out of the ordinary or in some way different from what it is expected to be. They can remain the first line of defense against the unexpected. Even executives with an impressive command of the big picture for the institution seldom see every change as it is occurring. Consequently, they routinely work on assumptions based on data that have changed. In the foregoing example, even though the six production facilities are old and scheduled for decommissioning, perhaps a new executive does not realize that these same facilities have larger footprints because the company owns the land where they are operating and has therefore placed all its maintenance spares and distributed all its emergency reserve inventory among the six plants, thereby making them much more critical than they otherwise appear. A line employee intimately involved with those sites knows this detail, however, and his or her opportunity for leadership coincides with communicating this knowledge so that it can inform the ultimate decision about just how critical those facilities are, after all. Consequently, with this additional information in hand, the executive now makes the call to defend 18 instead of 12 sites at a higher level based on their value to the institution.

Start Somewhere

The leader who opens the door to any problem soon finds problems entering and arraying themselves without order or labels to distinguish the crucial from the insignificant. Even with competent assistance and triage protocols to help separate what is important from what is simply annoying, leaders may still find themselves overwhelmed when it comes to taking on challenges in the realm of insider threats. What should they attend to? Should proper vetting through pre-employment background investigations receive the first priority? Should corporate sentinels be reorganized, retrained, or even purged until they can be made more effective? Should line managers be told they will in some measure be graded based on how well they engage their team members to transform them into copilots who take a hand in their own protection as well as in the continued welfare of the entire institution, as measured through objective criteria including higher unit performance and lower grievances, absentee rates, and other such indicators of personnel troubles? The answer is to start somewhere.

Not only does the journey of a thousand miles begin with the first step, the journey nowhere looks identical to just standing in place. In the case of insider defense, attaining perfection is an illusion. Perfection would require developing all aspects of a program in parallel and fine-tuning them ad infinitum before launching into implementation. Such a process, in turn, could easily spawn endless consultation, debate, reworking, and antibodies, thereby losing momentum and advocates in proportion to its latency. It could even mean going out of business to protect the business. Because insider defense can be interpreted so broadly as to affect everything, it soon becomes daunting. Leaders inured to bureaucracy may also find it tempting to refuse to do anything without supplemental funding or extra staffing. This approach is a recipe for failure. It is therefore best to start somewhere and without grand announcements or inaugural proceedings. Indeed, one leader who earned the popular title America's Mayor in the immediate aftermath of the September 11, 2001 attacks on the World Trade Center repeatedly advised withholding announcements of any initiative until the results are in and then announcing results rather than intentions.[9]

If a leader allows thoughts of budget and staffing and timing to overshadow taking action, he or she misses an opportunity to at least show a single improvement by starting somewhere. That point of departure could be as simple as restoring the probation period to what it was designed for: weeding out poor or questionable new hires. Selecting at least one area for executive attention in this manner gives the leader a point of action and influence, which in turn flow into developing employee support for the all-important momentum to follow once a full-fledged program is underway.

At Least Ask

Even the cash-strapped, resource-poor leader without a penny to spare for a new program or initiative has the power to improve results just by periodically asking about a given concern. It does not matter what legitimate business interest that concern represents. It could be as obscure as the signs for fire exits or as bottom line–oriented as reducing overtime by 20%. The first time the leader asks about this subject, whoever fields the question may be caught off-guard and have to promise to check in order to return an accurate response. But after the question has been heard a second, third, and fourth time, the question will be anticipated and the reply instantaneous. Such is the power of executive attention. What gets asked about regularly merits ongoing scrutiny, and what is routinely scrutinized cannot long be left in a wretched state. Consequently, once an executive commits to starting somewhere with insider threat defense, whether it be the probation period realignment or any other process, all it takes to assure some level of positive action is to keep asking about the same subject on a recurring basis. Naturally, providing reinforcement for positive results will accelerate improvement all the more.

WHY LEADERS FALTER

Making headway in instituting a No Dark Corners program, as the foregoing three recommendations suggest, need not be a complex undertaking. It begins with simple steps that align with traditional management tasks and responsibilities. Depending on the exigencies facing the institution and the executive at any given point in time, however, formal and informal leaders in a given organization may struggle to see the benefits of instituting a No Dark Corners program or, even if seeing them, make little progress in realizing the dividends. Why is this so, not only for insider threat defense but for any number of beneficent initiatives which, although acknowledged, slip into corporate cul-de-sacs where, starved of light and nutrition, they perish in obscurity? Perhaps editor, reviewer, and early television impresario Clifton Fadiman hit the mark more than a half century ago when observing, well before the dawn of the Internet age,

> With so many signals crowding in among us there is no time, and soon no inclination, to arrange them in order of importance, reflect upon them, and take proper action. Eventually the alert reception of the signal suffices. We delude ourselves into thinking because we know a thing we have done something about it: our equivalent of the primitive's belief that to name is to control.[10]

If seeing yet failing to act is one possible affliction, surely another equally counterproductive executive tendency is that of seeing through all things. In philosophical discussions ranging across religious and secular themes, one observer thus summarized this tendency and its pitfalls:

> If you see through everything then everything is transparent. But a transparent world is an invisible world. To see through all things is the same as not to see.[11]

These twin tendencies have the effect of placing the institution on autopilot. As long as the skies are clear with no imminent hazards or need for careful navigation, the formal leaders or pilots of the organization may relax their grip on the controls and, for a time, allow the institutional vessel to steer itself. When a hazard appears suddenly, however, whether the pilot–leader or a copilot–team member reaches the controls in time and manages to avoid self-destruction becomes a matter of time, chance, and that part of training and experience that constitute readiness. Failures occur just as much from overcorrection as from tardiness of response, as holiday traffic fatalities repeatedly demonstrate: a motorist falling asleep at the wheel awakens and suddenly swerves in the opposite direction of a discovered hazard, only to trigger an even worse pile-up. Institutionally, overcorrections take the form of grandiose programs launched with fanfare after a significantly adverse event has occurred. Thus, the enterprise-wide ethics program comes on the heels of a discovery that corporate marketing staff were caught issuing bribes or "facilitation payments" in order to close a multimillion-dollar order with a foreign government client whose only way of doing business is to build into every deal not only some ostensible off-set provisions but also brokerage fees to relatives or cronies of the regime in charge. Even if this transaction is standard practice in the host country, one's own government may see it as a violation of the Foreign Corrupt Practices Act and accordingly issue sanctions that damage one's corporation from doing business domestically. As a result, the corporation negotiates down its domestic penalties through the prominent launch of a new institutional ethics program. Similarly, an organization losing a discrimination case against a plaintiff who was badly treated on the job for an affliction or condition that was aggravated by bullying may lose a civil case in court. In addition to compensatory damages, the court may order or a settlement may stipulate that the employer must ensure such abuse ends at the job. How? The employer institutes a very prominent program to teach team members and managers how not to harass other people, to document this instruction, and to put in place a system for reporting violations and concerns.

In this context of institutional overcorrection, there emerge self-limiting to any programs that are perceived as token, knee-jerk reactions to negative press and external pressures. There is a predictable arc to these programs, and most employees can chart this trajectory: alarmed discovery, rollout of a new program, loss of interest, and rote compliance until another cycle begins with an event that raises eyebrows once more, leading back to alarmed discovery. Explanations for this phenomenon vary, but one compelling expression of this occurrence is the issue–attention cycle. For leaders, the importance of this cycle is in understanding how *not* to introduce a No Dark Corners strategy—or any other approach intended for lasting effect.

THE ISSUE–ATTENTION CYCLE MEETS INSIDER THREATS

In this cycle, attention to a given matter follows five stages: pre-problem, alarmed discovery, awareness of difficulties, gradual decline of public interest, and post-problem, with the latter resembling and flowing into the pre-problem stage. From this point, the cycle repeats.[12] As an illustration, assume a case of espionage where a trust betrayer managed to worm his way into a low-level position that nevertheless provided access to sensitive material that the betrayer was subsequently able to misappropriate and sell, through an intermediary, to realize financial gain while causing great harm to his employer and possibly to other stakeholders beyond the immediate employer. How would corporate reaction to such a case follow the issue–attention cycle?

Phase 1: Pre-Problem

Although this may only become widely known after the fact, in all likelihood there is vulnerability in the vetting process that had to exist in order for the trust betrayer to get inside the targeted institution. Someone within the organization probably knew about this but either went unheard or withheld this knowledge for any number of reasons. Leaders often have difficulty processing information that is miscommunicated or presented in such a way as to invite more disbelief than credence. If the person knowing the vulnerability cast herself as a whistleblower with an agenda, including furthering of personal grievances at the expense of her management, senior leaders would be inclined to discount even accurate warnings—particularly if such warnings were buried in an avalanche of invective and exaggerations. Alternatively, the same individual in the know, aware of other naysayers whose careers became stalled in a shoot-the-messenger environment, might judge it wise to remain mute on the issue unless asked for an opinion. In any case, a weakness had to exist for it to be exploited, but the weakness was either not widely recognized or just left unaddressed, perhaps because it was not regarded as a priority at the time.

Phase 2: Alarmed Discovery

Sooner or later, the problem captures marquee value. The trust betrayer makes a mistake, gives himself away, and faces incarceration along with a very public courtroom trial. In this process, events take on a life of their own and the employer is one day portrayed as victim and another day pilloried in the press for demonstrating the naiveté to fall prey to the trust betrayer. Meanwhile, the media alternatively portray the trust betrayer as callow and misguided one day and as calculating and ruthless the next day. In any event, the institution suffers a compounded loss: not only of the assets compromised but of an equally compromised reputation in the eyes of current and prospective clients, business partners, or stakeholders. Consequently, top management at the victimized institution, pressed for media comment and mindful of the need to mitigate reputational risk, expresses outrage at the betrayal and pledges to get to the bottom of this, cooperate fully with investigators, and see that nothing like this ever happens again. With this very public demonstration of support from the highest level of the institution, leaders, work team members, and corporate sentinels alike rally to the cause and prepare to put forth a maximal effort to keep from making a liar out of the chief executive. If any such problem is on the verge of breaking out, all these employees have reason to see that this does not happen on their watch. The tide has risen in the direction of insider threat defense, resources are flowing, and all at work have very vivid images of how important this matter is to the chief executive and the institution itself.

Phase 3: Awareness of Difficulties

Announcements are one thing, realities another. There is core business to handle, payroll to make, deliveries to see to, and a myriad other legitimate operations and priorities to address as part of doing one's job and staying productive. After the initial tide of alarmed discovery has subsided, the swirl has diminished and the waters have cleared. Pronouncements made with the rising tide of alarm and emotion are now seen for what they generally are: easier said than done. Spirited pledges with high-sounding but vague objectives, once assigned to action officers to convert into workplace reality, now unmask themselves as the kinds of organizational mission statement that was a "hero sandwich of good intentions."[13] An assigned leader or task force assumes responsibility for delivering a solution that will satisfy institutional expectations. The first thing these people realize is that recognizing the problem alone or recognizing it and simply announcing the intention to do something about it will not suffice. In other words, to name is not to control. Indeed, developing a plan of action and associating milestones with resources demonstrates that this insider threat problem by no means lends itself to an overnight solution. Instead, difficulties loom on the horizon. There must be a coherent strategy, alignment of corporate sentinels and work team members to work together toward shared objectives, an overhaul of a pre-employment background screening and new employee probation process that are falling short, and some cultural shifts that will require buy-in at all levels, including the top. These are just the immediate hurdles. Additional, larger hurdles may come in the form of senior managers and executives who see in this new program a challenge to their authority or erosion of their prerogatives. Accusations of draconian measures and lost productive time being imposed by one camp generate counteraccusations of lip service and myopic defense of turf as being artificially interjected to undermine the chief executive's wishes. It is even possible that the solution may come to look more burdensome than the problem it was intended to solve.

Phase 4: Gradual Decline of Public Interest

Time passes and the glaring attention powered by a voracious news media has gone off to another story. Just as no soldier can stand 24-hour watch indefinitely with fixed bayonet, so, too, no sentinel, leader, or work team member can continue to keep insider threats foremost in mind every day. Something invariably happens to diminish the original momentum that fueled alarmed discovery. Somewhere, somehow something worse has now captured the spotlight. Perhaps the leader who was at the fore of the institutional response has retired, rendering his or her promises and vision a matter more for archives than for action. External and internal clamoring for getting to the bottom of all this has dissipated to the point that attention has shifted elsewhere. It is not so much that no one cares. They just no longer care that much. Nor does any leader, team member, or sentinel save the most monomaniacal have the tenacity to remain single-issue focused in the face of the shifting priorities attending the press of business. Time passes. Priorities change. Absent a rekindling of the initial fire that raged to give the insider threat issue its intensity and glow, the embers cool and even an occasional spark falls on damp kindling.

Phase 5: Post-Problem

With the exception of an employee or a group indelibly affected by the betrayal, the institution allows its insider threat defense program to slide into dormancy. It seemed a good idea at the time, but there are now other problems to solve and, as top management reasons, the problem does not appear to be recurring. Thus, the program may be declared a success and then wound down to a maintenance level of support from which it can be once again ramped up by management fiat should the need arise. What if the keepers of the flame, including sentinels, leaders, and team members, point out that this program needs consistent application over time to sustain positive impact? To the bureaucratic executive hearing this remonstrance, the objection merely signals the need to install a more complaisant manager and better disposed team in the place of the malcontents. After all, sometimes people lose their perspective after working too long in one area of specialization, and it is a management truism that a fresh set of eyes and ears can produce needed epiphanies—even on demand, if properly directed. Such circumstances, in turn, place those with capabilities and institutional memory on the sidelines, where they will hopefully still be around as the issue–attention cycle gradually begins to repeat itself.

CASE STUDY: MANAGING AN INSTITUTIONAL PROBLEM INTO THE GROUND

Peter Drucker has said that good intentions are no substitute for organization and leadership, accountability, performance, and results.[14] Here follows an illustration of how well-intended but misapplied leadership can take the product of an alarmed discovery and make matters worse than they were at the outset. In this case, the alarmed discovery was that interoperable radio communications were in a state of disarray—something a small cadre of informed, internal users and a few leaders were trying to address with indifferent support until an infusion of executive attention altered events. Such was the case at a major public utility over the course of a 5-year period. The two lessons that follow are (1) how *not* to achieve the desired interoperability and, inferentially, (2) how easy it is to undermine interoperability without appearing to be an agent of sabotage.

PROBLEM

We begin by calling the organization studied Regional Utility Exchange (RUX), in the interests of discretion and of sparing many good contributors from embarrassment. In 2003, RUX found that its two-way radio system had turned into an obsolescent horror. This was the situation. RUX's analog low-band and UHF radios with radio repeaters served a diverse user community of about 700 users. More than 60% of the system was used on a daily basis and about 2000 radio calls were made daily. The radio system was procedure-intensive and cumbersome to use. Initiating a radio call required knowing which numeric codes to use for access to radio repeaters and exact knowledge of the call recipient's location. Range was limited to less than 25 miles in most locations. Daily congestion was common, and unacceptable performance was noted in emergencies such as earthquake response. In mute testimony to how dysfunctional the radio system had become, RUX patrol crews independently came to rely on personal cellular telephones to communicate at their own expense with their supervisors and other work crews. Some even preferred to use a pay phone to call in than to spend half an hour fussing with the two-way radio.

GOOD FAITH EFFORT AT SOLUTION

Regional Utility Exchange established a radio task force to address the problem. The head of the task force was a bright plant manager with sound engineering credentials and a can-do attitude. The individual who investigated the options and carried the laboring oar for most of the task force's technical work was an emergency manager and FCC-licensed radio operator (general class) who was very much mission-focused and well respected. The task force included heavy representation of the user community and RUX's telecommunications staff. This task force ultimately proposed a trunked radio system and developed different alternatives and a timeline for funding it. At the point that this effort was ready to move forward for upper management approval and allocation of capital funds to underwrite the new system, a series of unfortunate events unfolded.

- The plant manager heading task force departed to a higher position with another agency.
- The emergency manager responsible for the task force's work product died.
- The telecommunications staff, perpetuating a tug-of-war between head-quarters specialists and field technicians, reversed positions on the proposed solution and, after a key retirement, attributed all previous missteps to the individual who had retired.
- Senior management deferred efforts to bring the task force's recommendations to its executive body until the telecommunications department made a formal endorsement of them.
- Telecommunications decided it needed to perform its own, independent study.
- Telecommunications sought and obtained approval for $50,000 for an outside contractor to perform an independent interoperability assessment of the radio system.
- Contractor took a year to study the radio system, ultimately reaching the conclusion that a trunked radio system was the preferred solution (at a revised cost of $70,000 for the study).
- Extra costs associated with the contractor's proposed solution raised the price tag to the point where senior management and the governing board felt the project had to be deferred because of high cost and new difficulties in availability of unused frequencies to allocate for RUX use.
- A year of negotiations followed with a law firm claiming to be able to obtain a radio frequency for exclusive RUX use, ultimately collapsing without result.
- RUX entered into collaborative discussions with other agencies to explore options for frequency sharing and a trunked radio system that would allow multiple agencies to share the same frequency for their internal communications and, potentially, for interagency communications on a shared channel. Outcome: pending.

LESSONS LEARNED

It appears that nothing is more fatal to a project such as this than the loss of momentum and advocacy. The two biggest champions involved in the original effort left the scene before the ball could be carried across the finish line. As a result, the agents of bureaucracy, always lurking beneath the surface, emerged unchecked from their primeval bog of work avoidance and inertia to effectively lure the program into a still pool where it could drown quietly out of the view of any remaining lifeguards.

ALTERNATIVE APPROACH

The issue–attention cycle poses a significant challenge to any program launched in haste to appease negative press and mitigate reputational risk, particularly if it is a narrowly focused and single issue–based solution. This is where No Dark Corners offers an alternative to the endless series of peaks and troughs that accompany most programs of the month. What makes No Dark Corners viable in any institution is the extent to which the program can be grafted onto the skin of the existing organization and grow into an integral part of its culture and how it does business. It is like reattaching a limb or perfecting a transplant, which only works if the body accepts it as its own and enjoys improved function for having the addition. Here, the No Dark Corners strategy offers benefits beyond insider threat defense, and it is these additional benefits that sell the program for long-term adoption:

- Improved productivity
- Lower absenteeism and workplace disruptions from grievances and personnel-related actions associated with hostile workplaces
- Improved morale
- Improved work team cohesion
- Better, mutually supportive relations between employees and corporate sentinels
- Anticipation of problems before they turn into crises

The key to making the case for a No Dark Corners implementation lies in aligning the innovations from its strategy canvas with outcomes that benefit the institution in carrying out its essential operations. Specifically, these innovations (see Figure 2.3) offer the following corresponding business value:

1. Background Updates—that is, periodic refresh of background investigations over time
   - Provide early warning of life events that are adversely affecting team members before they become problem employees with degraded performance and potential trust betrayers. Example: Financial irregularities surfacing in a credit report may result from the individual succumbing to substance abuse or providing heroic medical treatments for a dying spouse. Uncovering the anomaly can trigger a discussion with a supervisor who can then channel the team member into an employee assistance program for rehabilitation, in one case, or to special institutional charity or loan programs in the other case. Result: An employee is saved from ruin and the employer benefits from sustained good performance without having to incur the expenses of involuntary termination and recruiting and training of a replacement.
   - Uncover information that may reveal that an individual in line for promotion may not be ready for new responsibilities, particularly if reckless driving has resulted in revocation of driving privileges, or additional education claimed while working has not produced the advertised credentials or licenses. Again, this information triggers a discussion with a supervisor and avoids placing an employee into a position where he or she may be overmatched, to the detriment of both the individual and the organization.
2. Not Only Sentinels Watch—that is, team and sentinel monitoring of employee performance over time
   - Early warning of workplace problems before they have time to fester. Example: An employee slams his locker and curses after a staff meeting. Rather than be ignored, he encounters a coworker or supervisor asking what is wrong and offering to listen, thereby giving him a chance to vent instead of stewing in his frustrations. This kind of concern for fellow team members and subordinates ultimately reduces grievances and surfaces areas of concern before they evolve into major problems.

- Improvement in workplace safety, as coworkers step in to assist when employees who do not realize they are impaired make errors in critical operations that if left undetected could create hazards, which in turn could lead to industrial or other accidents and corresponding financial losses for the institution.

3. ID and Work Verification—that is, careful vetting before the formal pre-employment background investigation has begun
   - Avoiding negligent hire of people who misrepresent themselves or their qualifications and could therefore cause harm in positions where they do not possess the requisite expertise.
   - Avoiding losses related to integrity issues that arise when applicants enter the workplace on false pretenses with hidden agendas.

4. Close Probation—that is, using probation as originally designed to weed out questionable hires
   - Avoiding cost in morale and resources associated with disciplining or terminating an individual who may be qualified but is obstreperous or disruptive with team members and thus counterproductive in the workplace.
   - Compensating for inevitable mistakes in the selection process, including interviewing of applicants whose flaws remain hidden until prolonged and direct exposure. As the seasoned chief executive who helped found Intel Corporation, Andy Grove, pointed out in acknowledging his own hiring shortfalls, "In the end, careful interviewing doesn't guarantee you anything, it merely increases your odds of getting lucky."[15]

5. Transparency on the Job—that is, keeping critical work within actual or virtual line of sight of a supervisor or team member
   - Error reduction, with corresponding decreases in avoidable losses, whether the losses are the result of inattention, mischief, human error, or equipment malfunction. Having an informed team member in a position to provide instant consultation and direct support means fewer mistakes made by guessing.
   - Rapid containment and mitigation of unforeseen problems and hazards. If one team member enters an area where a gas leak results in a loss of consciousness, there is a much better chance of timely rescue of the individual and isolation of the problem if a teammate is in a position to provide immediate assistance. This individual can also summon reinforcements and sound the alarm, which a lone, unconscious colleague cannot.

6. Self-Monitoring Team—that is, self-policing and internal team promotion of performance to a shared set of values
   - Establishment of a foundation to enable effective delegation and, in turn, the need for fewer layers of management, thereby improving cohesion and enterprise-wide communication, without the signal loss and make-work that typically attend having the reverse: too many intermediate managers without enough productive work to do.
   - Overall improvement of individual performance, whether in an orchestra or a combat platoon, because the people in the work unit refuse to let their team down.

Another Opportunity: Rotational Assignments

The whole world changes when one takes charge. Although it may not be practical to abdicate executive responsibility in order to give subordinates a chance to see things from the leader's perspective, in the interest of transparency and improved communication throughout the organization, it may indeed be useful to reserve certain assignments as rotational opportunities for employees in the core business as well as for corporate sentinels. Such positions also offer the equivalent of an indirect probation period for veteran employees long past proving their worth formally but perhaps still being uncertain quantities when considered for promotion or transfer to other duties. For top management, a staff assistant operations officer who serves for 6 months to 1 year can provide a welcome infusion of field truth when the executive so served can ill afford the luxury of making as many field visits as he or she would like. For the staff member filling the temporary, rotational position, this role represents exposure to other people and activities in the enterprise that might otherwise be understood only through rumor or secondhand reports.

How does the rotation work? First, the opportunity is open only to volunteers and only to those coming with high endorsement from a supervisor and two peers. Second, no promises of certain rewards or advancement come with the assignment. On the contrary, the default is that the assignment will provide broadening and then return the assignee back to the home team. Third, the leader and assignee are very clear about expectations and rules of conduct from the outset, with all interactions to be kept businesslike and within certain bounds. Fourth, whatever the incentive for participating in this program may ultimately be for all involved, exclude financial compensation at the outset. Otherwise, applicants will multiply, not out of interest in learning and doing more, but out of mercenary impulses. Moreover, introduce money into the equation and labor relations take a turn for the worse as malcontents formulate grievances to allege that they were unfairly denied an opportunity for financial gain out of some unfair or discriminatory practice. Instead, eliminating an immediate financial incentive has the beneficial effect of turning away egoists animated only by short-term self-interest. It also gives the indolent and half-hearted a businesslike rationale for taking themselves out of the competition for a rotational assignment, as the argument of an insufficient, immediate return dissuades all but the visionary willing to see the job as something more than a paycheck. The net result is that such eliminations also reduce burdens on sponsoring executives. Most executives would prefer to choose from a smaller pool of highly motivated applicants than from an order of magnitude of more contenders where the highly motivated are outnumbered by those looking to only line their pockets.

What of the employee serving in the rotational capacity? At a minimum, he or she completes the assignment with a much deeper understanding of the responsibilities and dilemmas facing a leader of the institution. At best, the assignee walks away animated with a desire to advance to higher responsibility and an ally to help achieve this end. The superior performer, impressing the sponsoring executive through energy and achievement, cannot help ultimately passing on a sense of what it means to be a working member of the organization, whether in a core business unit or as a sentinel. The alert executive, in turn, takes in this information as a means of refreshing an otherwise dated understanding of what motivates the workforce and what issues matter most to its rank and file. Informed with this understanding, the executive in turn makes smarter decisions affecting the employee population, thereby depriving unseen potential trust betrayers of the spark or kindling necessary to ignite the fires of insider hostilities. In the end, the rotational assignment helps the leader at least as much as the assigned employee. The experience helps the leader remember why he or she should care about setting a good example and working hard to leave the institution better off than it was before.

QUESTIONS FOR ONLINE OR CLASSROOM DISCUSSION

1. Identify a good leader and a bad one who held the same job at different times. What traits did they share? Where did they differ? How might the good leader have done a better job preventing or minimizing the damage of an insider threat?
2. Can a good leader's example serve even in the leader's absence? How might that example affect a work team member rising to the position of copilot when no one else is around to take charge during a crisis?
3. Why might even a good leader fail to adequately defend against insider threats despite early detection of warning signs?
4. Can you think of an example where a leader's poor resolution of a conflict between a corporate sentinel and a work team member may make matters worse? Discuss.
5. How can an informal leader with great credibility but relatively no formal authority on the job act to negate the impact of a trust betrayer?

EXERCISES FOR GROUP PROJECTS

1. From an executive perspective, develop a job description and interview questions for a hypothetical vacancy of a chief sentinel in your organization. Assign one group member to exemplify the ideal candidate and another to represent the worst possible choice. Interview each and then, on the basis of the interviews, establish rating criteria and, if necessary, revise your questions to hone in on the desirable traits the process should identify. What has this process taught you?
2. Look at the career arc of the average employee who comes sailing into the institution without any adverse information in the background check or any difficulty in passing probation. At some point, though, this employee becomes jaded, dyspeptic, and begins to be seen as more a liability than an asset to the work team. What causes the transformation? Does it matter? What can or should the problem employee's boss do about the situation? What can or should team members do about it? Analyze options and make a clear recommendation of how to handle the individual, making any assumptions you like about information not given to you.
3. Chart a major issue affecting your industry or sector through the issue–attention cycle. Where in the cycle do you now find it, and where can you anticipate it going in its next evolution?

ENDNOTES

1. Indeed, some observers started seeing the workplace of the late 1990s as increasingly becoming an "if you don't, no one else will" environment. See, for example, H. Bergmann, K. Hurson, and D. Russ-Eft, *Everyone a Leader*, New York: John Wiley & Sons, 1999, p. 10.
2. P. F. Drucker, *Management: Tasks, Responsibilities, Practice*, New York: HarperBusiness, 1993, pp. 462–463. Harper & Row published the original version of this classic in 1973. It remains one of Drucker's longer works because he evidently designed it as an introduction to and reference about management as a profession.

3. T. Zambito, E. Benjamin, and H. Kennedy, "Governor Spitzer Tied to Prostitution Ring," in *New York Daily News*, March 11, 2008. Retrieved June 6, 2011 from http://www.nydailynews.com/news/2008/03/10/2008-03-10_gov_spitzer_tied_to_prostitution_ring.html.

4. Canadian psychologist Gerald Wilde appears to have coined the term risk homeostasis in discussions with Frans Johansson, who used it in his *Medici Effect*, Boston: Harvard Business School Press, 2006, p. 167.

5. Johansson, *The Medici Effect*, pp. 168–169.

6. For application of these recommendations in the context of a national advisory body, see N. Catrantzos, "Security for Water: A Personal Distillation," in U.S. Environmental Protection Agency, *Recommendations of the National Drinking Water Advisory Council to the U.S. Environmental Protection Agency on Water Security Practices, Incentives, and Measures*, 2005, pp. 65–66, at www.epa.gov/safewater/ndwac/pdfs/wswg/wswg_report_final_july2005.pdf.

7. G. Sutton, *Corporate Canaries: Avoid Business Disasters with a Coal Miner's Secrets*, Nashville, TN: Thomas Nelson, Inc., 2005, p. 127.

8. See Sutton, for example, who avows that better controls does not mean more controls (op. cit., p. 132).

9. See R. W. Giuliani, *Leadership*, New York: Hyperion, 2005. Giuliani repeats this point in different forms throughout his book.

10. C. Fadiman, *Any Number Can Play*, Cleveland, OH: World Publishing Company, 1957, p. 10.

11. C. S. Lewis, *The Abolition of Man*, New York: Macmillan, 1947, p. 91.

12. C. Bellavita, "Changing Homeland Security: The Issue–Attention Cycle," *Homeland Security Affairs* I, no. 1 (Summer 2005). Retrieved July 1, 2008 from http://www.hsaj.org/?article=1.1.1.

13. P. Drucker, *Managing the Non-Profit Organization*, New York: HarperCollins, 1992, p. 5. Drucker avers that it is one of our most common mistakes to make the mission statement into one of these, a mistake because one can only do so many things in any organization.

14. P. F. Drucker, *The Essential Drucker*, New York: HarperCollins, 2001, p. 40.

15. A. S. Grove, *High Output Management*, New York: Random House, 1983, p. 209.

PART **III**

Making a Difference

CHAPTER 5

Rethinking Background Investigations

To know what you know and know what you don't know is the characteristic of one who knows.

Confucius

INTRODUCTION

A background investigation is a snapshot in time. It provides a necessarily finite view, seldom a panorama revealing all the peccadilloes and skullduggeries beneath the surface yet accessible only through deeper probes which few institutions can afford as a matter of routine. Thus, the typical background investigation is only as good as the accuracy and scope of the information it uncovers, the degree to which areas of investigation meet the needs of the institution commissioning the probe, and the extent to which the individual receiving the results of that effort can interpret and make beneficial use of its results. Doing all this is a tall order and, as Delphi research suggested, the entire process radiates exploitable vulnerabilities. Even a first-rate investigation performed by a competent investigator becomes worthless if identity documents were not properly verified and the investigation has thus been unable to uncover any data prejudicial to the applicant being considered. Similarly, if the investigation returns arcane indicators of financial or personal irresponsibility, such as codes for late credit payments or failures to appear in court for repeated traffic offenses such as speeding, and the poor clerk receiving such details lacks the capacity to interpret these indicators or the authority to pause the hiring process pending further inquiry, the institution deceives itself in assuming that the background investigation process is barring entry to bad actors or future insider threats.

To the uninitiated, misinformed by television programs or motion picture fictions about the extent to which voluminous data on any person are to be had with a few keystrokes, it will also be surprising to discover that, in reality, such details do not reside in a single database and some, such as arrest records, are illegal for employers to see let alone use.[1] Nor should it be otherwise, if one reflects that in a free society operating under the presumption of innocence, even an applicant arrested for the most heinous crime remains innocent until proven guilty. This is why arrests do not count, but convictions do in employment-related background investigations. Anyone can be accused of anything. Conviction, however, occurs after due process. What about leveraging personal or corporate networks to have a "friend" in law enforcement discreetly obtain arrest reports or other nonpublic information in order to inform a hiring decision? Such a maneuver is not only illegal but jeopardizes the friend's career while providing little more than the grounds for an eventual lawsuit against the employer. Besides, as the Delphi panel's reflections indicated, an adversary selects its infiltrators for their unblemished records and ability to sail through applicant screening.

What if the hostile insider is not an infiltrator but a future malcontent? Would a no-holds-barred investigation not reveal telltale signs that could prevent negligent hire? Perhaps. But most future malcontents enter the institution smiling and even malleable, awaiting work-related vicissitudes to influence their behaviors positively or negatively at some distant point in the future. Consequently, the ethical and reputational risk attaching to using "friends" to develop illegal information generally proves out of proportion to the benefit sought. Nor is this necessary, if the institution instead has in place a robust probationary employment system and a work team inured to spotting and mitigating trouble before small problems turn into big ones.

TRADITIONAL BACKGROUND INVESTIGATION PROCESS

The pre-employment background investigation is not a single inquiry that returns an unambiguous signal to hire or not hire a given applicant. Instead, it is a process of which the investigation itself forms only one of many components.[2] The process begins with open solicitation of data from candidate new hires via the job application. Normally, both applicant and employer agree that all information supplied in the completed application is subject to verification and, if found untrue, constitutes grounds for an adverse hiring decision. Depending on the employer and jurisdiction, the application may include substantial detail about the applicant's right of review of all information produced in the course of a pre-employment investigation and even the options for challenging investigative findings or for supplying exculpatory or mitigating clarifications.

In this context, the individual or organization performing the background investigation has reason to be circumspect from the outset. Once they recognize that their best results may be shared in unpredictable levels of detail with subjects of their probes, investigators incline to telegraphic reports that satisfy client (i.e., employer) requirements by releasing the most minimal detail—and certainly no information that is not specifically requested or could in any way be used to embarrass the investigator or investigating entity. In practice, then, this system actually incentivizes the producer of the investigative report to be as arcane and succinct as possible. Consequently, for the human resources clerk at the receiving end of the background check's results, the chance of obtaining an understandable report in plain English diminishes greatly. Nor is it likely that the background investigation report will include any but the most miserly amplifying information that might otherwise put the results into useful context. This means that the clerk will scarcely benefit from what a savvy investigator knows but is constrained from sharing. For example, say an applicant claims law enforcement experience for a year and then indicates he went on to become a reserve sheriff's deputy while pursuing private sector opportunities. The investigator, being familiar with how the local sheriff's department operates, may be able to reasonably infer that the applicant was most likely released from probation after that 1 year of service, because the sheriff's department considered him unsuitable for any number of reasons. However, this information does not reach the clerk, and an applicant who may have been considered too unstable for police duty gets hired and assigned to the protective detail of a corporate executive. Not that this kind of contextual information should necessarily be the only factor to influence a hiring decision. However, given the full picture, the employer can interview the applicant for further information, to ascertain integrity and check more closely for suitability for a given corporate role. The employer can even use such fuller information to watch for any additional signs of instability during the probationary period. Absent the additional data, however, the hiring decision proceeds with a possible red flag suppressed out of a real or perceived fear of generating liability.

IDENTITY VERIFICATION

Another part of the entire background check involves identity verification. From the recruiting office's perspective, this is something done to satisfy legal requirements to verify that the applicant does indeed possess a legitimate right to work at the place of employment. Sometimes, this occurs in parallel with the acceptance of the job application for processing. At other times, the identity verification may be reserved only for applicants who have passed initial screening to form a candidate pool for interviewing by the hiring manager. Then again, perhaps only the successful candidate for whom a job offer follows after the interview will be the only one asked to supply necessary identification. In a workplace where the job itself may be geographically removed from the supporting human resources and other sentinel functions, how does this part of the process unfold? Electronically. The clerk from the recruiting office asks for facsimile or scanned copies of acceptable identity documents, which the applicant duly provides. Such a process magnifies opportunities for introduction of counterfeit identity documents whose holograms or other distinctive security watermarks can be masked or obliterated once the ID is copied for electronic transmittal. Add to this mix the likely chance that a long-distance hire is already taking more time than usual and that the hiring manager may be exerting pressure to expedite the hiring action, and it becomes almost inevitable that the identity verification will become a perfunctory check to be completed with maximal speed and minimal scrutiny, thereby creating yet another dark corner from which to insert a malicious insider.

WHAT GETS INVESTIGATED AND HOW

With the application in hand and a release from the applicant that consents to a background investigation to be performed for the purposes of employment, the human resources clerk in the recruiting function is now ready to hand off the process to the designated investigating function. Although this investigating arm may be internal, it is increasingly more effective to contract the work to a professional firm that has the resources and wherewithal to perform the most comprehensive check in the shortest period.[3] Turnaround time varies depending on how many types of inquiries are contracted for and how many places have to be searched to obtain requested information. An uncomplicated case can easily be concluded within 24–48 hours. A case where, for example, the applicant resided in several counties over the period of investigation and worked in other counties as well will invariably take longer, as records of criminal conviction rest with counties of residence and counties of employment. The more counties to check, the longer the delay in obtaining results. Background investigation firms typically offer moonlighting opportunities to courthouse employees for off-hour records retrieval, particularly when the records in question are not retrievable via online data-bases. Depending on the county where the records of interest are contained, however, there may be a need to commission a physical search, including a review of pending files or files checked out or otherwise in circulation for county business. All of this takes not only time but inside knowledge that make courthouse employees particularly valuable as occasional resources for a background investigations firm. If the pressure for rapid turnaround is great, and a time-consuming records search through multiple counties is necessary, the investigating firm finds little margin for error. Thus, a name that is reasonably close to the one supplied may be taken for the applicant, with the wrong files being searched. If the result is that the investigation returns adverse information that the applicant can clearly refute—such as a felony conviction on a date when the applicant was living in another country as a minor—this circumstance can be corrected and then overlooked. However, if a similar mistake results in having an applicant with a troubled past confused with someone else whose background is pristine, the applicant will be the last to complain. The opportunity, here, for an infiltrator is to develop a cover using a common name that traces to an unblemished past. How does the infiltrat-ing organization manage such a feat? One approach is trial and error. Craft a plausible but false identity under the name Smith or Garcia, for example, and then test it out at several employers as they run the name through their own screening process. Along the way, fine-tune the legend, or cover story, until applications sail through this screening process.

Another related problem is exploitable for trust betrayers: recurring mistakes poorly redressed by background screening service providers. If cases of mistaken identity do occur, as some victims report,[4] their resolution may not be as professional as provider and employer protocols suggest. In the case cited, for example, an individual whom the background investigations service confused for someone with a felony conviction who apparently shared the same name and birth date had to take the onus to correct the error. Had the person investigated not taken the effort to pursue matters doggedly, the error would have gone unaddressed, leaving him with a repeated message, "Our HR department has notified me that you aren't hirable."[5] As the related comment thread indicates, other applicants report similar experiences and frustrations. Under the cir-cumstances, a sophisticated trust betrayer unmasked in the attempt to infiltrate an institution need only point to such cases of mistaken identity and botched resolution of anomalies to erode the credibility of a background investigation and cast the entire process in doubt.

CREDENTIALS AND CREDIBILITY

Verification of licenses and credentials numbers among the standard checks that an investigative function performs. Surprisingly, though, owing to the proliferation of degree mills and coin-operated credentialing businesses, credential verifications are at times easily bypassed. In one case that earned media scrutiny and public scorn, for example, several degree-conferring institutions that sold baccalaureate and graduate degrees did so without accreditation and under the guise of granting college credit for life experience, taking years for several government employers (including the military and the Department of Homeland Security) to take notice.[6] One of the schools not only accepted tuition assistance payments but also restructured its billing to give the appear-ance that school credit awarded for life experience was actually being doled out over several quarters or semesters, thus furthering the illusion that the degree purchaser was actually completing coursework over time and earning instead of purchasing a degree.

WHERE BLURRED ACCOUNTABILITY COMES WITH A PRICE

In the foregoing case, what person or agency is responsible for uncovering phony educational credentials? Although the obvious answer would be to place this responsibility squarely on the shoulders of the background investigator, as a practical matter, it may well be misguided and contractually unsupportable to do so. The business of performing background investigations is highly competitive, with profit margins that decline in proportion to competitive pressures. Thus, service providers structure their most competitive offerings around bundles or packages of standard checks that they are able to offer at attractive pricing.[7] In some cases, the employer may not realize that verification of education is not even part of the pre-hire background check. In other cases, it is very likely that the service provider has only contracted to verify that the applicant did receive the degree claimed from the school identified on the job application. In such circumstances, the service provider is under no contractual obligation to check the school's accreditation, nor would such effort be cost-effective—unless specifically requested and sponsored by the client. Why? Even legitimate, degree-conferring schools experience problems with their accreditations, and an academic institution accredited to confer a given degree today may not have been capable of doing so yesterday, or vice versa. To attempt to make this determination would burden the service provider because this status would likely be difficult to ascertain with a keystroke and might require a probe generally out of proportion to the object sought. Moreover, sophisticated impostors working in concert with savvy diploma mills soon learn to use short forms of school names, the better to elude scrutiny. For example, one exposed diploma mill in Wyoming evidently chose the name Hamilton University. At the same time, Hamilton College operated in New York as a legitimate school. A deceptive applicant purchasing a degree from Hamilton University could easily just write "Hamilton" in the part of the job application requesting identification of schools attended.[8] This increases the chances of the diploma mill being mistaken for the legitimate college and would even allow the applicant to express indignation while denying misrepresenting educational credentials if caught.

   Under the circumstances, it would appear that the task of validating the legitimacy of the diploma-conferring school tends to be either unrecognized or unassigned. Nor is it practical to assign this extra task to every recruiter in HR, to the security department, or to the internal or contract background investigator. Recalling that trust betrayal remains relatively rare, there are more practical alternatives than making a career out of what should only be an occasional task. In a No Dark Corners approach, the work team and hiring manager would be among the first to raise eyebrows at educational claims that were suspect. Moreover, in a mutually supportive collaboration between the hiring organization and corporate sentinels, if a recruiter did not spot the inadequacy of "Hamilton" in the application asking for college name, the hiring manager or assigned investigator certainly would, and by the time the applicant was considered for an interview, details such as "Which Hamilton?" would already figure prominently among questions for the applicant to answer completely—not only verbally, but also in a writing as a correction to the job application. Even if "Hamilton" eluded scrutiny at this juncture, at the first sign of any question during the application or probationary process, it would become the subject either of an additional item of investigation or at least flagged for expanded discussion with the applicant in a follow-up interview.

OTHER RED FLAGS OFTEN UNSEEN

The increasingly litigious specter that haunts today's employers makes the latter hesitate to return any but the most curt and unobjectionable responses to requests for employment verification. In the author's own experience, for example, corporate policy dictated that the only formal reply to such inquiries would be to this effect:

> It is our corporate policy to supply only the following information: Mary Jones worked as a senior analyst at _____ location from June 2003 until December 2003.

Consequently, the most useful questions of previous employers often come back with no answer or with a formulaic reply to the effect that corporate policy forbids providing anything more than minimal data. Did the applicant do a good job while working there? No comment, per corporate policy. Is the applicant considered eligible for rehire? No comment, per corporate policy. Did the applicant ever do anything to disadvantage the past employer, whether by action or omission? No comment, per corporate policy. Was the applicant paid as much as claimed on the present job application (a figure often used to base a salary offer)? No comment, per corporate policy. Consequently, a bad employee with a history of stealing, fighting with coworkers, and disrupting the workplace with false allegations of maltreatment—all of which are known and many of which may have been the basis for parting ways—remain concealed at the future employer's expense. Ironically, withholding of adverse information about bad apples, although lamented, is repeatedly legitimized even further through the imprimatur of the former employer's legal advisers who have negotiated a termination agreement stipulating that the former employer make no unfavorable disclosures about any part of the former employee's work history.

ADJUDICATION OF ADVERSE FINDINGS

Given the constraints of time and legal reticence surrounding what a background investigation may be able to uncover, negative or adverse reports still reach competent investigators and their clients. What happens next, however, may be surprising to anyone removed from the entire process. In most places for most cases, time and hiring pressures supply positive reinforcement for only one action: approval. The hiring manager is champing at the bit to fill a vacancy that has already taken too much productive time for her to justify, revise, post, and otherwise facilitate with the assigned HR recruiter. At this juncture, further delay only represents more lost productive time. Meanwhile, the background investigation provider is already moving on to the next case, while HR continues gathering up all the forms necessary to keep the hiring process moving at full speed. At this point, any anomaly grinds the entire process to a highly visible and undesirable halt. If there have ever been any tensions between HR and the hiring organization, this delay now takes on the character of a declaration of war. Moreover, the hiring manager, rooted in the core business and generally occupying a higher rung on the institutional ladder than the HR clerk or analyst tasked with reviewing the background check and continuing the hiring process, has and will use positional authority to browbeat the clerk into dismissing any but the most blatant anomalies. Under the circumstances, it takes a rare HR clerk, recruiter, or other sentinel to derail the hiring express train over the discovery that something questionable surfaced in the background investigation. Anything short of murder or treason—and these only if within the past 7 years, the typical reach-back of the average pre-employment investigation—tends to be considered something that can be forgiven by the hiring manager or safely ignored by corporate sentinels whose job it is to support the needs of the core business. However, it is precisely the small signs that are potentially the most useful in defending against penetration by a trust betrayer.

Small signs may not rise to the level of an immediate threat but nevertheless invite the kind of circumspection that ultimately uncovers trust betrayers. A big sign is flagrant. Shooting coworkers, being convicted of embezzlement, and defaulting on business obligations are the kinds of big signs that an average background investigation will capture via criminal convictions, credit reports, news media search, and even word-of-mouth discussions that percolate through a given industry or workplace. A litigation search—at times used only for senior positions or as an extra probe if there is a need for an expanded investigation—may reveal a pattern of an employee whose greatest income results from bringing or threatening to bring legal actions against employers. Such individuals are unlikely to constitute an existential threat to the organization. After all, they need the institution to stay in business in order to be able to pay legal settlements or awards of damages. However, a mercenary malcontent whose only aim is to line his/her pockets at the employer's expense seldom hesitates to infect the workplace with mistrust, deception, and hostility—to the detriment of the work team. Even if past history does not support denying a job offer to an otherwise qualified applicant, it certainly can alert team members and their supervisor to the need to take full advantage of the probationary period.

The decision to withhold a job offer based on the findings of a pre-employment investigation is seldom within the purview of a single corporate sentinel. If the sentinel making this case is an HR recruiter or clerk shepherding the clearance process, he or she will invariably require the support of a supervisor, of the hiring manager, or both in order for the hiring decision to be reversed. This support may be grudgingly yet reasonably offered in cases where there exist several equally qualified applicants for a given vacancy. However, when the applicant in question possesses a unique skill or qualification that the hiring manager covets, the latter will resist recommendations against hiring this applicant and may well indict the entire background verification process and its stewards for being obstructionist and insensitive to the needs of the core business. Absent a clear, inclusive protocol for adjudicating questionable results from background investigations, it is quite possible that the decision to hire an applicant with a problematic background will hinge on relative rank or influence within the larger organization. Alternatively, the decision may rest on an informal referendum whereby the direction taken reflects the consensus of managers and staff in the room where a meeting convenes to address the case. Naturally, if one camp or another stacks the room with more senior or more influential staff members, that camp's chances of prevailing increase for most hierarchies. However, a No Dark Corners approach would offer a better result through institutionalized transparency and consultation.

TRANSFORMATIONAL OPPORTUNITIES WITH A NO DARK CORNERS APPROACH

Making a Team Out of Warring Camps

The fundamental difference between the traditional background investigation process and one following a No Dark Corners approach comes from close consultation and transparency whose strongest expression finds life in a different way of adjudicating adverse findings.

Alternative Process: Adjudication by Team vs. Fiat

In the old way, a background check surfacing red flags is glossed over by default or settled by the loudest and most powerful voice in the room. The new approach, however, makes it clear from the outset that every interest will be represented in the adjudicative process, with the larger interests of the institution taking overriding precedence and with a provision for escalating to the very highest executive levels of the organization if circumstances warrant.[9]

In the new, No Dark Corners way, hiring decisions become a responsibility shared between the business unit with a vacancy and corporate sentinels supporting them. The shared responsibility begins on a working level with as few as three people, the hiring manager or designated team member from the organization with the vacancy, the HR recruiter or individual charged with seeing to satisfaction of all screening criteria (which could include identity verification, a drug test, gathering of taxpayer information, and the requesting of the background investigation as well as receipt of its results), and a background investigator or representative of a security or other function with value to add in interpreting investigative findings. Working level representatives of the three functions meet at the outset to understand their roles and protocols. Chief among the latter is regular consultation among the three whenever a scrutiny-triggering event occurs. Does the applicant's driving record suggest multiple unpaid violations that suggest irresponsibility or worse if the applicant is expected to drive on behalf of the employer? If so, then this event is worth a discussion among the three. Is the applicant's information incomplete, indicating there may be something amiss or concealed? Again, this may warrant a brief, three-way consultation. Whenever any event causes any of the three to raise an eyebrow, the default question they must ask themselves is, "Is this the only person for the job, or can we just go on to another candidate?"

Resolving Differences

What happens when the hiring manager or representative insists—with or without justification—that an applicant who has triggered scrutiny is the only one for the job and no one else will do? At this point, the three meet, face to face, and attempt to work out their differences, respectfully arguing for and against moving forward in spite of the adverse information discovered. If at the conclusion of this meeting, the difference of opinion remains unresolved, then the parties escalate to the next level—but only after the hiring manager has spelled out in writing the case for accepting the risk of proceeding with the hire. This case need be no more formal than an e-mail to the next level of reviewers, namely, the managers of the people representing the three functions already consulted. Why? At the management level, or even at the next management level up if managers were already involved in the impasse, one is expected to look beyond the immediate press of business and to consider the greater good of the organization. Thus, the next level of review engages people whose positions put them beyond the immediate fray, without the kind of emotional investment that clouds judgment and ignites tempers. This distance keeps the ultimate decision from being about a contest of wills, particularly if the next reviewers receive a written (e-mail) business case articulating the reason they are being asked to authorize an exception to a general rule. After all, managers exist to make sensible exceptions to general rules. To balance the e-mail advancing the case for authorizing an exception, corporate sentinels may either summarize the investigative findings at issue in another e-mail to the same audience or present the adverse material directly, without filters.

What does this protocol do? First, it compels the person seeking an exception to choose words carefully and think through a business case to go to his or her boss—surely an assignment that will give passions and antipathies a chance to cool in deference to reason and businesslike arguments. Second, the protocol requires even corporate sentinels to reevaluate their objections in order to be able to support them before another level of management, including their own bosses. At the same time, standardizing a process like this where all principals know that there is a structured escalation that will require level-headed arguments and the coherence of giving management something in writing to review will impress upon all concerned that it is to their advantage to do their best to resolve such differences among themselves as an alternative to consuming management time unnecessarily. To the more senior managers convened for reviewing such a matter, the process signals that subordinates are taking the screening process seriously. They only escalate after making a good faith effort to resolve their differences over the risk the applicant represents. Finally, putting a process like this in place assists the institution by assuring that hiring decisions in the face of adverse information are not the result of what one observer might characterize "willful ignorance, which is different from lack of knowledge."[10]

If further escalation is necessary because of continued impasse, it now falls to the boss of the hiring manager to send an e-mail to his or her executive superior indicating support for the requested exception.

In any of these escalations, if the hiring organization's representative is unwilling or unable to generate the e-mail making the case for going through with hiring the questionable applicant, the process stops right there. Failure to produce the written, e-mail justification constitutes tacit admission that making an exception is not worth the effort, which means that it is time to go to the next best qualified applicant.

Ramifications for the Entire Process

Once the foregoing method of resolving anomalies through consultation is institutionalized, the foundation exists for encouraging across-the-board collaboration on the entire background investigation process. In addition to the collaborative framework made inevitable by this consultative escalation process, the stakeholders and institution benefit from a final failsafe to compensate for the occasional hiring mistake. This failsafe is a robust probationary period that, when exploited to its fullest, does what it is supposed to do by culling out not only bad but suspect and questionable performers. As noted in Chapter 2, once the No Dark Corners innovation of turning probation on its head takes hold, then instead of being a formality, this period becomes one of intense scrutiny where the default action is to release the new hire from employment absent total work team endorsement of his or her value.

Who Should Perform the Background Investigation?

Institutional line and staff employees can always be found to array themselves on opposing sides of the debate over whether internal investigators or a contract background check service should carry out this task. The author has witnessed both as a corporate security manager looking into the suitability of prospective corporate employees and a public and private sector new hire being vetted by government or private firms engaged in vetting as a prelude to award of a security clearance. In most cases, for most institutions, using a contract service is the better option. In-house resources are costly to maintain and seldom have sufficient volumes of new hire investigations to be able to specialize exclusively in this discipline. Consequently, they have to take on other work that their investigators may well prefer to the mundane aspects of background checks. Nor will in-house investigators develop and maintain the same level of proficiency that employees of a contractor will if the latter are handling an order-of-magnitude more background investigations from week to week. Indeed, as studies of expertise in any field have revealed, it takes 10 years or 10,000 hours of practice or experience to become a virtuoso in a given discipline.[11] Absent a voluminous case load in a very large institution that is always hiring new employees, few internal investigators will attain this level of experience on pre-employment investigations on the job. Nor will their employers necessarily see fit to invest in keeping pace with the latest investigative tools and annual subscriptions to online databases that enable a contract background service to turn an investigation around in 48 or fewer hours. Yet, not all background investigation service providers are the same. Here follows a case illustrating contrasting features.

CASE STUDY: A DAVID TAKES ON GOLIATH IN PRE-EMPLOYMENT BACKGROUND INVESTIGATIONS

The Setting

A gathering of corporate security directors has time set aside on different days for two different vendors of background investigations to present their capabilities to an informed audience predisposed to do business with whichever firm offers the better service. Two different managers of the corporate security organization each take on the assignment to bring one qualified firm to present. The first to present will be All-Find Investigations (pseudonym), the Goliath of the two.[12] The second, presenting on another day of the conference will be a newer and smaller David of the background investigations, Pro-Back Investigations (pseudonym).

All-Find's Approach

All-Find prepared for its session by asking about conference attendees, ordering leatherette folders and other leave-behind logo items such as pens and paperweights in sufficient quantity to distribute to each conference attendee. All-Find also reproduced marketing brochures in quantity to leave with each attendee and customized an existing, polished presentation with multiple references to the hosting corporation by name, wherever the word "client" might otherwise appear. All-Find sent three personable representatives to the conference to present, including an attractive male and female junior executive and a polished, more senior male executive. At the conference itself, All-Find representatives presented impressive statistics making a case for how thorough pre-employment investigations essentially paid for themselves. While openly soliciting questions, all representatives said they could not commit to pricing or turnaround times although, unofficially, one did affirm personal confidence that All-Find was on the verge of being able to promise returning a background investigation's results within one business week. Another representative pledged to ensure attractive, volume pricing if given a corporate endorsement and sufficient business across the corporation to warrant preferential treatment for all the assembled operating companies represented by the security director attendees. All three representatives joined the audience for lunch, projecting a very upbeat attitude and confining themselves to generalities whenever touching upon the subject of background checks.

Pro-Back's Approach

Pro-Back prepared for its session by offering a free sample investigation, soliciting the name of a new hire from its corporate host upon which to run a background investigation. Pro-Back's chief executive himself initiated and sustained the corporate communication. When the day arrived for his presentation, he arrived alone, without a formal presentation to deliver or logo items to distribute. Instead, he spoke about his business, how he had recently started it after graduating with an advanced degree in business and working in the background check business between one of his years of graduate study. He noted how Pro-Back had selected its headquarters based on demographics and cost, pointing out that this part of the country had a very stable workforce and a relatively low cost of living. Pro-Back supplied details and commitments, including pricing. Although he did not distribute glossy brochures, he did supply no-frills descriptive literature and contact information. The chief executive explained how he could already turn over the majority of pre-employment investigations within 48 hours. Thanks to automated, real-time coding and tracking of transactions, Pro-Back could also tell whether it was processing 1 or 50 background investigations in total for the corporation on any given month. Thus, when Pro-Back offered volume discounts, even an operating company that only contracted for a single pre-employment investigation all year could nevertheless benefit from the corporate discount if the total number of investigations that Pro-Back was performing that month for the entire corporation crossed the threshold points for different levels of discount. Thus, if one discount level was available for, say, 10 investigations a month and another, deeper discount for 25, the operating company with a single investigation all year stood to potentially qualify for either discount if it happened that during the month where the investigation took place other operating companies within the same corporation caused the total number to exceed either 10, 25, or another such price point. What Pro-Back's executive did not do was to sell the concept of background investigations to an audience more experienced and already sold. Instead of speaking in generalities when joining the audience for lunch, he answered direct questions on pricing with quotes and options. One security director from an operating company asked if Pro-Back would accept single assignments or only work on the basis of a contract. Pro-Back's representative replied that he was equipped to do business in whatever way made the most sense for his clients, including purchase orders, large contracts, or piecework.

Business Outcome

At the end of the day, Pro-Back's chief executive walked away with immediate business and with the promise of more new business that he ultimately captured and executed. The sample investigation that Pro-Back had performed to demonstrate its capabilities also won praise, as it uncovered adverse information that corporate security's internally conducted background check had missed. Explaining how he incentivized his employees, Pro-Back's chief explained his "extra-mile program" whereby he encouraged supervisors to catch employees displaying initiative and reward them with bonuses and recognition for obtaining hard-to-get data or producing results in record-breaking time.

Feedback after the security director conference revealed that as much as the security directors had been initially impressed by the apparent polish of All-Find's first appearance, goodwill began to evaporate as All-Find's representatives began using unattractive sales tactics. The most unwelcome of these proved to be wasting the time of the assembled security audience by selling the concept of background investigations to people who were already believers and probably possessed a deeper understanding of the value of background investigations than All-Find's staff. Audience members also found it frustrating for All-Find staff to dodge all questions on pricing and to revert to generalities whenever questioned on specifics. By contrast, they appreciated Pro-Back's no-nonsense focus on specifics and on addressing questions directly and substantively. They noted that it was refreshing to meet a provider who had the authority to commit to means of contracting and turnaround times without the kind of evasion that, by contrast, made Pro-Back's competitors appear to be sales people only marginally attentive to client interests or needs.

Conclusion

Pro-Back was operating in No Dark Corners fashion with its clients and employees before the term came into existence. Pro-Back's chief executive was engaging clients directly with a high level of transparency, working with them through whatever contracting method made most sense to them, and with engaged employees working as a highly motivated team to turn out the best background investigations in the shortest time.

In a No Dark Corners environment, the pre-employment background investigation is demystified, stripped of its plumes and spangles, and rendered intelligible to the end-user relying on it as well as to the people involved in every step of arranging for it and seeing it through from initial request to final report. The assigned investigator is accordingly neither functionary nor third-party scapegoat, but part of a collaborative team seeking to deliver his or her part in a mutual exchange of value, in this case defending against a bad hire, hence mitigating the potential for at least some exposure to insider threats.

AN OVERLOOKED PROBLEM: INVESTIGATING THE NONEMPLOYEE

Even if an institution possesses a robust pre-employment background investigations program backed by an enlightened internal review process, an unaddressed vulnerability may arise in the form of nonemployees whose roles may give them de facto employee access without subjecting them to comparable scrutiny. After all, few employers enjoy the resources or business model that permits hiring internal resources to perform every important task—particularly if the task is infrequent or requires a level of specialization best handled with contract labor or specialized consultants. If the hiring manager or corporate sentinels of the institution attempt to subject such outsiders to the same internal process as internal employees, the outsiders should rightly balk at co-employment, unless the institution's own legal staff does not anticipate the objection first. In other words, once an organization starts to impose on nonemployees the same conditions of employment and direction of activities that it does on its own people, this action opens the door to the outsiders seeking the same benefits and privileges as the regular employees themselves.[13] In general, however, it is seldom a practical alternative to subject nonemployees to the same vetting and background investigation process as one's own employees. However, what many managers and sentinels do not recognize is that there are feasible alternatives readily available to serve the same purpose.

ACCESS THE REAL ISSUE

The real issue from the view of protection is not whether a given individual is an employee, vendor, temporary employee, contractor, or consultant. The real issue is access. Does that individual, by virtue of his or her work, gain the same access to people, facilities, or operations that a full-time inside employee would? If so, then the institution is well within its rights to insist, that as a condition of access, the actual employer of that consultant or nonemployee perform the same level of pre-employment background investigation and certify successful completion to the institution. In other words, if your consultant is to have unrestricted access to my place of business for a day, a week, or a year, then before I grant this access, I should be able to insist on documented reassurances to the effect that this outsider has passed pre-employment screening standards comparable to my own. How do I know that this has indeed taken place and that the job shop or contractor sending me a consultant is not just issuing an affidavit like this without substantiation in order to meet a requirement superficially? There are ways to address this dilemma.

One way to ensure that comparable vetting is taking place before granting unrestricted access to an outsider is to spot check the documentation for background investigations. Require the outsider's true employer to perform the background check, to document this in an affidavit to your institution, and to then make background investigation files for all of its people assigned to your employer available for your own corporate sentinels to review on reasonable notice—say, 24 hours. Then spot check periodically to ensure that the background checks are being performed and meet your own standards of accuracy and completeness. Alternatively, depending on sensitivities and circumstances, insist on seeing the background investigation itself before granting unrestricted access to the individual in question, returning or destroying the documentation after reviewing it, particularly if the outside organization has sensitivities about having personnel information of its staff being held outside of its direct control.

The most expeditious way to address such vulnerabilities without having to occupy one's sentinels with an outside organization's fidelity to proper vetting is to simply insist that all outsiders be given access to critical areas, assets, or operations only when under knowledgeable escort. This means that the outsiders never receive unhampered freedom of movement if they are not employees. However, in order for such a restriction to produce the desired protective effect, escorts for outsiders must be knowledgeable escorts—not just any employee available to watch the outsider. Escorts must be able to recognize inappropriate activity and intervene in time to prevent damage. Thus, a mechanic is not a suitable escort for a computer programmer, nor is a physician the right escort for an alarm technician. A proper escort must have the knowledge and judgment to instantly spot mischief and the authority to put a stop to it before adverse consequences ensue.

SELF-QUIZ: MYTHS AND COMMONLY HELD ASSUMPTIONS

Test yourself with this true–false quiz.[14] Give yourself 10 points for every right answer. If you score 70% or below, maybe it is time to rethink your assumptions. Look at the end for the Achilles' heels that are often forgotten.

1. A friend in the local police department can always get you better information than a background check company.
2. A good background investigation keeps threats out.
3. Every employee should be reinvestigated every 10 years.
4. Today's insider threats are primarily interested in financial gain.
5. Background investigations can uncover those who sell you out for money.
6. Human Resources is best suited to manage the background investigation process.
7. All contractors need the same background investigation as my employees.
8. I cannot legally fire a new employee you happened to discover on Megan's List who was convicted of a sex crime and completed a prison sentence in 1998.
9. A good background investigation will prevent hiring terrorists.
10. I cannot legally warn other employers about an individual whom I fired as a workplace violence threat.

ANSWERS AND DISCUSSION

1. **A friend in the local police department can always get you better information than a background check company.**
   False. It is illegal for police officers to provide arrest information to you, and it is illegal for you to base a hiring decision on it. You can only use convictions, since not everyone arrested is ultimately convicted, and since the American system of justice presumes everyone is innocent until proven guilty. Legitimate background investigations uncover convictions. Most background check firms rely on courthouse employees who can easily and legitimately search pending and public files as a side job.

2. **A good background investigation keeps threats out.**
   True—to varying extents. Although an investigation can keep some threats out, it is not perfect. Investigations will keep out demonstrably unstable, dangerous, or high-risk people—who likely know they cannot pass and will avoid the hiring process. If the process includes drug screening, keeping out drug abusers saves time and money by reducing absenteeism, tardiness, and performance problems that may include unsafe actions.

3. **Every employee should be reinvestigated every 10 years.**
   False. Not everyone needs to be investigated every 10 years, and those who do need regular reinvestigation need it more often. National security clearances are refreshed every 5 years and third-party consumer reporting agencies (background check firms) typically review a 7-year history. So waiting 10 years means that 3 of the years will not be examined, or you need to pay extra for the additional history. Who should be investigated? Employees occupying a position of trust. Some employers require successful background checks as a precondition of promotion to higher responsibility.

4. **Today's insider threats are primarily interested in financial gain.**
   False. Although most Cold War era spies and betrayers were motivated by money, research shows that in the past 10 years, the principal motivation for insider espionage has been divided loyalties, and many of the trust-betrayers have been self-funded. This means that financial indicators may not give away the hostile insider the way that they used to in the past.

5. **Background investigations can uncover those who sell you out for money.**
   True. If you can ask for and properly interpret financial status indicators, you can identify employees living beyond their means or demonstrating financial irresponsibility. This can also be done through common sense observations, such as looking at what type of car a person drives or other conspicuous indicators of a lifestyle that one's paycheck cannot support.

6. **Human Resources is best suited to manage the background investigation process.**
   False. No one office or department handles this well in isolation. A team approach is best, bringing in the recruiting function within HR, a security function, and the hiring organization. If a background investigation identifies a prospective employee as risky, the default decision should be to move on to the next qualified applicant. Otherwise, the onus should be on the hiring manager to make a compelling business case for hiring the applicant who has raised red flags.

7. **All contractors need the same background investigation as my employees.**
   False. Ideally, all contractors should be screened by their employer, although you should reserve the right to spot check for proof that this is taking place. One way to reduce overreliance on background investigations is to limit unescorted access for contractors, or anyone else. However, escorts must always be knowledgeable, per Pitfall C (below). For example, do not assign a mechanic to oversee a computer programmer reconfiguring your network.

8. **I cannot legally fire a new employee you happened to discover on Megan's List who was convicted of a sex crime and completed a prison sentence in 1998.**
   False. You can fire the employee if he falsified his employment application. Much depends on whether the job application asks for felony convictions only within the past 7 years or whether it asks for a full disclosure of all felony convictions with no time limit. If the new hire served his time and did not falsify his application, you may still legitimately release him from probation or fire him for cause.

9. **A good background investigation will prevent hiring terrorists.**
   False. A competent terrorist organization will select operatives without criminal convictions or long audit trails of questionable behavior. They may even be overqualified for the job.

10. **I cannot legally warn other employers about an individual whom I fired as a workplace violence threat.**
    False. You may be prohibited from disclosing personnel information by employer policy or by terms of a legal settlement. You can also advise other employers that you require a notarized, signed release by the individual before providing the requested information, and recommend the prospective employer obtain that release. Consult your legal counsel to avoid

crossing the line into defamation, but recognize that you could just as readily be sued by victims or their survivors for contributing to the negligent
hire of a dangerous person whose violence was foreseeable.

ACHILLES' HEELS FREQUENTLY IGNORED OR FORGOTTEN

Identity Verification

Identity documents are easy to fake or purchase and often undergo only the most
casual scrutiny by the lowest level clerk involved in the hiring process. Employment
law requires establishing a right-to-work by the new hire's presentation of only
certain types of official government identification. Pay more than token attention
to this process.

New Hire Probation

By default, most new hires are under probation for a certain amount of time (6
months, for example). In theory, this is the time to get rid of them for any reason whatsoever, without the rigors of progressive discipline or grievance processes.
However, many employers are reluctant to fire probationary employees. There may
be a substantial burden of time and resources necessary for obtaining approvals
to fill a position, and a cumbersome recruitment process. There is also a natural
tendency to give the new hire the benefit of the doubt. Resist these dynamics and
put every new hire on trial for his or her life, with a release from employment being
more the default than the exception. It prevents serious and expensive problems
later and conditions the employer to use the probation process as it was intended.

Knowledgeable Escort

Not everyone needs to be cleared or vetted, only those people working unescorted
in areas where they could cause harm. However, many organizations assign escort
duty to the most junior employee available. Escorts must be able to recognize
inappropriate activity and to intervene in time to stop it. As mentioned above, a
mechanic is not a suitable escort for a computer programmer. A proper escort must
have the knowledge and judgment to instantly spot mischief and the authority to
put a stop to it before harm results.

Adjudication of Adverse Background Checks

Doing a background investigation is useless if there is no internal protocol for how to
interpret the results, particularly those that are negative or questionable. Most background screening processes become perfunctory, with many falling on the desk of the
lowest level employee of the recruiting organization whose main priority is to keep
the process moving. Instead, there needs to be a thought-out adjudication protocol
that brings together the HR recruiter, someone representing security, and the hiring
manager to handle adverse information that the background check has uncovered. If a
prospective hire raises a red flag, the default should be to move on to the next qualified
candidate. Otherwise, the hiring organization must make a compelling business case
that the questionable candidate is the better hire or only right hire for the job. This represents a witting acceptance of risk, instead of ignoring risk in the name of expedience.

QUESTIONS FOR ONLINE OR CLASSROOM DISCUSSION

1. Thinking like an adversary, identify three exploitable vulnerabilities in your own organization's pre-employment background investigation process.
2. What is an example where a perfunctory escort may inadvertently give an outsider a chance to penetrate defenses in a way that may mistake the consequence for the work of a hostile insider?
3. How would you distinguish between a good background investigation and one that is inadequate?
4. How would you distinguish a good provider of pre-employment background investigations?

EXERCISES FOR GROUP PROJECTS

1. Compare and contrast background investigations from two very different environments. What are your two examples? What kinds of probes are unique to one organization that would not work for the other? Are depth and expense for one unsupportable for another? Why or why not? Can you craft a hybrid approach that would deliver a single background investigation that would serve the vast majority of the needs of both environments?
2. Assume that you can design a work environment where no pre-employment background investigation is necessary. What would that environment be like? How would it operate in a way that compensates for the absence of vetting? What are some possible real-world applications where you could test such a design?

ENDNOTES

1. See *Pre-employment Background Screening Guideline*, Alexandria, VA: American Society for Industrial Security, International, 2006, pp. 20–24, at http://www.asison line.org/guidelines/guidelinespre-employ.pdf.
2. For additional information on this subject, one would do well to consult a variety of readily available references, including *Pre-employment Background Screening Guideline*, op. cit.; U.S. Department of Justice, June 2006, *The Attorney General's Report on Criminal History Background Checks*, http://www.justice .gov/olp/ag_bgchecks_report.pdf; and U.S. Small Business Administration, 2011, *Performing Pre-Employment Background Checks*, http://www.sba.gov/content/ performing-pre-employment-background-checks.
3. The author was able to validate firsthand not only the contract option's cost-effectiveness but also faster turnaround and overall improvement in quality of investigative results while serving as a security manager overseeing all pre-employment investigations for corporate employees of Lockheed. This occurred by means of a competition using actual background checks performed by internal resources and then by two competitive background investigation firms as a prelude to presenting the capabilities of such firms to assembled security directors from other Lockheed operating companies during a corporate-wide security conference.

4. Anonymous, November 9, 2010, user-submitted review and related comment threat on Pissed Consumer, "Lexis-Nexis Background Investigation Screwup," http://lexis-nexis.pissedconsumer.com/lexis-nexis-background-investigation-screwup-20101109206427.html.

5. Ibid.

6. R. J. Cramer, "Diploma Mills: Federal Employees Have Obtained Degrees from Diploma Mills and Other Unaccredited Schools, Some at Government Expense," Government Accountability Office Testimony, May 11, 2004. Retrieved June 27, 2011 from http://www.gao.gov/new.items/d04771t.pdf.

7. For a commercial offering available with minimal effort on the buyer's part, see Inquisitive Research Corporation's price list and recommended bundles at http://www.iqresearch.com/background-check-pricelist.html and http://www.iqresearch.com/docs/IQ%20Research%20Pre-Employment%20Starter%20Kit.pdf.

8. Cramer, "Diploma Mills."

9. The author had an opportunity to apply the new adjudication approach firsthand in a company that was facing both exponential growth and a business need to make sure it was taking no shortcuts in due diligence while making new hires. Accordingly, it fell to the author to design a system which met the requirement to allow for no more than three levels of escalation to reach top management while, at the same time, actually reaching that top level very infrequently, so as to respect business demands on executive time. Company affiliations and company-specific or -revealing details are withheld in deference to client confidentiality.

10. W. F. Buckley, "O.J. Simpson and Other Ills: An Address at a Dinner Honoring Henry Salvatori, Hosted by Claremont-McKenna College, the Four Seasons Hotel, Los Angeles, May 7, 1995," in *Let Us Talk of Many Things*, New York: Basic Books, 2008, p. 482.

11. Called the 10,000-hour rule in Malcolm Gladwell's best-selling *Outliers*, this assertion derives its analytical heft from the work of researchers whose work predated Gladwell's. See K. Anders Ericsson, Michael J. Prietula, and Edward T. Cokely, "The Making of an Expert," *Harvard Business Review*, July–August 2007, p. 4. Retrieved July 1, 2011 from http://hbr.org/2007/07/the-making-of-an-expert/ar/1 and from http://www.coachingmanagement.nl/The%20Making%20of%20an%20Expert.pdf.

12. This story is true. The names of the firms were altered to avoid distraction or confusion of present capabilities with those of a given point in time. As of this writing, both firms have undergone rebranding, including name changes as a result of reorganization or, in one case, acquisition by a larger competitor.

13. For a more comprehensive and tailored understanding of one's employer concerns with co-employment, consult assigned labor attorneys or employee relations staff of the given institution.

14. From N. Catrantzos, "Background on Backgrounds," posted August 2010, www.NoDarkCorners.com, under Tools and Self Help. Reprinted by author's permission. Retrieved July 3, 2011 from http://www.nodarkcorners.com/8.html.

CHAPTER 6

Deception and the Insider Threat

I tell only useful lies, and only those not easily exposed.

Rex Stout

INTRODUCTION

Trust betrayal is impossible without some level of deception. At the very least, under the most benign of circumstances, this may mean self-deception comingled with ambiguity or equivocation. Thus, the cheating spouse seeking to mask infidelities by openly claiming to have spent last night in an illicit liaison cannot possibly mask the betrayal unless his or her audience engages in the kind of self-delusion that discounts the admission as a tongue-in-cheek remark. At the same time, the one offering such a remark by speaking true words in jest knowingly commits an act of deception by presenting a truth as a lie, perhaps even concealing the declaration in a forest of incredible statements, such as, "just before I won the lottery and gave religious advice to the Pope." To an infiltrator or saboteur, deception is the *sine qua non* for transforming what might otherwise be a powerless opponent into a serious threat. Why? At some point, hostile insiders must deceive their targets into granting or continuing to grant trusted access that they do not deserve but intend to exploit.

DECEPTION'S ROLE

Some observers find that average people without a nefarious agenda mislead, fabricate, or otherwise deceive in as many as 25% of their daily interactions.[1] Although this level of deception no doubt accounts for white lies to elude undesired social obligations without giving offense, there remains a self-serving element to deviating from truth and, if the occurrence is indeed so ubiquitous, routine exposure to lying inures defenders to it as a phenomenon both prevalent and socially excusable. To the trust betrayer, this circumstance affords low-risk opportunities for practice, for honing of skills to manipulate the truth without raising eyebrows. The more lies that enter into daily social intercourse without inviting challenge or rebuke, the more difficult it becomes for alert team members or sentinels to probe into fabrications, particularly if doing so takes on the appearance of a personal invasion. For the deceiver, one of the best ways to deflect such a probe is with a simulated expression of outrage or other such ebullition, as one expert has found that the best concealment technique is a mask of false emotion that is much easier to feign than keeping one's cool when caught in a lie.[2]

Recalling the principal tasks of the trust betrayer bent on carrying out a serious insider attack in Chapter 2 (as shown in Figures 2.1 and 2.2), deception plays a key role in enabling an infiltrator to penetrate a targeted institution. The infiltrator's first task is to pass the background screening process, including a hiring interview, and background investigation. This process itself begins with proper verification of identity and credentials—things that an infiltrator must be prepared to alter, embellish, or falsify altogether as occasion warrants. Even to the long-term disgruntled employee whose aim is to misappropriate employer assets or to harm an internal rival while not necessarily representing an existential threat to the institution, deception remains a vital means to those ends. After all, this individual must at least appear sufficiently normal or innocuous to be allowed within range of his target. At the very least, this kind of goal-oriented activity requires cloaking one's rage or predatory impulses until the moment comes to strike. Without deception, there is no concealment of ulterior motives but there is instead a strong chance of behavioral leakage that may give away the hostile insider and increase the likelihood of intervention by defenders.[3]

INADEQUACY OF DEFENSES

Given the importance of deception to carrying out insider attacks, it would stand to reason that institutions would cultivate and deploy the capability to detect deception in time to thwart trust betrayers. Research findings indicate otherwise, however.

> More than two decades of research examining deception detection has indicated that law enforcement officers (as well as citizens) barely perform above chance levels of accuracy.[4]

Indeed, experiments involving studies on the detection of deception indicate not only that lay individuals and police fare poorly, but also that police assumed to have received training in this skill often prove worse than those without such training. The explanation underlying this counterintuitive turn of events is that most of this training involves few opportunities for practice or demonstration in order to absorb and apply the skills assumed to be imparted, with the exception being for members of the U.S. Secret Service.[5] One reason for this finding is that law enforcement officers tend to receive marginal feedback on the accuracy of their determinations of truth or deception. Once a suspect moves out of their hands for prosecution, officers may never learn whether suspects they judged to be deceptive were actually truthful or whether others they deemed truthful turned out to be deceptive.[6] Another reason offered by some critics is that police interview techniques tend to be overly coercive, thereby eliciting false confessions and producing inaccurate information that make the techniques themselves suspect, particularly if misapplied.[7]

Another problem in gauging adequacy of defense against deception is that controlled, experimental studies suffer from a dearth of ecological validity. The actual situation when deceiver and truth detector engage in a battle of wits invariably calls forth different behaviors from all parties. The stakes are high for trust betrayer and attacker in the real world, whereas experimental subjects participating in research efforts remain insulated from the dire consequences of being found out or the equally serious consequences of failing to detect a threat in time. Conditions and observations like these lead some analysts to infer, "Conclusive measures of verbal and nonverbal deception do not appear to exist," while at the same time concluding that deceptive indicators nevertheless decrease "when a person is deliberately lying."[8]

REPRESENTATIVE METHODS FOR DETECTING DECEPTION

Although deception remains a subject of constant study in popular culture and social sciences research, three representative methods continue to surface in studies and critiques: the Reid technique, the Wicklander–Zulawski (WZ) method, and scientific content analysis (SCAN). Before considering these methods individually, it may avail the reader to examine a common feature that they all share: Each was spawned by a polygraph examiner. Even critics of these methods acknowledge their wide use.[9] More interestingly, special forces officers finding themselves tasked with obtaining time-sensitive intelligence from enemy interrogations but with little training on how to go about gaining this data recently reported resorting to the better known Reid technique after taking any available course of instruction they could find, namely,

> Later we would certify most of our people conducting interrogations on the Reid Technique. Although these law enforcement models did not fit well in Iraq, they still built confidence in the team members and helped fill an obvious need.[10]

Eventually, the limitations of the Reid approach's focus on eliciting confessions was recognized as not necessarily making it the ideal technique to apply to intelligence collection, yet it was still considered a very useful stopgap measure in the absence of any practical alternative.[11]

WHAT DO POLYGRAPH EXAMINERS KNOW ABOUT DECEPTION?

Finding arguments challenging the legitimacy of the polygraph is as easy as discovering any jurisdiction where a polygraph is not legally admissible evidence in a court of law. However, there remain sensitive occupations, including compartmented intelligence work and police antidrug task forces and vice squads where successful passing of a polygraph examination is a condition of acceptance and continued employment. Regardless of what position one adopts regarding the validity of using the device, a small exercise in arithmetic soon reveals what advantages a polygraph examiner stands to develop over other interviewers. These advantages are volume of experience and availability of feedback.

To begin with volume, a polygraph examiner fully engaged in performing examinations for an intelligence or law enforcement agency could easily perform several of these probes a day. For ease of calculation and conservative estimating, however, assume only two polygraph examinations per day, leaving time for administrative duties, travel, or other work that may spread out over the course of a year. In a week, then, the polygraph operator has conducted 10 examinations. In a 50-week year, this works out to 500 polygraph examinations. Five years at this rate leads to 2,500 and in 10, to 5,000, culminating in a career of 20 years to 10,000 interviews where the interviewer obtained visible, immediate feedback of how the subject interviewed responded to questions through not only visible behaviors but also changes in speech pattern and corresponding measurements of physiological reactions, such as galvanic skin response and changes in heart rate. These discernible indicators give our polygraph examiner two very significant benefits denied to every interviewer other than a cross-examining attorney who has just pierced through a false alibi while questioning a deceiver on the witness stand. The polygraph and the attending structure of the interview process give the examiner instantaneous feedback. Recall that one of the reasons that even trained law enforcement interviewers do a poor job detecting deception is that they seldom get to find out if their judgments were right or wrong about whether a suspect was telling the truth.[12] The polygraph examiner, by contrast, receives more feedback on the direction of his or her interviews in a week than counterparts in detective or patrol units do in a year. Moreover, receiving not only this kind of feedback but performing interviews focused specifically on detecting deception gives the polygraphist the kind of edge that can separate competence from virtuosity. That edge is in what Anders Ericsson first identified and then Malcolm Gladwell more recently popularized as the 10,000-hour rule.[13] In essence, this rule offers the number of hours of practice as a key factor that distinguishes the proficient violinist from the world-class violinist or from an average computer programmer to a Bill Gates who had obtained more computer experience by his teens than older contemporaries had obtained after a career in computer science. Under the circumstances, it becomes no acrobatic feat of logic to conclude that a superlative and analytical polygraph examiner who masters this craft may eventually come to the point of being able to detect deception without having to strap subjects to a measuring device. Indeed, the more adroit examiner should be able to use the polygraph to calibrate postulates and theories, observing indicators of deception first and then checking the apparatus for independent confirmation of whether that personal observation was right or wrong.[14] Such may well have been the case for John E. Reid and his Reid technique, David Zulawski and Douglas Wicklander for their Wicklander–Zulawski approach—a Reid variant—and for Avinoam Sapir, the author of Scientific Content Analysis (SCAN). Each of these techniques offers defenders some tools for uncovering deception. Each also comes with an element of risk, for not every technique optimized for one setting will apply seamlessly to another.

THE REID TECHNIQUE

Background

The Reid technique is largely the product of a police polygraph examiner turned entrepreneur, John E. Reid. Essentials of the method are available in one of the editions of *Criminal Interrogation and Confessions*, coauthored by a law professor, Fred Inbau, and Reid and Associates executives, including Reid himself, Joseph Buckley, and Brian Jayne.[15] The company also markets seminars on this technique across the country and a certification in its own technique. Reid and Associates continues to offer polygraph examiner services as well. Access and details on offerings appear on www.reid.com. John Reid learned the polygraph from Fred Inbau, who headed a laboratory for Chicago's police at the time. After launching his own polygraph business in 1947, Reid developed a structured interview process whose popularity rose with the 1988 passage of the Polygraph Protection Act, which restricted employer reliance on polygraphs in addressing labor issues. Reacting to the rough kind of police interrogations of the 1930s that apparently generated suspicious levels of false confessions, Inbau worked together with Reid to develop an interrogation technique that would produce results without the same level of intimidation. Many police and private sector organizations came to adopt the Reid Technique as a means of structuring interviews to single out wrongdoing, particularly in circumstances where limited evidence or investigative options were available.

Key Features

Key features of the technique include distinguishing between interviews and interrogations, with the interviews first taking place to gather information in a way that is non-accusatory yet seeks to provoke telltale behaviors indicative of deception. The Reid technique then follows interviews with select interrogations, which are accusatory in nature and designed to culminate in confessions from the guilty. The technique hinges on positive confrontation that draws one set of behaviors from the guilty and another from those not guilty. For example, the innocent subject told he is the prime suspect for any misconduct is expected to launch immediately into vehement denial. The guilty, on the other hand, is expected to become evasive and give himself away with grooming gestures, shifting in a chair, or other signals indicative of stalling in order to find out just how much the interrogator knows about the wrongdoing. Certain questions in the Reid sequence also elicit different answers, depending on guilt. Asked whether she would know anyone well enough to consider above suspicion, for example, an innocent subject would be expected to offer several names, whereas a guilty subject would offer none. Similarly, when asked what should happen to the individual ultimately proven responsible for the wrongdoing, the innocent tend to insist on harsh penalties while the guilty tend to talk of second chances or more vague consequences. Finally, the Reid technique includes development of a theme to offer the guilty as a rationale for misconduct that may appear more socially acceptable than the actual motivation for the misdeed. Although such a theme ultimately has no exculpatory leverage in corporate or criminal proceedings that accompany an admission of guilt, psychologically it is more likely that an admission will follow if tied to a palatable rationale. Thus, a thief will be more inclined to confess if the interrogator hints at understanding that he stole in order to help an ailing parent rather than to indulge in parties and luxuries at another's expense. In either case, the guilt and punishment faced may be the same, but one theme sounds more lofty and forgivable than another, hence its manipulative use by interrogators adept at coaxing admissions of guilt.

Limitations

Critics claim that the Reid technique is capable of producing false confessions, particularly if misapplied. Also, for applications outside of a custodial or law enforcement setting where interviewee cooperation is essential and where employee rights are vigorously defended, the necessarily confrontational application of the technique may foreclose its use in many corporate or institutional environments. One cannot level accusations at three of four people in a given work environment without eventually alienating not only all employees but also their management and their ombudsman, labor association, or other advocates. Finally, because the technique aims at coaxing an admission from a guilty person, its use in obtaining information unrelated to confessions may be limited. In other words, if the principal value that the interviewee has to offer is an article of information that has nothing to do with being guilty of an offense or of having collusive knowledge about one, then a Reid application may fail to unearth this detail. Reid also incorporates interpretations of body language, and to those doubting either the value or the variation in interpreting kinesics in an interview setting, there remain questions raised about whether a given body movement of a subject reveals guilt or whether it is an innocent means of reducing stress in unfamiliar circumstances, particularly in the face of accusations to which one is unaccustomed.

THE WZ METHOD

Background

The WZ method is a non-accusatory variant of the Reid technique whose exponents began their careers as polygraph examiners for Reid and Associates before practicing the Reid technique themselves and then incorporating independently. This method is much more palatable in a corporate setting where accusatory interviews and confrontational approaches run counter to the institutional culture. Essentials of the WZ technique are available in one of the editions of *Practical Aspects of Interview and Interrogation*, coauthored by creators David Zulawski and Douglas Wicklander.[16] While at Reid, Wicklander and Zulawski claim to have developed paper-and-pencil testing survey tools to evaluate employees within a company or organizational setting. The company markets seminars on its technique across the country and, like Reid, a certification in its own technique. WZ does not offer polygraph examiner services but does offer training tapes and videos. Access and details on offerings appear on www.w-z.com.

Key Features

The WZ technique shares many of Reid's features but differs in one: It is non-accusatory. It also begins with fact-finding interviews to narrow a suspect pool and then transitions into select interrogations of likely guilty parties. Once in interrogation mode, the WZ practitioner goes to great lengths to keep the subject from making any denials, even suppressing these by talking over the subject and explaining the investigative process. This explanation is calculated to instill uncertainty and apprehension in the subject without ever communicating precisely what investigative tools were used to arrive at this point, which is a determination that the subject committed the wrongdoing in question. What Reid calls themes WZ calls rationalizations, and the WZ interviewer offers the subject a palatable rationalization that appears to parallel the subject's circumstances, thereby offering the subject a means of making an admission that can then be developed into a full-fledged confession. WZ works particularly well in circumstances where there are no other investigative tools available, such as surveillance video or forensics, or where the use of such tools would generate expense out of all proportion to the object sought. Instead, skillful application of WZ convinces the subject that his guilt has already been established and that the only reason he is being interviewed is because of his employer's interest in knowing not the what but the why and in giving the wayward employee a chance to come clean or give his side of the story. In the end, however, as cathartic as the attending confession may become, once guilt is established the interviewer leaves punishment to higher authority, which typically focuses exclusively on the misdeed, not its stated or airbrushed motive.

Limitations

Although WZ is much more conducive to professional environments where accusatory approaches are unacceptable, issues of guilt are woven deeply into the method's fabric. Thus, like Reid, the method may not necessarily avail if inexpertly administered in areas where the principal goal is to develop information. It may also be difficult to distinguish between the deception uncovered because of actual guilt rather than deception that comes of possessing collusive knowledge.

INTERVIEWING TO DETECT DECEPTION

The suggestions below represent a synthesis of recommendations from many schools of thought, including Human Intelligence (HUMINT) collection, Reid, and WZ techniques. The reader is encouraged to selectively consider those suggestions appropriate to the particular workplace and ambient conditions.

PHYSICAL PREPARATION OF INTERVIEW ROOM

1. Prepare by selecting a space that will offer
   - Minimizing of interruptions, including sufficient privacy to allow not being seen or overheard by others
   - Conducive surroundings, including privacy and a comfortable place to talk
   - Paper, relevant diagrams, or computer access if the interviewee may need these to supply complete information
2. Place the chair of the interviewee nearer the door than yours. This helps diffuse potential claims of false imprisonment if the interviewee later alleges having been trapped in the room and being unable to exit.
3. Avoid having anything between you and the interviewee. [This advice runs counter to custodial-style interviews where the interviewer traditionally interposes a heavy desk or table to gain separation from the interviewee on the theory that the latter may lunge at any moment. Such things rarely happen in a noncustodial setting, and the separation imposed by the table limits your ability to adjust your proximity or position relative to the interviewee, which can limit your effectiveness.]
4. Select a chair with wheels for yourself and leave one without wheels for the interviewee. This allows you to adjust your relative position so that if the interviewee becomes agitated or defensive, you can adjust your chair to be perpendicular to his and then gesture away from both of you while saying an unseen "They" want or expect something that you are trying to moderate on behalf of the interviewee. This position also allows you to move imperceptibly closer to the interviewee if at a point of trying to apply subtle pressure.
5. If you must conduct the interview in the presence of a witness, such as a manager or union representative, position the witness(es) off to the side and, if possible, out of the interviewee's line of sight. This prevents the witnesses from distracting the interviewee or from coaching with nonverbal signals. Ideally, it will also make it easier for the interviewee to ignore their presence and speak as if only the two of you are there.
6. Plan to openly record the interview and set up your materials so that they are visible and in easy reach for you to turn on or off in a matter-of-fact manner.
7. Have writing materials close enough for you to hand to the interviewee if and when needed for a written statement or to draw a diagram, but not so close as to allow the interviewee to use them for taking notes, scribbling, or doodling.

FOR NEUTRAL WITNESSES OR COOPERATIVE SUBJECTS/ INTERVIEWEES WHO CAN HELP SPOT DECEIVERS

1. Open with a few standard, noncontroversial questions to establish a conditioned response and that you are in charge and are the one asking the questions that the interviewee is expected to answer. These questions may include confirming name and some other nonsensitive, work-related details. You could also issue mild commands such as, "Please close that door and take a seat," which will be inoffensive but condition the interviewee to accept direction from you.

2. Relate interviewer's purpose to the motives of interviewee to encourage cooperation. Begin by giving some motivation for cooperation, such as solving a problem of mutual concern so that everyone can get back to the regular job.

3. Be friendly. Make the interviewee feel an equal and, within reason, adapt to his or her intellectual level.

4. Begin with pleasant or innocuous topics.

5. Control your own feelings of distaste or disagreement.

6. Take or appear to take the interviewee seriously.

7. Listen. Always give the other person a chance to talk. Do not rush into silences. Let them tell their story.

8. How to get past an unsupported opinion to obtain verifiable detail: "How do you know that to be true?"

9. Way to lead into interview: "Please tell me everything you think I should know about ____." Then avoid interrupting and just listen.

10. Way to conclude: "Is there anything you didn't tell me because I didn't ask you?"

GOING ACCUSATORY

This is when what may have started as a benign fact-finding interview begins to assume elements of an interrogation because the interviewer suspects the interviewee is being deceptive and seeks to prevent the latter from locking into a lie or misleading statement.

1. Do not allow the interviewee to make a denial. Hold up a hand and say, "Let me finish." Talk about the investigative process and all the ways the organization has of finding things out, including reports from witnesses, computer audit trails, surveillance cameras, anonymous tips, and other methods that will make the interviewee start thinking you already have all the evidence of deception.

2. Instead of making a direct accusation, offer a theme or rationalization that will be easier for the interviewee to admit to than what may be the real motive behind the deception. One approach:

    "Look, there are three types of employees we find in these situations:
    a. "The ones who are telling the truth, and our investigation will clear you.

    b. "The ones who lie outright, and we won't give you a single break. You might as well go out that door right now.

    c. "There's the kind who find themselves between a rock and a hard place, where there are extenuating circumstances. If they come clean, give us their side of the story, then maybe they deserve a break."

3. Minimize the seriousness of the deception but assume that the individual has committed multiple deceptions. The interviewee is more likely to admit to other incidents if suspecting that these have already been discovered. Also, remember that most people do not get caught after the first time, as it is likely a pattern of deception that has led to their exposure.

4. Contrast the deception you want the interviewee to admit with a more serious one, as if by admitting to the lesser instance he is acknowledging something relatively minor and is thus avoiding being blamed for a more serious offense. Example: "What's the worst thing you've been lying about? It wasn't about running over those two kids in the parking lot after close of business that day, is it? [Interviewee denies this.]… That's right. I didn't think so. Because you were just in an area where you didn't yet have authorization to be—and at the same time that that tragedy happened, weren't you?" [Note word selection, such as "an area where you didn't *yet* have authorization" instead of "trespassing" or "violating security." The word selection minimizes the apparent seriousness of the offense and of the denial of it that formed the basis for the related deception.]

5. Use these kinds of expressions if looking for words that offer a palatable way to admit deception:
   - "Anyone in this situation could have…."
   - "Everybody makes mistakes, and you know it's the cover-up that gets them into more trouble than the mistake itself."
   - "Only you can tell your side of the story."
   - "Anybody would have seen it that way."
   - "It wasn't you who started this, was it?"
   - "People always ask themselves later, when it's too late, 'Where would I be if I had told my side of the story while I still had a chance?' If you wait, a story gets out, but by then it isn't your story, is it?"

6. After obtaining an admission, continue to press for more details. Then get the interviewee to put down the details in his or her own words in a personal "account of events" if the term "statement" would appear too formal or risk having the individual withdraw the admission. Remember, however, that the recording you have made will most likely enable taking action even if the interviewee refuses to give a written statement.

SCIENTIFIC CONTENT ANALYSIS

Background

The brainchild of Avinoam Sapir, an Israeli polygraph examiner who honed his skills working for police and intelligence superiors in Israel, SCAN parts ways with many popular techniques by discounting body language altogether. Himself a student of psychology, Sapir mistrusts the near-infinite variations in body language and their corresponding potential for misinterpretation. Instead, he concentrates on what people say, with particular emphasis on the open statement and even some structured questionnaires that can whittle down suspect pools from say 100 possible malefactors to 10 or fewer likely suspects. Sapir does not publish his work but makes it available in seminars and workshops at his Laboratory for Scientific Interrogation. He also provides ongoing support to graduates of his programs. Access and details are available at www.lsiscan.com/.[17]

Key Features

Sapir takes a contrarian approach to average investigative interviews, which he sees as susceptible to producing poor information by leading subjects in their statements. Instead, SCAN promotes open statements, even to the point of letting subjects take them home, complete them in private, and return them the next day. Based on his continuing capture of statistics, Sapir finds that the average statement is one and a half pages long. Truthful narratives also follow a similar pattern, with a relatively small introductory preamble, an equally brief conclusion, and the lion's share of the story focusing on the main issue. By contrast, deceptive statements alter this pattern dramatically, often compressing the main issue at the expense of lengthy preambles or overly long conclusions. Pronouns also figure prominently in SCAN, as when the personal pronoun is missing, the person telling the narrative is also likely to be out of the story, hence deceptive.[18]

Limitations

Most criticisms of SCAN tend to be comingled with explanations of why the technique does not fit well with investigative interviewing methods already in place.[19] SCAN also does require a baseline understanding of semantics and an eye for spotting shifts in tense, self-reference, and other uses of language. This skill is not always readily accessible nor typically cultivated in many or even most individuals who come to assume investigator roles that ultimately make them into protagonists in the detection of deception.[20]

OTHER TECHNIQUES FOR DETECTING DECEPTION

The foregoing techniques piloted by former polygraph examiners by no means constitute the entire universe or constellation of methods of detecting deception through interacting with people who have something to conceal. Academics like Ekman fascinate readers with their studies of microexpressions in controlled laboratory settings unavailable to anyone—other than, perhaps, world-class poker players adept at divining "tells" at high-stakes tournaments.[21] Reviewers of cutting-edge lie detection technology note, however, that new science still faces old hurdles, including questions of accuracy and legality.[22] Moreover, even Ekman's claims of attaining 76% accuracy for his facial action coding system fall short of the polygraph's claim of 85–90% accuracy—yet the polygraph remains largely questioned or inadmissible, and stroke victims or the physically challenged may be unfairly disadvantaged by application of experimental technologies.[23] Psychologists whose methods gain cultlike followings, as accompanied Bandler and Grinder's debut on the pop culture scene with neurolinguistic programming, may for a time enjoy such a cachet that their ideas percolate into government training programs.[24] If one instead examines alternative techniques that have remained in practice over time with some credibility, two rise to a level meriting discussion: courtroom cross-examination and Israeli-style behavioral detection. Both offer lessons and limitations for defenders against the deceivers who become insider threats.

CROSS-EXAMINATION

Background

In legal parlance, cross-examination is the interrogation that opposing counsel carries out immediately after a witness has been directly examined by the other side's attorney. Just as direct examination of that witness seeks to establish a fact or compelling article of information that will advance the case of the attorney calling that witness to testify, so does cross-examination permit the opposition to impeach the credibility of the witness or to uncover different facts than those presented in direct examination.

Key Features

Since proportionally few attorneys actually try cases in court, the legal profession tends to respect cross-examination as an art that not every lawyer can master.[25] The cross-examining attorney must not only attempt to uncover perjured testimony but also demonstrate where the witness and opposing party may be honestly mistaken. As uncertain as the outcome may be, "no substitute has ever been found for cross-examination as a means of separating truth from falsehood, and of reducing exaggerated statements to their true dimensions."[26] Discerning inconsistencies in testimony, questioning the purportedly unassailable expertise of expert witnesses, and raising doubts about what facts witnesses are swearing to or about the credibility of the witnesses themselves are made possible by competent cross-examination.

Limitations

Cross-examination involves an element of theater, as its effectiveness is based on influencing judge or jury in a formal, public setting. The formal setting supplies the cross-examiner an edge, as he or she performs on familiar ground with a superior grasp of the rules than most witnesses subject to questioning. It is also a one-sided technique, where an adept attorney can box the witness into replies that favor the cross-examiner's case without allowing the interviewee to add contextual clarification. That the process includes a formal swearing to tell the truth under penalty of perjury adds a degree of stress for anyone being cross-examined, regardless of guilt. Take away the formal setting, the audience, the rules of engagement, and the legal trappings of this Procrustean bed, and it is arguable whether any deceiver would willingly recline upon it or otherwise risk damning self-revelations.

BEHAVIORAL DETECTION

Background

Behavioral detection, sometimes called behavioral profiling or predictive profiling (which bear no thematic linkage to racial profiling, despite the pejorative reputation the latter has extended to almost any modern use of the term "profiling"), is a technique owing its celebrity to successes of Israeli airport security agents from the early days of hijacking in discovering terrorist adversaries in time to neutralize their attacks. The signature case epitomizing this technique involved an unwitting, pregnant Irish national whose Palestinian boyfriend had manipulated her into boarding an El Al flight with a concealed explosive whose existence was unknown to her. This lack of even collusive knowledge safeguarded the woman from the kind of self-betrayals or "tells" that a witting attacker or supporter might be expected to reveal. Yet the behavioral detection interview uncovered enough anomalies in the woman's story to trigger further scrutiny, which led to discovery of the bomb. The woman herself, perhaps rendered more gullible or suggestive through the blurring veil of romance, was more deceived than deceiver—a circumstance highlighting the power of this detection technique.

ISRAELI BEHAVIORAL DETECTION—THE SIGNATURE CASE

Ann-Marie Murphy was an Irish maid working for Hilton in the United Kingdom. Nezar Hindawi, her Jordanian boyfriend of Palestinian roots and sympathies, manipulated her into becoming an unwitting mule to take a bag laden with Semtex explosive aboard an El Al flight from London to Tel Aviv in April 1986. Hindawi convinced Murphy that they needed to travel separately but would link up in the Holy Land, from there meeting his parents en route to getting married and enjoying a honeymoon. Evidently, Hindawi received the Semtex and the suitcase to conceal it via the Syrian embassy in London. Several sources offer a similar narrative about how the plot was discovered and thwarted by El Al security. This 1989 version is from Daniel Pipes.[27]

RED FLAGS LEADING TO DETECTION
   A. First, Murphy's ticket had been rebooked, an action which automatically invites additional scrutiny by El Al.
   B. Murphy's standard security interview raised more eyebrows, although she passed x-ray inspection without problems and reached the gate with the bag still on an airport cart. There, an El Al representative asked her the company's standard questions.

Detecting Deception with One Dozen Questions
   1. Q: Did you pack your bags yourself?
   A: No. (Hindawi had done this for her, including a calculator detonating device which was supposed to be a "gift for a friend" but would also function as a calculator if examined by airport security.)

2. Q: "What is the purpose of your trip to Israel?"
   A: (As coached by Hindawi...) "For a vacation."
3. Q: "Are you married, Miss Murphy?"
   A: "No." (Finding an unwed, pregnant Irish woman vacationing in Israel struck the questioner as unusual, hence suspicious, triggering an additional probe.)
4. Q: "Traveling alone?"
   A: "Yes."
5. Q: "Is this your first trip abroad?"
   A: "Yes."
6. Q: "Do you have relatives in Israel?"
   A: (Hesitating) "No." (At this point, every reply appeared more farfetched.)
7. Q: "Are you going to meet someone in Israel?"
   A: "No.
8. Q: "Has your vacation been planned for a long time?"
   A: "No."
9. Q: "Where will you stay while you're in Israel?"
   A: "The Tel Aviv Hilton."
10. Q: "How much money do you have with you?"
    A: "Fifty pounds [about $70]."
11. Q: "Do you know how much a room costs at the Hilton?" (The cost at the time was at least $100 per day.) Then, not waiting for an answer, he asked,
12. Q: "Do you have a credit card?"
    A: "Oh, yes." (Murphy then drew from her purse a check-cashing card valid only in Britain.)

SECURITY RESPONSE

At this point, the El Al representative concluded that Murphy's answers had reached a threshold-crossing point. He emptied her bag, finding it "quite heavy," with "a sort of double bottom." He directed Murphy to a body search and took her bag to a staff room. Although she had nothing on her person, inspection of the luggage revealed a plastic bag at the bottom full of a yellowish, oily substance, that is, Semtex. On further scrutiny, El Al determined that the detonator was concealed in the Commodore calculator.

Key Features

Israeli-style behavioral detection is more elicitation than interrogation. Akin to getting to know someone on a first date, it consists of asking questions without revealing what triggered suspicions in the first place. Questions are not so much scripted as tailored and interactive, based more on the answer to the last question than on a formal script. The purpose of the questions is to validate or disprove a potential red flag. When the answer is reasonable and makes sense, no red flag emerges. However, when the answer is incongruous or inconsistent with what most people say in similar circumstances, more probing questions follow. This technique, in essence, is how one pierces cover stories of hostile intelligence officers, spies, or impostors who have learned enough to elude casual inquiries but do not know enough about their cover to be able to reply to detailed questions. In a financial context, for example, an individual may pass herself as a bank vice president by showing a business card and referring to a legitimate-looking business address and telephone where someone stands ready to vouch for her. However, if pressed to explain how the bank in question selects its investments or how it uses bond ratings to guide investment strategies, she may falter and give herself away if unschooled in the more arcane aspects of the banking world. In the signature Israeli case discussed here, a tourist who is going to Tel Aviv without any of the usual preparations, foreknowledge, or funds for a vacation and who also appears in no condition (i.e., pregnant) for this kind of travel presents red flags that only multiply as her answers—although rehearsed—remain inconsistent with the story she is giving to account for her actions. In acknowledgment of the effectiveness of this approach, the head of the Transportation Security Administration (TSA) announced that TSA would be incorporating more elements of Israeli-style behavioral detection at airports as an alternative to invasive searches that have been widely regarded gratuitous or, at the very least, controversial.[28]

Limitations

The Israeli-style method of behavioral detection demands a great deal of training, verbal skill, and discretion on the part of the agent entrusted in its application. Criticisms in applying this method to American airline security frequently arise in the form of disparate feasibility. In other words, Israel is of necessity inured to the terrorist threat and operates in a constant backs-to-the-wall mentality where national service, conscription, and the daily prospect of reacting to suicide bombers permeate civilian life. Given these circumstances and only two international airports, Israelis find it prudent and cost-effective to engage in levels of security that would elsewhere appear draconian. Moreover, given that larger countries such as the United States have exponentially more airports and airline passengers, imposing the same level of scrutiny and training airline security staff to the same level as El Al counterparts would be cost- and time-prohibitive. In other words, the argument hinges on an it-won't-work-here argument for application to airports. For wider application to detecting trust betrayers, the Israeli technique may appear beyond reach because its demands for on-scene judgment, verbal skills, and discretion exceed the capacity—or at least the expectations—of both corporate sentinels and work team members. In other words, nobody teaches or expects anyone at the job to demonstrate the kind of finesse it takes to regularly carry out this kind of behavioral profiling or few institutions provide the questioner the backing to do something about anomalies uncovered through this style of detection. Additionally, absent a controlled setting such as an airline security checkpoint with armed responders prepared to intervene, and the prospect of missing a scheduled flight if one fails to comply with security screening, most interactions on the job offer sentinels and work team members alike few opportunities to follow up on any anomalies they discover, at least to the point of enabling them to legitimately detain or search suspect coworkers.

THE DECEIVER'S EDGE

What, then, makes a good deceiver? He or she may already find that those in the best position to detect the trust betrayer are constrained by real or perceived internal rules that limit defender ability to probe, ability to intervene, or both. Intervention in the form of lawful disruption is the subject of the next chapter. Finding a legitimate means of uncovering the deceiver in this context, however, remains important if one hopes to have any chance of first detecting deception and then doing something about it to thwart insider threats. We next look at what makes a good liar.[29]

WHAT MAKES A GOOD LIAR

An epiphany that surfaces when matching psychological studies of deception to didactic literature on doing well at job interviews is that those who do best in both cases are actors who exhibit confidence and find no difficulty in misleading others.[30,31] Indeed, the ability to project confidence is key and often facilitated through the kind of literature that advises aspiring job applicants on how to present themselves to prospective employers, in terms such as, "Believe in yourself. Even if you don't believe in yourself... make the interviewer think that you do."[32] In other contexts, such as the workmanlike production of fiction, at least one expert advises, "Sometimes, it's easier and just as effective to avoid research altogether and bluff your way through."[33]

Long-term researchers into deception and deceivers offer these traits as some most likely to smooth the path of fabricators or prevaricators:[34]

- Likable personalities, including actors, expressive people, and physically attractive people. They disarm suspicion.
- Positive behaviors, namely, demonstrating behaviors associated with likability and honesty.
- Ability to mask nervousness or fear in tense situations and also the ability to camouflage their emotions and give convincing expressions of feelings that they are not experiencing. Expressive people tend to do better in this area, but they are also more susceptible to giving themselves away by their expressiveness, which is why the ability to camouflage feelings is important for them.
- Capacity for managing cognitive load (that lying may produce) by making statements impossible for others to verify and by tending to conceal information more than to tell outright lies.
- Ability to read others through nonverbal cues, so as to adjust deceiver responses to allay suspicions.

NO DARK CORNERS APPLICATIONS

As the foregoing review and sampling of techniques indicates, even experts are divided on the effectiveness of tools when applied in the environments for which they were designed, which are often in a legal or other controlled setting where the primary objective is to obtain an admission of wrongdoing that has already taken place. Even in cases such as courtroom cross-examination or Israeli-style behavior detection, the operating conditions include elements of formality and armed enforcers who are in a position to heighten the trappings of authority and to exercise deadly force in the event that confrontation leads to open hostilities. Such an environment differs categorically from the average workplace where work team members as well as corporate sentinels need a means to expose deception without alienating the entire workforce. Where does one turn for the right approach?

Intelligence collection through human sources, also known as HUMINT, offers some tools more conducive to these operating conditions. One of the cautions to consider in weighing the applicability of HUMINT collection techniques, however, is the relative importance of language skill over interviewing aptitude for most intelligence agencies. For most intelligence agencies, it remains more practical to recruit primarily for language skills and then graft onto the individual hired other necessary training, including instruction on interrogation, debriefing, and interviewing. Why? It takes years of exposure and regular use to master a language to the point of fluency, and few instructional programs can impart such fluency. However, questioning skills may be taught much more rapidly, and these also serve collectors who must conduct interviews or interrogations via an interpreter. Thus, the intelligence agency can craft or choose a single training program to impart questioning skills in a single common language within days, months, or a year. This training applies equally to people with specialized language skills as well as to those who will have to operate through interpreters. This training investment, in turn, is much more feasible than the much larger investment necessary to take seasoned interrogators and teach them new languages with any hope of attaining the necessary fluency to have them operate as native speakers. The net result is that such practical considerations may often result in force-fitting an individual with valuable foreign language skills into a collector's role regardless of how poorly he or she may be suited to obtaining and assessing intelligence from other people.

One intelligence officer, Frank Stopa, posits an information collection spectrum in terms of invasiveness of the associated collection effort.[35] In this formulation, the poles of the spectrum range from interrogation to conversation, with interrogation representing the most invasive option and conversation, the least. Second to interrogation in invasiveness comes debriefing, followed by interviewing, elicitation, and, finally, conversation. The same categories similarly appear in a military intelligence manual on interrogation, although the manual treats debriefings, interviews, and elicitation as "forms of intelligence interrogation."[36] A brief look at each of these techniques along this invasiveness spectrum will quickly indicate why the more invasive approaches are only partial solutions in a No Dark Corners strategy in the workplace.

Interrogation

Interrogation typically resides in the arsenal of tools used by police, military, or intelligence questioners who are in a position to control the setting or freedom of maneuver of the person questioned.[37] It is also typically an adversarial process where the principals are hostile to one another and where the individual questioned is or may safely be assumed to be unwilling to provide information.[38] In a criminal justice context, interrogation "seeks to get the guilty to admit to their involvement."[39] Recent guidance for military intelligence collectors goes on to categorize interrogation as the HUMINT subdiscipline responsible for military intelligence "exploitation of enemy personnel."[40] Clearly then, interrogation is generally not an option in a noncustodial setting such as the common workplace, where imposing the same controlling force on subjects would represent the kind of false imprisonment that would open most employers to civil or criminal penalties. Moreover, to the average public or private sector place of business, interrogation evokes the kind of coercion or intimidation that alienates the innocent and guilty alike.

Application

In a No Dark Corners milieu where actively engaged team members perform self-monitoring, transparency on the job reduces avoidable errors as well as opportunities for mischief, and corporate sentinels pursue collaborative relationships with employees transacting core business, who would interrogate whom? Team members inured to acting as copilots would be stepping out of their purview and expertise to take on such a role, namely, that of inquisitor. Managers weighing the alternatives could hardly embrace a role that would threaten to jeopardize esprit de corps by turning management into the personification of employee maltreatment. Only corporate sentinels would remain available to take on such a role, and many would find it incongruous with their professional duties and training. Moreover, in the kind of workplace operating under open conditions with due respect given employee rights, the sentinels from one's own legal department would either militate against taking on interrogation as a labor relations debacle in the making or would so closely monitor and constrain the technique as to make its actual use first rare and ultimately extinct. Besides, whom would an institutional questioner interrogate?

Interrogation denotes severe treatment not to be taken lightly, casually, or frequently. In effect, this consideration highlights how undesirable and impractical it becomes to interrogate all but known malefactors. Consequently, if interrogation were to be applied to an insider threat, the technique would come into play only after the discovery of trust betrayal or an actual loss had occurred. The net result is that this technique offers the average institution little value on the frontlines of detection of deception and thus no utility as a means of triggering early warning and interdiction.

Debriefing

Debriefing is interrogation applied to a cooperative subject. Thus, if interrogation deals with enemies, debriefing deals with people on one's own side, such as soldiers or cooperating informants.[41] Sometimes, the difference between interrogation and debriefing may amount to little more than a legal distinction based on the subject's combatant status.[42] Absent an environment where cooperative subjects routinely gather information and present themselves for debriefing, this technique is also likely to be alien to the average workplace.

Application

In a No Dark Corners milieu as above, who debriefs whom? As with interrogation, the technique is likely beyond the capacity and comfort zone of team members and almost as unattractive to managers as interrogation would be, for similar reasons as before. However, debriefing of work team members who come forward with concerns to report suspicions or seek expert counsel may be performed discreetly to the institution's advantage by corporate sentinels possessing the appropriate proficiency and finesse. Over time, however, the existence of a debriefing program such as this would lend itself to being construed as the active cultivation of informants in the workplace by management, which could be deleterious to the employer's aims and inconsistent with the kind of culture that the employer is trying to promote within the workplace.

Interviewing

Interviewing, as distinguished from interrogation, is a process aimed at obtaining information. As such, it is neither accusatory, nor focused on obtaining a confession.[43] Instead, the interview stands apart from the interrogation by being non-accusatory and free-flowing, in contrast to the interrogation's accusatory and structured format. Accordingly, individuals assuming the interviewer role tend to appear less domineering or intimidating than interrogators. Another point of contrast is that, unlike interrogators who tend to accord great priority in exerting control over the venue where the questioning takes place, some interviewers actually find it beneficial to question subjects in their "natural environment," particularly in cases where they may be assessing the interviewee's potential as a threat, as does the Secret Service.[44] Hiring managers and journalists also perform interviews, and the level of give-and-take is more variable than for interrogations or debriefings.

Application

In a No Dark Corners milieu, interviewing is more palatable than either interrogation or debriefing, as it is already an accepted tool regularly used in the recruitment process and in such business process improvements as safety reviews following accidents on the job. However, team members and managers may still distance themselves from taking a lead in the process. Their rationale would be that since sentinels already possess the training to conduct interviews, whether to arrange for screening of job applicants or to conduct internal investigations following a loss or a safety problem, sentinels should be the ones to perform this task. The non-accusatory nature of interviews and their flexibility in being conducted under conditions of mutual acceptability—contrasted with the more controlling aspects of interrogations and debriefings—also render interviews more palatable within most institutions. It is the rare corporate culture that cannot accommodate a fact-finding session under the auspices of legal counsel, internal audit, or employer security as something done as a matter of course as circumstances warrant. To varying degrees, managers and supervisors may also embrace the need to hone their own interviewing skills as a leadership responsibility that goes hand in hand with performing job-related diagnostics after problems occur and, ideally, to avoid problems in the first place. Transferring the interviewing role beyond the manager or designated corporate sentinel, however, appears unlikely. It would be like asking a copilot not so much to take over the controls when the pilot falters but to also take on the responsibility for seeing to the training or compensation of all crew members. In other words, it would be a task inconsistent with promoting highly collaborative, peer-level relationships where one of the reasons team members work well together is that there is no inherent system of giving one artificial ascendancy over another—an inevitable consequence of trying to turn some team members into interviewers to unmask hostile insiders.

Conversation

Conversation, here, is taken out of sequence because it involves undirected, desultory exchanges that may or may not yield informational value and that occur in the absence of a guided collection effort.[45] Conversation takes place ubiquitously and with little restraint or channeling, save in areas where critical safety or other operational mandates require the kind of concentration that prohibits casual speech between coworkers. Although conversation can be revealing, it becomes something other than conversation if it is directed.

Application

In a No Dark Corners milieu, conversation is already taking place as part of social and business intercourse. Who holds conversations with whom? Everyone converses across all levels. There is neither a need nor benefit to tailoring conversation, per se, to the end of detecting deception, as the effort to do so trespasses against spontaneity and transforms the exchange into a probe. Deftly handled, that probe may steer conversation into a lane where telltale revelations may debark after which the banter resumes and the conversation finds its way back to the open road of free-flowing dialogue whose momentary detour went unremarked. The technique that begins as conversation, veers into a subtle probe, and concludes as conversation is elicitation.

Elicitation

One intelligence collector characterizes elicitation as conversation with an agenda where the questioner steers the discussion without revealing the underlying agenda.[46] Another way of representing this collection method is as an oblique way of prompting revelations without drawing attention to them or to the potentially adverse ramifications that might accompany the same. Thus, a parent wanting to learn which of a group of children threw a baseball through a window may find it more productive to ease into the matter by discussing the street game in general terms rather than starting with an outright confrontation or demand for the identity of the window-breaking offender. Another trademark of elicitation is that it allows a skilled practitioner to leave the subject unaware of the collection agenda and even whether the subject actually made any revelations. How is this possible? On the likely theory that most people remember the beginning, the end, and possibly those parts of a conversation that underwent repetition, then the best way to elicit information and minimize the chances of the probe being recalled is to make a single probe toward the middle of a dialogue and then not revisit the same topic again.[47]

Application

In a No Dark Corners milieu, the answer to the question who elicits information from or about trust betrayers parallels the answer to the question who operates the lathe or who bakes the soufflé: the one who can. The dispositive element in elicitation is interpersonal skill—not organizational role or title. The necessary interpersonal skills include not only the ability to converse but a capacity for listening and creating openings in the dialogue to gently probe without giving away one's true area of inquiry. For an insider case, this process could involve a team member, sentinel, or manager having a social chat that elicits details about the subject's credentials, identity, or experience by offering up a story about one's own experience and then inviting the subject to share his or her own comparable story—without appearing to pay more than polite attention to the details that are captured and later verified or disproven outside of the interchange that just took place.

WHERE TO EXPECT DECEPTION FROM TRUST BETRAYERS

Given the plethora of techniques available for detection deception and their variable usefulness depending on ambient conditions, defenders of institutions seeking to unmask the perfidy of hostile insiders could easily find their prospects unpromising. However, by harkening back to the essential tasks of the hostile insider as depicted in Figure 2.1, defenders may subdivide an otherwise daunting task into manageable elements from which to navigate toward more promising shores. We thus begin with the infiltrator as the hostile insider poised to be the serious existential threat, for reasons cited in Chapter 2, and then consider the disgruntled insider who may also present danger to the institution or its employees. Although there are some areas where both types of trust betrayer must deceive in order to further their destructive aims, there are other areas where they differ. Table 6.1 lays out the differences in abbreviated form.

THE INFILTRATOR'S DECEPTION

The infiltrator must pass the background screening process, survive a probation period, and then exploit vulnerabilities in order to strike. On the surface, doing all these things appears very demanding. However, given that the infiltrator comes with a support structure, it is likely that he or she has been selected for the particular betrayal with an eye to how well the individual infiltrator fits into the targeted institution. It is also a near-certainty that this infiltrator will receive the benefit of formal training or ongoing coaching to deal with each of the obstacles where detection of deception could spell defeat. These are the areas where deception is necessary in order for the infiltrator to advance to either the next level or to final striking position.

Deceptions Possible in Screening Process

This area (which includes identity, credential, education, and employment verification, a job interview, and a background investigation) covers the following:

- Presenting false identity documents or credentials and struggling to remember the legend or cover story that accompanies an assumed or carefully structured identity.
- Presenting and maintaining an engaging demeanor, including controlling any signs of ideological hostility to the employer or country of employment.
- Repressing outward expression of political, religious, or other beliefs and practices that would invite scrutiny or suspicion.
- Concealing knowledge, training, equipment, and communications channels with which the infiltrator maintains connectivity to the controlling cell directing his activities. This includes mastery of basic tradecraft, the same kinds of personal security skills essential to espionage, so that one does not give oneself away by leaving evidence of one's true purpose or affiliation where it can be discovered. This may also include feigning a lower level of intelligence or lack of interest in politics, world affairs, or other passion where zeal would be difficult to suppress.

Possible Indicators
- Well rehearsed in answering questions on the employment application but falters or gives non-answers when asked about side issues not included in cover story
  - Q: I see you went to Georgia Tech for a year. Didn't you hate how busy Hartsfield gets during the holiday season? What did you think of that crazy ordinance that made Kennesaw famous, you know, the one about gun ownership?

TABLE 6.1   Deceptions of Infiltrator vs. Disgruntled Insider

	Infiltrator	Disgruntled Insider	Remarks
Screening Process	• Masking real identity, hostile intentions • Avoiding revealing details or indications of attachments	• Concealing any part of prior work history pointing at instability	The screening process, properly handled, is a greater challenge for the infiltrator than the employee who eventually becomes disgruntled. Most new hires walk in smiling, happy to get the job. Only later do they sour.
Probation	• Avoiding personal revelations that deviate from rehearsed script used for application • Appearing eager while remaining socially distant • Using newcomer's unfamiliarity to mask entry into sensitive areas or operations	• Suppressing dyspeptic or abrasive tendencies long enough to pass probation	Either one having something to hide will likely exhibit counter-elicitation behaviors, i.e., giving limited responses, feigning ignorance, giving rehearsed responses, and redirecting conversation away from areas of discomfort. This may require more work for the infiltrator who has the added complications of a double life and of getting to learn an unfamiliar environment.
While Seeking Vulnerabilities	• Using pretexts for probing into areas outside of purview • Manipulating others into supplying information or access • Offering to cover for other workers in order to be alone and unmonitored	• Claiming overriding interest in quality of work, safety, or other lofty concern as excuse for probing into restricted areas • Concealing saboteur tendencies as whistleblowing or concern for safety • Using grievance and hotline complaints to deter coworkers and managers from taking disciplinary action • Professing or inflating expertise to justify deviation from or malicious compliance with instructions	This becomes more difficult now for the disgruntled insider because he or she will have developed a reputation without necessarily having a say in what others think of him or her. The disgruntled insider is unlikely to be believed as much as ignored or avoided, particularly if having a reputation for being abrasive or dyspeptic. Either the infiltrator or disgruntled insider may inadvertently invite scrutiny by deviating from the norm when it comes to taking time off. Those who never do often remain in place to conceal misdeeds, particularly in cases of embezzling or espionage.

- A: Hartsfield … yes, very busy. (Has little else to say because no direct knowledge of the airport in Atlanta. Parrots interviewer's words in order to avoid having to produce specifics.)
- A: Well, I'm against that sort of thing, guns, you know. (Offers an abstract assurance[48] instead of answering question specifically, because does not know that Kennesaw had a law making it illegal *not* to own a gun in the community.)
  A: [Saying nothing and waiting for interviewer to move on to another subject. As noted in some HUMINT-related accounts of how operatives are trained to deal with questions on occupation or clandestine involvements, "The simplest thing was to say nothing."][49]
- Avoids words that convey attachment[50]
  - Q: This job has a pretty generous number of vacation days. Are your folks in town or do you end up traveling to see them for the holidays?
  - A: No, there is no family. I don't mind working extra hours. (Avoids saying *my* family or offering personal information. Shifts subject. Talks about *the* job, not my job when asked about previous work. Leaves out the point of view of others in any stories and does not ask questions.)[51]

Deceptions Possible during Probation Period

- Avoiding self-revelations that could compromise true intentions and affiliations
- Keeping social distance yet conveying appearance of being eager to work and fit in
- Going to great lengths to appear teachable and proficient while at the same time not standing out so much as to invite undue attention that leads to questions that may put cover story in jeopardy

Possible Indicators

- Rarely deviates from a story line or mentions what went wrong when telling a story[52]
  - Q (from new coworker during a lunch break): So, my last job was pretty lousy. They had me working really long hours and I guess that made me surly. The boss and I didn't get along, and I guess I didn't help matters much with my attitude. But I still run into my old boss, now and then, and we get along. Do you stay in touch with your old boss?
  - A: No. Everything was OK at my last job. I just wanted to get more money and work some place that looked like it had a better future (sounding like something rehearsed for the job interview).
- Reluctant to socialize after business hours because of need either to make contact with planning cell or because of concern that real feelings of distaste for coworkers or employers could leak out, even through facial expressions if not in words[53]
  - Q: Hey, a couple of the guys are getting together at the diner with their wives for a beer and a burger Thursday night. Want to join us? You could bring your wife or girlfriend if you want.
  - A: No. Sorry. I have to take a friend to the airport that night (or other excuse—unremarkable unless part of chronic evasion).
- Shows uncommon interest in doing jobs others avoid in order to gain favor

- Strays into areas where does not belong and just says, "Sorry, I'm the new guy and still don't know my way around," or words to that effect to excuse minor trespass
- Pays more attention to facility diagrams, access routes, layouts, and access points not only for own job but for areas outside of purview, paying extra attention to sensitive areas or those housing high-value assets
  - Q (from coworker): How come you're so interested in that manual about the control room when we end up doing most of our work in the field switchyards?
  - A: I guess I'm just interested in everything, as the new guy. If I get an idea how everything connects, I'll do a better job and won't let any of you down.

Deceptions Possible after Probation While Seeking Vulnerabilities

- Probing into sensitive matters or areas to learn more about them and to test defenses to identify gaps or weaknesses under some pretext or by feigning ignorance
- Manipulating others into becoming information sources or providers of access otherwise unavailable
- Exploiting open work environments to gather up more data than the job requires on facilities, operations, schedules, and security—particularly for critical areas or operations

Possible Indicators

- Finding pretexts for going into sensitive areas outside of normal purview
  - Q: Why are you in the vault by yourself? Shouldn't you be here only with someone assigned to this area?
  - A: I heard there was a problem with one of the duress alarm switches and wanted to see if I could help out. Sorry, I guess I'm still new and don't know all the rules yet. No offense.
- Working or offering to work extra, uncompensated time, or to cover for coworkers who need to leave early on personal business in order to be able to be alone and unmonitored
  - Q: Are you sure it's OK if I leave you on your own so I can get to my daughter's soccer game in time? And you won't tell the boss?
  - A: No problem. I might want to ask you to do the same for me some day.
- Cultivating venal or shy employees to be able to manipulate them into giving information or access otherwise unavailable
  - Q (from venal employee): What's your angle? Why should I tell you anything about this process instead of reporting you to my supervisor?
  - A: Hey, I didn't mean anything by it. My brother-in-law works for our biggest competitor and said he was having a problem in this area. I just figured if you could help me help him out on this, maybe he would show his appreciation to both of us. Nobody here loses, but maybe you and I come out ahead. But, hey, if you can't use a little extra money....
  - Q (from shy employee responding to advances): How come you're so interested in going out with me, when no one else here seems to know I'm alive?
  - A: I'm kind of shy myself and really have no interest in show-offs. You look to me like someone I might have more in common with, someone who's interesting and smart and has enough sense of self not to have to go around flaunting it.

THE DISGRUNTLED INSIDER'S DECEPTION

Deceptions Possible in Screening Process

- Masking any part of prior work history that would point to instability or otherwise send red flags to a recruiter or hiring manager.
  Rationale: Most disgruntled insiders start out as average employees who enter the institution smiling and only later cultivate resentments that make the employees themselves obstreperous and result in declining performance or even counterproductivity. Thus, only the new hire with a history of being a problem employee would have reason to be deceptive in the hiring process. This deception may involve concealing misconduct that was the reason for termination, with the subject confident that the typical background check will only return information to the effect that the individual worked at this location in that job title from this date to that date—a modern-day nod to fears of litigation. Similarly, if the individual was dismissed after making threats of violence against peers or supervisors, the termination may have been negotiated for the convenience of all parties and stipulated that the former employer reveal no details of the case and tell future employers nothing more than the bare minimum to verify past employment.

Possible Indicators
- Concealing dismissals and gaps in employment
  - Q (by recruiter accepting application): I see here that you worked for one of our competitors in this industry before but left something out. Why did you leave them? And what did you do afterward?
  - A: My mother was dying of cancer in another state and I had to take extended time off in order to help with the family during her last days. I cashed in my retirement savings to help out until I had to get back to work.
- Refusing to accept blame for own misfortunes
  - Q: It seems you left a couple of previous jobs because of personality conflicts. What can you tell me about that?
  - A: Just one of those things, I guess. I'm a workaholic and at some of the places I was at, they didn't like me coming in as the new guy and doing more work than old timers did who had been there for 20 years. Sometimes, other people resented that, and I couldn't help it because I have a strong work ethic and I wasn't raised to take a paycheck for doing less than my best on the job.

Deceptions Possible during Probation Period

- Suppressing dyspeptic or abrasive tendencies long enough to pass probation

Possible Indicators
- Never has a tardiness or absenteeism problem until after successfully passing probation.
- Takes unusual interest in employee hotline, ethics, grievance, and whistleblower programs, often appearing to make retaliatory or pre-emptive allegations in order to draw attention away from own asperity or recalcitrance on the job.

These kinds of acts may follow or in some cases precede disciplinary actions that the insider knows or suspects may be forthcoming, including an impending decision not to retain the individual at the conclusion of the probationary period.

- Q (from internal or external investigator following up on a complaint): So, what exactly happened and what evidence do you have of discrimination against you by your boss or peers?
- A: Well, I have it all written down right here on my calendar. On that Tuesday, the foreman made a snide remark about mafia gangsters—and you know I'm the only one on the team with Italian heritage. (Or, ...)
- A: The guys told me that the only ones who get this lousy assignment are the ones the bosses don't like and want to drive out of the company. Go ahead, ask anyone. (Or, ...)
- A: I was reading my Bible on my lunch break and I heard the boss say out loud, "I would not have you, ignorant brethren," when the actual quote should be, "I would not have you ignorant, brethren." And she was looking right at me and smiling when she said that. It's religious discrimination.

Deceptions Possible after Probation While Seeking Vulnerabilities

- Probing into sensitive matters or areas under the pretext of concern over quality, possible misdeeds of management, safety, or even citing ethics concerns[54]
- Claiming whistleblower protections when fearing negative reactions
- Abusing grievance, hotline, and other vehicles for bypassing chain of command as means of browbeating peers and bosses into overlooking deficiencies or abnormal actions
- Feigning misunderstanding or using malicious compliance as means of furthering own ends and sidestepping direct guidance or standing orders

Possible Indicators

- Getting involved in an institutional task force, committee, or grievance-handling process as a representative, solely in order to skirt normal duties and probe into areas unrelated to own technical area of concentration
  - Q (by supervisor): Why are you concerning yourself with access for that control room, since neither of us works there?
  - A: As a union steward, I may one day have to represent those employees, especially if their usual reps are on vacation or out of town. Are you trying to hide something? I heard one of the people working there is Fred, who lost his hand in an accident, and I wouldn't want to see him discriminated against because he doesn't have a hand to use on that palm scanning biometric reader at the door to the control room. Are you telling me you condone that kind of discrimination?
- Alleging retaliation when caught in suspicious activity, thereby deflecting negative scrutiny
  - Q: What are you doing with the plans to the network operations center? You know those aren't supposed to leave the area.
  - A: Oh, sure. I get it. It's OK for me to be a floor warden, and take extra training on my own time, but I'm not supposed to know where the exits are, in case of a fire? Hey, this isn't about the plans, is it? You're after me because I

went to the ethics officer and reported that lunch you had with a vendor last Christmas. I was only doing what they told me to do in the annual ethics briefing, and now you're taking it out on me. This is retaliation. I won't stand for it. I'm going straight to the auditor, the union, and, if necessary, getting my own lawyer. There are laws against this kind of harassment.

- Using malicious compliance to cover suspicious actions
  - Q: We're not supposed to take any of those files home or make copies, so why are you downloading them on a flash drive?
  - A: Was I the only one there when the boss said he wants all our work turned in by Friday, or else? He told all of us to do whatever it takes, didn't he? OK. Well, there's no way I can concentrate on my project and finish it here, during the day. So the only way I can meet the deadline I'm supposed to meet, is to do it this way: Take it home. Now you're telling me *I'm* wrong? Well, why doesn't somebody make up their mind around here? You want the job done on time, or not? I'm just trying to do what I'm told.

THE DETECTION DILEMMA

As the foregoing examples illustrate, defenders may suspect anomalies or even discern that an answer to their probes appears deceptive. Yet any answer by and of itself seldom affords incontrovertible proof that the subject of inquiry is being deceptive. There is seldom a single action, response, behavior, or revelation on the part of an insider that categorically establishes maleficence or betrayal. Even someone caught in a lie can turn out to be innocuous. The applicant nervous about identity verification could be not so much a nefarious infiltrator as someone who changed his surname because his brother discredited the family name by defrauding pensioners of millions in a Ponzi scheme or by murdering patrons at a shopping mall in an outbreak of workplace violence. Similarly, the woman airbrushing reasons for leaving her past employer could have herself been the target of harassment who really suffered in a hostile work environment and prefers to set that experience aside rather than to keep revisiting it by going into the details of past grievances and legal action. It is even possible that the employee who strays into a sensitive area absentmindedly really possesses no ulterior motive other than curiosity about someone working there with whom there is a mutual attraction and a possible dating opportunity. One dilemma, then, is not only detecting the kinds of anomaly that point at the possibility of deception but also deciding at what point deception really is evident—a dilemma of calibration. The answer to this dilemma, in a No Dark Corners setting, is similar to the answer that schools face when called to make determinations of risk in order to anticipate outbreaks of violence from students: using a multidisciplinary assessment team.[55]

As studies of school violence have shown, the keys to timely identification of potential danger are to

- Use multidisciplinary teams—rather than rely on a single expert
- Concentrate on whether the subject under inquiry *poses* a threat, not on whether the subject actually made a threat
- Give every threat prompt attention[56]

There is no single expert, nor can any institution reliably expect a single team member, manager, or sentinel to assess in a vacuum the deception and threat potential of all suspect insiders. Indeed, an assessment process drawn from that used in schools can assemble a diverse talent pool among which to parcel out aspects of the assessment that best match available skill sets. Thus, it may fall to a security sentinel to perform a discreet investigation into allegations of a subject's inexplicable behavior while it falls to a trusted team member to interpret whether the behaviors are indeed inconsistent with the job and to a coworker better acquainted with the subject to serve as an ad hoc assessment team member, while a senior manager with decision-making authority chairs this assessment team.[57] The multidisciplinary team offers the advantages of keeping threat assessments grounded in common sense, so that inquiries into every anomaly do not take on the ravings of paranoia and also offers the institution a desirable alternative to questionable programs of making snoops out of fellow employees. One such program, the passive listening post, for example, came about in the aftermath of the discovery that a naval intelligence analyst was delivering classified material to a foreign power. The passive listening post idea was supposed to work as a tripwire whereby fellow workers would watch for security violators. However, the program ultimately faltered and was discontinued after running afoul of Privacy Act concerns.[58]

CONTEXT-BASED ANOMALY DETECTION

The keys to parrying an insider threat are timely detection and intervention. Intervention, which permeates the discussion of the next chapter, is impossible without detection, and recognizing deception remains at the heart of early warning that something is amiss. Ultimately, the key to uncovering the deceptions a hostile insider must perpetrate in order to enter into striking range of a target resides in the ability to gauge whether statements and actions are consistent with workplace expectations. In some cases, this means gathering independent data and matching them with what the deceiver has offered, uncovering inconsistencies and even culminating in a face-off with the deceiver to ascertain intentions. More often, however, the most valuable and timely indications of deceptions will leak or be brought to the surface before work team members who have the greatest exposure to the hostile insider, regardless of whether the latter is an infiltrator or a disgruntled employee. In either case, trust betrayers lower their guard sooner or later and, being human, make mistakes. These mistakes are most likely to happen before the employees with whom the insiders spend the most time, that is, peers. As we have seen, though, peers may write off such signs, particularly if there exists no system to encourage them to notice or act upon their suspicions.[59] Also, as in school violence warning signs, research suggests that different people may have different pieces of the puzzle, hence the need for multidisciplinary assessment teams and a means of reaching out to all available sources for relevant input before undesirablez.[60] Yet how are these multidisciplinary teams to function, particularly in an environment where application of the more aggressive techniques for detecting deception would appear draconian and run counter to a culture of transparency and collaboration?

One promising approach is to take the multidisciplinary approach pioneered for dealing with threats of school violence and blend it with those detection techniques that work effectively in the given situation. By using one of the least invasive techniques, for example, one would expect coworkers to elicit information from and about potentially hostile insiders. Because they take a proprietary interest in their work and in the success not only of the individual but of the entire work unit, these team members are in the best position to spot anomalies. All they need is the encouragement to probe further and to then communicate any concerns without delay. The necessary incentive, then, comes to them in terms of seeing someone in the organization take their information seriously and at least assess it. In the arena of workplace violence prevention, including the school violence research discussed, one option for demonstrating this level of engagement is to make the reporting coworker an ad hoc member of the threat assessment team. Since the assessment team is composed mostly of internal employees, it is more feasible to convene it rapidly for a quick review of concerns than to await the arrival of consulting experts whose contracts may have to be renewed or travel schedules accommodated.

From this point, the reporting coworker is interviewed about his or her concerns. Who performs the interview? Ideally, a respected manager who is in a position to make decisions about actions to contain any threats should also lead this process. However, there may be occasions when the manager elects to instead defer to a more experienced corporate sentinel to take in the information, particularly if that sentinel is also in a position to launch a parallel investigation that can prove or disprove suspicions raised. Is there room for a debriefing in this process?

Indeed, the manager in charge of the assessment or the corporate sentinel acting on the manager's behalf can and should debrief the supervisor of the individual exhibiting the behavior of concern. However, this debriefing may best occur after the supervisor has been brought in as a member of the multidisciplinary team and has returned to the workplace to make personal, direct observations of the individual in question, which would include eliciting answers to questions that inform further assessment.

Is there room for content analysis, such as SCAN? Content analysis is likely to be more helpful in examining products of the disgruntled career employee whose statements, e-mails, or reports may be revealing to the trained eye and also indicative of whether the individual poses a threat. The technique may offer less value in assessing an infiltrator who is relatively new to the organization and has as yet little to offer in the way of statements or other material to analyze for indicators of deception.

What about interrogation? In most cases, interrogation would only follow after the fact and occur at the hands of authorities, either after the insider had already caused a loss or had been apprehended before striking. If matters arrive at a point where the assessment team determines that the insider has indeed betrayed trust and poses a threat, it may avail to have an experienced corporate sentinel convene an interview that may include some of the accusatory aspects of an interrogation. In most institutional settings where critical assets are involved but institutional culture prohibits heavy-handed tactics, the only interrogation approach likely to be permissible and to yield results will be the WZ approach. The WZ technique may offer little productive yield when applied on an infiltrator, however, as this kind of individual may be thoroughly schooled on how to resist probes and may also be immune to the portion of WZ that sets up alternative rationalizations for coaxing admissions of guilt. The disgruntled insider, however, is much more likely to succumb to the WZ method, as this individual typically feels underappreciated and misunderstood, thereby easily playing into the hands of a deft questioner with the finesse to show empathy and tailor a rationalization that plays to the insider's ego.

When all else fails, there may be nothing to lose and everything to gain from confronting the insider with direct questions and then, in deference to SCAN's guidance, listening to the answer that follows. However obvious this latter guidance may seem, what makes it worth emphasizing is that the average length of time that a skilled investigator will spend before interrupting the person he is interviewing remains about 8 seconds.[61,62]

AT LEAST ASK

Another useful practice for experienced investigator and neophyte alike, is to conclude interviews by asking whether there is anything that the subject "didn't tell me because I didn't ask?"[63] A variation of this tactic, offered by a psychologist specializing in piercing through deceptive narratives, is to make reference to an undefined, higher authority in soliciting additional details by saying, "They're going to want to verify everything. Even the slightest exaggeration will work against you…. What specifically needs to be revised so it's perfectly accurate?"[64] Because psychologists theorize that lying produces stress on the deceiver, it stands to reason that there may come occasions when the hostile insider has grown weary of deception and may be receptive to making disclosures or admissions that only await the prompting of having someone ask. Although obtaining incriminating admissions infrequently happens this way, the rare admission turns into a virtual impossibility if one does not at least ask. This, in turn, recalls the counsels for leaders in Chapter 4, as a useful point of departure, viz., know your world, start somewhere, and at least ask.

KNOW YOUR WORLD

In detecting deception, it is seldom difficult to overrate common sense and a sound grasp of what is incongruous in the ambient environment. One particular place where this knowledge avails in penetrating through fabrications is in retaining the wherewithal to recognize the kind of glaring oddity that goes unremarked for fear of being branded insensitive or giving offense. In financial crimes, this phenomenon has been called the "curse of the indelicate obvious."[65] In other words, a fear of violating perceived standards of political correctness or generating exposure to lawsuits makes otherwise reasonable employees ignore blatant signs of aggression (a possible precursor to workplace violence), lavish spending beyond one's salary level on cars and jewelry (a possible indicator of embezzlement or even treason), and display of tattoos or clothing favored by criminal gangs (a sign of affiliations that are unlikely to place a high value on the employer except as a target). Managers eager to avoid the disruptions of legal or personnel actions will often expand their tolerance of unusual behavior before reporting it or taking action. They do this not so much out of liberal, laissez faire attitudes regarding individual expression as out of a desire to spare themselves the hassle of raising red flags that corporate sentinels and upper management will refuse to act upon for fear of offending some aggrieved party or of inviting negative publicity. Meanwhile, the hostile insider benefits from this diffidence by gaining and exploiting more freedom of maneuver, perhaps even more so in the case of the disgruntled career employee who is more familiar with what kinds of negative publicity the institution most fears, as opposed to the infiltrator who has not had time to develop so keen a sense of institutional antipathies.

START SOMEWHERE

The difficulty in even the most enlightened workplace equipped with the tools and resolve to counter insider threats by piercing through deceptive layers is that the worst way to launch capabilities is to do it all for the first time in a high-stakes, real-world event. A better place to start is in a training environment, where members of a multidisciplinary team can establish personal relationships and a foundation of shared knowledge of procedures to follow before encountering their first real case.[66] As a truism in crisis management pronounces, the best time to make a friend is before you need one. Even a relatively minor insider threat gives rise to high emotions that flow out of feelings of betrayal. It is therefore better to think through the process of assessment and how different team members will go about conducting probes and validating suspicions in a stress-reduced, scenario environment that follows interactive training and discussion with instructors who have more experience and can answer questions on the spot.

THE WHAT-IF DISCUSSION

Even the organization bereft of outside resources and short on staff to dedicate to due diligence efforts and detecting deception can improve its capacity to identify deceivers through a single step: running through a what-if scenario. Managers, team members, corporate sentinels, and informal leaders all meet from time to time for a variety of personal and professional exchanges. "What would we do if that new guy we hired turned out to be a rotten egg looking to steal our trade secrets?" might be one such scenario to discuss in a round table session. "If our chief financial officer wanted to bankrupt us and transfer our contingency funds to a personal offshore account that no one else could touch, who other than she could tell?", might be another scenario to ponder. From the discussions that follow, one could then infer what deceptions would be necessary to carry off the betrayal and what potential early signs would be worth monitoring.

SAMPLE SCENARIOS

Each of the scenarios that follows has a different subject who invites suspicion but essentially the same core cast of people who are evaluating the particular subject for signs of deception that may signal an insider threat.

Core Cast

Cody	Concerned coworker
Sandra	Supervisor for Cody and subject
Harry	Higher manager to whom Sandra ultimately reports
Pauline	Protective services (i.e., security) representative and investigator
Edna	Employee relations (i.e., Human Resource subunit) representative
Bernie	Behavioral sciences specialist (consultant) who gets called to evaluate some cases
Lorraine	Legal department representative, a labor attorney

Scenario 1: A Bad Feeling Early On

Cody is having coffee with Sandra on Friday after a busy week, as they both look to wrap up the documentation for all the work orders their unit handled during the week. After finishing the documentation, they chat about how things are going and what they have to look forward to in terms of next week's anticipated work load. Sandra then asks her usual question about how things are going with the other team members, particularly the new hire, Ian.

Cody: You know, I've got a funny feeling about him.
Sandra: Oh … (puts her pen down, and just listens, waiting for Cody to go on).
Cody: Yeah. Can't put my finger on it exactly. But there's something a little off about this guy. What he does—I mean he seems to do the work OK. Maybe he even knows more about it than some of the old timers. It's not the work exactly. It's how hot and cold he runs in the way he talks.
Sandra: For instance … ?
Cody: Well, for instance, he gets real chatty when it comes to work things and structures, like the Ames Plant we showed him on Wednesday—asks all kinds of questions and even warms up to the old war stories some of the guys start telling about those unexploded bombs we used to find there from the days when Patton trained his army before shipping them out to fight WW II.
Sandra: Ooookay. So far, that doesn't seem to be a big deal.
Cody: Absolutely. It's not. The hell of it is, we get back to the barn and guys start talking about their RVs or what they want to do to blow off steam or to kick back for the weekend, and all of a sudden, Ian is like a different person. No talking, kidding around. Doesn't ask a single question. Shows no interest in anyone or anything. Brushes off invites to have tri-tip at Louie's Barbecue or any other outside stuff. Not that he's mean or anything. It's just that if he was all quiet all the time or all chatty all the time, I guess that would look normal. But the way he goes up and down—it's not like any of the other people we've ever had on the team. Probably nothing to it. But it just makes you wonder.

Sandra then goes over this account again with Cody to make sure she understands what is bothering him and then tells him she will give the matter some thought and get back to him next week.

What happens next? Sandra talks this matter over with her boss, Harry. Between the two of them, they reason it may just be odd enough to be worth a closer look. So Harry calls Pauline over to join them because she has had a lot of experience with investigating problem employees, and Harry would rather get ahead of any problem situation than wait for it to flower on his watch. Pauline talks briefly with Harry and Sandra, in Harry's office, and then takes on an action item to take a second look at Ian's application package and background investigation, just to see if there's anything there that may have been missed. Meanwhile, Harry gives Lorraine a call, explaining the situation.

Lorraine: So, Harry, I had a feeling this wasn't entirely a social call. Are you asking me what your legal options are with Ian or whether I recommend we convene a threat assessment team on this case?
Harry: Both, actually. I know we're coming up on the weekend, but I hate letting these kinds of thing fester, and if there is a problem, I'd rather map out the next move than be blindsided or, worse yet, end up blindsiding my own boss.
Lorraine: If it's a question of starting a threat assessment, I'd say to see what Pauline finds out and let that be your guide. As far as legal options with Ian, well, that's what we have a probation system for. You know how we run it. You can release him at any time. I'd say we use the system the way it was designed and

intended, where release is the default—not just keeping someone on because it's the easy thing to do. Let Sandra and Cody go over the situation again after the weekend and, if the bad feeling is still there, don't expect it to get better 5 or 6 months down the road once Ian accepts an offer of permanent employment and no longer has to be on his best behavior. Let the people on the front lines take a lead in making the call. They have to live with the consequences, either way.

Early in the afternoon, Pauline comes back to see Harry with a couple of folders in hand.

Harry: Well, Pauline, find any smoking guns?

Pauline: Not at all, Harry. In fact, if there's anything about Ian's background that bothers me, it's that it's too lean and clean. He's only had three other employers. But two of them refuse to verify anything other than dates of employment and the job classification they hired him into. The third employer is his uncle, an independent consultant, who gives him a glowing recommendation—big surprise. See how he went to work for the uncle each time he left a big company. What does that tell you? To me it suggests using family to gloss over periods of unemployment. I called the security director at the last big company Ian worked for and asked for any professional courtesy he could give me on this case. Know what he said?

Harry: No, what?

Pauline: It is company policy to release no information other than job classification and dates of employment, unless you have a signed, notarized release from the former employee in question—

Harry: Blah, blah, blah. Just the usual bureaucratic song and dance, right?

Pauline: Yes,…and no. He said one more thing after chanting that particular litany and pausing just a little.

Harry: What was that?

Pauline (Shifting through her notes.): Here it is. I quote, 'I *encourage* you to get that signed release.'

Harry: Meaning?

Pauline: Meaning there's something probably wrong, here, and he probably is legally prohibited from talking out of school about it. But he's telling us to be careful, just the same.

Questions to Explore

1. What action should Harry take from this point? Consider these alternatives, at a minimum:
   A. Clear the way for Sandra to release Ian from employment before Ian completes probation, leaving exact timing up to her.
   B. Convene a threat assessment team including Pauline, Lorraine, Sandra, Edna, Bernie (if available), and possibly Cody to answer the question: Does Ian pose a threat? What if he does? What if he does not?
   C. Have Cody and Sandra both keep an eye on Ian, with Pauline giving them some guidance about discreet inquiries they may make and how to make them (i.e., elicitation). Then, after a week or so, have Pauline debrief them

and bring the information to Harry and the threat assessment team for a closer look at whether Ian poses a threat.

    D. Write this matter off as work team xenophobia, which the work unit has to learn to suppress in order to get by and thrive in the real world.

2. What may be going on with Ian to account for his curious behavior?

    A. He may be fundamentally introverted, awkward at socializing, and just more interested in things than people.

    B. He may be an infiltrator tasked with gathering up all available data on potential targets of the institution and under strict orders to avoid socializing because it could expose him to discovery and thereby compromise his mission.

    C. He may be someone who had a serious problem in his previous employment, perhaps including unwanted attention directed at a fellow employee that led to charges of stalking and a restraining order taken out by the employer because the target of Ian's undesired attention was too frightened to do this directly. Ian may have been forced to resign in lieu of termination but negotiated an agreement that the former employer would disclose nothing of the matter in answer to future employer inquiries.

    D. He may be brighter than but disdainful of peers who are 15 or more years his senior and whose interests have nothing in common with his own.

    E. He may be an undercover reporter or investigator for a tabloid news agency or a congressional committee seeking to unearth evidence of illegal contamination at one particular plant.

    F. He may be a troubled soul struggling to recover from a difficult past that included a prison sentence he served out but did not list because it was beyond the 10-year scope of experience required in the job application.

3. In light of the foregoing possibilities, what are the lowest-risk options for Harry to pursue in addressing the situation with Ian? Most options would involve cutting losses at the first opportunity. Otherwise, at best the institution becomes saddled with a future problem employee likely to detract from team performance or, at worst, a ticking time bomb bent on visiting harm on the employer in some way.

Scenario 2: A Rising Tide of Concern

Sandra is worried about Vince, an employee with considerable seniority who has been increasingly vocal in his objections to converting to a new maintenance management system and is now asking for the lead position in the system rollout, because it comes with a pay increase. Cody shares her concern, and the two are talking to Edna, because they are worried about the ramifications of giving or withholding that particular job from Vince.

Edna: I guess the first question I would have from a labor relations viewpoint is whether Vince meets the essential qualifications for the new job?

Sandra: Technically, he comes close.

Cody: But he's been throwing monkey wrenches in the way at every previous upgrade of the system. He goes into every meeting asking what is going to get screwed with next, and disrupts trainers before they have even had a chance to answer his questions. After the last training session, he even slammed his manual on

the table and said, "I'm going to show you bozos what training is all about."
It scared the temps who were coming on board, the way he said that. Now, all
of a sudden, he's smiling and saying he gets it and is on board with everything.
I don't buy it.

Sandra: Neither do I. Vince has complained about everything in the past two years and
made more hostile work environment allegations than anyone—and none of
them panned out. Yet here he is, a week later, acting like he is taking happy
pills and looking to turn captain of the cheerleading squad for the new system.
Something just isn't right about it.

Edna: Well, it's your work unit, and I don't want to second-guess you. But you do know
there are liabilities for our employer if someone is qualified for a job and doesn't
get a shot at it because he is, well, difficult. After all, people do change, and we
should give them a chance when they do. We can always consult Lorraine for a
legal opinion and Harry for upper management's take on the situation.

So Cody goes back to work and Sandra and Edna go off to touch base with Harry
and Lorraine. Meanwhile, Sandra also calls in Pauline, because she has a feeling that
if they have to end up giving Vince some bad news about his not getting the new job,
there might be some security concerns that protective services may want to prepare for
in advance.

Harry: Well, it looks like we have enough of the right people here to convene a threat
assessment. You all know the case. Bottom-line it for me. Does Vince pose a
threat?

Sandra: He hasn't actually *made* a threat—at least none I know about. Team members
have come to me about Vince before. Sometimes, it's the way he says things.
Like he loves the new system in a way that makes you know he hates it more
than his worst enemy.

Lorraine: If we're meeting as the threat assessment team, I guess we look at the threat
potential. What about giving Vince a chance at the new position and the higher
compensation that comes with it? Isn't that a separate issue?

Sandra: I'm not comfortable with handing it to him just because he asks for it. That position comes with a lot of access and the ability to take down more than just the
new system.

Edna: Our policy on these kinds of openings is to give everyone a fair chance at advancement, though, even if they haven't been model employees in the past.

Pauline: Maybe that's true, but if this guy is unstable or wants the job not for the money
but for a chance to really take the system down....

Harry: OK. Let's cut to the chase. We're asking for a grievance or legal problem if we
don't give him a chance at the new job, right, Lorraine?

Lorraine: Most likely.

Harry: Handing him the system is a risky proposition for the organization, though, is
that what I'm hearing?

Pauline and Sandra: Right.

Harry: Here's my call, unless anyone gets me better data. Vince doesn't get the job. I don't
like the idea of leading him on by pretending to interview him seriously for it
if, at the end of the day, putting the system in his hands represents an unacceptable risk. Lorraine and Edna, that might make some extra work for your
departments, but sometimes we have to choose what's in the organization's

best interest, even if it makes our situation more difficult. Now let's get back to the other question: Does Vince pose a threat?

Sandra: I think so but maybe I'm not qualified to make the call by myself.

Pauline: I can interview him and his coworkers to take an initial look and bring the results back to the threat assessment team.

Harry: Fine, Pauline. Do that. Then let's meet again and get Bernie in to join us with his reading of what we have heard so far and what else you gather up. Let's do this sooner rather than later. Everyone got their calendars handy?

Everyone returns to respective duties, with Pauline taking on the fact-finding role. She discovers that coworkers have grown increasingly apprehensive about working with Vince and, at the same time, gradually distancing themselves from him while also writing off his rants as "just old Vince blowing off steam." After her third interview and an abortive meeting with Vince where he stormed out of the conference room while Pauline was talking to him about workplace conditions and reports of employees getting upset over the new system, Pauline is ready to take her findings to the threat assessment team. In Pauline's judgment, Vince has little interest in the success of the new system but a great deal of interest in scuttling it.

Questions to Explore

1. What action should Harry take from this point? Consider these alternatives, at a minimum:

    A. Direct Sandra to give Vince a chance at the new job after all, without any restrictions.

    B. Seek Bernie's input on what, if any, threat Vince poses. Direct Vince, through Sandra, to report to Bernie or even the organization's employee assistance program to address his angry displays on the job. Also direct Sandra to monitor progress and draw the line for Vince so that he knows what behaviors are and are not acceptable on the job.

    C. Test Vince for the new job, along with other contenders, by including not only technical questions but a practical exercise where the applicant has to demonstrate how he or she would teach others how to use a new system and also present a 10-minute briefing (to the selection panel) as though selling the system's benefits to new users. Although putting together such a selection process for the new position would be very demanding, it might offer a chance to both uncover latent talent among promotion seekers in the organization as well as expose Vince's thinly veiled contempt and abrasiveness. This would essentially give Vince the chance to disqualify himself from the new job instead of providing him with a new focus of resentment, that is, being denied the opportunity to compete for the position. Additionally, this alternative would accommodate the concerns and equities of the legal and employee relations members of the assessment team who retain a vested interest in maintaining fairness and transparency for all promotional opportunities, even when frontline supervisors have serious misgivings about some of the contenders.

    D. Place Vince on a corrective action plan for violating the institutional workplace violence policy with his angry actions and displays. Schedule the selection process for the new job to run concurrently with Vince's corrective action plan, thereby making Vince ineligible to apply (since employees under disciplinary action are typically barred from any transfer, promotion, demotion, or other change of status until they have completed their action plan).

2. What may be going on with Vince to account for his volatile behavior?

   A. Like much of the workforce in general, he could be suffering from a substance abuse problem, including alcohol, drugs, or both, in addition to the financial and family pressures that such problems create.

   B. He could be a nascent workplace violence threat with poor coping skills who is seeing personal insults behind normal workplace vicissitudes and lacks a sounding board or other means to calibrate his views or relieve his frustrations.

   C. He could be in a desperate financial situation that he seeks to remedy by clandestinely offering to sabotage his employer's annual production for a foreign competitor who may be amenable to paying for this kind of unorthodox competitive advantage.

   D. He could be a resentful employee whose chronic resistance to change threatens his personal vision of competence and who, hungering for his old glory days, would like to stage a demonstration of his worth by causing the new system to malfunction just enough so that Vince can come charging in to save the day by showing all how to handle manual backups. This would be somewhat akin to a firefighter setting a fire to be seen as the hero who arrived in time to put it out.

3. In light of the foregoing possibilities, what are the lowest-risk options for Harry to pursue in addressing the situation with Vince? Should the overriding concern be to cut losses or to make every possible effort to rehabilitate a long-term employee?

DECEPTION'S ROLE IN SCENARIOS

In Scenario 1, if Ian is an infiltrator, then his entire self-presentation and actions constellate around a web of lies. Ian as infiltrator might be too well trained to give away revealing details in an interview, regardless of whether Pauline, Sandra, or Harry conducted it. Nor does he appear likely to reveal much in elicitation to coworkers like Cody, although this could change over time. The worst-case scenario, that Ian is an infiltrator targeting the institution, requires deception for Ian to gain access and exploit that access over time in order to stage an attack. Depending on the institution's actual operation of its probation system, however, Harry has the option of cutting losses without a prolonged debate or inquiry that may be inconclusive if Ian is careful enough. Harry, as the voice of the institution, can back Sandra in making a release from employment at any time during probation and, with proper backing from Lorraine, this action is virtually impossible to stop or reverse. The worst threat is averted on the basis of likely deception. At the same time, even if the worst threat proves not to be realized, the probationary release has averted a burdensome disciplinary process that would otherwise be required to deal with a future problem employee.

In Scenario 2, if Vincent is a disgruntled employee on the verge of posing a threat of violence or sabotage, giving or withholding a promotion may be a secondary concern. The main objective becomes to safeguard the people and institution from the threat. Denying him the promotion, if this also means denying him the means to inflict harm, is nevertheless important. The more serious threat comes first, however. Elicitation may help early on in such a case, where a concerned coworker or boss can help arrive at the source of Vince's trouble obliquely and steer him along a more supportive and less destructive path while Vince is still receptive to advice. The time for finesse may have passed, however, and it may instead be time to draw lines and establish clear objectives for Vince to meet in order to save his current job, let alone considerations of advancement for which he appears ill-suited. Vince's deception is in a less than credible reversal of antipathy toward the new maintenance system. His deception is obvious, perhaps indelicately so obvious that a bureaucratic tendency may be to avoid drawing attention to it out of fear of some violation of privacy or employee rights. Nevertheless, the employer's own best interests dictate taking some positive action and at least not ignoring this deception and the ramifications to which it may lead. The institution at its discretion may generously try to help Vince, but it must as a matter of due diligence ensure that other people and operations do not come to harm once warned of Vince as a potential threat.

QUESTIONS FOR ONLINE OR CLASSROOM DISCUSSION

1. Thinking like an adversary, where might you be most likely to give yourself away in an institution you were targeting?
2. What are some outside resources you could tap to test the veracity of someone you suspect of being a trust betrayer?
3. What are some of the benefits you can derive from an open statement?
4. What makes the WZ method potentially more conducive to a modern workplace than the Reid technique?

EXERCISES FOR GROUP PROJECTS

1. Pick an organization with a good mix of corporate sentinels, managers, and access to outside resources. Now, to whom (by function) would you assign these roles: interrogation, debriefing, interview, and elicitation? Explain why the people you have in mind would be better suited to one role than another because of the function they currently perform. Are there people who could perform well in more than one of those roles? Who and why?
2. What might be some good places to use for attempting to obtain information from a subject you suspect of being deceptive?
3. What kind of documents could expose a hostile insider by indicating deception?

ENDNOTES

1. B. M. DePaulo and K. L. Bell, "Truth and Investment: Lies Are Told to Those Who Care," *Journal of Personality and Social Psychology* 71 (4), October 1996, pp. 703–716.
2. P. Ekman, *Telling Lies*, New York: W. W. Norton & Company, 2001, p. 33.
3. Ekman, pp. 43–44, suggests this leakage may take the form of changes in facial expressions, vocal inflection, or other slips—some of which can be controlled and others unanticipated.

4. L. H. Colwell, H. A. Miller, P. M. Lyons Jr., and R. S. Miller, "The Training of Law Enforcement Officers in Detecting Deception: A Survey of Current Practices and Suggestions for Improving Accuracy," *Police Quarterly*, 9 (3) (2006): 275–290, DOI: 10.1177/1098611104273293.

5. Colwell, p. 276.

6. Colwell, p. 286.

7. S. M. Kassin and C. T. Fong, "I'm Innocent: Effects of Training on Judgments of Truth and Deception in the Interrogation Room," *Law and Human Behavior* 23 (5) (1999): 499–516. Also see R. Milne and R. Bull, *Investigative Interviewing: Psychology and Practice*, Chichester: John Wiley & Sons, 1999, pp. 104–105, for identification of Kassin's bias that may be influencing his critique of any methods used by police.

8. N. Smith, *Reading Between the Lines: An Evaluation of the Scientific Content Analysis Technique*, London: Home Office Police Research Series Paper 135, January 2001, p. 5.

9. R. Milne and R. Bull, *Investigative Interviewing: Psychology and Practice*, Chichester: John Wiley & Sons, 1999, pp. 104–105. Milne and Bull also repeat criticisms leveled by Kassin, op. cit., in the process highlighting Kassin's personal belief that there is no adequate protection in the United States for innocent people interviewed as suspects.

10. Major N. R. Dotti, "The Accidental Interrogator: A Case Study and Review of U.S. Army Special Forces Interrogations," *Interrogation: World War II, Vietnam, and Iraq*, Washington, DC: National Defense Intelligence College, September 2008, p. 197.

11. Dotti, p. 210.

12. Colwell, op. cit., namely, Colwell, pp. 275–290, 276, and 286.

13. M. Gladwell, *Outliers*, New York: Little, Brown & Company, 2008. Gladwell points out how such different achievers as Microsoft founder Bill Gates and the musicians who became the Beatles made comparable investments of time honing their respective expertise to the point of attaining proficiency unavailable among peers in their fields.

14. A cautionary reminder may avail at this point. Just as not every practitioner of a craft is necessarily the best at it, there is no reason to infer that every polygraph examiner is equally proficient or even possessed of the analytical proclivity that leads to an intellectual journey out of the box and into detecting deception without benefit of the polygraph. Some may resonate with the box analogy, here, more than others, as a colloquial term for the polygraph in intelligence circles has long been "the box."

15. See, for example, F. E. Inbau, J. E. Reid, J. P. Buckley, and B. C. Jayne, *Criminal Interrogation and Confessions: Essentials of the Reid Technique*, Sudbury, MA: Jones and Bartlett Publishers, 2005. The author has also attended a one-day Reid seminar co-sponsored by a chapter of the American Society for Industrial Security.

16. See, for example, D. E. Zulawski and D. E. Wicklander, *Practical Aspects of Interview and Interrogation*, Boca Raton, FL: CRC Press, 2002. The author has also participated in a three-day Wicklander–Zulawski seminar.

17. The author has attended a week-long course on SCAN at LSI.

18. A number of academic findings that parallel Sapir's appear in D. Rabon, *Investigative Discourse Analysis*, Durham, NC: Carolina Academic Press, 2003.

19. N. Smith, op. cit., for example, a key aspect of criticism was not so much that SCAN was ineffective as that the system of taking statements in the United Kingdom at the time, 2001, was not conducive to encouraging the kind of open statement which SCAN favors.

20. Here the author is offering a professional observation as a licensed investigator and also as a 30-year security and intelligence practitioner. By and large, the educational level, language skills, and writing ability on tap among intelligence collectors have tended to outpace those demonstrated by investigators in security-related functions, although education and changing exigencies of professional credentials may be altering this condition.

21. Ekman, *Telling Lies*.

22. J. Kluger, "How to Spot a Liar," *Time*, August 20, 2006. Retrieved July 3, 2011 from http://www.time.com/time/magazine/article/0,9171,1229109-1,00.html.

23. Ibid.

24. R. Bandler and J. Grinder, *The Structure of Magic, Vol. 1: A Book about Language and Therapy*, Palo Alto, CA: Science & Behavior Books, 1975. Bandler was at least partially discredited when implicated in the murder of a woman with whom he had apparently been involved in illicit activities. However, his manipulative techniques received a measure of validation after a jury acquitted him of the murder with Bandler's own gun under suspicious circumstances. Nor did it help Bandler's credibility to pretend to a doctorate in interviews and court testimony. In the early 1980s, the author recalls an intelligence training activity's embrace of NLP for some of its case officers going through a strategic debriefing program. Evidently, students would come out "mirroring" people they interviewed, in the belief that this would advance the creation of rapport. Reports that having a junior interviewer instantly and robotically cross his or her leg to mirror interviewees who had just done the same, however, excited more mirth than credibility among seasoned practitioners.

25. F. L. Wellman, *The Art of Cross-Examination*, New York: Macmillan Company, 1903, p. 9.

26. Ibid., p. 12.

27. D. Pipes, "Terrorism: The Syrian Connection," *National Interest*, Spring 1989. Retrieved July 8, 2011 from http://www.danielpipes.org/1064/terrorism-the-syrian-connection.

28. J. Gerstein, "TSA readying new behavior detection plan for airport checkpoints," *Politico*, July 28, 2011. Retrieved July 29, 2011 from http://www.politico.com/blogs/joshgerstein/0711/TSA_readying_new_behavior_detection_plan_for_airport_check points.html.

29. A. Vrij, P. A. Granhag, and S. Mann, "Good Liars," *Open Access Journal of Forensic Psychology* 1 (2009). Retrieved July 20, 2011 from http://web.me.com/gregdeclue/Site/Volume_1_2009_files/2009-excerpt-Vrij.pdf.

30. Vrij et al., p. 60.

31. J. T. Molloy, *Live for Success*, New York: Bantam Books, 1982. Molloy attained commercial fame with his 1975 *Dress for Success*, which offered advice for aspiring professionals based on experiments that Molloy conducted with graduate students introduced into various workplaces and looking identical with the only alterations being whether they dressed in styles perceived to be of high or low socioeconomic status. By the time he had made a corporation of the revenue generated by his books and consulting, Molloy was advising companies on selection of security guard uniforms and interviewing chief executives on the kind of behaviors that facilitated advancement up their corporate hierarchies. His experiments suggested that the two classes of people who performed best in job interviews were, first, professional actors and, second, professional athletes. Both groups exuded confidence and a surer sense of themselves in one-on-one interactions.

32. H. A. Medley, *Sweaty Palms: The Neglected Art of Being Interviewed*, Berkeley, CA: Ten Speed Press, 1984, p. 97.
33. L. Block, *Telling Lies for Fun and Profit*, New York: Quill, 1994, p. 216.
34. Vrij, p. 61.
35. F. Stopa, *The Human Skills: Elicitation and Interviewing*, Smashwords, 2010, Barnes & Noble Nook edition, p. 14.
36. *Intelligence Interrogation Field Manual* 30-15, Washington, DC: Headquarters Department of the Army, 29 September 1978, p. 1-4.
37. Ibid., pp. 1-4 to 1-5.
38. Stopa, pp. 14–15.
39. N. J. Gordon and W. L. Fleisher, Effective Interviewing and Interrogation Techniques, 2nd ed., Burlington, MA: Academic Press, 2009, p. 34.
40. Human Intelligence Collector Operations Field Manual 2-22.3, Washington, DC: Headquarters Department of the Army, 6 September 2006, p. vii. This manual supersedes FM 34-52, 28 September 1992, and ST 2-22.7, *Tactical Human Intelligence and Counterintelligence Operations*, April 2002.
41. Stopa, p. 15.
42. FM 2-22.3, 2006, p. 1-1.
43. Gordon and Fleisher, pp. 33–34.
44. R. A. Fein and B. Vossekuil, *Protective Intelligence and Threat Assessment Investigations*, U.S. Department of Justice, July 1998, p. 38. Fein is a psychologist for the Secret Service and Vossekuil was a Deputy Special Agent in Charge for that service.
45. Stopa, pp. 16–18.
46. Stopa, p. 18.
47. Stopa, pp. 49–55.
48. D. J. Lieberman, *Never Be Lied to Again*, New York: St. Martin's Press, 1998, p. 30. Offering an abstract assurance is a common way to avoid a specific question.
49. G. Jonas, *Vengeance: The True Story of an Israeli Counter-Terrorist Team*, New York: Simon and Schuster, 1984, p. 55.
50. Ibid., p. 36.
51. Ibid., pp. 42–44.
52. Ibid., p. 43
53. Ekman, pp. 43–44.
54. The world of counterespionage offers some lessons, here. See, for example, Olive, R. J., *Capturing Jonathan Pollard*, Annapolis, MD: Naval Institute Press, 2006, p. 3, where the traitor Pollard showed signs of instability to coworkers who tended to write off odd behaviors as the harmless quirks of a bright peer.
55. R. A. Fein, B. Vossekuil, W. S. Pollack, R. Borum, W. Modzelski, and M. Reddy, *Threat Assessment in Schools*, Washington, DC: U.S. Secret Service and U.S. Department of Education, 2002, p. 37. Note that the first two authors were the lead formulators of the Secret Service's threat assessment guidance, as noted in Gordon and Fleisher, pp. 33–34.
56. Ibid., p. 33.
57. Ibid., pp. 37–38.
58. Olive, p. 268.
59. See G. Jonas, *Vengeance: The True Story of an Israeli Counter-Terrorist Team*, New York: Simon and Schuster, 1984, p. 55.
60. Fein et al., pp. 19–20.

61. Milne and Bull, p. 3, found that the average time before a detective interrupted such a statement was 7.5 seconds.
62. B. Bedard, "Detecting Deception: Interviewing and Interrogation Techniques," presentation at the annual meeting of the American Society for Industrial Security, San Diego, September 26, 2006. Bedard, a retired investigator with the Royal Canadian Mounted Police, started his career as a polygraph examiner and was a senior investigator for Shell in Calgary at the time of his presentation. In Bedard's experience, the average elapsed time before a policeman interrupts an interviewee is 8 seconds, hence the importance of holding one's tongue and listening.
63. Ibid.
64. Lieberman, pp. 111–112.
65. N. Catrantzos, "Defending against the Threat of Insider Financial Crime," *Frontline Security*, October 2010 (pp. 17–19). Retrieved July 20, 2011 from http://www.frontline-security.org/publications/10_SEC2_Money.php.
66. Fein et al. recommend this kind of joint training and interpersonal interaction in advance of having to act for the first time in the midst of a threat of school violence.

CHAPTER 7

Lawful Disruption of the Insider Threat

A man with his house on fire and a man dying of thirst would put a different value on a glass of water.

John D. MacDonald

INTRODUCTION

First detect deception and the potential of an insider attack. Then what? Derail. However, ours is a society that complicates to simplify. Despite a 9/11/01 epiphany that soon left the U.S. Attorney General and the FBI Director both avowing that the new national priority must shift from making a case for successful prosecutions of terrorists to actually preventing them from realizing attacks,[1] 10 years later the prosecutorial bias continues to permeate through the ranks of those charged with countering terrorists at home.[2] Consequently, prevention takes a back seat to the overriding concern for the legalistic burden of launching investigations and gathering evidence, the better to facilitate defensible arrests and successful prosecutions—with little consideration for one staggering ramification for institutions at risk. The ramification is that the perfect prosecutorial effort occurs post mortem, missing fleeting opportunities to prevent an attack and its catastrophic losses in the first place. To the asset owner or steward, whether it be of a critical infrastructure, trade secret, or cash reserves necessary to make payroll and stave off bankruptcy—to this frontline defender, the offer to consider opening an investigation in hopes of making an eventual prosecution is the equivalent of presenting a glass of water to save a house on fire. Yet this kind of response is precisely what has become the default reaction from those charged with taking the lead in thwarting terrorist attacks, owing to a fundamental disconnect that will be described later (below). What alternative, then, is open not only to officially designated counterterrorist officers but also to defenders and any concerned team member in the presence of an emerging insider threat? The answer is lawful disruption.

WHAT IS LAWFUL DISRUPTION?

Lawful disruption is the short circuiting of pernicious activity through legally permissible actions aimed at preventing adverse consequences, including the sharing of intelligence that a high-ranking political leader has differentiated as being gathered on a prophylactic basis as opposed to a prosecutorial basis.[3] In the arena of insider threat defense, lawful disruption may include statements or actions that impinge upon the hostile trust betrayer in such a way as to introduce obstacles to the intended attack. Such obstacles may come in the form of providing actual or embroidered indications of target hardening that delude the would-be attacker into abandoning or altering plans to strike for fear of failure or apprehension. Similarly, defender-produced disruptions may include convincing the trust betrayer that he has been discovered and has lost either the element of surprise or previously available access to critical facilities or operations, thereby making his plan of attack futile. Even in circumstances where defenders have few resources and the insider knows it, lawful disruption remains possible by introducing an element of doubt through the use of ploys that magnify the would-be attacker's inevitable apprehensions or wreak havoc on his timetable.

Indeed, sometimes this kind of lawful disruption may be nothing more than an adaptation of the technique of "thought interruption" that gained notice when police responding to suicide threats and hostage-barricades would interject non sequiturs into conversations that were showing signs of escalating into violence.[4,5] Thus, an individual working up the nerve to leap from a rooftop or to start shooting hostages in a bank may be deflected from spiraling into danger by being asked a neutral question or engaged on unrelated topics of weather or hunger. Even a temporary interruption of the spiraling sequence often suffices to diminish the likelihood of a negative outcome or, at the very least, stops one particular act from being carried out. Similar obstruction of the flow of an insider's action or thought process offers an opportunity for preventing loss. Why, then, do the counterterrorism experts frequently decline such opportunities, leaving institutional defenders on their own? Much of the answer lies in mindset and functional programming that even Attorney General and FBI Director mandates appear powerless to erode.

A CASE IN POINT: WHY A FUSION CENTER WILL NOT DISRUPT BUT (PERHAPS) INVESTIGATE INSTEAD

Note: Fusion centers are regional intelligence clearinghouses co-staffed by FBI, Department of Homeland Security, local police, and local fire service agencies with the stated purpose of sharing intelligence to prevent attacks. Their official charter:

State and major urban fusion centers (fusion centers) serve as focal points within the state and local environment for the receipt, analysis, gathering, and sharing of threat-related information between the federal government and state, local, tribal, territorial, and private sector partners.

Located in states and major urban areas throughout the country, fusion centers are uniquely situated to empower frontline law enforcement, public safety, fire service, emergency response, public health, critical infrastructure and key resource protection, and private sector security personnel to understand local implications of national intelligence, thus enabling local officials to better protect their communities. Fusion centers provide interdisciplinary expertise and situational awareness to inform decision-making at all levels of government. They conduct analysis and facilitate information sharing while assisting law enforcement and homeland security partners in preventing, protecting against, and responding to crime and terrorism.[6]

So much for the theory. The reality diverges from the stated goals as illustrated below.

What's in a lead about suspicious activity, and whence the gulf between how defenders and official lead processors react to it? The answer says a great deal about how far our homeland security partners have advanced in gearing their efforts for preventing terrorist attacks instead of focusing top priority on prosecuting attackers. The way one answers also reveals instantly whether one is a defender or an official unburdened by direct responsibility for protecting a target of terrorist attack. Take this example and follow its course to appreciate the difference.

EVENT

A person drives up to a fenced facility whose purpose is to control electricity, water, or telecommunications serving millions of citizens. This person, who may apply for a job at that facility or be a confederate of someone already working there, then takes several photographs of that facility and of the entrance to it before driving away. Staff or security cameras at the facility capture the photographer's description and license plate number. An employee from that facility then reports these details through channels that ultimately reach the local fusion center. This center is where homeland security partners take in and presumably do something with all the information generated by their bosses' "See something? Say something!" campaigns. What should happen next? It depends.

IF YOU ARE A DEFENDER . . .

An analyst or duty officer calls up the license plate number and hands the details to a law enforcement officer on duty. This officer immediately calls the registered owner of the vehicle driven by the photographer, communicates official interest and concern over the actions of the photographer, and ascertains the photographer's intent while clearly signaling that such activity is monitored, acted upon, and taken very seriously. Result? Deterrence. Even if the photographer's actions trace to some innocent, plausible explanation, a clear message goes out that somebody is watching and that suspicious actions trigger real time response. If a terrorist was taking pictures as part of a target selection or pre-strike surveillance operation, the dividend is greater. The same message goes out disrupting the attack and in effect causing the would-be attacker to pick a softer target. But there is an alternative reaction that misses this deterrent while consuming much more time and resources.

IF YOU ARE A LEAD RECEIVER AND PROCESSOR . . .

You see the situation differently. You see your job not as deterring attack but as launching investigations that take attackers down and put them behind bars. So, what happens? Well, you evaluate the lead. Let us see, there is not too much there to justify an investigation. There are more of these leads than investigators to handle them. Besides, you probably need a supervisor to authorize an investigation. This means more processing delay. Net result? Note and file. Thank the defender for the lead. Not enough to go on, though. Maybe next time. . . .

RAMIFICATIONS

What signal does the latter approach transmit? To the photographer—innocent or nefarious—it says no one will stop or question you or stand in your way. To the defender, it communicates indifference and bureaucracy that disincentivizes future participation in passive or one-sided homeland security "partnerships."

To the public at large, the handling of such events reveals just how much our organs of homeland security have in reality taken to heart the message of the Attorney General in November 2001 when he announced that, henceforth the new priority would be prevention, not prosecution. If the second approach is crowding out the first, this is not necessarily the fault of fusion centers and lead processors. It is a failure of leadership to incentivize timely responsiveness for deterrence that is difficult to measure over traditional investigative case handling that lends itself better to metrics but not to the object sought. And so we chew and chew on the very leads that a quick bite and swallow would handle better, leaving our vaunted partnerships infused with a bovine incapacity to deliver the value they were created to produce.[7]

DEFENDER DILEMMAS

Derailing insider attacks through lawful disruption need not rise to the level of prosecution, progressive discipline, or even the kind of direct confrontation that makes for high drama in theaters but in real life only dissuades employees from wanting to get involved. In the ideal or fictional world, the only intervention to stop insiders from doing their worst culminates in a mortal or near-mortal contest between good and evil. In the real world of employers and institutions, of people with work to do and families to feed, pyrrhic struggles attract few defenders from any level. So the objective remains, first and foremost, to prevent the loss or derail the attack. Seeing to the comeuppance of the hostile insider comes a distant second, in terms of consequential priorities. If the work team, corporate sentinel, or boss has achieved the first objective, the institution has more reason to rejoice than it would if instead undergoing devastating losses and learning that authorities ultimately apprehended the responsible trust betrayer and are planning a vigorous prosecution. Prosecution seldom produces regeneration of human casualties or irreplaceable capacity.

Under the circumstances, defenders of institutions and authorities bent on prosecution must, at times, find themselves at odds with prime objectives—no matter how much they empathize with each other's situation. Authorities remain unabatedly focused on pursuing the greater public safety goal of bringing malefactors to justice. Defenders are concerned with the more immediate demands of survival. Reconciling the two is like offering the defender a glass of water to extinguish a house fire. No degree of sincerity can render the offer serious or useful in the eyes of the homeowner. Consequently, before the defending institution and its employees advance down the path of lawful disruption, it may avail to think through the following questions:

- What three biases of authorities risk undermining the institution's own efforts to defend against an insider threat, and what can the institution do about them?

- Where does decision-making authority reside in determining whether to risk institutional employees and equities at the behest of authorities or in determining how far to go in accepting such exposures? This is the question regarding the decision of how far to go in accommodating external direction in insider threat cases.
- What risks of failure in analysis and problem-solving may occur at the institution's expense? How does the institution safeguard against this contingency?
- What are the representative options for lawful disruption open to defenders for their own use?

We will now focus on each of these questions in search of options that enable the institution to not only take a hand in its own protection but to assume the lead in defending against hostile insiders through lawful means.

THREE BIASES OF AUTHORITIES THAT RISK UNDERMINING THE INSTITUTION

Prosecutorial Bias

As illustrated in foregoing discussions, the prosecutorial bias accords top, or even exclusive, priority to making the perfect case for prosecution at all costs. Where this bias jeopardizes the institution's equities the most vis-à-vis insider threats is in the potential gulf between operations at the targeted site and burdens imposed by authorities. As an expert on resiliency of supply chains has observed, the overarching principle behind all security measures is that they must work in tandem with the organization's main mission. Outsiders unconnected with governance, investment, or scrutiny of the organization beyond the instant case of their efforts to arrest the hostile trust betrayer and flex the muscles of the justice system through a successful prosecution have little reason to concern themselves with the degree to which they burden the institution.

A request for secrecy and for a prosecutor or detective to act as gatekeeper for all information relating to the insider may seem innocuous enough to the requestor. To the employer with a cohesive work team, transparency, and highly collaborative relationships among team members, corporate sentinels, and managers, honoring the request means leaving in the dark valued employees at an outsider's discretion—and not just excluding the suspected trust betrayer. As the institution accommodates one request after another, a conditioned response pattern arises in which the employer accommodates any request that does not appear to impose a direct or extraordinary burden. Soon requestors, adapting to these conditions, widen the boundaries of their requests, intermingling convenience with exigency. Thus, the detective who asked for office space for occasional use, eventually displaces another team member for a temporary office with a door and locking file storage. Next, the detective obtains free space in the employer's coveted downtown parking garage. When the detective finds that parking in this garage is more convenient and affordable than his usual options, he takes to using it as a matter of course, even on days when he may not be working on the insider threat case. Similarly, clandestine surveillance devices and additional investigative aides find their way into the workplace, sometimes with a clear focus exclusively on the suspected trust betrayer. At other times, however, devices and people are introduced by authorities because they are available and because they form part of the net that these agencies are accustomed to cast in their routine fishing in a boundless sea. Meanwhile, once the institution cedes all oversight or influence over the investigation, its pace may lag or accelerate because of resource constraints or internal politics of the investigating authority—with no coordination of or regard for the impact on the institution's blameless employees, its core business operations, or its critical assets. Under ideal conditions, the investigation is expeditious, discreet, and flawlessly managed without danger to employees, compromise of critical assets, or damage of any institutional equities. How often do plans and outcomes approach such an ideal, however?

Detectives and prosecuting attorneys share all human limitations, including staffing challenges. Consequently, things can and do go wrong. The lead detective or prosecutor is out sick when an unprepared stand-in steps into the fray and inadvertently exposes the investigation to the trust betrayer. Or perhaps a transfer in the middle of the case replaces an experienced counterpart with a callow junior who proceeds to conduct his education at the institution's expense. What happens next? The tipped-off hostile infiltrator recalibrates, strikes a secondary target, inflicts substantial although not catastrophic damage, and then escapes before any arrest or prosecution is possible. Alternatively, the malicious insider, if not an infiltrator but a disgruntled employee, reconsiders an attack plan on the fly and, angered by the discovered betrayal, decides to shoot his boss, the two coworkers he most resents, and then himself in order to relieve his frustration. Yet another alternative, in the case of a financial insider threat, may be that an alerted trust betrayer cuts her losses and flees the country with only a third of the funds she had intended to illicitly transfer into her offshore bank account. As such events unfold, the brunt of the negative publicity, stakeholder outrage, and other hallmarks of reputational risk visit the institution with laser-like penetration, while authorities distance themselves from the fallout— whether by choice or by direction. Authorities may write off such misadventures as the anticipated cost of doing business, secure in their public safety jobs and legal protections that may accord them a proprietary interest in those positions. As for institutions, however, whether public or private, careers do not survive such fiascoes. At least one manager or sentinel will see a promising career stalled or witness an involuntary career event that means a loss of responsibility, face, income, or all three.

What can the institution do about the prosecutorial bias? First, recognize its likely existence in order to gauge the concomitant risk to the organization and to oneself if the collaboration with authorities arrives at an unfortunate denouement. Second, do not under any circumstances cede control of the institution's employees and facilities or second its primary mission to any outside entity unless legally and formally obligated to do so. Weigh the relative merits and risks with your own multidisciplinary team and make a business case for or against supporting authorities infected with an overarching prosecutorial bias. Assure that the institution has two places at the table for major decisions affecting the employer: on the executive side, with peer-to-peer consultations at the chief executive level and an open channel to rapidly escalate any situation that threatens to get out of hand, and on the front lines with one's own designee and operational liaison with authorities. Set ground rules and document them sufficiently to foreclose the potential for future misunderstandings or assignments of blame. At no time impose needless burdens on team members for the convenience of authorities, as the long-term loss of goodwill may never replenish itself in the workplace. Periodically remind authorities of the institution's mission and objectives in the collaboration, and convene regular status meetings. Establish a general timeline and a sunset period so as to communicate an expectation of closure rather than of indefinite involvement in the absence of results.

Investigative Bias

The investigative bias is distinct from the prosecutorial bias in that it reflects a law enforcement predisposition to answer calls for preventive action with referrals to detectives and their protocols, which typically are time- and labor-intensive, before even hinting at results. In practice, this means that when defenders attempt to engage a law enforcement agency in helping prevent an insider from causing harm, they will recognize the investigative bias if the response is to refer the matter to a detective bureau for consideration of whether to open an investigation. As noted in a preceding example about fusion centers, this kind of reaction misreads defender intent and urgency. Thus, if a custodian of a critical asset calls for police assistance in tracking down which insider is attempting to sell a proprietary lock or process diagram that she happened across on eBay, how does the investigative bias interpret the request? Instead of accepting it as a case where law enforcement authority may be beneficially exercised to obtain identifying information from eBay's security department, the recipient of the call defers any action until the matter may be discussed with a supervisor. Then the supervisor will only consider the case in terms of whether it is worthy of opening an investigation into the matter. At that point, the decision will hinge on the monetary value of the item or items on eBay. In the meanwhile, the moment for action has passed, unless the custodian of that asset decided to bypass bureaucratic delays by arranging to purchase the proprietary item herself, in hopes of uncovering details that eBay cannot release to her and detectives will not even request unless they have determined that an investigation is warranted. That the value of the item in question may be insignificant compared to the losses that could be enabled by having it fall into the wrong hands is a concept that a detective may grasp yet still be powerless to act upon because of the limits of discretion that the investigative bias imposes. This bias expresses itself not in averting catastrophic losses but in counting investigations opened and successfully closed—all of which militate against delivering meaningful assistance to defenders in real time.

What can the institution do about the investigative bias? First, recognize its existence and seek to engage a counterpart who can understand and support the institution's priorities. Failing that, remain guarded in the manner and depth to which defenders engage with counterparts affected with that bias, as the resulting burdens will tend to be unidirectional and the value to the institution difficult if not impossible to demonstrate. Engage to the extent required by law or policy, but be prepared to treat this engagement as an act of corporate citizenship rather than a partnership.

Intelligence or Need-to-Know Bias

The intelligence bias springs from a perpetuation of the myth that just because some information bears restrictive markings such as those first used within the intelligence community, it may never be shared with any person or institution lacking the same need-to-know as demonstrated by having the same pedigree. In one sense, there is validity in restricting dissemination this way. After all, there are laws that govern the protection and unauthorized release of classified material, such as Title 18 of the U.S. Code.[8] However, the mature classification system in use for protecting national security information from unauthorized disclosure to foreign powers differs from the reflexive application of restrictive labels whose origin and value may be more tenuous. Thus, LEO (Law Enforcement

Only), Security Sensitive, Sensitive But Unclassified, and labels tailored by a given public agency for their own perceived needs lose credibility when disassociated from the kind of established classification systems that include reference to a classification authority, portion marking to distinguish what is classified from what is not, and some means of requesting a classification review or release of the data to a stakeholder who does not possess a need for the material even if not recognized by the system. In the seasoned world of classified material management, there are such things as limited access authorizations and the capacity to sanitize what may be a minute part of a report that makes it classified in order to share it more broadly with an audience that neither has nor requires the clearance to read that portion. In practice, the kinds of reports circulating through authorities who are in a position to support defenders of institutions are controlled either because they contain very specific details—which the institutions and their employees do not require—or because the reports include traces of data that could compromise sources or methods used in their collection—again, something that most defenders neither require nor seek. Many reports circulated widely, including to counterparts at institutions not involved in policing, are indistinguishable from media stories on the same topics, lag behind news stories by hours or days, and yet continue to bear restrictive markings as if to suggest that the information contained therein is somehow more valuable than it would be without dissemination restrictions. The perpetuation of this reporting process and implied exclusivity attending it disadvantage both law enforcement perpetuators and institutional defenders.

For the defenders, the principal disadvantage comes in repeatedly encountering an at times glib retort to the effect that one's law enforcement counterpart is prohibited from sharing relevant details on a subject of moment because the information is "law enforcement sensitive" or otherwise restricted. Although this may be true, the capricious manner in which variegated restrictions are applied eventually comes to the surface. Consequently, before long, defenders begin to wonder whether these need-to-know restrictions relate to actual information that could be meaningful although withheld, or instead constitute a convenient way to mask ignorance of the matter under discussion. The person or agency that manifests a chronic tendency to hide under this need-to-know mantra disadvantages itself through progressive erosion of credibility.

The first such mutual disappointment typically occurs when a defender reports information developed internally to a law enforcement or regional intelligence agency counterpart. This report may include, for example, discovery in a break room of a low-voltage blueprint showing placement of lights and surveillance cameras to one of the institution's control rooms. That the material was left in a break room gives rise to concern over an insider who may have hostile intentions. Although the law enforcement or regional intelligence representative may take in this information, when the defender calls a week later to discuss it and possible developments, he or she hears that such a discussion cannot occur because the defender is not cleared or does not possess the proper need-to-know— even though the information itself would never have been absorbed into these channels but for the reporting of the person now denied the chance to discuss it.

Another manifestation of this need-to-know bias periodically infects otherwise well-meaning employees within the institution who are made to feel part of an elite fraternity by virtue of having law enforcement or regional intelligence counterparts convey, in hushed tones, that these employees alone are briefed and trusted with certain information that cannot be shared with their institutional bosses. Young in age or experience, employees who succumb to this tactic soon lose sight of whom they are really working for, particularly if carefully cultivated or even self-recruited into a world they perceive as more exotic in contrast to their mundane duties. The challenge, then, becomes one of sufficient oversight and engagement with the institution's own employees to safeguard against divided loyalties and the inadvertent creation of an informant who may cross the line in risking employer's equities without adequate guidance.

What can the institution do about the need-to-know bias? Remain guarded and selective about which intelligence or law enforcement "partners" to bring into one's circle of trust. Engage as law and policy require, but do not casually accept one-way information sharing burdens imposed on one's own employees or chronic refusals to provide meaningful and needed information. Be prepared to take responsibility for cultivating one's own information or support resources, whether via consulting or institutional liaison channels. Insist that burdensome requests—even for one-time information—come through formal channels, including on letterhead stationery signed by an officer empowered to make decisions and commit resources. This approach will curb ill-considered requests made by junior counterparts under color of authority that their own agency has yet to confer upon them. Finally, make it abundantly clear to employees in liaison positions, whether sentinels or managers or work team members, that collaboration with outside entities that is unsanctioned by the institution and unreported to the appropriate level of management constitutes grounds for discipline or even termination. One must only have a single boss in such matters.

DECIDING HOW FAR TO GO

In addressing the foregoing issues of bias, the institution's decision makers must of necessity determine the extent to which it is necessary or advisable to collaborate with authorities and, in some cases, whether to involve external agencies at all. There are times when there is no legitimate alternative but to accept such involvements, as when a court order or other official edict leaves no doubt. Many or even most cases, however, are not so clear. Consequently, a decision to go outside the institution for assistance and possible collaboration in countering an insider threat is a judgment call which, like most important judgment calls, will generally require executive involvement when recognized as a high-stakes decision. At this juncture, a determining factor in deciding how far to go becomes an accurate assessment of which alternative has the potential to lead to the worst mistake. Analysis of high-stakes judgment calls shows that the best decision makers seek to avoid the worst of possible mistakes.[9] Under the circumstances, the dispositive question may be whether minimizing potential loss by removing the hostile insider means less risk for the institution than collaborating in an externally controlled sting operation that carries with it the potential that otherwise preventable loss may occur in order to catch the insider red-handed in the commission of a crime (hence facilitating prosecution). Here, it may be instructive to consider the kind of insider threat where some blend of internal and external collaboration is necessary yet going it alone or mismanaging the collaboration may produce unacceptable consequences for all concerned.

Say an adversary group wishes to harm an organization that handles or produces a consumable product, such as water, food, or pharmaceuticals. Its attack vector is through product contamination, and this contamination may be actual or simulated. The adversary's goal may be political, through inflicting mass casualties or through causing a loss of confidence in the targeted organization, thereby resulting in economic harm. Alternatively, the adversary's goal may be extortion by threatening similar consequences unless the target meets specific demands for an extortion payment. In either case, why is an insider particularly valuable to the adversary in furthering its aims? The assistance of an insider is useful in making the threat believable, since the targeted organization's first obligation upon receiving a contamination threat is to assess its credibility.[10]

Most contamination threats are hoaxes and may often be discounted because the individual making the threat lacks sufficient, realistic detail to make the attack appear possible or believable. However, with the help of an insider, the attacker may gain enough process or production details to be able to pinpoint how best to introduce contaminants. Moreover, with the assistance of this confederate from the inside, the attacker can also introduce a sample contaminant and then use this sample to demonstrate his bona fides when calling in a threat or making extortion demands. A vague threat tends to be dismissed as a hoax. A specific threat accompanied by a sample containing a toxin or poison in a concentration sufficient to kill compels defenders and authorities to take the threat maker much more seriously. Furthermore, if the product contamination has the possibility of affecting the public, the institution receiving notice of the threat has a moral and legal obligation to alert authorities and to do its best to protect the public—and its customers—from any avoidable endangerment. In this situation, the organization cannot go it alone because of possible threats to public safety. At the same time, authorities cannot assure a low-risk response, particularly if the officers involved lack experience in product contamination and product extortion cases. Finally, if executives at both the corporate and public authority level deem that the best course is to make some kind of extortion payment in the interests of public safety, it will most likely fall to the asset owner to gather up the funds for the payment. At the same time, the situation will demand of both organizations to make the most of any professional relationships that they have cultivated over the years with the news media to request sensitivity on reporting that could give rise to a widespread panic—again, in the interest of public safety. In situations such as these, experience counts more than affiliation or relative position in a given hierarchy, so it is not at all uncommon to find key decisions hinging on the input of otherwise obscure players, such as law officers of the Food and Drug Administration's Office of Criminal Investigation (who typically contend with more product contamination cases than their FBI counterparts) or specialty consultants (who respond to these kinds of extortion threats and assist clients and other responders with individual and corporate expertise).

The bottom line in deciding how far to go is identical to any other high-stakes judgment call: It is a case-by-case decision made by or with consent of the executive in the institution who has the authority to deal with the level of reputational risk that an unfavorable outcome would produce. The one who has to live with the decision and who has the most to lose is the one who must make the call.

RISKS IN FAILURE ANALYSIS AND PROBLEM SOLVING

Groupthink, whitewash, and going through the motions are the kinds of counterproductive hallmarks of even the best combinations of ostensibly peerless talent assembled to solve a complex problem. If such counterproductive approaches are possible in prestigious fact-finding commissions, there is no reason to expect that collaborations of internal and external experts will be immune from similar tendencies. Institutional leaders on the point of entering into such collaborations would do well to study the candid impressions of the Nobel laureate and physicist, Richard Feynman, that fill half of his second autobiographical work, *What Do You Care What Other People Think?*[11]

Asked to participate in a presidential commission chartered to investigate the under-lying causes of the obliteration of the *Challenger* space shuttle shortly after liftoff on January 28, 1986, Dr. Feynman was disinclined to accept the invitation. After overcom-ing personal reservations, however, he did accept and found many technically competent luminaries among his new peers. However, the former statesman and political being chairing the commission soon validated Feynman's misgivings by running the commis-sion along rigid lines where members attended informal meetings followed by public meetings and were fed set piece presentations by NASA and its contractors. Feynman, bristling at this rigidity and wanting to actually get to the bottom of why the *Challenger* exploded, costing seven lives and horrifying a nation, performed his own probes inde-pendently, eschewing formality and talking to engineers who could answer his questions without bureaucratic delay or obfuscation. As a result, it was Feynman who discovered a temperature-induced failure in the O-ring seals between booster rockets and also uncov-ered systemic failures in the way space shuttle workers across multiple organizations took in and acted upon information such as this. Indeed, at one point a Senate committee summoned the commission's chairman to upbraid him for "sitting and reading" instead of more vigorously pursuing Feynman's approach for active data gathering.[12]

Feynman's story also chronicles the introduction of unsupported political recommen-dations in an area reserved for technical recommendations in the commission's report. More significantly, it concludes with reflections arrived at over time about how a highly energized institution populated by committed employees—the NASA of the early 1960s, in this case—can lose its way once its cohesive sense of mission fades—as had happened by the time of the *Challenger* disaster. Thus, in NASA's early days, "everybody's inter-ested in everybody else's problems."[13] After NASA had met the challenge to land a mor-tal on the moon within 10 years, however, the bureaucratic imperative of convincing Congress of the continuing merits in funding the organization inevitably led to a culture of exaggerating capabilities and suppressing the upward flow of any information that might "look bad."

But reflecting on Feynman's observations and epiphanies, one arrives laterally at several analogues that translate into lessons applicable to how a No Dark Corners workplace may learn from imperfect consultation of experts and outsiders summoned to address an insider threat. First, in the arena of insider threat defense, expertise in one subject area may not mean expertise in another area of greater significance for the defender. Just because Feynman's commission chair was superior at navigating through political and public relations reefs, this did not equip him to use his skill set for getting to the bottom of a technical problem that was beyond his grasp. Similarly, a prosecutor adept at taking down rings of organized crime or drug dealers may be at a complete loss about the tactics and support structure behind an infiltrator. Equally, a detective with expertise in arresting perpetrators of armed robbery may not necessarily be equally adept at catching embezzlers or workplace rampage killers before either has done his worst.

Second, beware the introduction into key positions of individuals lacking organiza-tional commitment, that is, bureaucrats. Just as Feynman found that the NASA of yester-day was different in kind from the less mission-oriented and more accountability-resistant NASA represented among many of the management ranks he dealt with, so is it vital to consider the impact to institutional culture if one overturns transparency and team self-monitoring in the course of chasing an insider threat by the externally imposed rules of a prosecutorial or investigative organization with no stake in the institution's survival. As another observer has noted, "the right corporate culture . . . is a crucial ingredient."[14]

Moreover, as another has pointed out, all high-stakes judgment calls involve trade-offs where there is no best choice.[15] Consequently, it is only at the institution's own peril that it risks undermining its own ethos and competitive competence by advancing down a path of suspicion and mistrust that outsiders may pave in setting their traps for the hostile insider.

In the end, involving the wrong people in addressing one's insider threat leads to the same outcome as ceding one's fiduciary obligations to an agency or individual who does not share those concerns: disaster. "Bringing in people with insufficient motivation will cause a plan of action to fail."[16] For this reason, any workplace dysfunction imposed in the hope of negating an insider threat must always be weighed in terms of whether the remedy is worse than the disease.

REPRESENTATIVE OPTIONS: WHAT DEFENDERS CAN DO THEMSELVES

In the context of the preceding admonitions, it may seem that a complex response to an insider threat may be so taxing as to dissuade the institution from taking timely action. However, much depends on the level of complexity one seeks to embrace. An insider threat may be sophisticated without being complex, and lawful disruption offers many uncomplicated alternatives limited only by imagination. Indeed, as one long-term observer of crime prevention has pointed out, "It is only in the relatively recent past that the general citizenry has *not* been the primary line of defense."[17] From the insider's point of view employer-induced disruptions broadly fall into these categories:[18]

- Changes that increase perceived effort for the desired attack
- Changes that increase perceived risk for the attacker
- Changes that reduce the anticipated yield of the attack
- Changes that alter the insider's guilt or justification for attacking

Why are these categories all described in terms of changes? Absent a change in one or more of the identified areas, the trust betrayer has already arrived at the point of deceptions and some level of preparation to cause harm, and would therefore experience no disruption in plan or momentum absent a perception of change. We next consider each of the change categories at length.

Changes That Increase Perceived Effort for the Desired Attack

Even a seasoned cutthroat plotting assassination will not ignore convenience. To the extent that a defender can harden the intended target by making it less accessible than the suspected trust betrayer first perceived, target hardening has occurred and a likely attack is postponed. To the extent that the defender introduces additional obstacles into the would-be attacker's path, postponement follows postponement to the point of compelling a reconsideration of targets altogether. If the hostile insider is an infiltrator, then his or her masters will have expectations about when the strike should occur. They will also have a sense of apprehension that the greater the delay, the greater the opportunity for exposure of the insider, of the planning cell, or of the plan itself. Additionally, delay brings demands on budget and other resources. As an analyst schooled in tradecraft has noted, terrorist groups always find themselves in needs of funds to support their lifestyle and their security measures, in addition to their travel expenses, safe houses, payments for informants, and need to buy or rent vehicles and other equipment.[19]

On the other hand, if the hostile insider is a chronic malcontent bent on actions calculated for self-enrichment or for exacting revenge for a real or perceived injury, the changes in accessibility will compel rethinking strike plans. To the committed trust betrayer, being unable to lay hands on purchase orders or to enter unseen into the office of a hated superior, may displace the strike to another time and place or refocus attention to a more accessible target. In either case, however, the defender has bought time and at least deflected one attack.

Even in the most serious cases, as one counterterrorist expert has found, vulnerability matters to the point that,

> Terrorists make decisions to attack or not to attack based in large part on how vulnerable they perceive a target to be, and thus how easy or difficult it would be to attack it. In at least one recent instance, terrorists cancelled plans to attack a U.S. embassy because they concluded that the security measures they observed were too formidable to overcome. Terrorists can be expected to make similar calculations about targets in the private sector, and with a target that is less symbolically significant than an embassy, they are more likely to be deterred by even a moderate level of security.[20]

How does a defender manage to increase perceived effort on the part of the hostile insider? Any of these tactics may avail:

1. Change the assigned work space for the attacker, the targeted person or function, or for both attacker and target.
2. Alter access protocols, so individuals not assigned to daily duty in the target area are no longer able to gain unescorted entry or enter at all without advance appointments.
3. Multiply the frequency and duration of field assignments for the suspected malicious insider, making the individual accountable for measurable work performance whose neglect would be rendered obvious by unauthorized detours to the target.
4. Interject unpredictable schedule changes in the targeted operation so that neither the suspected betrayer nor the uninitiated can chart schedules to the point of certainty, thereby making an attack exceedingly difficult to time to attacker satisfaction.

Changes That Increase Perceived Risk for the Attacker

An attacker willing to kill is not always willing to die, and one willing to die is likely to be very particular about the time and place for such a sacrifice. If the defender manages to increase the chances of premature capture or unmasking of the hostile insider before the latter is ready to strike, then the entire attack has to be reassessed as a trade-off. No insider who has invested time, energy, or other resources in preparing to harm or incapacitate a target wants to risk premature exposure and the humiliation of being twice branded: once for perfidy and once more for ineptitude.

How does a defender manage to increase perceived effort on the part of the hostile insider? These tactics may avail:

1. Institute random security measures into the targeted work area, including brief-case, package, and parcel inspections, and inventory of materials brought into and taken out of the area.
2. Increase visibility and frequency of security patrols.
3. Install an open work area or kiosk with telephone, charging station, and coffee for the use of local police officers, inviting them to take breaks there at their convenience as long as they are in uniform. The institution gains public relations value from doing this as a community service, and most employees welcome the presence of law enforcement, particularly after normal business hours or in the hours of darkness. To a hostile insider, however, this introduces an unpredict-able element to account for in any attack scenario. It also seriously increases the chance of being caught or retaliated against by someone better trained and armed than the intended victim.
4. Increase or alter the placement of visible surveillance cameras and invite security vendors to test new detection technology in the target area through pilot pro-grams, without giving away details yet without concealing the new infusion of detection technology in the workplace.
5. Conduct visible security and operational audits to identify and shore up vulner-abilities that may have gone undetected.

Changes That Reduce the Anticipated Yield of the Attack

Once a trust betrayer's deception has been exposed, likely motives behind an insider attack become relatively easy to adduce, if only because betrayal compels closer obser-vation. If the inside attacker is after financial gain, instituting tighter controls to make funds less accessible without cosigners or to alter spending authorization thresholds may be all that is necessary to alter the attacker's cost–benefit analysis to read all cost for little benefit. If, instead, the trust betrayer seeks revenge by attacking a specific target or targets, distributing these so as to keep them from being geographically concentrated in a single location frustrates the targeting process and again reduces anticipated yield. (In security parlance, this is known as avoiding a high target-value concentration.) Finally, adding secondary security controls that use biometrics (such as an iris scan or hand geometry in addition to institutional access cards or badges) can mean that even if the insider manages to reach a target area, he or she will be unable to activate controls or open safes that are necessary to carry out the intended attack.

In summary, then, tactics for reducing yield may include

1. Instituting tighter controls over funds and critical assets
2. Distributing targets to avoid a high concentration in a single place
3. Adding secondary security controls, including biometrics, so as to deny ability to operate safes or systems even if the insider manages to enter the target area without interference

Changes That Alter the Insider's Guilt or Justification for Attacking

This final category involves erecting psychological barriers, which may not work equally well with all populations. There is potentially inestimable protective value to be derived from treating insiders with a level of fairness and decency that, although reflexive to the defender in a No Dark Corners milieu, nonetheless runs counter to the narrative that guides the hostile insider's antipathies. Thus, if part of an infiltrator's indoctrination cites a level of ruthlessness and incivility on the part of institution employees that the infiltrator cannot independently verify or detect, this absence may eventually cause the infiltrator to question his masters and the underlying justification for their planned attack. Similarly, if a disgruntled careerist harboring resentments for old wrongs comes to the realization that none of the hated conditions are in evidence within the ambient work environment, the internal narrative of injustice and ill treatment becomes difficult to sustain. Sometimes, the difference between workplace anger that festers into resentment and culminates in rampage killings may be altogether defused if a supervisor or team member had taken the time to show interest in the troubled employee and ask, "What's wrong?" at the first sign of a problem instead of ignoring the situation. The principal difficulty in benefiting the institution through subtle campaigns of civility or charm offensives, however, rests in the highly unpredictable, hence unreliable, yield of positive results. After all, in assessing the effectiveness of this kind of deterrent—whether upon the hostile insider or upon a supporting structure such as a terrorist organization behind an infiltrator—deterrent value presupposes an assumption of rationality on the part of the adversary organization.[21] Under the circumstances, it would appear prudent to take advantage of opportunities to lower hostilities through fair treatment, yet stop short of relying on such an approach as a sole defense. An extraordinarily charismatic boss or coworker may possess the talent to nip hostile insider tendencies in the bud through deft application of interpersonal skills. However, the institution cannot afford to risk its survival on results that only the extraordinary employee can deliver, since such conditions cannot be perpetuated.[22]

TECHNIQUES OF LAWFUL DISRUPTION BY EMPLOYEE LEVEL

Leaders and corporate sentinels have options that may be unique to their roles and consistent with the resources that the institution places in their care. Thus, they are in a position to disrupt daily activities of others and frequently do so in the ostensible interests of the organization, as when requesting a special report or enforcing a new mandate. Team members, as coworkers in any workplace, regularly exert influence on those around them by the way they interact with one another and with employees outside of the immediate work team. Just as any employee can make another's day with a helpful response or an unsolicited compliment, so too can anyone ruin another's with distressing information, a slight, or refusal to cooperate in an expected collaboration. On a more specific level, words and deeds perceived as ruining one's day seldom constitute a daylong barrage of rapid-fire personal attacks. Instead, the perception of having a bad day traces to one or two events that violate expectations or in some way compel an undesired change in plans, with attending burdens thrown into the equation. The value to defenders in appreciating such workplace banalities emerges when defenders harness such otherwise trivial forces to the plow of disruptions that are lawful and permissible to deploy as obstacles to a hostile insider's objectives. The finesse in using such techniques is in derailing the insider attack without unjustly harming others in the process. These techniques include opportunity denial through workload shifting, a tactic traditionally reserved for the leader's repertoire; open surveillance with oblique probing, suited more to corporate sentinels whose responsibilities include such activities; and a variety of team-level options ranging from ostracism to catalysis that can either isolate the hostile insider from an intended target or complicate the timetable and arc of an attack through introduction of unforeseen variables.

Leader Disruptions

Ideally, the prime disruption is complete removal of the hostile insider by any legitimate means, even if the consequence is legal action alleging job discrimination. To the leader seasoned in weighing such risk, such extreme measures are an infrequently used option but one where the exposure is to the organization's purse instead of to its people or critical assets. Often, such extreme measures are not immediately available, and leaders must temporize. Fortunately, leaders in the institution have positional authority and, with it, the organizational imprimatur to subordinate individual preferences to the needs of the job. Thus, if one of the essential management functions is to make work productive,[23] then leaders are well within their rights to transfer, rotate, or otherwise manage the physical placement and circumstances of their subordinates to maximize their productivity. In practice, this means that the leader suspecting a trust betrayer at large can take some or all of these actions to limit the insider's deleterious impact:

- Terminate or indefinitely suspend the hostile insider pending formal termination proceedings.
- Reassign the insider to less sensitive duties or away from a high-value target area.
- Rotate the insider into different, remote job assignments on a frequency that will impede developing expertise necessary to target those areas effectively, and ensure that security protocols change or increase after each transfer.
- Offer up the insider in question for time-consuming, make-work assignments, and committees in order to limit the individual's contact with core business and productive team members.
- Change the individual's work shift to accommodate greater scrutiny and oversight.
- Add burdensome but noncritical duties to the insider's portfolio to consume time and effort that might otherwise be available to invest in studying targets and harboring resentments.

Corporate Sentinel Disruptions

Although sentinels lack the overall authority of the institution's formal leaders, they usually have the power to exercise considerable discretion in enforcing work rules and in steering investigations and audits to expose untoward activity. Accordingly, sentinels—in full coordination with affected leaders—can complicate the hostile insider's attack plans and impede the latter's freedom of maneuver through these lawful disruptions:

- Catching the insider in procedural infractions and then fastidiously documenting successive infractions to the point where they constitute actionable misconduct that, in turn, triggers greater, unrelenting scrutiny of the individual.
- Instituting random operational audits that compel the insider to account for activities that had previously eluded scrutiny.

- Visibly increasing surveillance to the point of convincing the hostile insider that the organization has discovered his or her attack plans, thereby denying the element of surprise, a technique that Canadian intelligence has evidently used with positive results to thwart terrorist attacks "before they materialize."[24]
- Arranging fitness-for-duty or other examinations permissible within institutional policy, such as reasonable suspicion testing for drug abuse if the insider displays the kind of erratic behaviors that would justify further assessment. (Note that in cases where the malicious insider is openly hostile and perceived a potential threat of workplace violence, it frequently happens that substance abuse plays a destabilizing role and, if caught in time, may actually help the employee turn around negative behaviors. According to one workplace study, substance abuse is the third leading cause of workplace violence.)[25]

Team Member Disruptions

Although leaders and sentinels possess tools at their disposal that the average employee may lack, work team members nevertheless retain a nondelegable power to influence any team member by virtue of comprising the social core of the work unit. All other factors being equal, it is team members who will interact the most with the insider, and that interaction can easily incorporate elements of ostracism, catalysis, or catharsis depending on the motivations and capacity of team members. Under ideal circumstances, management removes the trust betrayer upon discovery, thereby protecting the institution's equities and sparing the work team from the deleterious impact of insider hostilities. However, employees left to their own devices are likely to adapt other typical behaviors to the malicious insider as a means of damage control, including the following:

- Shunning, a form of ostracism that often arises spontaneously when employees feel that one coworker has brought harm to a more popular coworker by making claims against the latter that led to discipline or termination. A representative case might involve a woman who has properly turned in a coworker for harassment, resulting in the latter's termination and in the woman then being shunned by coworkers to the point of distress that is not necessarily actionable.[26] In the case of disrupting an insider's attack plans, shunning could make it impossible for the trust betrayer to obtain cooperation or information about anything not immediately related to job performance, making it difficult for the adversary to elicit information about schedules or to maintain a low profile by blending in a group that wants no part of him or her.
- Catalyzing the attack to run prematurely is possible by giving the trust betrayer to understand—directly and obliquely—that the work team is alert to deception and is collaborating with sentinels and management to remove the insider at the first opportunity.
- Malicious compliance with work instructions to honor them on a superficial level while withholding any assistance that the suspected betrayer would otherwise expect from the team under normal circumstances. This means the team works with the individual as directed, and only as directed, thereby forcing the individual to perform his or her assignments without any extra help at any time, which could lead to exhaustion, frustration, or mistakes that compromise the insider and attack plan all the more.

• Facilitating catharsis, in those cases where the suspected insider threat is known to have bonded with a work team member whom he respects. The latter may informally broach the subject of deception and suspicions in a way managers and sentinels would be loath to attempt and unable to carry off successfully. The focused social pressure applied by a respected peer or mentor, however, could produce an admission and even lead to the insider questioning of his own motives, awakening though by no means ensuring the possibility of a change of heart. Used in coordination with and support from the right manager and sentinel, this approach could lead to recruiting the hostile insider around to the point of making him a double agent, although the institution should be wary of being duped by such an offer as a means for the insider to reach the intended target despite having been discovered and ostensibly neutralized.

TECHNIQUES BASED ON EXPLOITING DISRUPTIVE BEHAVIORS ALREADY IN THE WORKPLACE

The difficulty with many techniques of lawful disruption is that they require of those attempting them a capacity for self-command in emotionally charged situations that few but professional actors may simulate convincingly. Some of the most competent team members got that way by being able to focus on their work with little taste for anything other than straightforward communications. For them, presenting one face to a trust betrayer and another to the rest of the world is an imposition or an impossibility. In such cases, where ambient conditions may supply few opportunities and fewer employees capable of the role playing that lawful disruption may require of them, there remains an underexplored option: making beneficial use of otherwise deleterious influences already present somewhere within the organization.

In this case, it falls to the defender to reverse-engineer behaviors that analysts have found sufficiently disruptive in the workplace to merit development of specific guidance on how to neutralize them.[27] In this application, however, the defender's objective is not to neutralize the particular behavior but to conscript it into service for the higher objective of lawful disruption. The behaviors themselves and their potential contribution to lawful disruption are what Brinkman and Kirschner have characterized as 10 behaviors that represent people at their worst:[28]

1. The Tank
2. The Sniper
3. The Grenade
4. The Know-It-All
5. The Think-They-Know-It-All
6. The Yes Person
7. The Maybe Person
8. The Nothing Person
9. The No Person
10. The Whiner

We now explore each of these to describe the behavior itself and, instead of looking for ways to suppress, we explore ways to use it to advantage to confound the hostile insider and either delay or frustrate attack plans until the institution is in a position to take positive action to remove the threat.

The Tank

Description

This individual epitomizes aggression and is very confrontational. As a personality, the tank is animated by a monomaniacal focus on the job and brands any impediment as a distraction worthy of a declaration of war. The tank attacks any individual or thing in the way of attaining an objective. Any attempt to counterattack inspires escalation on the part of the tank.

Disruption Value

Positioning the hostile insider into the path of a tank puts the insider on the defensive, potentially leading to a confrontation that will result in disciplinary action for both employees. Alternatively, the insider unaccustomed to such an overbearing personality is likely to experience great frustration and to set aside other plans and activities while trying to figure out how to handle the new work environment. An infiltrator will tread carefully in order to avoid a blunder that embarrasses him or his masters. A disgruntled employee will add the situation to a list of real or perceived grievances, potentially moving the tank to the top of this list. This reordering will accordingly occasion a change in attack scenarios. A more subtle, venal insider whose activities focus on personal enrichment through embezzlement or other misdeeds will have to take a leave of absence from such activities to deal with harangues and interruptions that the tank specializes in generating.

The Sniper

Description

The sniper focuses sarcasm or teasing to gain attention at another's expense. The sniper's effect is to undermine the individual speaking or the individual's program by attacking from the sidelines with caustic remarks that may be thinly veiled as joking.

Disruption Value

Positioning the hostile insider into the path of a sniper introduces the frustrations of being undermined for no apparent reason by someone who may have little stake in the subject under discussion. This interaction creates frustration and complicates the insider's work life by placing undue demands on one's self-control in order to avoid a loss of temper and the kind of exaggerated retaliation that would expose the insider's hostile intentions. As for the tank, the sniper will cause an infiltrator to tread carefully in order to avoid a blunder that embarrasses him or his masters. A disgruntled employee will add the situation to a list of real or perceived grievances, potentially moving the sniper alongside the tank on an enemies list. This reordering will accordingly occasion a change in attack scenarios. A more subtle, venal insider whose activities focus on personal enrichment through embezzlement or other misdeeds may discount or shrug off the sniper, unless suspecting that the sniper may focus greater scrutiny on the insider, even inadvertently, by the mischievous drawing of attention on the insider's perceived foibles.

The Grenade

Description

The grenade is a character who explodes with out-of-control emotional outbursts that tend to be out of all proportion to the triggering event. A grenade will become equally upset and launch into a tirade regardless of the appropriate or trifling nature of the issue at hand.

Disruption Value

Because the grenade suffers from feeling underappreciated, outbursts may multiply over time, as others try to avoid this individual. Leaving the hostile insider in the path of the grenade imparts a degree of emotional stress and frustration, particularly if the insider is unaccustomed to encountering such behavior in a less dysfunctional team setting. As with the tank and sniper, prolonged exposure to the grenade exacts an emotional toll that can interfere with concentration and divert the trust betrayer from the focus necessary to gather data and carry out hostile action.

The Know-It-All

Description

The know-it-all is results-oriented, competent, yet overly assertive with low tolerance for contradiction. Hostile to new suggestions or alternatives, this character takes any challenge as a personal affront and takes in new information poorly.

Disruption Value

Positioning an insider with a know-it-all ensures that the insider will be doubted, challenged, and drawn into pointless arguments. As with the other disruptive personalities, the know-it-all will make undue demands on the hostile insider's time and energy, in this case for self-justification and for counter arguments, which take time away from attack planning and preparations.

The Think-They-Know-It-All

Description

This character is a blowhard who lacks the expertise of the know-it-all but pretends to a knowledge or experience level that is lacking. Although most people see through the pretense, some do not, as the think-they-know-it-all does master the argot of a given subject area.

Disruption Value

This character can be particularly frustrating to a hostile insider who can legitimately lay claim to competence in an area that the think-they-know-it-all simulates unconvincingly. By adding insult to injury when raising objections or just interrupting the insider, this character may inadvertently draw the insider into protracted efforts to discredit the pretender which, in turn, mean time and energy diverted from attack scenarios or preparations.

The Yes Person

Description

This individual is so interested in seeking approval and avoiding conflict as to agree to everything, with little regard for the capacity to satisfy all resulting obligations. As a result, the yes person is in perpetual agreement and in perpetual default, seldom meeting any commitment but always agreeing to do so next time.

Disruption Value

This type of character poses minimal disruptive value, as the perceptive insider will see the yes person's limitations and navigate around them.

The Maybe Person

Description

This individual is incapable of reaching a decision or taking a position, offering little value when others are seeking an opinion or input.

Disruptive Value

As with the yes person, the maybe person poses little disruptive value for the insider, who can navigate around this individual with relative ease.

The Nothing Person

Description

This character is a low reactor who offers no verbal or nonverbal input or feedback absent extraordinary coaxing.

Disruptive Value

As with the two preceding types, this character poses marginal disruptive value and presents no real obstacle to distract or delay the hostile insider.

The No Person

Description

This individual is a champion of futility, gravitating reflexively to a position that rejects any ideas or suggestions out of a belief that they will not work, and instead aiming for perfection by avoiding the risk of a mistake.

Disruptive Value

The no person has the effect of draining morale out of individuals with a bias for more action than debate. Given prolonged exposure to the no person, the insider could grow weary or withdrawn. The disruptive value may be greater than for the preceding three types of character, but the savvy insider could equally learn to ignore this individual and move forward with hostile actions.

The Whiner

Description

The whiner seeks perfection but sees only its opposite and dwells in misery awash with misgivings about everything that can and does go wrong.

Disruptive Value

Faced with a whiner, the hostile insider can either learn to bypass this individual or be drawn into shared misery. Thus, disruptive value is similar to that of the no person.

THE LAYERED OFFENSE

Accepted wisdom avers that no security measure suffices in and of itself, hence the case for having multiple layers in place with each supporting other layers that are redundant and coordinated.[29] By applying the same principle in reverse in the case of interjecting lawful disruption in the aim of derailing an insider attack, one may infer that the same kind of layering that works for defense should offer offensive value in parrying an insider attack. Layered offense, then, consists of weaving a multiplicity of legitimate disruptions into a net that will either snare the hostile insider or sufficiently retard the planned insider attack to mitigate its impact or neutralize it altogether. A few representative illustrations of how to deploy such a layered offense may thus be instructive.

   As in the preceding chapter, each of the scenarios that follows has a different suspected trust betrayer but essentially the same core cast of people who evaluated the particular subject for signs of deception that may signal an insider threat and are now in a position to introduce lawful disruption pending a senior management decision about what action to take with the employee.

Core Cast

Cody	Concerned coworker
Sandra	Supervisor for Cody and subject
Harry	Higher manager to whom Sandra ultimately reports
Pauline	Protective services (i.e., security) representative and investigator
Lorraine	Legal department representative, a labor attorney
Edna	Employee relations (i.e., Human Resource subunit) representative
Bernie	Behavioral sciences specialist (consultant) who gets called to evaluate some cases

Scenario 1: Disrupting a Suspected Infiltrator

Ian has given his employer, the city water and power utility, reason for concern. Although well into his probation period without showing any performance-related flaws, Ian has established an erratic conversational pattern that led his peer, Cody, to suspect that Ian is too inquisitive about one particular power plant, the Ames facility, while remaining unusually close-mouthed and aloof on all other occasions. Cody discussed his misgivings with his supervisor, Sandra, who shares Cody's concerns. Their upper management, in the person of Harry, heard them out and had Pauline from the security function take a closer look at Ian's background investigation. Pauline, noticing some subtle anomalies, made inquiries and came to the conclusion that something was amiss (as noted in the preceding chapter). Taking in all these data points, Harry is weighing removal of Ian by exercising the employer's full rights during the probation process.

However, it now turns out that a recent dismissal of someone of the same protected class as Ian was alleged to be discriminatory and a related civil lawsuit proved very embarrassing to the employer. As a result, Harry has been warned to move very cautiously in this matter so as to avoid giving the appearance of a pattern of discrimination with Ian's removal. A member of the board of directors is particularly sensitive to this issue and is causing quite a stir over the matter, making professional life very difficult for Harry's bosses. The net result is that instead of being able to move forward with sending Ian on his way, the institution is now forced to defer this action pending lengthy executive and legal review. Meanwhile, Harry and Sandra are determined that Ian should have no opportunity for mischief, so they convene their assessment team of frontline supervisor Sandra, labor attorney Lorraine, protective services investigator and security representative Pauline, and employee relations representative Edna to lay out a course of action for introducing lawful disruption to safeguard people and critical assets.

Harry: Thanks for coming. We're leaving Bernie out for now because I'm not altogether sure we need our consulting psychologist, just yet, for what is fundamentally an internal, management decision. You all know the basic situation. The new hire in Sandra's team, Ian, is looking suspicious and has given his coworkers cause for alarm. Under normal circumstances, Ian would be gone and we wouldn't be having this conversation.

Lorraine: But with the recent scandal and board action...

Harry: That's right. Our hands are tied—for awhile, anyway. So, we'll tackle this as a management problem, and that's why this brain trust is here. How do we keep Ian at arm's length from the Ames plant and from anything sensitive until we can take more permanent steps? And I mean legitimately, without causing grief for our executives or doing anything we shouldn't be doing?

Edna: Obviously, then, we want to be careful not to give Ian ammunition to later claim discrimination or violation of his rights.

Harry: Absolutely.

Sandra: At the same time, we have a first-rate work team that's getting very unsettled about one of their own who not only doesn't seem to fit in but is also starting to make them look over their shoulders and worry about talking shop when he's within earshot.

Lorraine (handing out a single page of bullet points): Well, here's a highlight sheet from briefings you've all attended before. It says what you absolutely cannot do with employees to deny them of due process, both legally and according to our own policies.

Pauline: Well, you don't need me here to decide NOT to do something. How can protective services help out?

Harry: I'm not altogether sure, yet. But I think we'll go back to my main objective of keeping Ian away from certain things and then you, Sandra, and I throw out some ideas, while Lorraine and Edna, you concentrate on telling me how we can achieve the objective without crossing the line.

Sandra: Well, as his boss, I can pretty much control his assignments, can't I?

Edna: Sure.

Sandra: Then there is no reason he has to go to the Ames plant for at least 2 months. And I can load him up with enough administrative and training assignments to leave him no time to spare but his breaks and lunch. We normally like to stay busy, and I think Ian just got busier.

Harry: Any problem there?

Lorraine: Probably not—as long as he's not the only one working while all his peers are lounging with their feet up on the lunch table.

Sandra: Not in my shop. That doesn't happen more than once, and no one remembers the last time it did.

Harry: Do we have any options for taking him out of Sandra's shop altogether? What about sending him to a focus group or one of those task forces we all have to sacrifice someone to for one of those pet projects that always seem to be designed to avoid productive work?

Edna: I know there are a couple of those coming around, but we have to be realistic. No one sends a new hire to participate in groups where everyone is drawing from at least 5 and as many as 20 years of experience in order to be able to talk about process improvements. Don't you think it would stand out like an elephant bleeding in the snow if you sent Ian to one of these?

Harry: You're right. Scratch that.

Pauline (to Sandra): How savvy is Ian? Do you think he already suspects someone may be on to him?

Sandra: I wouldn't be surprised.

Pauline (to Harry): Then do you see any value in maybe trying to scare him off or back down on whatever his timetable is by having us watch him, without being too subtle about it?

Harry: What did you have in mind, Pauline?

Pauline: Well, we recently got an offer from our integrator to test some new surveillance cameras, and we *could* happen to sort of randomly pick Ian's work area—or wherever Sandra wants to assign him to spend most of his time. Depending on how subtle you want to be, we could even kick off the pilot program there first and you could assign him there right after. We could also do a random security audit, find him on our radar, and then keep looking—see what other anomalies we discover. If we catch him in a security violation, or violations.... Well, that gives you more ammunition if you have to justify a release from employment, doesn't it? We don't make those things up, but anyone who goes snooping around and gets caught once has always ended up getting unauthorized access anywhere from 3 to 10 times where he wasn't caught, at least in my experience. So all we have to do is catch him once and keep looking, and that could reveal a lot.

Harry: I like the sound of that. Any objections from you two (looking at Lorraine and Edna)?

Lorraine: None, with the proviso mentioned earlier.

Edna: No, sir.

Harry: OK. Let's make this happen. But, you know, part of me would just like to sit this guy down and have him come clean. What do you think?

Lorraine: Bad idea, chief. If he really is up to no good and was inserted into this place to perpetrate an act of sabotage or worse, all you would be doing would be telegraphing your punches—

Sandra: And maybe leaving him some time to still do some damage before bolting out the door. I'd feel better isolating him from the Ames plant and our sensitive areas and keeping him under a microscope while loading him up, especially if Pauline's folks could also keep an eye on him. If Pauline's people end up giving him the idea that he's being watched, he'll be a lot more worried about that than if it's just Cody or the guys he works with. These guys aren't about to win any Oscars, but I can get Cody to play up that story about that temp that Protective Services caught trying to sell drugs in the parking lot. That story gets bigger all the time, to the point where some people are insisting the only way the temp gave herself away was because your folks had a bug in her latte.

Pauline: Illegal and too expensive—plus we just don't have the staff hours to listen to every dull conversation on the job. But we let some of those urban legends get a life of their own, just to keep the dishonest people guessing about what we really can and can't do.

Harry: OK. I think we have the makings of a plan of action. Let's put two things in motion. Sandra, you handle the assignment change. Pauline, you set up the increased surveillance. Meanwhile, Sandra, let me know how the team is reacting to all this. The last thing we want to do is put all our focus on Ian at the expense of the people doing actual productive work. Let's make sure they're not disadvantaged while all this is going on. And don't anyone sell Ian on something as if it's a favor or special benefit. I don't want even the hint of a precedent getting out there about questionable employees getting preference over good, trusted employees—even if it's just because we want to watch them. The most Ian can be allowed to infer about any changes that are coming his way is that they are neutral, or maybe even negative—but definitely not any kind of undeserved reward. Let's review status a week from now. I'll send out a meeting notice.

Discussion

What has happened in the foregoing meeting? Management has identified a problem, sought consultation, taken some promising inputs, and identified a program of disruption to use in the case of a suspected infiltrator. The senior manager, Harry, even established a follow-up timeframe. What about the work team, however? Has their role been adequately covered? Harry is concerned about insulating them from the hostile insider, but their involvement appears to be peripheral at this point. However, under the circumstances, it may be prudent to avoid placing coworkers in a situation where, as frontline supervisor Sandra noted, they may have to act differently toward the suspected betrayer than they normally would, and this is no troupe of actors. Moreover, given governing body concerns over avoiding another discrimination scandal or similar event that would invite negative scrutiny, keeping Ian away from likely targets without involving his coworkers may indeed be the rational first choice. Have some elements of the problem received insufficient attention, however? For one thing, Pauline did not appear to have received clear direction on the degree to which her surveillance of Ian should be obvious or undetectable. Could this ambiguity lead to problems or missteps? For another, no one addressed how Ian's movements could be constrained after normal business hours. If employees in Ian's position typically receive 24-hour access to plants and facilities on the theory that they may have to respond to trouble calls at any hour, then failing to take this dynamic into account could leave in place an exposure that Sandra's reassignment and monitoring of Ian will not address fully. On balance, though, Harry's meeting and plan of action represent a reasonable way to go about introducing lawful disruption. when other options are temporarily unavailable.

Scenario 2: Disrupting an Insider Threat of Workplace Violence

Vince, a long-term employee who has been increasingly vocal in complaints and fault-finding, suddenly reversed himself by offering to take on a lead role in converting to a new maintenance management that, up to this point, has been anathema to him. As his boss, Sandra is worried about Vince. Although the new role would come with a salary increase, Sandra sees indications that Vince may be less interested in the extra money than in an opportunity to sabotage the new system or, worse, to use such sabotage as a launching point for a destructive rampage. Cody shares her concern, and the two spoke with Edna, because they worried about the ramifications of giving or withholding that particular job from Vince. When the usual assessment team met and consulted Harry, he made the call that Vince would not get the new job nor be falsely led on to think that he was in serious contention for it. Now Vince is even more erratic. His personal hygiene has declined. His side conversations at work are focusing on the recurring theme of wronged individuals who took matters into their own hands to obtain justice, such as a news story about a wife who shot her abusive husband and another story about a worker at a state lottery commission who shot three executives on the day that his wages were garnished for child and spousal support incidental to his failed marriage.

The assessment convenes in Harry's office, this time including Bernie, the consulting behavioral psychologist on speaker phone.

Harry: We all know the basic situation but, Sandra, why don't you bring us up to speed on that has been going on in the workplace with Vince?

Sandra: Well, he's getting pretty cranky and he's scaring people, me included. He used to have a couple people he would at least say hello to. Not anymore. The rest of the team walks on eggshells when forced to be in the same room with him. Otherwise, they make themselves scarce. I don't think it's like they're consciously isolating him. I really believe they're worried that he is going to go off, like a ticking time bomb.

Bernie: Has any intervention of any kind been tried with Vince?

Edna: It looks like his previous supervisor gave him the number to EAP (the outsourced employee assistance program), but EAP has no record of any contact. We've had two recent hotline complaints about him.

Bernie: Did they give you anything to go on?

Edna: No. Both anonymous. "He's going to go postal." Click. That kind of thing.

Pauline: From everything I've heard and seen, Vince poses more of a threat today than when he was at least going through the motions of being civil in order to compete for the maintenance system rollout job.

Harry: I tend to agree. I just read over our workplace violence policy, and if ever there was a case it applied to, this looks like it. Here's how I see the priorities. Tell me if I'm wrong, anybody. Number one, we get Vince away from the other employees—all people on our premises for that matter. Number two, we get him some help—if we can. Comments?

Lorraine: Legal can support that. We certainly have precedent with other cases, and it would seem that the totality of circumstances would be in favor of such a move as the prudent thing to do.

Edna: What about a directed referral to EAP?

Pauline: Wouldn't that still leave him at large in the workplace, as a potential threat?

Bernie: We've also seen a lot of stalling when employees like Vince get these referrals. Some just take the time off work and skip their appointments. Depending on the confidentiality system in place, it may be quite some time before the employer finds this out.

Pauline: Also, isn't EAP designed to do everything possible to help the employee get back to work? I mean, that's great when the employee is cooperative. But is Vince even close to being cooperative?

Edna: Well, it is our policy to do everything we can for the employee, Vince included.

Sandra: But what about the rest of the employees, and other people who happen to be around? I'm thinking of visitors, contractors, and even the cleaning crew or cafeteria staff. If Vince really poses a threat. . .

Bernie: I'm fine with making a firsthand assessment of him, but it doesn't have to be at the job site.

Sandra: That would sure make it better for the rest of the team.

Harry: OK. I can see some workable options. Unless someone can talk me out of it, here's what we'll do. Sandra, as his boss, you remove him immediately, with one of Pauline's people—preferably armed, but discreet—going along to deter any outbursts and to escort him out the door. Edna, you draft an official letter of instruction to be personally handed to Vince that spells out the following:

1. He is out on paid administrative leave until further notice.
2. While in this status, he is to make himself available at his home telephone during the hours of his normal work shift.
3. He is not to appear at this work site or any of our other locations for any reason unless coordinated—and approved in advance—through Employee Relations. This also means he turns in his badge, keys, parking pass, and any employer assets on the way out the door.
4. He is to participate in an assessment interview as coordinated by Employee Relations. Let's be ready with one scheduled date. and one alternate. That's where you come in, Bernie. And Pauline, you find a site that is off-campus and capable of being secured, for Bernie's protection.

Now, what else? What am I missing?

Lorraine: You probably want to reference our workplace violence policy or at least give some indication of why this is happening and what due process he will have.

Harry: OK, Lorraine. Work with Edna to get that in. Anything else?

Bernie: Based on what's been reported about him before, I'd recommend two things. Make that letter as brief and generic and emotively neutral as you can. Vince is going to read it and reread it and reread it. He's going to have a lot of time on his hands to do nothing else. Also, it may be better to have your signature block on it, Harry, instead of Sandra's.

Sandra: Why's that?

Bernie: Well, in addition to his history of being something of a misogynist, Vince appears to most resent people he sees every day, you included, Sandra. On the theory that he hasn't interacted all that much with Harry, Harry's name may be a little more neutral to see on the bottom of that letter. Your building is in another part of the campus, too, isn't it, Harry?

Harry: Right. And probably not one he is that familiar with. I'm fine with that. Let's move.

Discussion

What has happened in the foregoing meeting? Management has identified a problem, sought consultation, sought inputs, and taken the onus to act promptly in the face of an insider threat judged to be imminent and potentially lethal. Disruptions in this case appear less feasible. Nor are spontaneous ones producing positive results. Spontaneous shunning of Vince by worried coworkers is having no positive impact on either Vince or the rest of the work team. Assigning him to EAP looks doubtful because it leaves the door open to him ignoring the mandatory referral while remaining at large and unconstrained. There appears to be some debate of priorities that reflect functional bias, with the human resources perspective leaning more in favor of focusing all available attention on the troubled employee, Vince, and with management and security taking the view that the welfare of all other employees and passersby comes first. In the end, Harry exercises leadership by deciding the matter in favor of those who could be potential victims. Legal liability is possible in either direction. Mishandle Vince's treatment and the institution faces a likely claim of wrongful discharge, discrimination, or violation of personnel rules relating to progressive discipline. Fail to remove an identified threat of violence and the institution faces even more claims from casualties or survivors, in addition to reputational risk as media stories of ignored warning signs appear in the event of a workplace rampage. In this scenario, the plan of action appears to take into account the realization that, pending more assessment and review, having Vincent on the premises at any time is not acceptable. There is even provision for an armed escort off the premises to deter Vince from hostile reaction or to be prepared to respond appropriately if that happens.

What is missing? Although this may be the subject of a separate planning meeting, no one has openly addressed what happens once Vince exits the workplace. Bernie has observed that Vince will most likely read and reread his instruction letter over and over again. If Vince then appeals to a union representative or engages an attorney to challenge the actions taken, the assessment team will probably exhale in relief, as this is a sign that Vince appears to be going down a rational path of nonviolent dispute. However, what if Vince decides to come to the job site after a week of paid suspension, and he comes armed and eager to settle scores with Sandra, his work team, and anyone else he can reach? Pauline, at the very least, should anticipate Harry's question about protective options and also about ways to monitor for Vince's unauthorized approach to employer premises, including discreet alert of security guards on site and protocols to follow for summoning police if Vince appears to be trespassing. If matters have deteriorated to the point that Vince appears to have the capability and intent to harm others that he begins to threaten while on administrative leave, it may be prudent to have Pauline, her staff, or even specialty consultants, teach targeted employees about spotting and reacting to signs of stalking and how to shelter in place or evacuate out of the line of fire.

Scenario 3: Disruption Taking an Unexpected Turn

Shifting gears, Harry and Pauline are now discussing an unexpected development. It did not involve Sandra's work team, or any other employees, directly. However, employer resources came into play at the request of a tenant organization seeking help with providing the kind of disruption that would intervene in a sensitive personnel action that could cause an embarrassing stir in the workplace. Or so Pauline was told, as she explains to Harry.

Pauline: So one of our team leaders, Eric, took an eleventh-hour call for assistance from the vice president of the credit union on campus.

Harry: That's across the parking lot from my building, right?

Pauline: It is.

Harry: Wait a minute. Aren't we complete walled off organizationally? I mean, sure, most of our employees have accounts there, but aren't they separately incorporated and have their own resources?

Pauline: They do. But, like any tenant, when they ask us for something, we try to help out if it doesn't look like it's going to be too much of a burden.

Harry: Understood. I'm with you so far.

Pauline: Eric walked into the situation because his team member who is assigned to this complex was out sick that day. So, being a good guy, in the interest of good tenant relations, Eric figured he would step into whatever it was and just step out if it turned out to be far afield of our purview.

Harry: Got it. So what was this about?

Pauline: Well, as it turns out, the credit union was going to terminate its branch manager for cause and wanted someone from Protective Services to be around to make sure he went quietly. It was going to be very low key, and they didn't want to have anyone upset by tempers or theatrics. So they figured a security professional could just sit in for about 20 minutes, quietly escort the branch manager out, and that would be it.

Harry: Why do I get the feeling it wasn't so simple?

Pauline: Probably because you've been around a long time. But you're right. So Eric found himself in the room with the guy, Arnold, and the VP, Vanessa. Vanessa was visibly awkward about this and had to read a script explaining why Arnold was being let go. She was almost apologetic about it, and it took Eric awhile to bottom line it to this: Arnold embezzled as much as $10,000, but the credit union wasn't really sure.

Harry: What? They're firing a guy for stealing but they can't even tell how much?

Pauline: Evidently. Eric figured that's why Vanessa was so tentative. She was asking Arnold about his company laptop, and Arnold was being polite, almost sympathetic toward Vanessa. Arnold told her he had left it at home but would go there and bring it right back this afternoon.

Harry: OK. So the hostile termination is looking very genteel at this point.

Pauline: Right, and that's where Eric's instincts kicked in. He was a cop for many years and taught at the academy. Unlike a lot of cops, Eric could be intimidating but, instead, tends to charm people into doing things his way. But his experience told him there was something awry. Why was Arnold going so quietly? What was missing here?

Harry: So somebody was holding out?

Pauline: Right. Meanwhile, Vanessa has to excuse herself for some business, and maybe to regain her composure in what must have been a most unpleasant situation for her. So what does Eric do?

Harry: What?

Pauline: He starts talking to Arnold. Neutral subjects, at first. Then he starts asking questions, probably the ones Vanessa should have been asking but didn't. Then, wonder of wonders, Arnold starts answering. You have to know Eric. It's hard not to respond once he gets you talking.

Harry: Interesting. But I'm going to have to ask you to skip to the end, as I'm running out of time. What was really going on?

Pauline: Bottom line? Arnold was embezzling from week one. He was signing checks to himself and directing subordinates to countersign them, since checks like that required two signatures. A couple of subordinates refused. So Arnold fired them. Eventually, he trained replacements to honor those checks with just one signature—his—instead of two. No one who was still around knew to do otherwise. Arnold got himself a new BMW, a day trader account with $80K, and a condo for his parents in Florida—all courtesy of the credit union. Eric got it out of him, bit by bit. But it all started out with Eric's experience saying that no one walks in stealing $10,000 period. He had to start somewhere smaller and work his way up. Eric was right.

Harry: And the credit union let this guy go home to get his laptop? Did he ever come back?

Pauline: Not exactly. Vanessa overheard enough to catch what Eric was picking up. So he wrote her a note and kept Arnold talking. The note told her to call the police to invite them to arrest the perpetrator of a major fraud case, which Vanessa did. Arnold left alright. But it was in handcuffs. They got the laptop with the search warrant that came later. At last count, the actual loss was about 40 times what Vanessa first reported. It seems Arnold had a passport and airline ticket to the Cayman Islands waiting with his laptop at home. Arnold got prison time, but a reduced sentence in exchange for making restitution. I think Vanessa took early retirement.

Harry: So, Eric was called in to de-escalate a situation. He was the designated disruption, but he ended up uncovering a deception that was the bigger part of the iceberg underneath the tip that everyone else was seeing, and he started a thawing process until the guys with the icepicks could come along to chip this thing off its glacier and haul it away. My metaphors may be lousy, but you've got a good guy in Eric. Well done.

Discussion

What has happened in the event chronicled above? An intervention that the security sentinel, Eric, was prepared to perform as a courtesy soon became something altogether different. Through conversational ploys, including elicitation and, from all indications, the application of interviewing or interrogation techniques, Eric uncovered a greater deception than what served as the original basis for action. In addition to developing an admission and uncovering details of skullduggery on the part of Arnold, Eric improvised a lawful disruption by keeping Arnold talking long enough to summon authorities to arrest Arnold and prevent him from making off with his spoils.

What may deserve further exploration? The question whether Eric was right to assist the credit union in the first place may deserve institutional scrutiny. On the one hand, he possessed no standing in the matter. On the other hand, his involvement made possible the discovery of a systemic problem and an opportunity for restitution, thereby sparing losses that would ultimately affect credit union members consisting mostly of Eric's fellow employees. Does Eric's finesse in reading the situation and deftly adjusting his actions and demeanor to meet its shifting demands suggest that tasks such as disruption and detection of deception may require a level of uncommon virtuosity? Perhaps, in their most accomplished expression, these tasks are best handled by virtuosi. However, there is a counterargument to be explored in that any attempt to perform these tasks to unmask and derail a hostile insider is preferable to none, and Vanessa's discomfort with the situation indicated a minimum of previous attempts.

Scenario 4: Disruption at the Top

Shifting gears once more to an entirely different setting, Elizabeth is a former Wall Street financial analyst who now sits on the board of a heretofore successful financial investment firm that also operates a viable bank. She has come to a consultant, Joe, because she and the rest of the board find themselves in the awkward position of having to unseat a chief executive and chief operating officer who started the firm but are now plunging it into bankruptcy. The chief executive, a popular wunderkind and patron of multiple charities in the local community, has hired a number of friends and relatives into the firm, including his father-in-law and his old high school buddies, distributing sinecures while also embedding these individuals into positions where they can inform him of any signs of a move against him or his second-in-command. For this reason, Elizabeth found Joe's operation attractive: headquartered 1,000 miles away, in another state, yet with a reputation for competence and discretion. What is Joe's task? Find a way to remove the two top officers of the firm at an upcoming board meeting without giving them forewarning or an opportunity to incur more debt to the point of leaving nothing to salvage.

There are complicating factors, however. The executives to be removed also have seats on the board. Independent of their role in the firm, both executives also head a real estate investment trust. Attorneys advising the board in its takeover plans determined that this other role is not necessarily a problem, except for a facilities sharing agreement. This agreement gives the two executives in question very liberal access to the facilities of the firm in question in return for a nominal annual fee, such as a dollar. In terms of removing the executives, these complications present two hurdles. One is that although the board may fire them as executive employees, it may not fire them as directors with seats on the board. According to corporate bylaws, any directors on the board may not be removed—even for cause—without receiving 2 weeks in which to vindicate themselves or present to the board reasons to reconsider the removal. Additionally, even if the board waits 2 weeks and still sustains its decision to remove the two executives, as long as they have a legitimate facilities sharing agreement in place or the real estate investment trust, they may be impossible to remove physically from the premises.

Joe as a security adviser and retained attorneys specializing in corporate takeovers each attend to different aspects of the executive removal problem, while Elizabeth and other board members engage a seasoned financial manager to run the company once the two wayward executives are no longer in control. What disruptions fall to Joe to arrange to facilitate an uneventful corporate takeover, since the chief executive is suspected of being both volatile and vindictive?

Joe makes arrangements for these things to prevent outbreaks of either violence or corporate self-destruction:

- "Suspension" (as opposed to termination) of all access for the two executives on receipt of a signal from the board that it has removed the two from their executive positions in the firm. Suspension, in this case, means temporary deactivation of badges and access cards, temporary removal of ability to use all corporate networks, and temporary denial of access to voicemail and other corporate communications. The reason these access curbs are temporary is that the executives legally remain on the board for 2 more weeks and also retain some rights to facilities under the facilities sharing agreement. However, Joe reasons that the firm can meet these access obligations by granting access under escort to a limited number of buildings rather than allowing the errant executives to range freely across all corporate sites.
- Arrival of a visible and somewhat intimidating protective detail consisting of trained executive protection specialists carrying concealed weapons and prepared to suppress any outbreak of hostilities.
- Staging of a forensic computer exploitation team to gather, copy, and extract all incriminating evidence from the company laptops and desktop computers of the two executives, who have been making investments counter to board directives and possibly running side businesses using corporate resources at the same time.
- Standby placement of a locksmith to change the locks on the doors of the offices of each of the two executives, thereby preventing them from gaining unescorted access to remove or destroy records once the board removes them from executive duties.
- Replacement of the firm's guard contractor with a reputable provider who will report to new management instead of to one of the cronies of the current chief executive.

All of these disruptions are calculated to deter impetuous action on the part of the two executives, particularly on the part of the chief executive, who is the youngest officer of the firm and a brilliant, though undisciplined, innovator of considerable talent. The disruptions succeed to such an extent that Joe is victimized by his own success. How is this possible?

First, the appearance of the protective detail takes the two executives completely off guard. Instead of reacting with their customary petulance upon receiving notice of the board decision to remove them, both pledge to go quietly without fuss or fanfare. In the relief that follows the attending lowering of tensions, the board elects to defer some of Joe's preparations because all present appear to be comporting themselves as ladies and gentlemen. As it happens, however, the mutual expressions of goodwill are short-lived. The executives quietly make the most of their local connections to obtain a legal order that prohibits their removal from the premises, citing the facilities sharing agreement of the real estate investment trust as justification. The interim executive retained to turn the institution around finds himself sabotaged at every turn, with a surly executive assistant who reports on his every move and middle managers—all owing their positions to nepotism—dragging their feet and misinterpreting instructions. Meanwhile, the two executives occupy their offices (made possible because the board had Joe send back the locksmith poised to change the locks on their doors) and act as if they remain in charge, disrupting the workplace themselves and frustrating the interim executive at every turn. Between the two executives and their loyalist cronies, the characters of sniper, tank, and grenade almost prove too much for the interim chief struggling to maintain order while turning around the troubled firm. Twice he threatens to resign if the disruptions cannot be contained. While retained attorneys prepare to contest these arrangements, what primary disruption to this counterattack does it fall upon Joe to handle? Joe must find a way to satisfy the legal requirements of the facilities sharing agreement while getting the two executives out of the way and containing the many acts of petty sabotage in the immediate vicinity of the interim chief executive. Ultimately, he manages this within 2 weeks and the two executives are removed from the board and from the productive flow of the organization to be saved.

Discussion

Of the many disruptions that occurred in the foregoing scenario, which proved the most effective? Ironically, it was the suite of disruptions that Joe originally developed, as these cowed the two executives into submission. The impact of these disruptions in chastening the two executives was no less forceful for them being out in the open at the point of the takeover. However, once the board relented and compelled Joe to defer executing the entire suite out of a misguided belief that the two executives would withdraw quietly, Joe briefly lost the upper hand and the two executives regained the initiative. Then their impromptu campaign of disruptions threatened to counter the corporate turnaround until Joe helped reverse matters once more.

In this particular case, the two executives availed themselves of multiple spontaneous disruptive influences, including in-house confederates whose sympathies turned them into embedded saboteurs until the interim chief executive had them removed as Joe identified untainted replacements.

COMPARATIVE OBSERVATIONS

The foregoing scenarios each differed yet also presented common elements. Among the differences: kind of insider threat (infiltrator, workplace violence, embezzler, leader turned saboteur), type of disruption necessary to achieve institutional objectives (protective and delaying action pending removal, immediate safeguarding of targets, stalling to reassess losses and prevent insider escape, thrust and parry of disruptions aimed at seizing control of company), and extent to which defenders revealed their suspicions to insiders (none, all and formally once insider isolated from work force, partially until further revelations changed understanding of extent of loss, fully but only at point of contest for control of company).

At the same time, each scenario came with unknowns and uncertainty of outcomes, requiring defenders to brainstorm, improvise, or to be prepared to redirect their disruptions on the fly. In some cases, defenders did not ostensibly address contingency plans on how to contain losses in the event their disruptions accelerated the hostile insider's timetable for a strike and triggered an early attack as an alternative to impending neutralization of the primary attack. In Scenario 4, by contrast, the defense did plan for such contingencies but was nonetheless overruled by an ingenuous board of directors which, eager to avoid unpleasantness, misinterpreted an early victory in battle as a surrender before the war was over.

The cases also included planned and unforeseen disruptions, with varying degrees of effectiveness for both. In Scenario 1, timely management and sentinel action isolated the threat through physical isolation from targets and increased monitoring on the job, without calling into play extensive intervention from work team members. What if Ian learned of the Achilles' heel of executive sensitivities that was preventing his immediate release from employment, however? Then he would be in position to disrupt the defender plan by seeking out an ally in one or more board members upon whose sympathies either he or his support cell could play. In the attending institutional frisson, Ian could end up maneuvering his way into a transfer to the Ames facility or another high-value target as a management gesture to appease board members irate at Ian's alleged mistreatment, thereby negating the original program of defensive disruptions.

Likewise, in Scenario 2 Vince's actions could deviate from what the threat assessment team anticipated. Vince could temporarily direct all his energies to exploiting the sanctioned means of institutional grievance resolution, including union action, ombudsman or hotline complaints, and even civil action against his employer. Consumed by the process of defending each charge Vince makes, defenders could lower their guard and fail to notice that after Vince has exhausted all his savings in legal battles without winning the big payout he feels he deserves, he arrives at a point of desperation where he feels he has nothing to lose by walking into his final administrative hearing with a concealed firearm, a suicide video, and the intent to take the lives of as many of his perceived mortal enemies as he possibly can.

In Scenario 3, Vanessa's aversion to confrontation and apparent reluctance to probe into the full extent of the losses Arnold has caused would likely have resulted in Arnold's quiet escape from major consequences or restitution if Eric had been asked to sit in a lobby without making direct contact with Arnold. But for the opportunity for Eric to interact directly with Arnold, professional curiosity of a sentinel would not have had the chance to evolve into uncovering more deceptions and the true extent of losses involved. Arnold would have acquiesced in an uneventful termination, departed from the premises, and made good his escape before the institution ultimately realized how much damage he had really caused. In this scenario, the employer planned and deployed no disruptions at all but those improvised by a sentinel providing support on no notice as a professional courtesy of landlord to tenant.

Finally, Scenario 4 illustrated how no amount of contingency planning and readiness to deploy disruptions can overcome the occasional misfires that result when hope overrules preparation. As good as a campaign of protective disruptions may appear, its effectiveness still hinges on timely implementation. Moreover, when dealing with agile and intelligent insiders as in the case of this scenario, one must also prepare to contend with improvised counterattacks. In this particular case, the executives fighting removal were able to take immediate advantage of cronies who were automatically predisposed to hurling monkey wrenches into the gears of new management, particularly since they owed their jobs to the disgraced executives and had little to lose by acting as saboteurs of a new administration that would (and ultimately did) replace them.

PRACTICE

Management icon Peter Drucker has observed that the habit of doing the new and different has to be kept alive by practice.[30] Otherwise, the capacity is not developed or it atrophies. Introducing lawful disruptions into the path of an evident insider threat requires an awareness of the likely presence of hostilities—usually obtained though the discovery of deception, some foundational, know-your-world sense of what disruptions are available and permissible for defenders to deploy, and a combination of imagination, experience, and tenacity to enable defenders to function effectively as they parry unpredictable thrusts from internal adversaries. As an example against which to apply the lessons of lawful disruption, here is a problem that may or may not involve an insider threat. After examining the problem, one should construct a palette of disruptions to introduce into the situation, while also considering potential outcomes as the disruptions are introduced. This situation is from an actual case.[31]

A DISTRESS CALL AND UNPREDICTED TURN OF EVENTS

Problem

Monique, a practice leader at a specialized consultancy fields a distress call from the chief executive of a prosperous company that is under siege. The executive is convinced that one or more ruthless competitors is carrying out a multipronged attack against his firm. The internal network is down, files are being lost, and there is evidence that confidential records are making their way outside the company. The company's head of information systems, Tony, is working around the clock to isolate the problem and recover the systems, but he is clearly overmatched. Tony is also nervous because he suspects he is being followed and has confided in the CEO that the combination of leaks and denial of service attacks would be impossible without insider collusion or some kind of clandestine monitoring. Tony is afraid he may himself be targeted for trying to sort out this mess, and the CEO wants immediate assistance. To this end, he is ready to commit to a preliminary expense threshold of $250,000 for this immediate assistance, as his entire business is at risk. Monique accepts the challenge and immediately launches into action.

Response

What resources does Monique begin to deploy to deal with the problem? Recognizing that there are several unknowns and potential threats to address, she taps her available resources to line up the following:

- A case manager to go to the site to oversee the deployment of all the resources to follow, while also interacting with the CEO and Tony to better assess the changing demands of the situation
- A technical surveillance countermeasures team, that is, specialty technicians who perform discreet sweeps of rooms and buildings to uncover the presence of clandestine monitoring devices or electronic bugs
- A protective detail, that is, bodyguards, to discreetly protect Tony while he meets offsite with the case manager to discuss preparations for bringing in the countermeasures team into the workplace that night
- A mobile surveillance detail to watch after Tony's approach to the meeting site and, later to and from the company, in order to spot hostile surveillance that may be responsible for following Tony

- A computer forensics exploitation expert to return from out-of-town travel that night and be brought into the workplace the next morning in order to examine the network under attack and work with Tony to diagnose the severity of the attack, so as to then bring on additional experts as required to restore the network and institute additional safeguards to defend against further attack

Disruptions

Which of the resources are disruptions? The countermeasures team performing the bug sweep is prepared to first detect and then exploit or neutralize any clandestine monitoring devices after examining key work areas overnight, including the CEO's office and Tony's work area where network servers and critical files are stored electronically and in hard copy. The protective detail is ready to intervene to defend Tony against physical attack, including kidnapping, extortion, or intimidation. The mobile surveillance detail is there to spot hostile surveillance targeting Tony and to follow the followers until identified and, if warranted, exposed or arrested. Finally, the computer forensics expert is en route to assist with damage control and to then follow digital audit trails that reveal the identity of the attacker or attackers while also providing options for safeguarding the network and systems from further attack.

Potential Outcomes

As resources come into place, Monique reviews these potential outcomes with the CEO:

- Monique's field resources will discreetly identify who is following Tony, where the bugs are in the firm, and whether the records lost or compromised give an indication of who is benefitting from this attack. Meanwhile, the field resources will also aim at protecting the CEO and Tony personally and the firm itself from further loss.
- Upon identification of a clear threat to life or property, Monique's resources will summon local authorities, in full coordination with the CEO, and act as a support resource within the scope that the law and the CEO's desires define.
- Monique's field resources may not be able to validate the threat as described. In this case, they may redirect their focus to expose an internal saboteur and will again be looking closely at who stands to benefit from the compromises under scrutiny.
- Some unexpected combination of unforeseen events may be causing the problem and none of them may be detectable by the resources Monique has deployed. This could include clandestine government or law enforcement surveillance of the CEO or Tony for reasons related or unrelated to what Monique has been told so far. If Monique's people uncover a clandestine operation legitimately under the direction of a government or law enforcement agency, she will call a halt to field activity once convinced of the legitimacy of the operation and either advise the CEO or, absent extraordinary circumstances, insist that the lead agency involved communicate with the CEO. If an unexpected sequence of events points elsewhere, Monique will have her case manager in the field consult with the CEO at the first signs of uncovering the root cause of the problem, before continuing to spend time, money, and energy of all the resources applied to the problem.

Sequence of Actual Outcomes

Here is what happened in the sequence of events that unfolded:

1. The protective detail of bodyguards found no signs of danger to Tony or to the CEO.
2. The technical surveillance countermeasures team found no bugs or clandestine monitoring devices, despite an exhaustive search. One team member interacting with Tony during the sweep observed that some of Tony's suggestions about where to look for what kind of devices were more than a little farfetched.
3. The mobile surveillance detail found no signs of Tony being followed to either the meeting site or to or from the place of business at any time of the night.
4. The computer forensics expert did confirm that the network was behaving erratically. As he was spending considerable time talking with Tony, he observed that Tony had relatively little professional schooling in his discipline and was more or less self-trained in the management of information systems. He also learned that Tony felt overmatched, had been recently promoted in responsibility with little extra compensation, and was struggling to keep up with his work before the network anomalies started to surface.
5. The forensics expert consulted with the case manager and then both started talking with Tony in a private conference room. Tony eventually revealed that he had few peers to interact with in trying to keep pace with the technical demands of his job. One of these peers was an outside computer enthusiast who had given Tony some freeware and also shown him some cracker tools. Eventually, Tony revealed that he had occasionally given remote access to this individual in order to obtain his advice on troubleshooting some network problems. While the forensics expert kept Tony engaged in conversing about the history of network problems, the case manager gave Monique the name of the outside computer enthusiast for any available traces.
6. Monique's investigators at headquarters found that the outside computer enthusiast had previously been convicted of computer vandalism and was active in hacker circles. Monique fed this information back to the case manager, who shared it with the forensics expert. The latter inferred that most of the problems experienced to date were most likely the result of the outsider hacking into the company network via a door opened by Tony.
7. The case manager and the forensics expert prevailed upon Tony to talk to the hacker in a conference call, which confirmed the forensics expert's suspicions about the cause of the problem.
8. The case manager and forensics expert consulted the CEO and revealed their preliminary findings, noting that there was no indication of malice on the part of Tony but, instead, that Tony was overmatched by his duties, in need of assistance and more professional training and support resources, and possibly in need of counseling to assist him with life management issues that were beginning to surface. The case manager recommended against taking punitive action, as Tony was still needed to help restore the network and was fully cooperating by this time. The forensics expert referred the CEO to a competent local systems administrator who could assist on a temporary basis while the firm decided how to help Tony with what ultimately turned out to be a combination of stress-induced paranoia and poor decisions in seeking technical assistance.

Lessons Learned

This case illustrated that there are times when one of the unknowns a defender may have to contend with includes when apparently existential damage is coming at the hands of an insider who does not realize that he has become an agent of destruction. Several disruptions introduced early on in the response were unnecessary, including bug sweeps, bodyguard protection, and mobile surveillance. However, until Tony was exposed as the underlying cause of the problem, it was impossible to predict that these resources would not be needed. Indeed, Tony had so convinced the CEO that the firm was experiencing a sophisticated attack, that the CEO insisted on taking every conceivable action possible to save his business. Although the computer forensics expert proved the most valuable of the resources deployed, his greatest value was not so much in what he was able to achieve technically but in his ability to elicit more revealing details from Tony and to then infer that all problems were tracing to Tony rather than to an outside competitor or calculated attack. Thus, a resource intended for disruption ended up reformatting in the field to detect deception—in this case including Tony's self-deception and errors of judgment that he had been concealing. What started out presenting itself as an outside attack with some insider-level of support turned out to be a non-malevolent insider threat that no one had foreseen. Deploying a broad array of disruptions, including some that were unproductive, nevertheless enabled the retained problem-solvers to arrive at the underlying cause of the problem and to contain the damage and lead the way to recovery.

QUESTIONS FOR ONLINE OR CLASSROOM DISCUSSION

1. Thinking like a sophisticated adversary who has caught wind of a possible investigation or sting involving authorities and closing in on the trust betrayer, how might you exploit the bias or biases of the authorities to your advantage?
2. What is an example of a creative approach you can take to disrupt a hostile insider's attack without revealing your true agenda or exposing your work team to danger?
3. What are some of the perils of asking team members to take the lead in using their wiles to disrupt the activities of a suspected insider threat?
4. How can lawful disruption be useful in dealing with a volatile situation where tempers give signs of escalating into violence?

EXERCISES FOR GROUP PROJECTS

1. Identify a case where the presence of a hostile trust betrayer would leave your organization no choice but to bring in authorities to assist with the response. How do you meet your legal obligations while also defending the organization's equities, as the authorities present specialists that they propose to put in charge of managing a sting operation designed to catch the trust betrayer in the act of sabotage?
2. Under what circumstances might it be wiser for the institution to go it alone in disrupting an insider threat rather than involve authorities in a response?
3. At what point might it ever become acceptable to move from lawful disruption to disruption at any cost? Is this ever advisable?

ENDNOTES

1. T. Frieden, "Ashcroft vows changes to focus on terrorism prevention," *CNN .com*, November 8, 2001. Retrieved 11-9-2001 from http://www.cnn.com/2001/ LAW/11/08/inv.justice.revamp.

2. C. Bellavita and N. Catrantzos, "A Chew-without-Swallowing Terrorism Defense," *Homeland Security Watch*, February 8, 2011. Retrieved July 4, 2011 from http:// www.hlswatch.com/index.php?s=chew+without.

3. Canadian anti-terrorism committee Senator Hugh Segal, in C. Addy interview, "Whither Anti-Terrorism," *Frontline Security*, Fall/Winter 2010, p. 12.

4. F. Bolz and E. Hershey, *Hostage Cop*, New York: Rawson, Wade, 1979, p. 57.

5. F. Bolz, K. J. Dudonis, and D. P. Schulz, *The Counterterrorism Handbook*, 2nd ed., Boca Raton, FL: CRC Press, 2002, pp. 177–178.

6. Department of Homeland Security. Retrieved July 27, 2011 from http://www.dhs .gov/files/programs/gc_1156877184684.shtm.

7. Adapted from N. Catrantzos, "Chew-without-Swallowing Terrorism Defense," *All Secure* blog, January 5, 2011. Retrieved July 27, 2011 from http://all-secure.blogspot .com/2011/01/chew-without-swallowing-terrorism.html.

8. Details available at http://www.law.cornell.edu/uscode/18/usc_sec_18_00000798----000-.html.

9. J. C. Mowen, *Judgment Calls*, New York: Simon & Schuster, 1993, p. 17.

10. While the author has participated in teaching private sector clients how to defend against product contamination and product extortion, some of the foundational concepts underlying the discussion in the preceding paragraph trace to a classic text, R. Clutterbuck, "Response to Product Contamination," in *Kidnap, Hijack and Extortion*, London: Macmillan Press, 1987, pp. 105–112.

11. R. P. Feynman, as told to Ralph Leighton, *What Do You Care What Other People Think?*, New York: W.W. Norton & Company, 1988, pp. 113–249.

12. Ibid., pp. 175–176.

13. Ibid., pp. 213–214.

14. Y. Sheffi, *The Resilient Enterprise*, Cambridge, MA: MIT Press, 2007, p. 15.

15. Mowen, p. 15.

16. Mowen, p. 248.

17. S. P. Lab, *Crime Prevention: Approaches, Practices and Evaluations*, 3rd ed., Cincinnati, OH: Anderson Publishing Company, 1997, p. 15.

18. The classification system that follows is adapted from seminal work by R. V. Clarke and R. Homel, "A Revised Classification of Situational Crime Prevention," in S. P. Lab, *Crime Prevention at a Crossroads*, Cincinnati, OH: Anderson Publishing, 1997, and also reproduced in Lab, *Crime Prevention*, 1997, p. 159.

19. G. Jonas, *Vengeance: The True Story of an Israeli Counter-Terrorist Team*, New York: Simon and Schuster, 1984, p. 121.

20. P. R. Pillar, "Is the Terrorist Threat Misunderstood?," *Security Management*, May 2001.

21. B. Ganor, *The Counter-Terrorism Puzzle*, New Brunswick, NJ: Transaction Publishers, 2005, p. 64.

22. P. F. Drucker, *Management: Tasks, Responsibilities, Practices*, New York: HarperBusiness, 1993, p. 683.

23. Drucker, *Management*, p. 41.

24. H. Segal and S. Joyal, "Interim Report of the Special Senate Committee on Anti-Terrorism," in *Security, Freedom and the Complex Terrorist Threat: Positive Steps Ahead*, Ottawa: Government of Canada, Committee Business—Senate—Reports, 40th Parliament—3rd Session, March 2011, p. 34.

25. "SHRM Survey Reveals Extend of Workplace Violence," based on the Society of Human Resource Management 1994 survey, *EAP Digest*, March–April, 1994, p. 25.

26. H. Zimmerle, "Common Sense v. the EEOC: Co-Worker Ostracism and Shunning as Retaliation Under Title VII," *Journal of Corporation Law*, April 1, 2005. Retrieved July 30, 2011 from http://www.allbusiness.com/legal/laws-government-regulations-employment/1011084-1.html.

27. R. Brinkman and R. Kirschner, *Dealing with People You Can't Stand*, New York: McGraw-Hill, 1994.

28 Ibid. pp. 3–11.

29. National Commission on Terrorist Attacks, *The 9/11Commission Report: Final Report of the National Commission on Terrorist Attacks upon the United States*, New York: W. W. Norton, 2004, p. 392.

30. Drucker, *Management*, p. 685.

31. The author served as the consultant managing the field resources deployed in the case described. Actual identities of individuals and employers have been masked in the interest of discretion.

CHAPTER 8

Existential Insider Threats

A society that cannot or will not focus on matters of life and death is a society whose survival as a free nation is at least questionable.

Thomas Sowell

INTRODUCTION

An existential threat poses a challenge to the survival of the institution, and a hostile insider serving as an extension or perpetrator of such a threat has the objective of carrying out an attack fatal to the institution. Such aims are by no means novel. In a handbook for terrorists created by the Brazilian, Carlos Marighella, translated into 15 languages, and disseminated globally in the 1970s, encouragement of the use of insiders for sabotage identified the objectives "to hurt, to damage, to make useless, and to destroy" that which is vital, including a country's economy, agricultural production, transportation, as well as firms and properties of businesses.[1] So, the intent to carry out existential attacks comes not only with a pedigree but with instructions for would-be attackers. From whom do we have the most to fear, however?

Terrorism authority Bruce Hoffman found in state-sponsored terrorism the most potent impact in advancing defined foreign policy objectives through violence without the constraints faced by attackers who must limit their lethality for fear of alienating the public or inviting a backlash in the face of too much carnage or destruction.[2] Thus, Hoffman concludes, "the state-sponsored terrorist and his patron can engage in acts of violence that are typically more destructive and bloodier than those carried out by groups acting on their own behalf."[3] By weighing Hoffman's finding against Marighella's exhortations to would-be saboteurs, one may infer, consistent with the Delphi panel's conclusions in the No Dark Corners research effort described at the outset of this book, that the infiltrator in league with a state-sponsored terrorist group is likely to pose a more serious, existential threat to the institution than, say, a disgruntled career employee. Consequently, it stands to reason that defenders accord first priority to such infiltrators as the most dangerous of threats.

FIRST THINGS FIRST

Faced with existential threats such as a terrorist infiltrator, then, what is the institution's first duty? One crisis management authority reasoned that the first duty is to employees and then to shareholders, since "If the firm does not give the prevention of human damage the higher priority, it is likely to lose more financially in the long run," and an organization that "fails to take care of its own people. . . will acquire an unflattering public image and face a disastrous decline in staff morale, and be unable to attract capable staff. . . ."[4] The implications, then, are that the institution must place a premium on defending its own employees. That premium, in turn, translates into an investment in prevention. Why? As a researcher in global policy discerned, "for most catastrophic risk, prevention is usually the most cost-effective strategy."[5] So, we know it is important to address the most dangerous threat, the state-sponsored infiltrator. We also know it is important to protect one's own people. Finally, we realize that the best strategy for doing these things is to focus mainly on prevention. Where do we begin, however?

PROTECTING PEOPLE AND PROPERTY

You cannot protect people if you cannot protect things. Why? Protection, at least in the long term, requires operating in a secure environment, that is, one that is substantially free from danger and defended from attack. Achieving this objective requires thinking through how to create and sustain protected spaces. Moreover, in a No Dark Corners milieu, it requires engaging team members to reflexively take a hand in their own defense. To do this effectively, everyone in the organization benefits from gaining a shared, foundational understanding of these security underpinnings. Tell employees the why and they will better manage the how.

Beginning with people, consider that the defender's challenge is to protect them in essentially three places: at work, at home, and in transit, with the most common exposure to adverse events being when someone is in transit.[6] As an authority in kidnapping response and prevention noted, adversaries look for softer targets, hence the value of being seen to take visible precautions, particularly since "the cost of being kidnapped will be many times greater than the cost of preventing it."[7] In cases involving high-net-worth individuals and prominent public figures, it may be feasible or even advisable to surround such targets with bodyguards and mobilize protective resources to supply 24-hour security. However, such resources are normally available in limited quantity or for limited occasions. Most people are expected to assume responsibility for their personal security most of the time, particularly at home and in transit, with employers taking the responsibility to afford some baseline level of protection at work. In fact, in the United States, the Occupational Safety and Health Administration (OSHA) regards it as part of an employer's fundamental obligation to provide a safe and healthful workplace, including taking reasonable steps to prevent or abate workplace violence hazards.[8]

This mandate necessarily returns us to places and the need to secure them for the sake not only of the people within but also for the safeguarding of assets in those spaces, including property, equipment, trade secrets, and any activities that require protection.

The first question in attempting to secure anything is a question of priority. What is critical? In other words, what most needs protecting? Resources and attention spans are finite, so to attempt to protect everything at the same level would be self-defeating. It could engender a lowest-common-denominator approach that leaves the trifling and easily replaced assets defended at the same level as the critical, irreplaceable assets upon which the core business or survival of the institution most depends. Another acknowledgment of reality compels realizing that facility operators seldom "have the financial resources to fully protect all their assets; therefore assets will in most cases need prioritization."[9]

After addressing what is critical, next consider questions of exposure. What adverse, existential fate must the critical asset be spared? In other words, what threats impinge on its successful operation or impede its capacity for delivering the value that makes it so critical to the institution? This could be loss of a trade secret, such as a formula for production of a wonder drug that cost years and millions in research and development to discover, refine, and bring to market. If compromised before providing a return on such an investment, this formula could spell ruin for the enterprise and mean loss of jobs for its employees. Another critical asset could be the founder of the pharmaceutical company that created the wonder drug and was able to attract the necessary investment to pay for development and trials and otherwise shepherd the product to market. At a critical phase in the debut of that product, losing the founder could spark loss of investor confidence at the critical moment, again resulting in ruin for all concerned. Alternatively, the critical asset could be a nuclear weapon whose capture by the wrong hands could kill thousands of innocents and trigger a global war. In such a case, the threat could be so severe as to justify significantly more protective resources than for the loss of a pharmaceutical whose worst impact would be loss of market share and eventual bankruptcy.

From this point, most security approaches embark upon a risk or vulnerability assessment as the next step.[10] The output of this assessment informs recommendations of what countermeasures to put into effect and what priority to accord them in order to defend one's assets. The next common starting place for any consideration of security measures to impose is to control access to the critical assets. With this understanding of why access control is important, all employees can better grasp the significance of denying access to infiltrators and to even curbing access of disgruntled career employees who show signs of betraying trust and inflicting harm.

DEFENDER'S ADVANTAGE IN DEALING WITH INFILTRATORS

An alert, engaged work force in a No Dark Corners environment communicates a copilot level of attention to how the business of the institution is moving along its daily flight path. In doing so, this involvement emits signals to adversaries that this particular institution is no easy target, which can act as a substantial deterrent. This deterrent value is all the more apparent when one realizes that the most dangerous adversaries, terrorists, prefer targets where "success is 100% assured."[11] Also, since terrorist groups seek targets they consider rewarding,[12] it stands to reason that visible precautions on the part of the work force will diminish the appearance of the apparent reward in an institution that makes itself a difficult target. Indeed, whether in business or government, the truism prevails that the greatest single factor in reducing one's risk is "to be seen to take active security precautions," because neither "political terrorists nor criminals can afford a fiasco," hence their perennial search for a soft target.[13]

SPILLOVER EFFECTS FROM DEFENDING
AGAINST EXISTENTIAL INSIDERS

Just as a rising tide lifts all vessels, mitigating existential insider threats of the most pernicious variety also flows into the broader reservoir of defenses against those insiders who may not necessarily pose an existential threat. By developing institutional knowledge, employee engagement, and the kind of muscular internal culture that actively detects and disrupts hostile trust betrayers, the No Dark Corners organization stands ready to parry insider thrusts in the manner of an adept swordsman making good use of a saber regardless of whether his attacker is wielding a foil or a machete. The defensive habits flow into muscle memory, and vulnerability declines as alacrity, readiness, and watchfulness become instinctive.

In practice, it may be impossible for defenders to ascertain unequivocally whether a trust betrayer was bent on annihilation of the institution until after the attack has been executed or defeated. Nor should defenders be responsible for diverting their energy from critical operations in order to become virtuosi at gauging whether every trust betrayer is an existential threat or whether the hostile insider is destined to escalate no further than the nuisance level. Instead, most defenders can satisfy themselves with making the organization what management authority Peter Drucker calls battle-ready.[14] Consequently, by making it difficult for existential insider threats to strike with impunity, defenders also improve their odds of prevailing over other insider threats—as long as they do not naively lower their guard on the basis of familiarity with a trust betrayer who raises fewer eyebrows or invites none of the xenophobia that may attach to an infiltrator. Further exploration of this line of inquiry will follow in the next chapter. In the meanwhile, however, it is necessary to begin with the most dangerous varieties of existential threat, the kind where collusion of a trust betrayer is necessary to maximize harm.

THE BIG THREE EXISTENTIAL INSIDER THREATS

Three kinds of insider attack requiring an infiltrator and offering disproportionally high return on investment for attackers are sabotage with cascading impacts, assassinations that result in political decapitation of key leaders, and espionage that supplies decisive victory to opposing forces. All three kinds of attack have homeland security components and, in the United States, the Department of Homeland Security (DHS) is most likely to have interests and assets to bear in dealing with all three, although espionage will more likely remain within counterintelligence purviews of the Federal Bureau of Investigation (FBI), the Central Intelligence Agency, and the Office of the Director of National Intelligence through its subsidiary functions of the National Counterintelligence Executive or even the National Counterterrorism Center. Nevertheless, to the extent that Americans find themselves on the frontlines of meeting and countering such threats on U.S. soil, some involvement of the DHS is likely to accompany state and local collaborations. Indeed, one analyst sees the way that the various federal agencies define terrorism as indicative of their predilections and likely concentrations in dealing with terrorist threats, from which we may infer similar organizational predispositions to dealing with insider threats.[15] Consequently, the FBI definition highlights the unlawful use of force or violence in its definition,[16] whereas the DHS definition focuses on any activity that is dangerous to human life, destructive of critical infrastructure or key resources, and seeks to influence government by mass destruction, assassination, or kidnapping.[17] We now look at each of these three existential insider threats in turn.

SABOTAGE WITH CASCADING IMPACTS

An individual act of sabotage may cause serious yet limited adverse impact. Environmental groups advocating sabotage in the name of protecting nature from exploitation, for example, go to some lengths to draw the line at targeting machines, not people, in their attacks dubbed monkeywrenching:

> Monkeywrenching is nonviolent resistance to the destruction of natural diversity and wilderness. It is never directed against human beings or other forms of life. It is aimed at inanimate machines and tools that are destroying life. Care is always taken to minimize any possible threat to people, including the monkeywrenchers themselves.[18]

A more serious attack targeting critical infrastructure, however, need not hobble itself with such self-imposed constraints. Predating the 9/11/01 attacks by several years, the President's Commission on Critical Infrastructure Protection acknowledged that inter-linked systems and dependencies—particularly within critical infrastructure—posed a vulnerability that would give an adversary incapable of prevailing in a military conflict the means to carry out devastating attack by instead targeting critical infrastructure. These introductory remarks to Presidential Decision Directive 63, Critical Infrastructure Protection, captured in 1998 a vulnerability that remains exploitable today (emphasis added via underscoring):

I. A Growing Potential Vulnerability
The United States possesses both the world's strongest military and its largest national economy. Those two aspects of our power are mutually reinforcing and dependent. They are also increasingly reliant upon certain critical infrastructures and upon cyber-based information systems.

Critical infrastructures are those physical and cyber-based systems essential to the minimum operations of the economy and government. They include, but are not limited to, telecommunications, energy, banking and finance, transportation, water systems and emergency services, both governmental and private. Many of the nation's critical infra-structures have historically been physically and logically separate systems that had little interdependence. As a result of advances in information technology and the necessity of improved efficiency, however, these infrastructures have become increasingly automated and interlinked. These same advances have created new vulnerabilities to equipment fail-ure, human error, weather and other natural causes, and physical and cyber attacks. Addressing these vulnerabilities will necessarily require flexible, evolutionary approaches that span both the public and private sectors, and protect both domestic and interna-tional security.

Because of our military strength, future enemies, whether nations, groups or individu-als, may seek to harm us in non-traditional ways, including attacks within the United States. Because our economy is increasingly reliant upon interdependent and cyber-supported infrastructures, non-traditional attacks on our infrastructure and informa-tion systems may be capable of significantly harming both our military power and our economy.[19]

Cascading impacts of sabotage represent the attacker's side of the interdependency coin. Just as the 9/11 terrorist attacks against the World Trade Center affected not only Manhattan but Wall Street, civil aviation, and the entire national economy, so can a successful attack against a primary, Tier 1 infrastructure such as water, electricity, or telecommunications, produce cascading effects on other sectors that cannot function without water or power, for example.[20] Thus, water's availability affects agriculture yet also the nuclear power, chemical, and manufacturing industries that need water for cool-ing. Nor can any automation-intensive activity operate long without electricity. Similarly, without telecommunications, remotely controlled operations and diagnostics cease to function.

Although the world of critical infrastructure protection recognizes the existence of interdependencies, hence the need to address them in risk reduction efforts, other institutions vary widely in their appreciation of how much they depend on others, including on the extent to which entire supply chains can be paralyzed if a major setback affects their weak and relatively obscure links. An authority on supply chain analysis, however, pointed out that intentional attacks against supply chains will target the least-defended place at the most inconvenient time.[21] Thus, to an intelligent adversary possessing the analytical tools to pinpoint such exposures, an attack that would not be possible against a well-defended headquarters or prime contractor may nonetheless be carried out by infiltrating a satellite office or subcontractor where there is less vigilance and where employees unaccustomed to being targeted neglect their own defenses as the ravings of headquarters that need not apply to the field.

HOW ONE EVENT'S CASCADING IMPACT ENDED A LINE OF BUSINESS

The difficulty in understanding and insulating one's operation from catastrophic impact of interdependencies is perhaps nowhere better illustrated than in the story about how a single calamity affected two competitors, Nokia and Ericsson, who both depended on the same supplier, Phillips. The sequence of events that followed resulted in cascading impacts that put Ericsson out of the cellular telephone business while its competitor, Nokia, retained its position as the global leader in the same market.[22] Corporate culture and advance decisions about risk had a hand in transforming what was manageable loss to one institution into fatal, existential loss for the other. Although the trigger for these developments happened to be a bolt of lightning, arson at the hands of a hostile insider could have produced identical consequences.

EVENT

Severe thunderstorms in March 2000 befell Albuquerque, New Mexico, the site of a Phillips semiconductor fabrication plant for multiple cellular telephone manufacturers, including Nokia and Ericsson, who together represented 40% of the plant's business. A bolt of lightning struck one of the plant's buildings, resulting in a furnace fire. Automatic sprinklers and an alert Phillips work force extinguished the fire before local firefighters arrived. Accompanied by plant employees, the firefighters performed inspections to make sure all flames were extinguished. To the firefighters, the damage seemed minor and the incident concluded with little fanfare and no media attention. However, the damaged furnace had eight trays of wafers that were ruined, with each tray representing thousands of mobile phones' enabling chips. More significantly, the smoke from the fire contaminated cleanroom facilities on a wide scale, ruining wafers in various stages of production and millions of chips for cellular phones. In addition to the smoke damage, cleanroom contamination spread even more because of the dirt brought in during firefighter and on-site staff inspections in the immediate aftermath of the fire.

NOTICE OF IMPACT

Phillips advised its customers, including Nokia and Ericsson, that the fire had caused lost wafers and initially projected a 1-week delay in production.

ERICSSON'S REACTION

Ericsson matter-of-factly accepted the notice of a 1-week delay from Philips as the sharing of information at a working, technical level. Ericsson staffers did not inform superiors about the loss, nor did they take action to monitor progress in recovery of Philips' capacity. Even after the delay had significantly exceeded the initial 1-week projection, Ericsson staff did not pass on the information to their management. Once Ericsson began to experience significant impact from the lack of chips, Ericsson asked Philips for additional capacity. Phillips, however, was unable to honor this request because Nokia had already secured all of Phillips' spare capacity by then. Ericsson then began looking for alternative suppliers but, having no preexisting relationships with such suppliers, was unable to find any available to make up for the Philips chips that came exclusively from the Albuquerque plant.

NOKIA'S REACTION

Upon receiving the same notice from Philips about the fire and projected 1-week delay, Nokia put the chips on a special watch list and increased its monitoring of Phillips' product deliveries from weekly to daily. Nokia also initiated daily status calls to Phillips to check on the situation with the Albuquerque plant. Although Nokia staff first learning of the situation in Albuquerque did not interpret it as a crisis, they did pass the information along internally because, as one Nokia manager avowed, "We encourage bad news to travel fast . . . (and) . . . don't want to hide problems."[23] Two weeks after the fire, when discussions with Phillips made Nokia realize that the situation could affect delivery of 4,000,000 cellular telephones and 5% of Nokia's annual production, the cellular phone manufacturer convened a team of chip designers and managers from across the corporation to address the growing problem. This team placed additional orders for three out of five parts with existing suppliers in Japan and the United States. The remaining two parts came exclusively from Phillips or a Phillips subcontractor, so Nokia held meetings with Phillips executives at the highest level to underscore how important this situation was. Nokia also probed into Phillips' capacity and insisted on rerouting this capacity and giving priority to Nokia. Meanwhile, Nokia also partnered with Phillips to develop new ways to increase production at the Albuquerque plant once it came back online, while Phillips factories in Holland and China freed up additional capacity to fulfill Nokia's demands.

ADDITIONAL INFORMATION

Ericsson had previously decided to cut costs by relying on single-source contracts, hence its lack of alternate suppliers at the time. Nokia had less confidence in the supply channel and kept multiple-source contracting in place while also monitoring the situation with Phillips recovery more closely.

OUTCOME

Within 6 months of the loss-producing event, Nokia's market share increased from 27% to 30%. During the same period, Ericsson's decreased from 12% to 9%. Within 1 year, Ericsson announced that it was exiting the cellular telephone handset production market and later entered into a joint venture with Sony for

Sony-Ericsson to design, manufacture, and market the products. Phillips lost sales from the Albuquerque incident amounted to 0.6% for the year 2000. Insurance compensated Phillips for the direct damage to the plant. Ericsson experienced more than 10 times Phillips' losses, with financial reporting of around $500,000,000 in losses before taxes owing to lack of parts.

LESSONS

Nokia recovered where Ericsson faltered because of a corporate culture that included:

- Rapid internal communication of problems*
- Close and collaborative monitoring of the difficulties Phillips was experiencing*
- Wide-ranging team engagement in approach to solving problems*
- Multiple sourcing to offset interruptions in its supply chain

* Consistent with No Dark Corners strategies.

DECAPITATION ATTACKS THROUGH ASSASSINATION

Political decapitation attacks aim to use human fatalities to produce the impact of sabotage with cascading impacts. Two aborted plots of this attack vector in recent years illustrate the significance of such strikes, the value of infiltrating agents where they can facilitate hostilities, and the difficulty of successfully carrying out such schemes. One plot unfolded in Toronto and Ottawa in 2006, and the other in Amman in 2004. The first targeted Canada's parliament, with attackers aiming to carry out bombings, shootings, and the beheading of the prime minister.[24] The second had the aim of destabilizing Jordan's government by killing not only Jordanian political leaders but also by targeting the U.S. embassy. In the eyes of Jordan's monarch, if the attack had succeeded, "It would have decapitated the government."[25] Both plots involved accumulation of explosives in significant quantities, with the Canadian plot apparently exceeding the destructive power witnessed in the Oklahoma City bombing of 1995. The cascading impact of such attacks would have potentially rivaled that of 9/11, with the Jordanian plot potentially resulting in casualties in excess of 20,000 if carried out in conjunction with a chemical weapon. In both cases, it is possible that an absence of attackers with insider access contributed to the plots failing to materialize before being exposed and thwarted. In the case of the Toronto plot, authorities managed to prevent the attack by infiltrating the terror cell.

Decapitation plots such as the foregoing have yet to succeed with the enabling force of well-placed insiders. Instead, as media reporting tends to highlight, their chief point of emphasis appears to be the extent to which plotters are homegrown as opposed to foreigners.[26] To date, such cases appear to involve insiders only to the extent that a country's own citizens turn against the nation or society writ large, without necessarily possessing the kind of insider access that delivers a decisive advantage in carrying out the attack. A parallel exists with Timothy McVeigh, the Oklahoma City bomber, whose life was chronicled in *American Terrorist*, which also included a letter from convicted Unabomber Theodore Kaczynski giving his impressions of McVeigh as a likable inmate.[27] In the private sector, corporate decapitation may result when leaders such as the cofounder of Akamai Technologies perish in terrorist attacks, as Daniel Lewin did on American Airlines Flight 11 from Boston when his plane became the first to strike the World Trade Center on September 11, 2001.[28] In practice, however, it is the rare executive's loss that goes beyond a personal tragedy to an event that spells the end of a business entity, particularly if that entity has in place sufficient management wherewithal to meet obligations, grow the business, and retain customer confidence—as apparently happened with Akamai over the years since 2001.

ESPIONAGE YIELDING DECISIVE VICTORY

In order for espionage to produce the kind of yield that would be fatal to a nation, it would be necessary for that yield to be on the order of betraying battle plans in a war to an adversary with the capacity to exploit them or to compromise a capability that gives one side an edge over the other. An example of the first would be to reveal the details of the Normandy invasion to Germany in time for the Nazis to defeat the Allied invaders. An example of the second would be to give Germany or Japan the details of the atomic bomb in time for either Axis power to use an atomic weapon against the Allies to force unconditional surrender and a resulting change in the history of the free world. As a long-term student of espionage cases has found, however, spying seldom appears to have delivered such decisive advantages to adversaries and may do so even more infrequently, since the modern trend is for betrayers of their country to be aiming at different levels and to be animated by different motives than in the past.[29] The change in motivation, as discussed in Chapter 2, indicates that today's trust betrayer is more likely to be animated by divided loyalties than by financial incentives. Not previously discussed but indelibly linked to this trend is that modern traitors are increasingly found to possess lower security clearances than in the past. Consequently, their access to national security information is at a lower level, hence increasingly less likely to rise to the order of a game-changing revelation that poses an existential threat to the country betrayed. Under these circumstances, the more likely arena for espionage to produce the kind of yield that can take an institution to its knees is in the corporate realm or in situations where compromise of a trade secret or proprietary information can mean loss of the competitive edge that makes the difference between profitable business growth and irrecoverable bankruptcy.

PROBLEMS OF THRESHOLD AND ACCUMULATION

In examining the three foregoing areas where existential threats traditionally offer the greatest return on deft use of a hostile insider, defenders face the twin dilemmas of establishing the threshold where an insider threat crosses into the existential realm and of assessing at what point a multiplicity of betrayals or combined effects of cascading impacts take an otherwise survivable attack and transform it into a juggernaut once it has exploited vulnerable interdependencies. As an example, attacking a single power plant of a large electrical utility or killing three executives involved in power distribution could be serious but not devastating for that utility. Then again, what if all things are not equal, and the targets include the only plant that serviced an adjoining water treatment plant that sustains a municipality with a large defense industrial base and chemical plant? Moreover, what if the executives targeted include one who was the heir apparent to the chief executive and another, perhaps more significantly, who was the only remaining engineer with detailed, hands-on experience of how to operate key facilities via local backup systems when there are major malfunctions with the supervisory control and data acquisition system that others rely on exclusively? Under such conditions, what may have started out as survivable losses may soon cross the threshold into irreplaceable losses, hence posing existential challenges.

On the other hand, what if a single loss in itself manageable begins to surface many times in multiple places, creating through accumulation an indefensible challenge? Losing one plant and one plant manager may be tragic losses; losing several at once or when they are most needed to provide redundancy that offsets the earlier loss can easily become catastrophic. In this context, it becomes apparent that not only is the threshold point for calling a threat existential difficult to establish with precision, it is also susceptible to shift as time passes and losses accumulate.

The answer to the question what constitutes an existential threat for the institution ultimately hinges on top management's tolerance for risk. This tolerance may vary considerably from one manager to the next, however, and may also change without notice to those on the front lines of protection. The one area that is almost certain to capture and hold executive attention, however, is reputational risk. Reputation, in turn, is "more likely affected by incidents caused by human intent rather than natural disasters."[30] If this is indeed the case, then the institution's threshold for identifying existential insider threats and marshaling resources to counter them aligns more closely with a homeland security mission, if one understands it to be a mission grounded in a defensive focus. To arrive at a practical grasp of this alignment, however, it becomes necessary to have a working definition of homeland security in the first place.

DEFINING HOMELAND SECURITY

Words convey meaning. The combination of two familiar words, then, should offer finite possibilities for defining the term composed of their mating. Consider:

HOMELAND *noun.* The country in which one was born or makes one's home.
adjective. Of or relating to homeland, or the country where one makes one's home.
SECURITY *noun.* 1. The state of being or feeling free from danger.
2. Protection against attack. 3. An organization whose task is protection.

Homeland security, in this context, refers to that part of security related to the homeland, that is, protection against attack on the United States. Thus, when "homeland," as in this usage, modifies "security" the resulting coinage tells us that the term is not just about security in general. Instead, the term relates to a subset of security. If we can agree on a working definition of homeland and a shared grasp of security along the foregoing lines, then defining homeland security need not become an exercise in semantic navel-gazing or ponderous speculation.

A PRACTITIONER'S VERSION OF AN EARLY, OFFICIAL DEFINITION

Homeland security is the discipline, study, or craft of protecting a nation from induced, existential catastrophe.

This definition draws on terms first introduced in a seminal work predating the National Incident Management System and establishing a framework for distinguishing between naturally occurring disasters and accidents as contrasted with intentionally caused, or induced, catastrophes.[31] This definition also dovetails with an early, official identification of homeland security as a national objective, namely,

> Homeland security is a concerted national effort to prevent terrorist attacks within the United States, reduce America's vulnerability to terrorism, and minimize the damage and recover from attacks that do occur.[32]

In practice, homeland security is achieved by reducing risk that would otherwise be fatal to the country, or homeland. This risk reduction, in turn, is a function of blending protective measures that reduce vulnerability with mitigation measures that reduce the severity of adverse consequences of an attack, an expression of fundamental principles of risk reduction where risk is a function of vulnerability and consequence.[33] Vulnerability and security possess an inverse relationship; hence the better the security, the lower the vulnerability. Reducing vulnerability, in turn, lowers risk. At the same time, reducing the consequences of an attack through mitigation measures also lowers risk. Ideally, both efforts work in tandem. Thus, if a power plant is a critical source of electricity, ideal risk reduction would result in protecting it with strong security measures on the one hand while, on the other hand, also keeping spare components available and developing a capacity to reroute the plant's load automatically to another plant. One analog of this risk equation relationship for homeland security functions is the mating of security-focused activities to vulnerability and of emergency management- or mitigation-focused activities to consequence. In other words, a homeland security function whose primary role is protective, that is, security, makes its contribution by reducing vulnerability. Examples include law enforcement and intelligence-gathering operations. On the other hand, a function that reduces the impact of adverse consequences makes its contribution by reducing consequence. Examples include public health and emergency management.

In the process of reducing overall risk, homeland security efforts often lower exposure to more than existential threats alone. This is a bonus, a collateral benefit not to be confused for a prime objective. If one is defending against an assassin, after all, the necessary protective actions may also reduce vulnerability to casual trespassers or vandals. However, losing the protective focus by beginning to concentrate on vandals instead of assassins will likely dilute security efforts and increase exposure to the more severe threat.

WHAT HOMELAND SECURITY IS NOT

Within the foregoing context, these activities could arguably fall outside the scope of homeland security:

- Protecting the homeland from existential threats that are not induced, such as accidents or natural hazards. Otherwise, it will not be long before scope creep begins to include automobile accidents as falling within its purview. After all, even in a forgiving year, such accidents account for at least 40,000 fatalities a year in America.[34] Similarly, one could argue that any other number of harmful activities do not qualify as a primary homeland security

function, such as saving the environment or promoting energy independence from oil-producing nations whose interests run counter to our own.

- Protecting from nonexistential threats. Thus, activities beneath this threshold of concern would include personal and property crime, such as workplace violence and arson whose targets may suffer death or destruction
  without placing the homeland in jeopardy.
- Protecting from broader, wide-ranging threats aimed at targets other
  than the homeland. Thus, an attack against an overseas trading partner
  would not merit primacy as a homeland security matter. An attack against
  a McDonald's restaurant in Jakarta or on an American Express office in
  Izmir should not be a matter in which a homeland security–focused organization assumes the response or investigative lead.

PITFALLS OF AN OVERLY BROAD DEFINITION

One curse that bedevils sideliners and gives them away at the same time is their
love of multiplying nuance and subtlety at the risk of becoming obtuse. This is
what accounts for a low bridge becoming "impaired vertical clearance" or a crook
becoming "ethically challenged." It is also why asking for a simple homeland security definition may unleash a ramble likely to include flu shots, Hurricane Katrina,
the emergency broadcast system, and fugues on all-hazard approaches. Moreover,
it is why such mental meandering loses sight of zealous adversaries bent on our
annihilation. Not that these extra themes are undeserving of attention. But to put
them on a par with the kinds of existential threat posed by terrorist adversaries with
blood on their hands, ferocity in their eyes, and adaptive intelligence in their heads
is to rob defenders of focus. The net result is a diffusion of effort and resources
to cover an ever-expanding purview that defines every underfunded initiative as a
homeland security matter. Meanwhile, this diffusion plays into the hands of any
smaller adversary focused enough to concentrate on objectives and targets and
attacks without our self-generated distractions. As our vision blurs, theirs sharp-
ens. We begin by seeing through the simple definition of homeland security. Then,
we continue trumpeting this potent vision, seeing through everything until finally
arriving at C. S. Lewis's conclusion, "If you see through everything then everything
is transparent. But a transparent world is an invisible world. To see through all
things is the same as not to see."[35]

BOTTOM LINE

In the foregoing context, one working definition of homeland security becomes:

> *Homeland security is the discipline, study, or craft of protecting a nation from
> induced, existential catastrophe.*

ALIGNING EXISTENTIAL THREAT DEFENSE WITH THE DHS

In addition to those portions of the role of the DHS that include protection from induced,
existential catastrophe, DHS is also the agency that defines terrorism in terms of a threat

posed to critical infrastructure (which aligns with the cascading impacts issue). DHS is also the home for the entity most adept at countering political decapitation attacks through assassination, the Secret Service. Finally, of the 17 critical infrastructures and key resources currently identified, DHS exercises the role of lead federal agency for 10 and nonetheless issues guidance supporting the defense of the ones for which it does not assume the lead.[36]

The institution that looks at nascent insider threats through the same lens that DHS counterparts focus on threats to infrastructure or would-be presidential assassins may find, like DHS, that the vast majority of what comes into view constitutes neither a danger to physical existence nor a threat at all. This realization bears mute testimony to the observation of a management analyst who noted, "Most people, most of the time, are neither saving the world nor exploiting it."[37] However, because DHS is a relatively new entity and one originally constituted to defend a nation against emerging existential threats, it embraces the focus, resources, and charter to at least accord priority to such threats when the hour sounds. Consequently, defenders are more likely to find a receptive ear within the DHS than within other governmental entities whose historical mission, training, and internal reward mechanisms reinforce roles and priorities that invariably take precedence over defense of the institution's critical assets. Thus, a traditional law enforcement agency will focus on apprehension of offenders, whereas its prosecutorial counterpart will accord top priority to winning convictions. These remain important societal contributions but, to the defender, they offer limited value because their greatest efforts and resources materialize only after the destructive loss has occurred.

WHAT MAKES IT AN EXISTENTIAL THREAT?

As the foregoing illustration showed in "How One Event's Cascading Impact Ended a Line of Business," existential threats may not be immediately recognizable, nor does the same threat necessarily amount to an existential one for two different institutions. The same event that culminated in putting Ericsson out of the cell phone business did no ultimate harm to Nokia's market share in the same business, partly because of the way Nokia managed its response to the chip supplier's catastrophe and partly because of Nokia's advance decision to multisource suppliers at the same time Ericsson had elected to single-source for short-term cost savings. To complicate matters further, "two people may differ persistently on what to do about" a given risk, especially "if they keep disagreeing on how big it is."[38] Under the circumstances, asking a team member, sentinel, or frontline manager to wait until ascertaining that a hostile trust betrayer may be posing an existential threat represents an unfair burden to the individual and a liability to the institution. Instead, it would appear wiser to adopt Nokia's motto of encouraging bad news to travel fast and engaging the right mix of employees with the skill sets for not only evaluating the problem but for devising options for solving it before it produces catastrophic impact.

If most employees are unfamiliar with the terms and distinctions of what constitutes a risk to the survival of the institution, they are likely to be more familiar with the ramifications, if not the terminology, of reputational risk. Formally, this kind of risk pertains to damage to an institution's reputation that has the potential to have cascading impact in its goods, services, financial performance, and other areas affecting the organization's capacity to function, hence, if uncontrolled, to survive. As some analysts have noted,

Coca-Cola's chief executive officer recognized the paramount importance of reputational risk in saying that his corporation could lose all its factories and trucks but keep the Coca-Cola name and still be able to rebuild the business; losing the Coca-Cola name, however, would cause the business to collapse.[39] More informally, savvy employees at every level of the organization soon learn that it is never a good idea to allow bad news to surprise the boss, particularly if the bad news has the potential to invite negative media or regulatory scrutiny. In practice, crisis management consultants also know that matters hinting of reputational risk quickly command executive attention because "if the public image is negative, the organization will be perceived as incompetent, inconsiderate, and unsuccessful."[40]

What is the lesson for defenders in a No Dark Corners workplace? Communicate suspicions of bad news rapidly, as at Nokia, and if unclear about whether the trust betrayer poses an existential risk, ask whether a worst-case impact would present a reputational risk to the institution. If so, then escalate the matter up the organizational command without delay.

ASSISTANCE WITH EVALUATING EXISTENTIAL MAGNITUDE

Contrary to popular fiction and adventure programs, there are no better qualified experts at assessing the severity that an insider threat may pose than the people within the institution who best understand its inner workings, critical operations, and interdependencies. There do exist, however, resources on a federal and local level that can offer perspective and connectivity to particular subject matter expertise with minimal risk of compromising the institution's equities. One of these resources resides within the DHS hierarchy; the other, at the local task force level. We now consider each it its turn.

DHS PROTECTIVE SECURITY ADVISORS

A small unheralded group of professionals who have begun to establish a certain cachet in infrastructure protection, Protective Security Advisors (PSA) exist to assist critical infrastructure custodians with their duties of stewardship. With no more than a handful of such individuals distributed across an entire state, DHS assigns each a portfolio of critical infrastructure organizations within a wide geographical footprint. The PSA visits his or her infrastructure clients, which consist of both public agencies and private companies, and also supplies them with training or guidance on site protection and topics of moment. Most of the training opportunities are free or heavily subsidized by DHS. Unlike other arms of DHS or law enforcement-related federal agencies, PSAs have no arrest powers or mandate to perform compliance inspections that result in citations or fines. Thus, their agenda closely parallels that of defenders seeking to safeguard their operations from hostile action, as opposed to eluding invasive or punitive action by government inspectors looking to find fault with facility owners and operators. As a result, the opportunity for establishing a peer-level collaboration with PSAs is significantly higher than it would be with, for example, OSHA inspectors, Fish and Game officers, or Transportation Security Administration freight or rail inspectors whose mandate to issue fines or citations can lose sight of the higher objective of assisting with prevention.

ROLE OF PROTECTIVE SECURITY ADVISORS, ACCORDING TO DHS

As of August 2011
Available to the public at http://www.dhs.gov/files/programs/gc_1265310793722.shtm

ENHANCING INFRASTRUCTURE PROTECTION

Regional Directors and PSAs assist owners and operators of critical infrastructure by coordinating requests for Department-provided services such as training, grants, and vulnerability assessments.

Regional Directors and PSAs provide an invaluable on-the-ground perspective to the Department's national risk picture by identifying, assessing, monitoring, and minimizing risk to critical infrastructure at the regional and local levels. They also assist law enforcement and state homeland security advisors with ongoing state and local critical infrastructure security efforts such as local exercises and planning initiatives.

Regional Directors and PSAs support security planning and coordination for National Special Security Events and other large-scale special events, including political meetings and economic summits (such as the G-20), sporting events (national championship games and series), and other national level special events.

ASSISTING WITH INCIDENT MANAGEMENT

Because Regional Directors and PSAs are strategically located across the country, they are often the first Department personnel to respond and deploy to emergencies and disasters. During an incident, they frequently work within state and local Emergency Operations Centers and at the Federal Emergency Management Agency Joint Field Office, where they:

- Advise the Department and other government and private sector representatives on interdependencies, cascading effects, and damage assessments concerning impacted critical infrastructure
- Help owners and operators, law enforcement personnel, and state and local officials prioritize and coordinate reentry and recovery activities

During the 2008 response to back-to-back Hurricanes Ike and Gustav, 32 PSAs were deployed from around the country to assist the impacted areas regular PSAs. This team helped reduce the extent of damage to critical infrastructure and hasten reconstitution and recovery. For example, they advised Department and other officials in real time on anticipated storm impacts to critical infrastructure and on how best to harness federal resources for the protection and reconstitution of infrastructure.

FACILITATING INFORMATION SHARING

Regional Directors and PSAs facilitate information sharing among all levels of government and the private sector. During steady-state (normal) operations, they conduct briefings and outreach meetings with critical infrastructure protection partners, help private sector personnel obtain security clearances, and disseminate critical infrastructure-related information such as protective measures reports.

Owner/Operator Requests

Regional Directors and PSAs also coordinate requests from owners and operators concerning Department programs and assistance, arrange for risk mitigation training, prepare critical infrastructure analytical reports and verification, and conduct security and vulnerability assessments.

Strengthening Regional Resilience

Regional Directors and PSAs actively promote and facilitate regional collaboration and information sharing, through the Regional Resilience Assessment Program (RRAP) and dedicated outreach to provide access to infrastructure protection (IP) programs and resources. RRAP evaluates critical infrastructure in specific geographic regions to examine vulnerabilities, threats, and potential consequences from an all-hazards perspective. RRAP assessments identify regional critical infrastructure dependencies, interdependencies, cascading effects and critical systems' ability to recover quickly from an event. More about regional partnerships and mission collaboration.

During Incidents

Regional Directors and PSAs are an important conduit of information on critical infrastructure response, recovery, and reconstitution resources. To inform decision making, they provide real-time data on ground conditions to the National Infrastructure Coordinating Center; Department leadership; and state, local, and private sector representatives.

Regional Directors and PSAs communicate directly with critical infrastructure owners and operators to assess damage to facilities and identify interdependencies and cascading effects, allowing responders to accurately prioritize and coordinate reentry and reconstitution efforts.

For example, during the response to Hurricanes Ike and Gustav in 2008, PSAs worked with the U.S. Army Corps of Engineers to prioritize generator requests from private industry, which allowed key industries to return to operation faster than anticipated. They also worked with Customs and Border Protection to organize helicopter overflights for the power company's survey of transmission lines. The flights captured imagery and data that permitted the companies to restore power faster than previously possible.

Of the three primary functions that PSAs serve, two offer the greatest potential to assist defenders in defeating insider threats, although somewhat indirectly. First, the PSA function to enhance infrastructure protection affords overall situational awareness that many employees of the institution may otherwise miss. This includes exposure to vulnerability assessments and training that might otherwise lie beyond the reach of smaller or financially strapped organizations. An institution finding itself excluded from the direct

purview of critical infrastructure may nevertheless, through business affiliations or community involvements, gain indirect access to PSA consultation.

Next, the PSA function to facilitate information sharing provides an independent
gateway to local and regional intelligence sharing and public–private partnerships that
the institution may otherwise find too esoteric or time-consuming to discover independently. Moreover, if a Terrorism Liaison Officer, Joint Terrorism Task Force, or state
fusion center relegates the defender to perfunctory attention out of reflexive habits that
rate as secondary any call originating outside of public safety channels, the PSA is in a
strong position to intervene. This intervention likely takes the form not so much of championing the defender but of conveying an analytical appreciation of how damage to the
institution could produce cascading impacts affecting the vital interests of all concerned.

PSAs will seldom be able to bring to bear special resources or finesse to expose the
hostile insider. However, they will be able to appreciate the defender's concerns about
what is at stake for a possible existential threat and will also be able to make common
cause with defenders to convey a sense of urgency to government agencies whose support
may be necessary to further a probe or interdict an attack.

LOCAL TASK FORCE ENTITIES WITH A PROTECTIVE MANDATE

Although the PSAs have a clearly identifiable role that remains supportive and constant,
local task forces vary in their mission, composition, resources, effectiveness, and longevity. A Joint Terrorism Task Force (www.justice.gov/jttf/) or Terrorism Liaison Officer
(www.tlo.org) program may offer linkage to the institution through corporate sentinels
and welcome the opportunity to collaborate on assessing emerging threats. Alternatively,
a program such as the FBI's Infragard (www.infragard.net) may offer more collaborative opportunities because of its aim to connect with the private sector, where many
other programs limit themselves to police-centric membership. Where such connectivity is uneven or one-sided, a local PSA may be able to spur improved collaboration as
noted above. However, there are other collaborative networks that may provide alternative pathways to resources otherwise inaccessible to defenders. Shortly after 9/11, for
instance, companies traditionally unallied with authorities sought a way to connect to
offer resources and exchange information, resulting in the ascendancy of the Business
Executives for National Security (BENS, www.bens.org). By engaging local authorities
at the police chief or special agent in charge level, BENS members found themselves with
a communications channel that vaults over bureaucratic hurdles when seeking priority
consideration for a concern of moment. Other work areas evolve collaborative networks
to address their constituents' particular needs within an industry or geographical area,
such as the California Utilities Emergency Association (www.cueainc.com), a utility-
supported nonprofit organization whose executive director is colocated with and serves
as a resource for the Governor's Office of Emergency Services. In addition to an endless
assortment of professional associations whose executives involve themselves with any
matter of urgent interest to their members, there are also informal groups that bring
like-minded professionals together and make useful referrals when necessary. One such
circle involved a gathering of Silicon Valley executives facilitated by McKinsey consultants who then advised a new chief executive facing unexpected wealth and prominence
on where to turn for answers to his concerns on how to avoid the kind of trauma a colleague in another business had previously experienced after being kidnapped. Similarly,

some Chicago and Milwaukee security directors started a monthly dinner meeting to discuss predicaments and exchange ideas on a non-attribution basis. The consistent value of all such relationships is that they afford direct, unencumbered channels for reaching experts and authorities when a defender is facing an existential threat and needs assistance without delay. One of the best such collaborations that predated 9/11/01, rose to international prominence, and then faded away in some jurisdictions as more formal, federally funded structures emerged to assume its role without always absorbing its ethos and effectiveness was the Terrorism Early Warning (TEW) Group under John Sullivan. Its leader's approach to unprecedented successes in collaboration is described in the text box that follows.

JOHN SULLIVAN AND EVOLUTION OF THE TERRORISM EARLY WARNING GROUP

This section is based on a 2008 interview with Lieutenant John P. Sullivan, Los Angeles County Sheriff's Department (LASD). Sullivan cofounded the first Terrorism Early Warning (TEW) Group, a collaborative network formed by and for local responders to monitor trends that could result in a regional terrorist attack.[41] The Los Angeles TEW became a national model, and John Sullivan gained recognition for leading well outside his immediate organization.

SULLIVAN'S RISE TO META-LEADER

In his work with the TEW, Sullivan epitomized what some observers say a meta-leader must be able to do: connect the purpose and work of different organizations, join diverse thinking into a coherent framework, and encourage a level of cross-agency collaboration that goes well beyond the leader's job description.[42] Moreover, absent the power of formal authority and a significant budget to subsidize his initiatives, this particular leader also had to call on personal credibility that stretched across organizational lines.[43] He linked organizations and people without the benefit of precedent or financing and, as meta-leader proponents would salute,[44] created something new that was mission-driven. How did Sullivan manage to do this, and why was he effective?

PERSONAL CREDIBILITY ACROSS ORGANIZATIONAL LINES

First, he began with a vision that leveraged his credible expertise. John Sullivan's interest in asymmetric warfare and the potential for radical organizations to threaten America traces to the 1978 Iranian Revolution, which focused his master's studies in policy analysis while he was working for the Port Authority in New York. His experience as a tactical medic informed his appreciation of what medical response teams need in responding to terrorist attacks. Later, as a deputy sheriff with the Emergency Operations Bureau at LASD, his knowledge, interests, and experience came together in 1996, when he played a lead role in piloting the TEW that would ultimately become the U.S. model for regional intelligence and security fusion centers. While still a deputy, Sullivan foresaw that it would take atypical and unprecedented networks and collaboration to address the growing terrorist threat. Based on some of the ideas of Arquilla and Ronfeldt[45] on the rise of networks to pose a threat in the post-Cold War age, Sullivan came to believe that collaborative, defensive networks of intelligence gathering for responders were the answer to the emerging threat. Fusing academic legitimacy through his own published studies with operational credibility through his law enforcement role in preparing for and responding to emergencies, Sullivan emerged as the natural champion of the TEW. With a handful of like-minded colleagues, he conceived a process for connecting multidisciplinary representatives into an inclusive setting with a flat hierarchy and a common purpose: defending against the emerging threat. Cutting across traditional barriers of rank and agency rivalry, Deputy Sullivan (at the time) brought together an unprecedented collection of more than 20 core and cooperating agencies, including the FBI, Secret Service, and multiple state and local response organizations.[46]

EVOLVING A CREATIVE FRAMEWORK BEYOND TRADITIONAL LINES OF AUTHORITY

At this point, Sullivan had enough interest and collaborators to shape the TEW into a forum for sharing information and ideas at the working responder level. Its trademark became the monthly plenary session of the TEW in Los Angeles. Although regionally focused from the start, the TEW came to host monthly speakers from across the globe. Since 1998, this author personally saw TEW presenters from Oklahoma City to London, Tel Aviv to Johannesburg, and Sydney to Washington, DC. Lacking the funds or formal authority to compel participation, he instead used his personal credibility, vast expertise of his growing community of interest, and an unprecedented culture of collaboration without regard for bureaucracy to make people want to join the TEW. Within one critical infrastructure organization, for example, John earned respect by following through on timely assessment of a threat of anthrax contamination in 1998. Whereas other, traditional response representatives of a larger agency took messages without returning calls and then took four hours more to deliver a message of concern but nothing else, the TEW was able to penetrate to the heart of the case and supply useful feedback within two hours. John Sullivan was able to gather and sanitize enough information on the maker and capabilities of the source of the threat to support utility decisions that would have had regional impact—and this without compromising a law enforcement investigation or any sensitive aspects of the case. From that point forward, the affected organization was not merely an advocate but a convert to the TEW collaborative process and supporter of its cross-agency value. Sullivan's monthly TEW meetings, offered free of charge and without frills, delivered more value in terms of subject matter and networking opportunities than comparable fee-charging meetings of three security and two emergency management organizations that this author and his colleagues attended in the same region.

Sullivan collaborated, communicated, and networked on many levels at once. He was the first to create a place for epidemiological intelligence in regional terrorism monitoring functions. He published papers and spoke at academic conferences on terrorism and preparations for chemical, biological, and radiological attack. His TEW model figured prominently in one Naval Postgraduate School thesis in the homeland security arena and in another in the realm of defense analysis.[47] His approach gained favorable notice of the Advisory Panel to Assess Domestic

Response Capabilities for Terrorism Involving Weapons of Mass Destruction (i.e., the Gilmore Commission), which devoted an entire appendix to the TEW model.[48] Most of Sullivan's influence gained momentum and adherents well before his promotions to sergeant and lieutenant—and also before 9/11/01.

EVOLVING WITH OPPORTUNITY

According to Sullivan, national attention followed his mention in the 2000 Gilmore Commission report. It opened the door to a pilot project for Sullivan to work on a six-city expansion of the TEW. Subsequently, Sullivan noted the strongest TEW successors emerged in Tulsa, Oklahoma, and in Snohomish County, Washington. After September 11, 2001, not only did the Los Angeles County Sheriff activate Sullivan's TEW as the primary entity devoted full-time to focusing on the regional terrorist threat, the Department of Justice's Office of Justice Programs also tied federal Urban Area Security Initiative grants to fostering of similar models. As explained by one observer, the TEW had

> . . . evolved from a small group of actors to a diverse, county-wide network bridging public–private, local–state–federal, and functional divides. The TEW demonstrates an example of organizational problem solving where a network facilitated collaboration in a wickedly complex and uncertain environment. The network's consensus-based innovation, collaborative processes, and meta-leadership helped the network evolve. These factors strengthened the collaborative ethos of the network and set the stage for success as the network meets current and future challenges. The TEW's bottom-up, consensus-based network expansion contrasts sharply with top-down collaborative approaches, such as the creation of the National Counterterrorism Center and Department of Homeland Security. Lessons from the TEW's well-paced evolution provide insight into how to facilitate collaborative action and build collaborative capacity for the future.[49]

WHAT MADE SULLIVAN EFFECTIVE

John Sullivan began with an idea larger than himself and, as Peter Drucker would have appreciated,[50] pursued that idea with a willingness to realize his relative unimportance compared to the task. He then placed a premium on collaboration and inclusiveness, with these highlights:

- He set an example for inclusiveness by inviting traditional rivals to not only participate but also set agendas. His recurring theme of "coproduction of intelligence" underscored his own conviction that prevention and response were better served by sharing information and analysis than by relying on isolated experts.
- The TEW cohesion was mission-driven and helped forge a common identity. A subtle but significant point as well, was that in 12 years of hosting TEW meetings, Sullivan never used these sessions to showcase his own scholarly publications or presentations, but instead kept the focus on the contributions of invited speakers and experts from a variety of disciplines.
- TEWs adopted, adapted, and promoted ideas generated from within. Following Sullivan's model, they thrived because they worked. He began

each monthly TEW plenary session with a reminder of house rules, including the treatment of all present as equals, with rank left outside the meeting room door. He also encouraged what some call ritual dissent[51] but Sullivan calls alternative analysis. In fact, at the suggestion of one of his military colleagues, Sullivan instituted an Alternative Analysis Cell in his LASD planning assignments to serve as devil's advocate and offer ideas distinct from accepted wisdom. Sullivan leveraged the Terrorism Liaison Officer (TLO) program for law enforcement agencies started by El Segundo Police Lieutenant John Skipper. Sullivan built on Skipper's six original police TLOs to promote TLOs for every city in Los Angeles County, and also brought fire and health department representation into the program. Today, TLOs are a nationwide fixture, although they may be called intelligence officers or Homeland Security liaison officers. Under Sullivan, TLOs became the outer sensing network of TEWs, and TEWs became the analytical heart of the first regional fusion centers.

LESSONS FOR HOMELAND SECURITY LEADERS

Homeland security leaders seeking to replicate the TEW's success at the grassroots level would do well to mirror Sullivan's collaborative and nonhierarchical approach to building a lasting network. The unifying trait linking John Sullivan's successes in attaining national reach with his TEW model repeatedly appear in his penchant for using "co-," as in cofounder of the TEW and coproduction of intelligence. It is the same kind of collaboration espoused in the strategy John Adams advocated in drawing popular support for a vision of independence that was a prelude to the American Revolution, where Adams

> . . . realized that if Congress told people what to do, then the outcome would be the responsibility of Congress. However, if they inspired others to act on their own accord, the responsibility and results would be the people's . . . With more people involved, there would be more ideas, more action to achieve the vision.[52]

Additionally, this collaboration led to the emergence of collective identity of TEW members and TLOs that, as some observers might suggest,[53] could be based on their mutual interactions and would easily have been lost if Sullivan had been forced upon the members as a formal leader. These values of Sullivan's would serve nascent leaders intent on producing successful collaborative networks beyond their immediate chains of command:

- Treat people as equals, as if their input is important. Avoid dictating to peers.
- Learn vicariously, by reading widely and listening to others willing to share their expertise in a specialized discipline. Promote such sharing by listening and by actively seeking it out.
- Use pilot programs to try out ideas of fellow collaborators. Embrace what works and do not hesitate to reengineer, overhaul, or scrap what does not work.

However, as useful as these channels may be, their value survives only as long as the channels are used judiciously and for serious matters. Thus, if the call goes out one day for what appears to be an existential risk and five calls follow the next day for assistance with threats that prove to be on the order of petty theft or vandalism, the bypass channel ceases to operate. The defenders making such calls then find themselves relegated back into the queue of bureaucratic name- and number-taking, where calls are taken in the order made and responses, if any, arrive in the fullness of time. Since one must not go to the well so often as to render it dry, it is useful for defenders to draw out in advance a number of scenarios that would allow a hostile insider to carry out existential damage to the institution. How does one do this? Consider red teaming.

RED TEAMING DEFINED

Red teaming enjoys multiple definitions that generally share common features. These features include the simulating of adversary thinking, tactics, approaches, and targeting to varying degrees, from conceptual consideration of alternatives up through carrying out mock attacks to test defenses. Within intelligence circles, red teaming is considered a subset of alternative analysis, which agencies presently encourage their analysts to perform as an alternative to groupthink or institutionalized myopia that contributed to the kind of failure to anticipate attacks such as the 9/11/01 use of passenger aircraft as guided missiles.[54] A periodical on this approach, which arose years before the 9/11 attacks, *Red Team Journal*, defines red teaming as

> The practice of viewing a problem from an adversary or competitor's perspective. The goal of most red teams is to enhance decision making, either by specifying the adversary's preferences and strategies or by simply acting as a devil's advocate. Red teaming may be more or less structured, and a wide range of approaches exists. In the past several years, red teaming has been applied increasingly to issues of security, although the practice is potentially much broader. Business strategists, for example, can benefit from weighing possible courses of action from a competitor's point of view. *Alternative analysis* is the superclass of techniques of which red teaming may be considered a member. As with red teaming, these techniques are designed to help de-bias thinking, enhance decision making, and avoid surprise.[55]

Other analysts see in red teaming a method of unmasking indicators of terrorist attack that should be observable but will likely go unnoticed in the absence of the kind of penetrating insight that red teaming produces.[56] Some key underpinnings of this school of analysis suggest that high-stakes targets—of the kind defenders would have reason to rate vulnerable to an existential attack from within—come with longer incubation periods, hence more opportunities for uncovering and potentially defeating attacks. Accordingly, the red team tasked with thwarting such an attack takes on the task of anticipating what kind of pre-strike attack indicators should be observable to defenders. This task the red team accomplishes by looking at the institution as a target through the eyes of an adversary. One of the challenges in adopting this approach is in enlisting into the red team the services of one or more individuals who possess the renegade's capacity for questioning assumptions, violating defender expectations, and probing for weakness with the eye of a skeptic and the daring of a buccaneer. If such talent exists within the confines of the institution, it resides in the contrarian who manages to subordinate predatory impulses in the service of the institution's core business and raison d'être. However, it is equally possible that even the most sophisticated organization composed of a diverse work force will nevertheless struggle to find an in-house red team member capable of at least the theoretical exercise of skullduggery, subterfuge, improvisation, and daring that an existential adversary would be prepared to unleash. Moreover, a good red team enhances this attacker's finesse with adaptive, forecasting skill—the kind that enables the opponent to stay three to five moves ahead in countering emerging defenses presented by the institution.[57]

WHERE TO RECRUIT RED TEAM MEMBERS

Where does one find ideal red team members? Answers vary. On the one hand, the benefits to looking inward and remaining strictly within the institution are manifest. Internal talent is readily available, easy to evaluate, and readily susceptible to taking on such an assignment with minimal fuss. Moreover, in the event that the red team unearths the kinds of exposure that would be embarrassing to the institution, keeping these vulnerabilities confined to a small internal audience is eminently feasible when relying exclusively on in-house talent. So is confirmation bias, however, which is the tendency for one's own people to see what they expect to see or to justify a conclusion already drawn.[58] The peril in infusing the insider threat team with employees operating with this confirmation bias is that doing so virtually guarantees that they see only those trust betrayers and opportunities for hostile action that are patently obvious or that the trust betrayer has scarcely bothered to conceal. Such discoveries are more likely to expose incidental threats of opportunists than existential threats devised by sophisticated adversaries and enabled by trained infiltrators.

Even in the rare cases where internal resources prove adept at sidestepping the culture that spawned them to simulate the innovative resourcefulness of a committed, freewheeling adversary, there may be more disincentives to red team victory than the institution may be prepared to recognize. In one vivid example of such an outcome, Malcolm Gladwell noted how a respected, senior military officer leading a sanctioned red team used unconventional tactics to defeat a superior force in an expansive, multiyear-planned military war game.[59] The red team victory evidently proved so humiliating to the Pentagon staff who had commissioned the red team, that exercise planners insisted on an artificial restart of the exercise and then serially altered the rules of play to render it impossible for the red team to repeat its victory. Extrapolating from this Pentagon experience to the average public or private institution, one may readily infer that there is little career benefit to be derived from being the red team leader or member responsible for embarrassing one's superiors. Indeed, the more spectacular the red team's discoveries on insider threat susceptibility become, the greater the implied criticism of other defenders—including bosses—who either did not discover the exposure or inadvertently contributed to its growth. Thus, only the independently wealthy, the callow stripling, or the tenured careerist with microambition would find themselves undeterred by the ramifications of being seen as the undefeatable adversary on the institution's red team.

Under these circumstances, it is probable that the institution will look to the outside for an infusion of perspective unencumbered by narrowness, confirmation bias, or apprehension over negative career consequences attending red team embarrassment of those in power. There are three principal sources of such outside assistance: government agencies, sister organizations, and consultants.

On the surface, government agencies offer three compelling advantages as purveyors of red team members. First, the vastness of government reach into temporal affairs assures that somewhere, someone cashing a public employee's paycheck will be compensated for earning a living at performing a task that the defending institution may find too specialized and arcane for doing itself. Whether it be for operating wiretaps or countersniper teams, there are tasks that could or should only legitimately be performed by government agencies. The second advantage that government agencies offer is that their services come with at least a perceived imprimatur that makes them difficult for the uninitiated to challenge. Thus, in the event that a red team makes the wrong call or goes astray, the presence of a government expert on that team diffuses liability and supplies cover for the rest of the team members. Finally, under the right circumstances, government participation can be affordable or free of charge—or at least unencumbered by an ostensible price tag. Sometimes, however, the avowed expertise offered up by a government red team may fall considerably short of its advertised capabilities, as the vignette in the text box illustrates.

A RED TEAM FADING TO GRAY

This is a true story illustrating a point in time, roughly 2003–2006, when a nascent arm of the Department of Homeland Security was finding its way with hastily assembled and deployed red teams for their ostensible benefit to critical infrastructure protection. Most of the principals have faded from existence, their employers have reorganized, and the related offers of expertise—at least to entities such as that described—have also declined to the point of oblivion, as of 2011. Precise identities are withheld in the interest of discretion.

THE OFFER

Office V (for Vulnerability, not an actual bureau), an arm of the DHS, eager to supply red team assistance free of charge, and to add into a national database the information gathered in the process, approached a large public utility, Utility X, with an offer DHS thought the utility could not refuse: a free, comprehensive vulnerability assessment conducted by a sophisticated red team composed of U.S. Navy SEALS and classified for protection of all the information that would likely result on vulnerabilities identified in the process.

HOW THE OFFER REACHED THE PROSPECTIVE BENEFICIARY

Office V, having little direct knowledge of Utility X and being innocent of its related industry and workings, turned to the Information Sharing and Analysis Center (ISAC) for that particular sector of infrastructure. Acting as V's broker, an ISAC representative made a call by reaching straight to the top. ISAC called the chief executive of X with an urgent request to have someone in infrastructure protection call V at the first opportunity on a matter of considerable moment. This call coincided with the second anniversary of the 9/11/01 attacks, thereby giving rise to executive concerns over whether ISAC's call was a prelude to DHS advice about an imminent attack on X or on X's sector.

THE DEVIL IN THE DETAILS

After resolving that V's call was not about any impending threat, X's security director scheduled a time to review the substance of V's offer and requirements at the latter's earliest convenience. This is what V proposed:

- Three weeks hence, a professional red team consisting mainly of Navy SEALS would descend on one of X's largest plants.
- The red team would study the plant extensively for vulnerabilities and engage in penetration testing, that is, trying to gain unauthorized entry. Time on site: one day, after which the red team would fly out of town to do the same thing for a different plant in another part of the state.
- The red team would write a comprehensive report of findings that would be classified, hence unavailable to the general public or potential adversaries.

EARLY MISGIVINGS

Although initially impressed by the red team offer, X's security director became circumspect, having had previous government service and having also conducted similar assessments for other public and private organizations. He asked probing questions, in answer to which the following additional details came forth:

- The red team would not actually consist of active duty SEALS or Navy personnel, but of military veterans working for a contractor to DHS which, at one point, had been founded by a retired service member who had some SEAL affiliation but may not have himself actually been a SEAL.
- The individual actually making the offer under the auspices of DHS was not a DHS employee but a contractor affiliated with the red team initiative.
- V was unfamiliar with the size and complexity of the billion-dollar plant he was proposing to have the red team analyze completely in a single day—a sheer impossibility if the findings were to be meaningful.
- V did not know that DHS was not the lead federal agency for X's critical infrastructure sector, nor had V nor anyone in his upper echelon coordinated with that lead federal agency, which had already required extensive vulnerability assessments to be conducted and submitted that year. Those vulnerability assessments, in the case of X, took almost 1 year to perform, analyze, and render into a comprehensive report. The report, in turn, had exceptionally limited distribution, controlled by the lead federal agency. Asked if he could arrange through DHS to visit that lead agency and first read that report before sending out the red team, V was caught off guard and said he would have to consult his superiors.
- V could not explain how he could manage to obtain national security clearances in a timely way to enable key staff from X to review V's report to (a) gain possible benefit from learning about undiscovered exposures and (b) to validate the accuracy and completeness of a "comprehensive" report of findings based on a single day's visit of a team that was flying off the next day to conduct another red team assessment.

VALUE ANALYSIS

In reviewing the cost vs. benefits of the proposed red team offer with senior management, X's security director reasoned that the V offer could at best produce one of three results. The V report could conclude that X's plant was underprotected, overprotected, or protected at about the appropriate level. However, it became clear that

V had a dilettante's grasp of the clearance process for national security which, at the time, was working off a backlog in excess of 500,000 or more background investigations to be completed for individuals already in the queue for security clearances in the aftermath of exponential demand after 9/11. As a result, X had no confidence that V would be able to arrange security clearances for anyone in X to be able to review the red team's report for accuracy and completeness before its publication and circulation in areas over which neither X nor the federal lead agency for that sector would be able to control. As a practical matter, this meant that if V concluded that X was ill defended, the first time X might find out about this would be through an elected representative seeking to find fault with X. On the other hand, if V's report concluded that X was overprotected, circulation of this conclusion— particularly if X had no opportunity to review or challenge this assertion—could reach X's governing body or lead federal agency and undermine long-term investments in infrastructure protection that X's governing body had just approved to be carried out with internal resources over a period of several years. Finally, if at the end of V's red team study and analysis the conclusion was that X was protected at an appropriate level, then the value of this finding was out of all proportion to the burden V was creating for X and, in any case, would hardly provide reassurance to any of X's constituents, since they would not have ready access to the classified report of findings.

FORMAL RESPONSE

Not wishing to appear an indifferent corporate citizen yet intent on performing due diligence and validating the worth of the red team offer before subscribing to it, X responded to V with the following conditions to meet before approving the red team effort:

- V was to issue a formal, written request from its government sponsor, presumably DHS, to an identified executive in X that spelled out who in V would perform what tasks, and for what objectives.
- The request would also explain in detail how V intended to safeguard from unauthorized release any vulnerability information that the red team produced.
- The request would stipulate that no red team report of X's facilities would be published without a formal review opportunity by X.
- Finally, V or its sponsoring agency would have to indicate coordination and approval of the lead federal agency for X's infrastructure sector.

OUTCOMES

While V was reviewing X's written statement of conditions to meet, X reached out to its lead federal agency, which expressed its own misgivings about this particular red team effort and the lack of coordination in launching it. Ultimately, V disengaged and retracted the red team offer. In subsequent years, when V's firm was being used to perform "assault planning" that was being used to justify DHS grants for funding of law enforcement investments to protect facilities such as X's that fell within a given police agency's jurisdiction, it became clear that the former red team members had turned into assault planners with little more unifying experience or credentials than one or two tours of recent military service. Eventually, V's firm lost its contract and faded from existence. Local law enforcement agencies took to performing their own assessments without V's "expertise." One witness to the process concluded that the biggest obstacle to V in arranging the red team visit to X's site was that none of the staff within V's organization responsible for arranging these visits possessed access to letterhead stationery or were authorized to issue formal communiqués on behalf of its DHS sponsor.

If government expertise for rounding out membership to a red team appears doubtful or comes with more strings than it is reasonable for the institution to accept (see preceding text box), then a useful alternative to groupthink and confirmation bias is to approach a sister agency to supply a red team member on loan. The advantage to such a course is that the red teamer on loan will be sufficiently familiar with the institution and the industry but not so inured to it as to be blind to what in-house employees may accept without challenge as the natural order of things. Thus, the red teamer on loan may question why a vendor making a delivery is left to range unescorted over a critical area, whereas everyone else on the team thinks nothing of this because "Everyone knows old Fred from UPS, and he won't hurt anything." Offsetting the value of such a loan is the possibility that intertwining relationships may influence the candor of the borrowed red team member. Thus, if the latter knows that her agency is about to enter into a joint venture with the institution assembling the red team, or if she has hopes of leaving her current employer for a better position with the institution in question, she may shade her red team contributions out of concern for adverse ramifications, particularly if at the point of presenting an embarrassing finding.

A consultant possessed of otherwise unavailable expertise can be an asset or liability to the red team. If he has a demonstrable command of how adversaries exploit vulnerabilities and skills of the renegade or contrarian to balance out areas where the team is lacking in diversity, there is a good chance that the consultant can be an outstanding contributor, particularly if it becomes the consultant who voices controversial findings that other red team members may be reluctant to raise for fear of embarrassing their bosses. However, even the best consultant can become a liability if the nature of the consulting agreement is such that it incentivizes identifying or creating more and more problems to solve in order to add billable hours to the consulting contract. Moreover, if not carefully vetted, any consultant may present the same kind of doubtful value that some government agencies offer—only with a much larger price tag.

RED TEAMING VALUE TO COUNTERING EXISTENTIAL INSIDER THREATS

The obvious reasons for engaging in red teaming to counter insider threats are twofold: (1) identifying vulnerabilities in the absence of the kind of incontrovertible evidence that only comes after an attack, and (2) raising organizational security awareness, hence improving defenses to the level of deterring or at least disrupting trust betrayers from hostile action. Less obvious but of no less consequence is that there may be occasion when, absent red teaming, defenders would be at a loss about how to react to suspicions of a hostile insider being at large but as yet undetectable with any certainty. This dilemma applies particularly to existential threats for which the institution has already implemented basic defenses. Thus, the fashion house that lives or dies by the safeguarding of its avant-garde designs until their scheduled debut shares some imperatives in common with the Secret Service detail protecting the target of an assassination attempt and with the intelligence agency holding the name of the general it has recruited from the enemy's camp.

All these defenders recognize that the assets in their care take top priority when it comes to being secured from all threats, including those from within. Accordingly, each defending organization must have already expended effort and resources in taking at least those prudent measures that represent the industry standard for protection against trust betrayers. The more diligent will even exceed whatever the standard happens to require. Thus, all may limit access to their vital asset and to any related information on whereabouts or secured locations without having to be told this is a good idea. They may institute two-person integrity rules to bar any single individual from having unmonitored, sole access to the vital asset at any time. They may overlay supplemental access controls on round-the-clock surveillance camera monitoring to increase to near certainty the detection of anything untoward that may impinge upon the irreplaceable asset. They may even redouble their vetting for all who get near the asset, making sure that such individuals undergo a supplemental background investigation and clearance process before being allowed to enter the innermost circle of trust. However, realizing that all security systems are fallible and seldom work 100% as conceived for 100% of the time, experienced defenders may still find themselves with a gnawing apprehension that they may be missing something and that the asset may be at greater risk than appearances suggest. This apprehension magnifies at the first adumbration of an anomaly. Someone opens the strong room's door to a janitor, who should never be allowed close to the asset. This event could be explained away as an accident. It could also be the result of an infiltrator making a probe as a prelude to striking. After double-checking all security measures in place, however, what options does the defender have under these circumstances?

Ratcheting up protective measures in the absence of an ostensible threat becomes redolent of the ravings of paranoia. No institution will long support rising security burdens that appear unwarranted or out of proportion to the object sought. Still, the defender may be intuitively detecting the makings of an attack by cues too subtle to process and articulate until after the fact. To the defender who cannot justify added security measures on the basis of intuition alone, however, red teaming may be the only viable option. By putting together a credible red team, the defender enlists other perspectives and substantially increases the chance that the red team will uncover under-appraised weaknesses or dispel unfounded apprehension. If it is the former, then the red team lends a full chorus to voice concerns upward, instead of leaving them to echo in the falsetto of a sole, worried defender. If it is the latter, then the red team reassures the institution and stewards of assets that no failures of due diligence have exposed the asset to undue risk.

In such a setting, it falls to the red team to focus its individual member and synergistic energies on the attacker's challenge from the adversary's point of view. For threats the institution clearly recognizes as existential, such as those postulated above, frontal attack is unlikely to be an option, although no one should prohibit the red team from considering it. Soon, however, the red team will turn to exposures from within as a more likely access point to the target. The more energetic red teamers will probe to uncover gaps in defenses by asking, "How does the security actually in place compare to what we think is in place?" From there, the team will begin to follow or, ideally, anticipate the steps an adversary would need to take in order to strike the targeted institution for greatest impact. Even though the rules may call for only certain, highly vetted security guards to be allowed near the targeted asset, for example, the red team may discover that when staffing levels fall short and one of those guards succumbs to food poisoning, a new guard who was in the queue for this assignment but has not yet undergone the entire vetting process will be allowed to fill in as a stopgap measure. To the rest of the institution, this minor personnel action may appear as an infrequent, acceptable risk because it happens so rarely that it cannot be reliably available for an adversary to exploit, and the new guard has shown signs of being nothing other than competent and trustworthy. Faced with the same circumstances, though, a red teamer assumes the personnel action was orchestrated, that the new guard administered food poison to the old guard when taking the latter out to dinner the preceding evening. Or perhaps it takes a red teamer to question the true motives of the insider who never takes a vacation and always happens to be available to fill in for peers working on a trade secret who need to leave the job for half an hour to arrange for daycare. Is this person being helpful, or is this a trust betrayer who is quietly taking advantage of others to benefit from the kind of unescorted access that the institution thought it had managed to prohibit? A red team could ask these indelicate questions that other employees would accept without challenge.

RED TEAM MEMBERS FROM WITHIN

Although an institution may rely on outsiders to participate in the red team to varying degrees, some internal involvement is inevitable. Only insiders can supply the details of which actions can produce what consequences, what cascading impacts result from which kinds of damage, and who might be irreplaceable at a moment critical for the survival of the institution. Moreover, since external red teamers have no authority to implement change or issue orders within the organization, the in-house employees who will be responsible for acting on red team recommendations retain a vested interest in charting these recommendations to benefit from a full understanding of their genesis and value. Consequently, the red team will require at least some internal representation from management and from subject matter experts.

DRAWING FROM THE RISK OR VULNERABILITY ASSESSMENT TEAM

In seeking out internal red team members, defenders may find themselves drawn to the same employees who informed a risk or vulnerability assessment. In the case of a relatively small organization, it may be impossible to do otherwise, as there may only be a handful of employees, with all routinely filling many different roles. Some cautions on filling both teams from the same bench may be in order, however. First, an employee who has made a material contribution to the organization's risk or vulnerability assessment has a vested interest in defending that product. By the nature of its proceedings, however, a fully functioning red team is obligated to unearth exposures that one of those other assessments missed. Overpopulating the red team with the producers of one of these previous assessments risks infecting the red team with a confirmation bias that will predispose the group to validate the status quo as captured in a previous assessment or at least soften any presentation of exposures that would retroactively cast doubt on the merits of the risk or vulnerability assessment. Under the circumstances, if the institution must draw on the same people to participate in the red team, it should at least ensure that the red team leader is uncontaminated by such bias and preferably unconnected with precursor assessments.

RED TEAMING MORE FOR EXISTENTIAL THAN NONEXISTENTIAL THREATS

If red teaming is such a useful approach, one might wonder, why not use it universally for anticipating and countering any insider threat? This question ultimately becomes an issue of quality and resource that only management can decide in favor of the institution's best interests. A red team is only as good as the quality of participation it engenders. In theory, the best red teams will draw on the best people, including internal employees and outsiders as needed. However, the best people tend to be the most valuable, the most productive, and the most in demand. One does not keep maximizing the strengths of one's best employees by assigning them to red teams in perpetuity. In practice, then, in order to be worth enlisting the best people for the red team effort, the effort itself must not present an undue or overfrequent burden that translates into lost productive time. Otherwise, faced with too many routine requests to give up employees for red team duty, managers will resort to the expedient of offering up mediocrity instead of excellence in the form of employees that they can afford to spare. In consequence, red teams composed of minor performers who lack the intellectual voltage, organizational insight, or industry experience to make more meaningful contributions will soon transform the red team from a capability to a liability, from a tool that maximizes creativity to a bureaucratic process that goes through the motions without adding value. The only way to prevent such diminishing returns is to limit red team formation to serious cases, that is, to existential threats or those threats perceived as reputational risks in the eyes of a senior executive.

What about threats that appear insubstantial on the surface but evolve into existential threats or produce significant reputational risk? One such case started out as a risk-taking trader—surely no unique problem in banking houses—yet ultimately evolved into an insider fiasco that resulted in the collapse of Baring's Bank. (See text box for details of the case and discussion of its escalation into a quintessential threat to the institution.)

UNCHECKED INSIDER RISK TURNED EXISTENTIAL THREAT

A 233-year-old merchant bank in London whose clients included the British royal family, Barings Banks collapsed in 1995 as the result of being overextended by rogue trader Nick Leeson. The latter's unauthorized trading in the Asian derivatives market produced approximately $1.3 billion in losses. Unable to recover from the magnitude of the loss, Barings closed, selling for a single British pound to a Dutch buyer. Evidently, Leeson rose from relative obscurity to progressively higher trading positions with financial houses because he appeared to understand a market that was impenetrable to his superiors and because his actions initially produced impressive profits for his employer. The institution gave Leeson a general manager's post in Barings' Singapore operation at a young age, along with chief trader authority and free rein to make complicated investments with virtually no oversight, circumstances for which Leeson blamed his own superiors in his tell-all memoir written in prison.[60]

Leeson did not appear to be an insider threat because he was in charge of both making trades and balancing accounts and had managed to create an account in which he buried his trading losses from scrutiny. Although in almost 15 years since his original memoir he softened his criticism of his Barings superiors as too proud to reveal their ignorance of the mechanics and perils of trading on derivatives or futures, he nonetheless continued to proclaim, "It was clear Barings were incompetent, and their lack of oversight was appalling."[61]

Analysts of the debacle,[62] supported by Leeson's own admissions, including in his latter-day appearances in a speaker's circuit where he lectures on the kind of financial risk he personified, find these consistent themes in his actions that led to the ultimate existential challenge for Barings:

- Absence of basic controls or checks and balances
- Poor understanding of the business Leeson was transacting
- Inadequate oversight, that is, no one was supervising Leeson's activities
- Unclear reporting lines, as he had different bosses in London and Singapore who nominally monitored Leeson's work

From a defender's perspective, it appears that if such basic due diligence was lacking, the institution victimized equally lacked the capacity to assess the presence or impact of this internal threat until catastrophic losses rose to a point of no return.

The lesson from the Barings case is that the dividing line between an existential and nonexistential threat is thin, gray, or even invisible if basic oversight is lacking. In reality, top management must decide whether a given insider problem has risen to the level of an existential threat or one that poses sufficient reputational risk to merit an extraordinary response or assignment of resources, including red teams. Such leadership decisions may ultimately find defenders assembling a red team to address a threat that may seem minor yet transform itself into an elemental issue of survival. Then again, the insider threat may seem severe enough to justify a red team yet devolve into a glorified nuisance. Because of the resources and potential ramifications involved, however, the decision to treat a given case as an existential insider threat rests with top management, whose prerogatives and responsibilities in the matter are dispositive. In any event, the institution will not be ready to assign its best employees to a red team constituted to uncover and thwart an insider unless the case bears the hallmarks of an existential threat: one involving reputational risk or command sufficient executive interest to merit executive support and institutional priority. In some cases, as with any of top management's prerogatives, employees may differ on whether they rate the matter the same way that their bosses do. However, if top management cannot be convinced of the significance of the threat, it will withhold the resources necessary to deploy every available tool to its resolution and, like Barclays, even march unaware to its own demise before recognizing any risk at all.

WORSE CASE AND WORST CASE SCENARIOS

Manifestly, as discussed up to this point, the infiltrator supported by a dedicated, professional cell of adversaries is in the position to deliver the most catastrophic blow to the targeted institution. Yet, worst case scenarios such as this are not necessarily the most probable, and the institution's top management may have sound business reasons for according higher priority to other kinds of threats. For example, a threat of workplace violence may be unlikely to culminate in events that are fatal to the institution. Rampage killings tend to be too personal, hence more limited in scope and intensity than what would be necessary to bring an entire institution to its knees. However, for the individual or individuals caught in the crosshairs, a workplace violence threat is very real and also a potential threat to one's existence. Thus, it gives the intended victims little reassurance to announce that just because their lives may be in jeopardy does not mean that the employer will face collapse. What is a theoretical worse but not worst case for the organization is a worst case for the individual. Additionally, left unaddressed, the outcome of such a threat can produce cascading consequences that result in reputational risk for top management and for the employer itself. The organization that ignores danger to its employees wins no awards for superior management or stakeholder confidence.

One of the difficulties in treating incidents of workplace violence as existential threats is their sheer frequency in the modern place of business. For many years in the United States, workplace violence has been the primary cause of job-related fatalities for women and the second leading cause of death in the workplace overall, with men as victims in three out of four workplace homicides.[63] Given that modern institutions have at least begun to address their responsibilities and options for contending with such situations, a channel already exists for organizational response to threats of violence from disgruntled insiders. Under the circumstances, the institution is unlikely to assemble a red team to anticipate how a hostile insider may go about attacking a supervisor or even a member of top management. However, the threat assessment team whose task it is to convene to evaluate whether an individual poses an imminent threat is likely to deliver the same value in safeguarding people at risk as the red team would in defending an institution in peril.

WHEN RED TEAM OR SPECIAL RESOURCES ARE NOT AN OPTION

All institutions exist to serve a purpose usually distinct from mere survival. The organization in the throes of a grand struggle to meet its core duties under adverse circumstances may have little to spare for even an agreed-upon defense against a likely existential threat. The platoon taking enemy fire has no leisure to relieve a private from feeding a crew-served machine gun as the enemy advances, just because that private acted suspicious. Nor may the company fighting a hostile takeover have time to assemble a red team to figure out how the opposition could have obtained confidential instructions from the board of directors. In these cases, the fallback remains to rely on the advance investment made in implementing No Dark Corners enhancements to the workplace so that team members, their supporting corporate sentinels, and first-line managers and supervisors are equipped and empowered to do their best to defeat existential threats as they arise. In these circumstances, it is important to take full advantage of transparency, team self-monitoring via the copilot approach, and collaborative engagement of all hands to defend against the threat even if it is not fully identified or traced. As one successful contrarian business leader said, "Secrecy is overrated as an asset and underrated as a liability."[64]

At the same time, when conflicting priorities make inordinate demands of scarce resources, the institution must engage in protective triage. This means not only prioritizing so as to focus only on the most dangerous insider threats, but also making tough decisions to take effect temporarily pending a return to conditions more conducive to other tactics. Thus, the beleaguered institution may find it necessary to staff its critical operations center around the clock during a period of crisis, thereby eliminating opportunities for a hostile insider to sneak in when the site is unattended while, at the same time, improving flow of information so that a team member is on hand at all times to report any new incoming information pertaining to the operational crisis. Distributing greater workloads across the board also takes away the time and opportunity that a hostile insider needs for carrying out mischief, and when everyone else is working at full throttle, the peer who is idling invites negative scrutiny and even disciplinary action.

AVOIDING WARNING FATIGUE

One unintended consequence of becoming proficient at mobilizing red teams or any resources to tackle an emerging insider threat of existential proportions is that this capacity may become overextended, resulting in warning fatigue, which can undermine insider defenses when most needed.

Warning fatigue is a phenomenon associated with "crying wolf syndrome," or the raising of a false alarm so many times that help fails to come when really needed. In application to existential threats, this phenomenon became associated with the Homeland Security Advisory System (HSAS) and its initial application. Indeed, HSAS's connection with crying wolf syndrome[65] contributed to the public loss of confidence or warning fatigue. Warning fatigue is by no means unique to homeland security matters or to HSAS. The phenomenon appears in alerts relating to severe weather natural disasters.[66] It has been observed in such diverse circumstances as the approach of the millennium[67] and U.S. Food and Drug Administration warnings that accompany new drugs entering the market.[68] The computer industry is also no stranger to this phenomenon, as there are even signs that software developers sensitive to it are cautioning fellow developers to be sparing in the number and theatricality of the warnings they present to average computer users.[69]

Warning fatigue occurs in many contexts and consistently emerges when a target audience feels it has been bombarded by cautions and predictions of dire consequences, whether these cautions are associated with drugs, health, weather, or terrorist attacks.[70] The more these dire consequences fail to materialize, the more likely are the warning's recipients to ignore warnings over time. Within the province of homeland security, policymakers fear that a jaded public, suffering from warning fatigue, will fail to act or take improper action, even if analysts provide sound, actionable intelligence. A by-product of warning fatigue is that policymakers become predisposed to heed warnings that confirm their preconceptions while dismissing those that do not.[71] As a result, absent careful attention to the manner and substance of existential insider threat warnings, it is increasingly probable that even the best warning will reach a receptive audience of defenders.

The full spectrum of options ranges from reserving warnings only for confirmed, imminent attacks to broadcasting regular warnings upon the first hint of a threat. The first, close-hold approach of withholding issue of warnings in the absence of absolute confirmation of an impending attack denies defenders the opportunity to save lives, bolster defenses, and at least mitigate those losses that they may not be able to prevent. On the other hand, the second, share-it-all approach of transmitting warnings whenever there is even a remote chance of an attack is equally problematic. Such an approach appears self-serving, in that it smacks of a bureaucratic attempt at self-indemnification against future charges of knowing but withholding threat information from potential targets and victims. Moreover, this approach exemplifies the crying wolf syndrome and, by contributing to warning fatigue, increases the likelihood that future, more credible warnings will be ignored after having inundated the workplace in a sea of doomsday caveats and false alarms. Finally, this approach plays into the hands of the institution's critics. Under the circumstances, either extreme is unsupportable.

Recommended: The Software Developer Approach

Although it is difficult to find the right balance and middle ground between the foregoing extremes, the computer industry appears to offer sound advice that can be adapted to warnings of existential insider threats.[72] Some examples follow.

- To prevent warning fatigue, avoid showing security dialogs in situations that are common and not actually dangerous.
- Use warnings with "scariness" appropriate to the situation. When a site is trying to install software, a dialog with bold warning text is appropriate.
- Minimize the amount of text on security dialogs. The more text a dialog contains, the more likely it is that users will ignore the text completely.

Synthesizing this advice into warnings of existential insider threats could yield the following courses of action:

1. To prevent warning fatigue, avoid inflation. Use warnings only for uncommon, dangerous situations, not for routine ones. In particular, avoid this kind of anemic warning often seen concluding official pronouncements: "We have no credible, specific information suggesting an imminent attack."[73] There is no value in perpetuating these kinds of advisories, but eliminating them would diminish warning fatigue.
2. Resist the tendency to make dire predictions that rely on fear to promote compliance—an ineffective technique. As keynote speaker and management authority Tom Peters observed at a security industry conference, "Fear is not the answer. In your business, it's easy to scare people. It's not wrong because it isn't moral. It's wrong because it doesn't work."[74]
3. Avoid padding warnings with extraneous matter and, instead, focus only on the useful and the credible. If a warning is credible, its informative content will stand on its own. The lengthier the indirectly related background material, the lengthier the time to process both for analyst and recipient. Besides, the actionable part of a warning is easier to distribute more widely if unencumbered with details that might give away intelligence sources or methods, which would require more restrictions on sharing the report. The resulting delay in and more restricted sharing of the warning serve no one.

CONCLUSION

Existential insider threats represent the greatest challenge for defenders because the stakes are high and the issues demanding. The infiltrator backed by a state-sponsored terror cell may well constitute the most formidable of existential threats using a hostile trust betrayer. However, the defending organization may not have the luxury of being able to categorize the precise nature of the threat as existential or its origin until it is too late to intervene. It generally makes sense to align oneself with the DHS in seeking government partners to assist with the evaluation or countering of an existential insider threat. DHS contains more agencies involved in some aspect of existential threat defense than any other single government entity. However, this by no means assures that the right DHS resource will match the institution's needs when an existential insider threat emerges. One way of marshaling available internal resources to anticipate the existential insider threat is to use red teams to uncover heretofore unseen vulnerabilities and to predict where an adversary would strike. The difficulty, however, is that such approaches are demanding of the institution and require the right kinds of participants to yield positive value. They may also divert resources from core responsibilities and can eventually become ineffective or counterproductive; hence, the wisdom of restricting their use to the more serious, existential threats that top management may alone be able to decide based on internal yardsticks or some determination of whether a given situation is beginning to pose a reputational risk. The fallback, when red teaming or other resources are unavailable to deploy, is to maximize No Dark Corners strategies in the workplace, relying on engagement at the team level and support from corporate sentinels and frontline managers to defend against trust betrayers without necessarily resorting to special instructions or resources that may not be available depending on what other circumstances are impinging upon the institution at the time. A final caution against warning fatigue illuminates the counterproductive aspect of focusing on existential threats beyond reason, to the point of losing internal support and inadvertently creating more maneuvering room for the hostile insider to operate while escaping notice.

QUESTIONS FOR ONLINE OR CLASSROOM DISCUSSION

1. When would a career employee who has turned criminal or mercenary be less of an existential insider threat than an infiltrator backed by a state-sponsored terrorist organization?
2. Why is prevention of an existential attack more important to the institution than apprehension of the attacker, particularly if it is possible to catch the hostile insider in the act?
3. In the case described in "How One Event's Cascading Impact Ended a Line of Business," what differences in outcome might have arisen for Nokia and Ericsson if Phillips' plant in Albuquerque had been damaged by insider-triggered arson instead of a storm?
4. What makes it wiser to begin security planning by asking what is critical instead of what is the threat?

EXERCISES FOR GROUP PROJECTS

1. Identify a case not mentioned in this chapter where red teaming offered defensive value and, at the same time, possible embarrassment to the larger organization. Comment on what factors may undermine the red teaming effort or improve its traction within the organization.
2. Under what circumstances could red teaming or other No Dark Corners approaches avail in a case such as the Barings collapse?
3. Why have decapitation attacks such as the two described here repeatedly failed, while other existential attacks with lesser objectives and fewer plotters succeeded?
4. Characterize the ideal red team and its opposite. Specifically, what attributes would virtually assure that a red team fails to add value in defending against an existential insider threat?

ENDNOTES

1. C. Marighella, "Minimanual of the Urban Guerrilla," in *No One a Neutral: Political Hostage-Taking in the Modern World*, ed. N. Antokol and M. Nudell, Medina, OH: Alpha Publications, 1990, pp. 229–230.
2. B. Hoffman, *Inside Terrorism, Revised and Expanded Edition*, New York: Columbia University Press, 2006, p. 261.
3. Ibid., p. 261.
4. R. Clutterbuck, *Kidnap and Ransom: The Response*, London: Faber and Faber, 1978, p. 88.
5. T. M. O'Sullivan, "Comparative Risk Analysis," in *Terrorism and Homeland Security: Thinking Strategically about Policy*, ed. P. R. Viotti, M. A. Opheim, and N. Bowen, Boca Raton, FL: CRC Press, 2008, p. 149.
6. R. Clutterbuck, pp. 91–96.
7. Ibid., p. 90.
8. U.S. Department of Labor, *OSHA Fact Sheet*, 2002. Retrieved August 8, 2011 from http://www.osha.gov/SLTC/workplaceviolence.
9. D. S. Fenn, R. Flynn, P. Taylor, and T. Moore, *Jane's Facility Security Handbook*, 2nd ed., Surry, UK: Jane's Information Group, 2006, p. 33.
10. See T. Williams, Ed., *Protection of Assets*, Santa Monica, CA: POA Publishing, 2000, pp. 2–1 to 2–50. This four-volume manual is a mainstay in the security industry, taking up four binders which some practitioners choose to update annually by subscription, while others choose to replace the entire manual every few years or as new content emerges.
11. O. Falluci, "Interview with George Habash," *Life Magazine*, June 12, 1970 and also cited in Hoffman, B., *Inside Terrorism, Revised and Expanded Edition*, New York: Columbia University Press, 2006, p. 249.
12. Hoffman, p. 229.
13. Clutterbuck, p. 89.
14. P. F. Drucker, *Managing the Non-Profit Organization*, New York: HarperCollins, 1992, p. 9.
15. Hoffman, pp. 30–33.

16. Ibid. and also noted in Counterterrorism Threat Assessment and Warning Unit, *Terrorism in the United States, 2000/2001*, Washington, DC: US Department of Justice, FBI Publication #0308, 2002, p. 3.

17. Ibid. and also in Public Law 107-296, November 25, 2002, p. 7 of 187. Retrieved August 10, 2011 from http://www.dhs.gov/xlibrary/assets/hr_5005_enr.pdf.

18. D. Foreman, "Strategic Monkeywrenching" in *Ecodefense: A Field Guide to Monkeywrenching*, 3rd ed., ed. Anonymous, 1993. Retrieved August 10, 2011 from http://theanarchistlibrary.org/HTML/Various_Authors_Ecodefense_A_Field_Guide_to_Monkeywrenching.html#toc3.

19. Presidential Decision Directive 63, *Critical Infrastructure Protection*, Washington, DC: The White House, May 22, 1998. Retrieved August 10, 2011 from http://www.fas.org/irp/offdocs/pdd/pdd-63.htm.

20. See T. G. Lewis, *Critical Infrastructure Protection in Homeland Security*, Hoboken, NJ: John Wiley & Sons, 2006, for additional discussion on how all infrastructures depend to some degree on the Tier 1 critical infrastructures.

21. Y. Sheffi, *The Resilient Enterprise*, Cambridge, MA: The MIT Press, 2007, p. 52.

22. Details on this case are increasingly cited in multiple references, including D. Apgar, *Risk Intelligence: Learning to Manage What We Don't Know*, Boston: Harvard Business School Press, 2006, pp. 47–49, and Y. Sheffi, *The Resilient Enterprise*, Cambridge, MA: The MIT Press, 2007, pp. 4–15.

23. Sheffi, p. 5.

24. G. Singh, "Bomb-laden Trucks Planned in Toronto Terror Plot," *Tha Indian News*, June 10, 2008. Retrieved August 10, 2011 from http://www.thaindian.com/news portal/world-news/bomb-laden-trucks-planned-in-toronto-terror-plot_10058809.html.

25. R. Collier, "Al Qaeda Warning by King of Jordan Abdullah Says His Forces Thwarted Major Bomb Plot," *San Francisco Chronicle*, April 17, 2004. Retrieved August 10, 2011 from http://www.windsofchange.net/archives/special_analysis_the_amman_plot_and_project_al-zabadi.html.

26. I. Teotonio, "Homegrown Terror Case Goes to Trial," *Toronto Star*, September 24, 2007. Retrieved August 10, 2011 from http://www.thestar.com/News/Canada/article/260004.

27. L. Michel and D. Herbeck, *American Terrorist: Timothy McVeigh and the Oklahoma City Bombing*, New York: ReganBooks, 2001, pp. 398–402.

28. D. Sieberg, "Akamai: Co-founder Dies in WTC Plane Crash," *CNN.com*, September 11, 2001. Retrieved August 11, 2011 from http://articles.cnn.com/2001-09-11/tech/akamai.founder_1_uniform-web-infrastructure-akamai-technologies-tom-leighton?_s=PM:TECH.

29. K. L. Herbig, *Changes in Espionage by Americans: 1947–2007*, Technical Report 08-05, Monterey, CA: Defense Personnel Security Research Center, March 2008.

30. Fenn et al., p. 57.

31. N. Antokol and M. Nudell, *The Handbook for Effective Emergency and Crisis Management*, Lexington, MA: Lexington Books, 1988, p. 3.

32. *National Strategy for Homeland Security*, Washington, DC: Office of Homeland Security, President of the United States, July, 2002, p. 2.

33. Analytical Risk Methodology (ARM) (n.d.). Booz, Allen & Hamilton and Risk Assessment Methodology for Water (RAM-W), Sandia Corporation, 2002. For

readers interested in details, both methodologies offer the basic risk equation, $R = V \times C$, where Risk is defined as a function of Vulnerability and Consequence. Vulnerability is the component most closely associated with security, since $V = 1 - Pe$ further refines the vulnerability component of the basic equation, based on the Sandia method (q.v.). Thus the original equation expands to $R = (1 - Pe) \times C$. The security component involves P, which stands for the protective system. Pe stands for the effectiveness of the protective system. The Sandia method assigns numerical values for ratings of High (0.9), Medium (0.5), and Low (0.1). Thus, if the effectiveness of the protective system is High, then its Vulnerability will be expressed as 1–0.9 (from the equation where $V = 1 - Pe$). The resulting value is 0.1, which equates to Low. This yields a quantitative representation to the effect that if a security system's effectiveness is high, its vulnerability should indeed be low—an inverse relationship.

34. Driving fatalities, according to statistics attributed to the U.S. Transportation Secretary, accounted for 42,642 deaths in 2006—during what was a record low year for traffic deaths. This information is from a news wire service article picked up by the *Earth Times* and published on July 24, 2007.

35. C. S. Lewis, *The Abolition of Man*, New York: Macmillan, 1947, p. 91.

36. *National Infrastructure Protection Plan*, Washington, DC: Department of Homeland Security, 2009, p. 19.

37. J. Badaracco, *Leading Quietly*, Boston: Harvard Business School Press, 2002, p. 3.

38. D. Apgar, *Risk Intelligence*, Boston: Harvard Business School Press, 2006, p. 28.

39. D. Atkins, I. Bates, and L. Drennan, *Reputational Risk: A Question of Trust*, London: Lesson Professional Publishing, 2006, p. 5–6.

40. N. Antokol and M. Nudell, *No One a Neutral: Political Hostage-Taking in the Modern World*, Medina, OH: Alpha Publications, 1990, p. 29.

41. The Gilmore Commission's second report (RAND, 2002) addresses these functions at greater length on pages G-1 and G-5, as well as in an entire section of its report, Appendix G. See Note 48, below, for additional details.

42. L. Marcus, B. Dorn, and J. Henderson, "Meta-Leadership and National Emergency Preparedness," in *Center for Public Leadership: Working Papers*, Harvard University: John F. Kennedy School of Government, 2006, p. 44.

43. Ibid., p. 45. This ability is another of the meta-leader's distinctions from the formally established leader.

44. Ibid., p. 46.

45. J. Arquilla and D. Ronfeldt, Eds., *In Athena's Camp: Preparing for Conflict in the Information Age*, Santa Monica, CA: RAND Corporation, 1997, p. v, Preface. Sullivan worked directly with these two analysts prior to the publication of their work and was also given a chapter in one of their subsequent publications.

46. Gilmore Commission II (RAND, 2002, op. cit.), p. G-6, lists the 20 agencies that made up the initial group.

47. Michael Grossman's thesis focused on the TEW as a smart practice for the Center for Homeland Defense and Security. Major S. Rust's thesis, Collaborative Network Evolution: The Los Angeles Terrorism Early Warning Group, was prepared for a master of science in defense analysis — not for a master's in Homeland Security. The quote that follows later comes directly from Rust's abstract.

48. RAND Corporation, *Second Annual Report of the Advisory Panel to Assess Domestic Response Capabilities for Terrorism Involving Weapons of Mass Destruction* (aka Gilmore Commission Report #2) Appendix G: Los Angeles Area Case Study. Arlington, VA: RAND Corporation, 2002, pp. G-5 to G-7.

49. S. Rust, *Collaborative Network Evolution: The Los Angeles Terrorism Early Warning Group*. Master's thesis, Naval Postgraduate School, Monterey, 2006, abstract.

50. P. Drucker, "Leadership Is a Foul-Weather Job," in *Managing the Non-Profit Organization*, New York: HarperBusiness, 1992, pp. 9–27. Drucker identifies this and three other basic leadership competencies that Sullivan also displayed in the TEW's formation, including willingness to listen, willingness to communicate, willingness to avoid alibis and re-engineer what is not working. These traditional competencies overlap with some other observers' views of meta-leadership traits.

51. D. Snowden and M. Boone, "A Leader's Framework for Decision Making," *Harvard Business Review*, 4–9, suggest that it is the role of leaders in complex environments to encourage dissent and diversity, including ritual dissent.

52. D. Phillips, *The Founding Fathers on Leadership: Classic Teamwork in Changing Times*, New York: Business Plus, 1997, pp. 35–36.

53. B. Lichtenstein, M. Uhlbein, R. Marion, A. Seers, J. Orton, and C. Schreiber, "Complexity Leadership Theory: An Interactive Perspective on Leading in Complex Adaptive Systems," *ECO* 8(4) (2006): 4–5.

54. National Commission on Terrorist Attacks, *The 9/11 Commission Report: Final Report of the National Commission on Terrorist Attacks upon the United States*, New York: W. W. Norton, 2004, p. 344. This part of the 9/11 Commission Report highlighted the need for "routinizing" the exercise of imagination in anticipating attacks.

55. M. Mateski, "Red Teaming," 2009 in *Red Team Journal* (online edition). Retrieved August 15, 2011 from http://redteamjournal.com/about/red-teaming-and-alternative-analysis/.

56. J. Sinai, "Red Teaming the Terrorist Threat to Preempt the Next Waves of Catastrophic Terrorism," February 12, 2003 presentation for 14th Annual NDIA SO/LIC (National Defense Industrial Association Special Operations/Low Intensity Conflict) Symposium and Exhibits, Washington, DC. Retrieved August 16, 2011 from http://www.au.af.mil/au/awc/awcgate/documents/sinai.pdf.

57. Ibid.

58. R. Nickerson, "Confirmation Bias: A Ubiquitous Phenomenon in Many Guises," *Review of General Psychology* 2(2) (1998): 175. Retrieved August 16, 2011 from http://psy2.ucsd.edu/~mckenzie/nickersonConfirmationBias.pdf

59. M. Gladwell, *Blink: The Power of Thinking without Thinking*, New York: Little, Brown and Company, 2005, pp. 106–125.

60. F. Norris, "Upper Class Twits Made Me Do It," *New York Times*, March 31, 1996. Retrieved August 17, 2011 from http://www.nytimes.com/1996/03/31/books/upper-class-twits-made-me-do-it.html?src=pm.

61. P. Culshaw, "Nick Leeson: How the Original Rogue Trader at Barings Bank Is Thriving in the Credit Crunch," *The Telegraph*, January 8, 2009. Retrieved August 17, 2011 from http://www.telegraph.co.uk/finance/4177449/Nick-Leeson-how-the-original-rogue-trader-at-Barings-Bank-is-thriving-in-the-credit-crunch.html.

62. S. Pressman, "Rogue Trader: I Brought Down Barings Bank and Shook the Financial World," *Entrepreneur*, April 1997. Retrieved August 17, 2011 from http://www.entrepreneur.com/tradejournals/article/19499019.html.

63. U.S. Postal Service Publication 45, *A Violence-Free Workplace*, November 1998. Retrieved August 17, 2011 from http://www.nalc.org/depart/cau/pdf/manuals/pub45.pdf.

64. R. Townsend, *The B² Chronicles: Uncommon Wisdom for Un-Corporate America*, New York: Perigee, 1994, p. 38.

65. L. Feldman, "Terror Alerts Run Risk of Crying Wolf," *Christian Science Monitor*, June 3, 2003. Retrieved August 13, 2011 from http://www.csmonitor.com/2003/0603/p03s01-ussc.html. Linda Feldmann summarizes the frustrations of a number of HSAS critics, including Randall Larsen, who was a senior fellow at the ANSER Institute, a precursor to the Homeland Security Institute. Larsen leveled his criticism at HSAS before publishing *Our Own Worst Enemy*.

66. Numerous sources treat different examples of warning fatigue in different environments, including weather and natural disasters, in the U.S. as well and in the United Kingdom. See J. Chadwick, D. Ernst, and J. Marshall, "All-Hazard Warning—Reply Comment," Docket No. 000609173-0173-01, *All-Hazard Warning Roundtable*, National Telecommunications and Information Administration. Retrieved June 2, 2008, from http://www.ntia.doc.gov/osmhome/warnings/comments/mitre2.htm and A. Clark, "Testimony of Andrew Clark, Minutes of Evidence," *Select Committee on Environment, Food and Rural Affairs*, British Parliament, January 30, 2008. Retrieved June 1, 2008, from http://www.publications.parliament.uk/cgi-bin/newhtml_hl?DB=semukparl&STEMMER=en&WORDS=fatigu&ALL=&ANY=fatigue%20myalgic&PHRASE=&CATEGORIES=&SIMPLE=&SPEAKER=&COLOUR=red&STYLE=s&ANCHOR=muscat_highlighter_first_match&URL=/pa/cm200708/cmselect/cmenvfru/49/8013006.htm. Clark also reports this in a terrorist threat context of the 2002 Bali bombings.

67. "Beware of Millennium Warning-Fatigue," *Oxford Mail*, November 20, 1999. Retrieved August 11, 2011 from http://archive.oxfordmail.net/1999/11/20/80419.html.

68. L. Funtleyder, "Wall Street Choice: Chantix Warning Boosts Fatigue, Amgen Big in Japan," *BNET*, March 2008. Retrieved July 14, 2011 from http://findarticles.com/p/articles/mi_qa5351/is_200803/ai_n25139566

69. J. Ruderman, "Security Tips for Mozilla and Extension Developers," n.d. Retrieved August 15, 2011 from http://www.squarefree.com/securitytips/mozilla-developers.html. Ruderman's related advice for Mozilla developers offers numerous suggestions, as noted later, whereas weather-related warning fatigue critics, like Clark, generally limit their recommendation to increasing the geographic precision of warnings.

70. W. Fishbein and A. Wenger, "Emerging Threats in the 21st Century," *Strategic Foresight and Warning Seminar Series*, December 2007, Global Futures Forum, Center for Security Studies, Zurich, pp. 19–20. Retrieved June 1, 2008 from http://se2.isn.ch/serviceengine/FileContent?serviceID=EINIRAS&fileid=4A4060DC-2BD8-EED5-C1F5-5A4F134F0A03&lng=en. Fishbein and Wenger indicate that most intelligence surprises result from a failure to act more than a failure to see, attributed to factors such as information overload, the "cry wolf" syndrome, and warning fatigue.

71. Ibid., p. 20.

72. Ruderman, op. cit.

73. For a representative warning of this kind, see R. Esposito and V. Walter, "Exclusive: FBI: Al Qaeda May Strike U.S. Shopping Malls in L.A., Chicago," *ABC News*, November 8, 2007. Retrieved June 2, 2008 from http://blogs.abcnews.com/theblotter/2007/11/exclusive-fbi-a.html where the authors discuss the warning issued prior to the end-of-year holiday and shopping season in late 2007.

74. T. Peters, speech on emerging security trends. Keynote address presented at the 2007 seminar and exhibits, American Society for Industrial Security, Las Vegas, NV, September 25, 2007.

CHAPTER 9

Other Insider Threats

There are two kinds of light—the glow that illuminates, and the glare that obscures.

James Thurber

INTRODUCTION

Not every hostile insider poses an existential threat, nor does every threat penetrating the organization represent an insider attack. If we accept the proposition offered in the preceding chapter that existential insider threats are the most dangerous and will likely require more effort and a longer incubation period, it stands to reason that the institution will experience such menaces less frequently than other threats from within or which appear to be from within. Thus, nonexistential threats, meaning those that do not jeopardize the institution's survival, are much more likely to surface and, by sheer frequency and weight of numbers, to propagate into a virtual forest of trust betrayal whose dense canopy may conceal a lone tree of existential insider threat.

Sadly for defenders, malicious betrayers of trust seldom announce in advance their intentions or severity. Consequently, it falls to the defender to take the measure of every insider threat to make certain determinations. First, the defender must determine whether the hostile insider poses an existential threat. If so, then the situation takes immediate priority for protective action in the interest of institutional self-preservation. If not, then the situation merits categorization into one of two realms. Either it is one that shows the potential to become an existential threat, typically through accumulation or cascading impact or crossing of some threshold. Such a case warrants continual monitoring. On the other hand, the situation may fall into any management queue, all of which have in common that the institution regards it as something other than an existential threat, thus meriting a different or broader range of responses. This chapter is about those other situations.

Three frequently occurring situations in the modern workplace that frequently arrive under the guise of insider threats are cyber attacks, threats of violence, and exploitation of employer assets for gain. To what extent does each of these categories enter the province of insider threat? Are they or can they become existential threats? We examine each of the categories before going on to propose a threat scale for assisting defenders in matching candidate responses with apparent threat levels.

CYBER ATTACKS—INSIDER OR OTHER THREATS?

Infection is not quite identical to infiltration, which is why cyber attacks launched from without do not necessarily become insider threats once they infect a network. The majority of cyber threats are neither insider attacks nor existential dangers, for reasons explained below. The institution is a castle, with watchful team members scanning for intruders from the parapets of a defensive structure optimized for seeing threats coming. Corporate sentinels man portcullis and drawbridge, with team members lending a needed hand to mobilize these defenses at the approach of an adversary. In cyber attacks, the portcullis is a firewall, and the drawbridge a suite of user-supported network security protocols. Why is it important to have user support? For the same reason that the castle's drawbridge cannot stand permanently raised or paved with spikes and glass shards: the occupants, after all, are the ones who most use it in innocent transit to and from the castle.

Is the spear or catapulted projectile that lands within the castle an insider attack? No, and neither is the externally driven cyber assault that happens to penetrate a firewall. The distinctions blur, however, when a castle dweller lowers the drawbridge or raises the portcullis and an opposing warrior charges in unopposed. Still, the analogy holds. One could argue that the castle dweller lowering a drawbridge unthinkingly, unaware of the presence of hostile forces, is no more an insider threat than the careless employee inadvertently compromising network passwords or naively falling prey to a phishing scam. In both such cases, otherwise robust defenses have succumbed to enemy guile—a form of intrusion presently called social engineering—but not the kind of attack requiring active collaboration of a hostile trust betrayer.

What of the foe who positions a turncoat into the castle precisely to alert opposing forces of when the moat is drained and to lower drawbridge and raise portcullis on a timetable or signal most advantageous to the adversary? This foe is now using an embedded insider who poses no less a threat than any other infiltrator. Alternatively, if the foe recruits a sympathetic castle dweller to spy from within or carry out acts of sabotage, the castle dweller ranks among insider threats that a No Dark Corners approach should be ready to expose and disrupt. When these defenses do their job, the insider's effectiveness and value to adversaries diminishes.

And so the foe returns to instruments of frontal attack or technologically supported attack enhancements, like the catapult in the case of the castle, and the cyber intrusion in the case of the enemy unable to launch a frontal or insider-supported attack on the institution. Most projectiles launched against a castle come from without, and most cyber attacks targeting the institution are similarly outsider threats in the main. How so?

As noted in Chapter 1, hackers and typical cyber intruders lack the position of trust that would qualify them as insiders. They therefore also lack the esoteric insider knowledge that would increase the destructive potential of their attacks. Under the circumstances, remotely based cyber threats who are not trust betrayers carry out actions akin to intrusion by stealth or outsider sabotage, on the order of the catapult launching at the castle. These are neither insider threats nor, for the most part, are they necessarily existential threats, since as reports cited in Chapter 1 suggested, many if not most cyber attacks aim lower than annihilation of the institution. As Chapter 1 also indicated, to the extent that insiders choose to involve themselves in cyber attacks, most appear to do so as a slam-the-door expression of a personal grievance at the end of their association with the targeted organization. In other words, their insider status is over or about to end and they are communicating their dissatisfaction with the employment or contracting relationship by striking out at the former employer. This is the equivalent of a laborer stealing tools or damaging construction equipment at the job site on the way out the door. Is either an insider threat? Or are both disgruntled former employees engaging in malicious acts whose criminality depends on the extent of damage inflicted on the institution? In either case, one could argue that a proactive termination process that engaged knowledgeable peers in anticipating mischief and securing the institution's assets before involuntary terminations would obviate the debate over whether such former employees' hostile actions constituted insider attacks.

What does a No Dark Corners workplace have to offer in the face of cyber attacks, particularly if it is not immediately clear whether there is an insider component to them or whether a given incident is rising to the level of an existential threat? The answer is the same for cyber insiders as for any other hostile insiders. The No Dark Corners innovations of increased transparency and copilot engagement at the team level offer prophylactic value in cyber applications as they do in any work involving interaction with other employees. However, the additional challenge that defenders face in contending with cyber insiders is one that applies equally to dealing with any specialized knowledge worker: greater potential that there will be no peer-level expertise available to serve as a counterweight at the working level where there is exposure to critical assets. This applies most commonly to situations requiring the infrequent call for outside specialists to handle episodic problem solving. For example, a physician working primarily at a research laboratory might hesitate to perform a tracheotomy while visiting a hospital. There would be other, more experienced peers who do this more proficiently, and any mistake on his part would be readily observed by experts in the medical field. However, the same physician might not feel so inhibited to perform the procedure if on a remote island with no one else available to do the job—and certainly no one qualified to do it better or criticize his technique.

Similarly, a cyber specialist invited into a critical area to perform a task that may be second nature to her but incomprehensible to the members of the work team encounters two opportunities.

She has a chance to render a needed and valued service that no one else can deliver or criticize. Like the research physician, however, she also has the chance to make a mistake— by accident or by design—and probably do so without anyone recognizing the mistake in time to intervene. In this kind of scenario, the normal exigencies of doing business impinge upon the institution's use of experts and specialists, particularly if the absence of knowledgeable oversight has become the norm rather than the exception. Thus, in the case of the cyber or other expert working alone in a position of trust and surrounded by an engaged work team that is nevertheless innocent of the expert's specialty, a dark corner emerges where there was none before. How does the institution deal with the resulting exposure?

One approach is to arrange knowledgeable oversight by remote means. For example, advances in the medical field have led to coining of the term "telepresence" as a new option for arranging physician visits with patients in remote areas, where "telepresence technology can help doctors use videoconferencing to have an in-person-meeting experience to quickly diagnose patients in distant locations or consult with colleagues."[1] Taking advantage of such an infusion of technology in the workplace would enable an institution's corporate cyber sentinel to consult in real time with the outsourced cyber contractor who is helping a work team in the field with a technology-related problem. Consistent with the No Dark Corners strategy outlined in Figure 2.3, this telepresence would increase transparency on the job. Moreover, not only would the cyber sentinel supply a degree of knowledgeable oversight to identify and deter untoward activity on the part of the contractor, the sentinel would also benefit from gaining a better in-house understanding of the problem. The net result would be value added both for insider defense and improving in-house diagnostic capability to benefit the organization in the future.

Another approach, in the absence of a telepresence, is to resort to overtly apparent monitoring that at least introduces the possibility that the institution is poised to detect mischief and react accordingly. As noted before, there is useful deterrent value for the institution from being seen to take active security precautions.[2] A team member escorting a visiting cyber specialist and a video camera monitoring the specialist's work at the same time introduce an element of uncertainty that serves the institution, since the visiting expert may not realize the full extent of technical knowledge or ignorance of the human and electronic watchers—unless someone gives these away. Thus, another challenge for defenders in this situation is to resist elicitation and avoid revealing limitations of the ostensible instruments of oversight. Thus, this situation calls for using the kinds of counter-elicitation behaviors that would elsewhere be part of the infiltrator's tool kit, such as, giving limited responses, feigning ignorance, giving rehearsed responses, and redirecting conversation away from areas of discomfort.[3]

THREATS OF VIOLENCE

Like cyber threats, most threats of violence are not existential in terms of their catastrophic potential for the institution. Nor are they insider threats if they involve intruders, trespassers, or armed robbers who force their way in from the outside to perform some villainy or misdeed. The line between insider and outsider may take on shades of gray, however, when hostilities come from the domestic partner of an insider, most frequently a husband, stalker, or even unrequited admirer who arrives at the employer's perimeter because his target has relocated away from him and concealed her residence to the point that the workplace is the only unchanged location he knows how to reach. Otherwise, the most common workplace violence events involve giving offense verbally. Only a small fraction of verbal threats escalate to physical confrontation.[4] However, although the rate of related fatalities appears to have decreased in the workplace, the rate of violent assaults in the U.S. workplace has risen.[5]

Domestic or Intimate Violence

Domestic violence has the potential to adversely affect not only a targeted employee but coworkers and anyone who is in the proximity of the hostile party in the midst of an ebullition or physical attack. Also called intimate partner abuse, this threat poses a societal problem that spills over into the workplace. Some statistical data indicated that women were 7 to 14 times more likely to experience serious acts of partner violence, and were significantly more likely to sustain injuries than men who were victims of intimate violence.[6]

Threats on the Job

The larger the institution, the greater the likelihood of management concern over workplace violence. Specifically, in one of its more recent, periodic surveys on workplace violence, the Society for Human Resource Management found that organizations with fewer than 100 employees showed that only 42% registered some level of concern over workplace violence, whereas those with 100–499 employees had 66% concerned over the issue, and organizations with 500 or more employees registered concern at the 73% level. In any case, however, the vast majority of threats were verbal, totaling 74%, as opposed to physical (7% total), with the latter dividing almost evenly between fistfights (3%) and pushing or shoving (4%).[7]

From the defender's perspective, there are two positive conclusions to derive from such studies. One is that the vast majority of reported incidents are verbal and by no means cross the threshold into existential threats for the organization. Another is that 90% of organizations presently have some form of workplace violence policy in place, hence some institutional means of addressing these matters in a way that spares defenders from taking on this particular kind of hostile insider as a situation without precedent requiring substantial diversion of management attention to evaluate and address.[8] Indeed, if the institution already has a policy and protocols in place for mobilizing a multidisciplinary team to assess the severity and options for dealing with threats of violence, defenders may find it expedient to tap at least some of the same team members for assessment of other insider threats where violence may not be at issue but where the potential for damage to the institution does require assessment or action.

EXPLOITING EMPLOYER ASSETS FOR GAIN

The third category of threats whose most likely expression results in some damage to the institution to benefit a trust betrayer does not typically start as an existential threat, although it may develop into one if left unchecked. The insider seeking to exploit the institution tends to benefit by stopping short of obliterating the source of his or her gains. Sooner or later, a dead host stops feeding all parasites. The mercenary insider involved in this kind of exploitation aims for financial gain, self-aggrandizement, or a combination of the two.

Financial Gain

Those aiming to exploit internal access and knowledge to line their pockets infect almost every workplace and are rational actors to the extent of being able to weigh risk vs. gain in a way that defenders also comprehend. Thus, the payment processing clerk who figures out a way to take advantage of rounding error to divert the odd penny to a personal account may feel the risk is warranted because few individual clients will make a fuss over a balance that is a penny off their own calculations. Merely entering into and auditing the process of reconciliation would consume more than the object sought. However, multiplied across enough accounts, this minor diversion of inconsequential amounts could enrich the clerk to the point of subsidizing a new sports car and an exotic vacation. The architect of this scheme, however, will be rational enough to know that getting away with a penny will not happen so easily when trying the same kind of diversion with thousands of dollars at a time. That level of discrepancy would not only invite greater scrutiny but would also make it worth the victim's time and energy to reconcile aggressively. On a grander scale, however, a hollow shell with the imposing edifice of a Potemkin village can produce an Enron whose trading in an unregulated market and concealment of losses bankrupt investors, employees, and even an overseer such as the Arthur Anderson accounting house ostensibly charged with defending shareholder interests and equity by keeping the corporation honest but blinded by lucrative profits from other Enron work.[9]

The clerk is an embezzler, whereas Enron's creators and perpetuators were something more, perhaps impostors operating a deception on a grand scale. To some extent, the difference between the two lies in relevant expertise or sophistication. The insider with the knowledge and finesse to establish and operate an Enron occupies a niche beyond the common embezzler, yet still maneuvers within the bounds of betrayal for financial gain, with self-aggrandizement necessarily growing in tandem with that gain. Pernicious insiders seeking financial gain take a variety of forms, including embezzlers, pilferers, and impostors who may be carrying out a grand deception, and nepotists.

Embezzlers breach trust by taking money or other assets entrusted to their care, with the terms embezzlement, peculation, and defalcation sometimes used interchangeably in describing their specific activities.[10] Popular misconceptions that such betrayals of the institution and thefts of its property occur because of need dissolve in the face of studies concluding that "accessibility rather than need triggers the desire to steal."[11] Small businesses may be more vulnerable to high-impact losses at the hands of embezzlers, as one report attributed to the U.S. Chamber of Commerce estimated that 30% of business failures result from employee theft.[12]

Certain situational factors exert significant influence on the frequency and pervasiveness of embezzlement in a given workplace. One factor is the lack of separation of responsibility and authority in the institution, resulting in a situation where one individual ends up ordering and receiving assets, or both authorizing and paying for goods or services, or handling both the cash and records of disbursements.[13] Another factor is the permissiveness of the dominant culture in the institution. In other words, embezzling is more likely to occur if the dominant culture is inclined to overlook internal theft because it regards such loss as a cost of doing business and, more notably, has a means of recovering losses by passing them on to clients or consumers in the form of higher prices or budget overruns.[14] Finally, organizational complacency often leads to management acting on the assumption that old and trusted members of the institution who might never have considered misappropriating employer property earlier in their careers may have experienced changes in their life circumstances and outlook. As a result, what may have once been an unthinkable breach of integrity to trusted members may now be considered something that they feel they deserve.[15]

Most embezzlement occurs over an extended period and often takes the form of systematic diversion of sums too small to attract management attention.[16] Although the application of basic management controls essential for the exercise of due diligence can deter and detect embezzlement, certain No Dark Corners measures also offer value in reducing exposure to this kind of insider-caused loss. Similar to their value mentioned in a foregoing chapter on lawful disruption, staff rotations frustrate embezzlers while offering broader value to the employer. The reason such moves interfere with embezzling is that they result in embezzlers losing control of records or audit trails of those aspects of the operation that allow them to cover their thefts, thereby exposing them to discovery in the next audit.[17]

Those No Dark Corners approaches that focus on transparency and building trust at the work team level also offer value in countering the situational and cultural factors that contribute to making embezzlement likely or even acceptable in the workplace. Specifically, as one professional association's study of the problem indicated,

> Establishing trust is a critical step toward controlling employee theft within the workplace. Employees are more likely to identify and report a thief if they believe the co-worker is stealing from their future. A thief may think twice if he or she believes management has earned the loyalty of its employees.[18]

Similarly, good internal relations among all employees within the institution play a positive role in preventing these kinds of losses, particularly if corporate sentinels are respected by employees and prompt investigations send a message that losses are a major concern.[19]

Pilferers are insider thieves operating on a lower scale than embezzlers. They generally act on a combination of impulse and opportunity, stealing items that are easy to conceal or whose loss will elude routine scrutiny. Typically, they conceal assets on their person before leaving the workplace.[20] Individuals whose jobs afford them great freedom of maneuver can be pilferers or even embezzlers. Often, the key to their ability to carry out financial crimes is not so much hierarchical position but ability to move through the institution without being observed. One observer suggested that employees at the top and bottom rungs of a given organization sometimes enjoy surprisingly equivalent freedom of maneuver.[21] Since pilferers are less sophisticated than embezzlers, most of their actions can be extinguished through the combination of a copilot work team environment that limits opportunities to make off with employer assets and the pervasiveness of a culture that does not tolerate stealing.

REPRESENTATIVE SCHEMES OF EMBEZZLERS AND COUNTERMEASURES

Hostile insiders seeking to realize gains at employer expense employ tactics that vary depending on their imagination and opportunities presented by exposures in the institution's system of controls.

SCHEMES

Schemes come in various forms including:[22]

1. Collusion of human resources and payroll staff to create false records of nonexistent employees or to keep terminated employees on the payroll while collecting associated salary payments.
2. Claiming unworked overtime and sharing the unearned income with the supervisor responsible for approving the timekeeping record.
3. Pocketing unclaimed commissions or bonuses of employees who have departed.
4. Marking usable equipment for removal as surplus and diverting it to sell outside the place of business.
5. Collusion of receiving clerks and delivery drivers to falsify count of items delivered, with extra items sold on the side.
6. Collusion of vendors and purchasing agents to falsify purchases and receipts, pocketing payments of goods and services never provided.
7. Collusion of contract administrators with contractors to pay inflated prices for goods or services or to rig bids that are supposed to be competitive.
8. Mailroom and supply staff shipping materials to themselves for resale outside the place of business.
9. Accounts payable staff paying fabricated invoices to dummy firms.
10. Making duplicate payments to creditors and then diverting the returned, second payment.

11. Appropriating employer checks, debit or credit cards for personal use.
12. Raising totals on vouchers and reimbursement forms after they have been approved.
13. Removing valuables from premises by concealing them in the trash.
14. Undercharging purchasers for goods or services and accepting a kickback in exchange
15. Manipulating accounting software to arrange transfer of funds from account overages into personal accounts
16. Paying a confederate cash or credit for returned merchandise that was not actually returned
17. Forging signatures on checks and destroying copies returned with bank statements

PREVENTIVE COUNTERMEASURES

Preventive countermeasures include the following:[23]

1. Screen applicants carefully and check not only their stated references but also independently develop references that can speak to the candidate's honesty.
2. Alert frontline managers and supervisors to possibility of insider financial crimes, insisting that they set a good example and refuse to tolerate even petty pilfering.
3. Avoid giving authority over high-value assets to employees experiencing financial difficulties.
4. Retrain employees who appear to be repeating errors involving sales or financial transactions.
5. Pay particular attention to employees who arrive early or stay late when there is no need.
6. Prohibit employees from handling transactions where they are making sales to themselves or where the same person is ordering and receiving materials.
7. Limit bringing in of briefcases or packages into high-value areas and inspect all packages and parcels leaving those areas.
8. Prohibit any single employee from having sole access to storerooms or repositories of critical assets.
9. Prohibit unescorted access of friends and relatives—even of those of executives.
10. Watch for theft contamination, that is, the spread of internal losses once they go unchecked.
11. Keep all storerooms and securable containers locked when not in use.
12. Maximize use of tamper-resistant seals and packaging.

Impostors may enter the institution without malicious intent but, because they falsify or inflate their credentials, they threaten to inflict financial damage by virtue of being overmatched. One could make the case that one such impostor was Nick Leeson, the trader whose gambling of Barings' assets resulted in the ultimate collapse of his employer's merchant bank. (See details in text box in Chapter 8.) In Leeson's case, once his gambles started to go sour, he resorted to creating a dummy account to conceal losses—a move indistinguishable from any embezzler who happens to control disbursement of funds and accounting for them, as Barings had permitted Leeson to do. A number of the most successful frauds have historically followed the model of Charles Ponzi, who pioneered the tactic of selling investors on the merits of complicated and impenetrable investments that produced high returns by paying the dividends of older investors out of the deposits of newer investors. Subsequent grand impostors in Ponzi's footsteps included Bernard Madoff and lesser known defrauders whose unifying traits were promising incredibly high returns on investments and, for a time, delivering impressive results while concealing losses or paying one set of investors with another's deposits.[24] Whereas the dilettantes in this category may deceive themselves to some degree until they are in over their heads, the virtuosi realize their limits and fabricate intricate deceptions to delay their exposure and maximize the number of investors they dupe. The most proficient, such as Madoff, can lead a career undetected and unopposed, until events such as an economic downturn expose their fraud.

An average impostor may fear exposure through a sound due diligence effort on the part of a prospective employer and even fear more from a No Dark Corners approach to close probation. However, it is unlikely that No Dark Corners innovations alone would unmask the highly proficient impostor operating on a grand scale. Instead, recognizing and exposing such a fraud requires extending the transparency beyond the work team level to a technical area of competence that corresponds to that of the impostor's purported subject matter expertise. Any convoluted profit-making scheme that can neither be explained to nor understood by one's counterpart to the alleged expert must be presumed to be either fraudulent or deserving of microscopic exploration until the person responsible for risking the institution's assets can fully comprehend and verify the soundness of what is being proposed. Most impostors would find a way to avoid such scrutiny under some pretext. Defenders can accordingly count themselves fortunate in being spared entanglement in any scheme that looks too good to be true.

Nepotists, from the Latin root for nepotism tracing to preferential treatment for nephews, may regard themselves innocent of mercenary motives when favoring cronies with insider information to win lucrative contracts or when manipulating competitions to give unfair advantages to their personal favorites. For them, the gain may be as modest as sparing themselves the burden of having to switch from a known contractor to a new one who will require some investment of time and energy to navigate the institution. At the other extreme, nepotists could insist on quid pro quo in the form of monetary payment or bartered favors, such as having the winner of a lucrative construction contract quietly assign workers to install a swimming pool into the nepotist's backyard in exchange for being allowed to pad the construction bid with extra charges.[25] Although the extreme cases range into the province of financial crime that includes embezzlement, the petty cases of unchecked nepotism nevertheless produce deleterious effects in the long run. They deny the institution the benefit of fair competition, whether in an unbiased recruitment process that hires the best over the well connected, or in a competed vendor or contractor selection process intended to deliver best value at a fair price, rather than perpetuating mediocre or insufficient value that is also overpriced.

A wily beneficiary of nepotism may even manage to recruit an inside confederate without revealing the intent to gain unfair advantage, as by cultivating the insider through ostensible displays of friendship. (Also review references to elicitation in Chapter 6 as an oblique way of prompting revelations.) Consequently, the same No Dark Corners approach that seeks to counter elicitation's success also avails when dealing with outsiders involved in competitive activities that are easily infected by nepotism. Specifically (as noted in Table 6.1), counter-elicitation behaviors include giving limited responses, feigning ignorance, giving rehearsed responses, and redirecting conversation away from areas of discomfort, or in the case of hiring or contracting decisions, redirecting conversation away from areas that are out of bounds. Additionally, with a No Dark Corners level of employee engagement, transparency, and copilot involvement of stakeholders, it becomes very difficult for the individual inclined to nepotism to play favorites in the midst of a work environment where bias is instantly evident and difficult to conceal.

Self-Aggrandizement

Not all gain is monetary, nor is financial gain the only kind of reward for perfidy. Although existential threats in the form of infiltrators directed by a terror cell may be animated by loyalty to a cause and group ties more powerful than the bond that the institution has with its own employees, these kinds of threats remain very infrequent, as noted before. More common, however, are the petty saboteurs within any sizable organization who may never pose an existential threat yet see it as their personal calling to undermine bosses, morale, change, or anything else that lacks their personal imprimatur. Some of the forms that these hostile insiders take include self-styled victims, whistleblowers (legitimate and otherwise), minor malcontents, and deflectors.

   Self-styled victims, as one observer noted two decades ago, are the natural product of a "no fault" and "no pain" society, where the "rush to declare oneself a victim . . . suggests a fundamental transformation" of cultural values, character, and personal responsibility.[26] Indeed, self-styled victims distort in the aim of self-indulgence what on the surface may appear to be legitimate concerns. As the same observer noted,

> The essence of egoism is imposing one's likes, dislikes, subtle prejudices, and whining annoyances onto others. Society exists to keep the ego from making itself the center of the universe; maturity is (or, at any rate, was) defined as the child's gradual recognition that his emotions, demands, and sensitivities are no longer absolute.[27]

   Why do such individuals continue to surface in the workplace? They belong to the class of employee that Peter Drucker defined as the "permanently immature."[28] As one may infer, to the extent that these individuals pose no existential threat, they still merit attention as a management problem. Although an environment of trust in a No Dark Corners workplace may produce the team dynamics that limit social reinforcement for self-styled victims, there are times when management must draw lines and put an end to the disruptions these individuals needlessly impose upon coworkers. As one executive coach advised, "As a boss you should stop trying to change people who don't want to change . . . people who don't think they have a problem."[29]

   Whistleblowers are insiders who disclose alleged misconduct or illicit activity to someone in authority or to the public, either within or outside of the institution. Public laws protect whistleblowers to varying degrees and prohibit retaliation against employees for making such disclosures. To the legitimate organization, whistleblowers may present burdens of investigation and corrective action as well as diversion of management time and other resources. However, just as the mature institution accepts the need and value of audit functions as an operating necessity, so must it make provision for allowing whistleblowers to raise what may be legitimate concerns for the welfare of other employees or the institution itself. An environment with the kind of transparency that No Dark Corners innovations promote reinforces team engagement across the board and should therefore offer more opportunities for employees to surface their concerns where fellow team members and frontline management hear them and address them openly, rather than suppressing these concerns until their advocate feels no alternative but to seek whistleblower attention. Because a given concern's legitimacy may not be immediately evident, and because of safeguards afforded whistleblowers under law and institutional policy, it is wise to develop internal channels for addressing whistleblower concerns, including such options as employee hotlines or specific offices, like that of an ombudsman or ethics officer who can serve as an independent sounding board for whistleblowers and an evaluator of their concerns. As for employees abusing whistleblower protections in service of an ulterior agenda, these people more properly belong in the deflector category (below).

Minor malcontents are dyspeptic saboteurs for whom reward is not necessarily direct gain but denial of another's objectives out of envy, spite, or sheer contrariness. Somewhat akin to self-styled victims, these individuals are naysayers but may not necessarily be labeling themselves as victims. The principal adverse effect that such individuals produce over time is erosion of the team ethos, like a corrosive acid that seeps between the joints of the collaborative spirit that otherwise cements the team together. Such individuals are sources of perpetual disruption, which is neither necessarily illegal nor actionable. Consequently, absent indication of an existential threat, the malcontent's negativity and complaining is not so much a defender problem as a routine problem for team and management to resolve. Transparency and copilot engagement at the work team level rob malcontents of much of their ammunition, leaving them unable to credibly allege being denied opportunities to be heard in decisions affecting work flow and workplace. However, as noted above, there are times when it falls upon management to draw a line between acceptable dissent and counterproductivity. Management's tools for disrupting these chronic disruptors include progressive discipline and increased attention to demanding productivity, as the busier the malcontent, the less time he or she has for filling idle hours with mischief. Similarly, the team may independently react by ostracizing malcontents, which management must take care to contain within bounds so that such social isolation does not interfere with core operations or give the malcontent a cause for action or any legitimacy to claim being victimized.

Deflectors include malingerers and decoys who interfere with productive work or escape doing any themselves while seeking to avoid accountability for nonperformance. Malingerers can make an art of pestering disputation, the tactic of appearing to be poised to work but stalling by launching into endless inquiries about details and fine points under the guise of seeking clarification.[30] Deflectors may be less pernicious to the institution than minor malcontents or self-styled victims, particularly if their focus remains inward and their primary objective the personal avoidance of hard work. They may also see it as a game to dodge work by alternatively feigning ignorance or confusion.[31] Again, unless they arrive at the point of posing an existential threat, deflectors are more a management problem than a defender concern. The transparency and collaborative engagement methods of a No Dark Corners workplace only give deflectors a culture to exploit in diffusing accountability or blame. Consequently, it falls to management to assign measurable work to deflectors and closely monitor performance, under the lash of progressive discipline as an incentive to perform. If such techniques still do not avail, the remaining options are terminating or sequestering the malingerer to at least avoid infecting a productive work team with noncontributors.

UNIFYING THEMES AND NEED FOR A SYSTEMATIC
APPROACH TO LESSER INSIDER THREATS

Several recurrent themes surface in the foregoing review of hostile activities attributed to insiders that fall short of being existential threats. First, not all technically require trust betrayal to succeed, thus opening to debate whether they qualify as insider threats. Second, the most commonly occurring hostile acts in the workplace appear to range more on the level of nuisance or disruption than the level of danger to people or assets. Additionally, it appears that the majority of such cases fall more squarely within the purview of management as issues of performance and discipline rather than as matters requiring the full array of defenses that the institution may choose to deploy against serious existential threats. Moreover, since no institution can afford to treat every insider disruption as a danger to survival while, at the same time, ignoring such matters is insupportable because it could speed their mutation into full-fledged catastrophic impact, something must be done about such cases.

If what to do is unclear, what not to do is more apparent: do not mobilize for garden variety insider threats the same level of effort and resources that existential threats command. The resulting diversion of resources would first interfere with the successful pursuit of core operations. Worse still, this diversion would eventually spawn a culture of perpetual witch hunts that would foreclose effective teamwork, thereby negating the No Dark Corners benefits of transparency and team-level engagement for defeating the existential insider threats when they arise. Under the circumstances, defenders may find

TABLE 9.1   Threat Scale

Rating and Level	Threat Perceiver Actions	Organizational Actions
0: Nuisance Level	• Ignore • Resolve directly • Mention to team or boss	• Write off • Talk to both parties • Monitor for change
1: Escalating Irritation	• Report to organization • Request assistance • Take recommended steps	• Assess • Set boundaries • Take some action to contain

2: Chronic, Active Disruption	• Report formally to authority
	• Take advice seriously
	  • Change patterns
	  • Avoid escalation
	  • Maintain confidentiality
	  • Follow guidance fully
		• Explore disciplinary and legal options
		• Institute multiple countermeasures (discipline, office moves, security surveillance, access controls, defensive briefings)
		• Establish tripwires to detect and respond to escalation
		• Evaluate response needs

3: Unacceptable, Proximate Harm	• Relocate to protected area
	  • Office
	  • Residence
	  • Secured areas
	• Support criminal action (testify, report)
	• Adopt lifestyle changes pending resolution
		• Suspend or terminate threat source
		• Make special accommodations for target(s) or for crisis negotiation
		• Arrange point protection for target
		• Arrange protective surveillance of antagonist
		• Actively engage police and prosecute

value in using a scale that at once helps gauge the relative business impact of the nonexistential insider threat and offers corresponding mitigation or countermeasures appropriate to that particular threat level, hence the threat scale that follows (Table 9.1).

THE THREAT SCALE

Perceptions of insider threats tend to be emotionally charged events—so much the case that interpretations of their severity often vary greatly among witnesses to the same event or circumstance. Although most reporters of threats tell the truth, experience suggests that they do not necessarily tell the whole truth. Nor is a person who is dealing with emotional involvement in a case the best equipped to arrive at an objective determination of its severity. Under these circumstances, institutions need a way to gauge severity based not only on the intensity of feelings that threatened employees report, but also on other factors that help isolate feelings from facts. Here is one such scale.

0	1	2	3

In this scale, intensity from 0 to 3 represents a steady progression from low to high. Here is how we apply the scale based on *actions* that the threat perceiver and the organization are willing to take, rather than on intensity of feelings expressed. In each case, if the threat perceiver is not willing to take on the corresponding actions listed in the perceiver action column, and if the organization (which may sometimes buy into the individual's emotions) is also unwilling to take on the actions of the next level, the severity of the case is likely to be at a lower level than initially portrayed.

USING THE THREAT SCALE: AN ILLUSTRATION

Employing the threat scale to gauge the relative severity of an insider event assists not only the organization but also principals who may otherwise temporarily lose their capacity for objective analysis while caught in the swirl of events. Here is one such example of an actual case where identities are masked in the interest of discretion.

Joanne is a junior supervisor of support staff in an engineering department. Appreciated as a hard worker and convivial subordinate, she has advanced ahead of her peers and also impressed her management with the tenacity and resolve it took for her to dismiss a belligerent malcontent, Bertha. Bertha had been intimidating others as a means of deflecting attention from her own indifference to completing her work assignments. It took almost a year of progressive discipline to terminate Bertha, and the process was unpleasant for all concerned, including Joanne's boss, Ralph. However, Ralph backed Joanne throughout the process and has become her mentor and chief advocate, regarding her as one of his rising stars. Today, however, a situation that all had thought behind them returns to the fore, and Ralph's initial sense is that this poses an urgent insider threat.

Ralph accordingly approaches Pauline, the head of protective services and the corporate sentinel in charge of leading employer response under the institution's workplace violence policy. Here are the details Ralph gives Pauline:

- Bertha no longer works at the institution but maintains an account in the organization's credit union. Today, while ostensibly visiting the credit union for a routine financial transaction, Bertha strayed into her former workplace, said hello to people she used to know well, and glared with great hostility in the direction of Joanne.
- Joanne was very upset by this unexpected appearance of Bertha and by the hostile glare. She left the work area and went to another floor, ostensibly to do some business with the accounting department in one of her routine checking of invoices from a construction contractor.
- Later in the day, after Bertha had departed and Joanne had returned from lunch, Joanne came to Ralph to report the incident and express concern for her personal safety, saying that she felt Bertha would do her harm and asking for protection under the employer's workplace violence policy's "zero tolerance" provision for threats.
- Ralph then recounted recent history involving Bertha's chronic performance deficiencies and how Joanne had first tried to work with Bertha but ultimately entered into a program of progressive discipline that ended with Bertha's dismissal, to the relief of Bertha's coworkers.

Ralph followed his recitation of the foregoing events with a request that Pauline arrange immediate protection for Joanne before she came to some harm from Bertha. Pauline, however, sensing that both Joanne and Ralph might be overreacting and reading more into a single event than they might from a more objective position, used the threat scale to arrive at a joint appraisal of the severity of this case.

Pauline: Let me understand just how big a threat you and Joanne consider this to be. Is this incident with Bertha something Joanne is so concerned about that she is ready to relocate to our field branch office in the next county in order to be harder for Bertha to see next time Bertha goes to the credit union? And are you willing to transfer her and her work to the field branch?

Ralph: Well, I don't know that we need to go that far.

Pauline: OK. Is this the kind of thing that has given her reason to be afraid of Bertha coming after Joanne at home? Is she ready to go to the police with her concerns?

Ralph: No, I'm pretty sure she isn't. She doesn't want to make a police report, although I can try talking her into it, if you think this would help.

Pauline: Well, what would Joanne be reporting actually?

Ralph: The glaring, you know, hostility and so forth.

Pauline: How much and how often has this happened?

Ralph: Well, only this time, I guess. But it sure rattled Joanne.

Pauline: Of course, I'm sure it did. So far, though, unless there is more that I'm missing—and I will talk to Joanne to check further—it doesn't seem that we have her feeling so threatened that she is prepared to go to authorities and make lifestyle changes, right?

Ralph: Right. I was thinking, maybe just getting some extra security around the work area . . . ?

Pauline: To do what exactly?

Ralph: I don't know, maybe just to reassure everybody?

Pauline: When and for how long? Do we just have someone standing around in case Bertha returns?

Ralph: I see how that might not look like such a great idea. How about a restraining order to keep Bertha out of here?

Pauline: We could certainly look into that. Typically, though, there's usually a police report before a restraining order, and if someone isn't willing to make a police report, it's unlikely that there will be sufficient justification for a restraining order. And if all we have to go on is what you told me, there does not seem to be enough here to allow our attorneys to try for a temporary restraining order on behalf of our employer.

Ralph: I see.

Pauline: OK, well it seems we don't have enough here for Joanne—or her department—to be willing to take the most serious protective actions that people in real and immediate danger would not hesitate to take. Have there been other instances of hostility against Joanne even remotely traceable to Bertha?

Ralph: Not really, when you put it that way.

Pauline: Well, as you have probably figured out, what I am trying to do is get a sense of how serious this case may be relative to others and to what the concerned individual and her organization are willing to do about it themselves. So we have essentially ruled out the extreme of having a round-the-clock bodyguard and putting Joanne into protective seclusion, right?

Ralph: Yes. That would be overkill.

Pauline: OK. We also see that this is looking more and more like a one-time event, meaning no chronic disruption and not even signs of some form of escalation, correct?

Ralph: Correct.

Pauline: OK. Well, that seems to leave us at the nuisance level: a one-time event that upset Joanne and that she reported with you. I think we can and should do something about this, but not necessarily go all out with the kind of security measures neither she nor you are ready for at this point. Suppose we put some things into place that won't draw a lot of attention but will still give us the ability to ramp up more protection if and when needed?

Ralph: Like what?

Pauline: First, while none of us can prevent a credit union customer from doing business there, we can arrange to pay closer attention to not letting credit union customers wander into work spaces that are for employees only. I can work that with our access control system and also have our guards keep an eye out for Bertha to make sure she doesn't easily sneak in where she no longer belongs. You can talk to Joanne and her work team and tell them to call Security if they see Bertha—or any unauthorized person—coming into their work area without a badge. We'll make sure to escort such people out, which usually happens quietly. When we talk to Joanne about this incident, we'll also go over some defensive actions she can take, like things to watch for, so that she can be alert to suspicious activity or circumstances that may expose her to risk—whether from Bertha or everybody else. And we can also monitor this situation and touch base in the next couple of weeks to see if the situation has changed. But if Bertha was just expressing herself inappropriately without making a direct threat—the kind of behavior that apparently contributed to her being fired—then do we really want to inadvertently make things worse by letting word get around that all she has to do to get petty revenge is to show up and send Joanne running? Or do we want to take this seriously and be ready to scale our response but not make things worse by over-escalating what we have just categorized as being at the nuisance level?

Ralph: I agree, and think I see your point.

LESSON:

By walking Ralph through the varying options in the threat scale, Pauline helped him frame the incident as something less than an exigent and existential threat, in effect bringing him back down to earth so that Ralph, in turn, could do the same with Joanne. However, Pauline also put in place some monitoring points to be able to tell if the situation changes or escalates to a different level on the threat scale, which would require corresponding different levels of response.

APPLICATION OF THREAT SCALE TO INSIDER THREATS BY CATEGORY

Scale for Cyber Attacks

0: Nuisance Level

Threat Perceiver Actions   A nuisance level threat from within could begin on the order of an employee using employer connectivity to the Internet to surf the World Wide Web for personal business or amusement. The likely perceivers of this circumstance would be either cyber sentinels (i.e., from the Information Technology security staff), coworkers, or a supervisor. What makes this a nuisance? The activity may be annoying to others but still fall within the institution's acceptable use policy, particularly if the surfing occurs during breaks or lunch and does not interfere with any other employee's legitimate duties. At this level, the threat perceiver would be wise to weigh whether the activity is really detrimental or an affront to personal preferences that need not escalate into an epic battle. Thus, the coworker annoyed may ignore the matter or quietly discuss it with the individual responsible for it to arrive at some resolution. If such a matter hinges on differing interpretations of the institution's acceptable use policy, it would be reasonable to ask for an interpretation from the supervisor of both offender and offended employees. If the threat perceiver is, instead, a cyber sentinel, it would probably be wise for the sentinel to first calibrate a potential overreaction with the boss of the individual involved or with his or her own supervisor. Why? Specialists tend to view the world through the prism of their specialty. Thus it is possible or even probable that a cyber sentinel would see in a minor nuisance a more dire threat than the larger institution would interpret the same way.

Organizational Actions   A clue to the relative severity of such a nuisance immediately arises by asking what the organization is willing to do about the reported incident. In most cases, if there is no resulting impact to work and the surfing falls within the bounds of the institution's acceptable use policy, the matter hardly merits attention let alone escalation. At most, if not writing off the matter completely, frontline management may communicate with offender or offended to clarify where the boundaries lie and then monitor for change.

1: Escalating Irritation

Threat Perceiver Actions   To build on the preceding example, suppose the individual who was previously using the Internet occasionally is now playing video games between work assignments, disturbing coworkers in the same area, and monopolizing a work station that other employees need to use for time entry before they drive out to the field. How serious is this situation? Although it by no means has risen to the level of an existential threat, it is unbusinesslike and deserving of some action to curb the attending disturbances. If the threat perceiver is of such a mind, then he or she will have no hesitation in reporting the problems experienced as a result of this activity. Nor will the threat perceiver legitimately decline to follow any recommended steps that management directs to resolve the matter, up to and including providing relevant, verifiable details of impact to the job.

Organizational Actions   The organization that concurs in the threat perceiver's report of escalating irritation will be willing to assess business impact directly, to set boundaries for the offender and to also keep the perceiver from responding inappropriately, and to take some action to contain the irritation so as to preclude further escalation. Management response may include such options as counseling the offender by setting unequivocal restrictions on use of organizational computers and network access and doing so in writing to foreclose debate or future misunderstandings.

Scaling Note   At this point, a workplace with engaged employees and managers should find itself with employees and immediate supervisors categorizing the majority of purported insider events as rating between 0 and 1 on the threat scale. This rating encourages resolving problems at the lowest level through open communication, without agonizing over perceived slights to the point of magnifying nuisances and irritations beyond reason or the capacity for the work team to address to mutual satisfaction.

2: Chronic, Active Disruption

Threat Perceiver Actions   Now the threat perceiver has reason for greater concern, as the apparently hostile insider is using another's work station to perform eBay transactions and surf pornographic web sites during duty hours. Additionally, the same insider is failing to log off computers left in areas accessible to visitors and custodial staff and has been caught using someone else's password and employee name—the perceiver's—to gain network access without being held accountable for unauthorized Internet activity. Now the threat perceiver has even more reason for concern, since these actions give the appearance of the perceiver sharing in the illicit activity. At this point, the threat perceiver gives indications of the severity of such disruption by making formal reports and taking seriously advice to make changes, such as changing passwords and automatic logoff settings in addition to other guidance from management, cyber sentinels, or even legal authorities who may be investigating the matter.

Organizational Actions At this point, although the threat may be a long way from being existential, it has crossed over into a matter that is at least disciplinary and may even be illegal. This is where the organization demonstrates its appreciation of severity by instituting multiple countermeasures at once, including discipline of the offender, possible office moves to separate offender from victim or victims if the latter require some level of insulation to be able to work effectively, and other measures to assess damage and limit its spread. This may include internal or external investigations, which may also involve computer forensics probes to uncover the scope of the insider's misconduct or abuse of institutional assets. It may also involve curbing the insider's access to computers and networks and using sniffer programs or other tools to legitimately capture and monitor every keystroke that the offending insider is making.

3: Unacceptable, Proximate Harm

Threat Perceiver Actions Suppose that a hostile insider has now misused her boss's electronic credentials to authorize a release of thousands of dollars to a contractor for a service never performed, or that another insider has allowed a former college roommate to infect the network with a virus that resulted in a denial of service that cost a month of operating revenue to unscramble, or that another insider was responsible for abusing a confidential personnel database to support identity theft of 20 employees and compromise of their private information to organized crime. At this point, perceivers of threats—particularly those feeling themselves directly disadvantaged—demonstrate their seriousness by receptivity to a number of actions they would not consider for a lesser betrayal. Such actions include relocation to other work areas if there is a chance that they may have been exposed to criminals who may retaliate against them, full collaboration with employer and authorities in such matters as giving testimony and depositions, and even adopting lifestyle changes to exercise greater caution and security awareness.

Organizational Actions Meanwhile, the organization signals how seriously it takes such matters by removing the immediate source of the problem via suspension or termination, making special accommodations for targets to make them whole if they have experienced personal losses at the hands of an errant insider, arranging point protection at areas where the hostile insider is likely to strike targets, and even arranging protective surveillance of the offender or engaging police and cooperating with prosecuting attorneys to eliminate the threat from the workplace while sending a message about how the organization will not tolerate such actions.

Scale for Threats of Violence

0: Nuisance Level

Threat Perceiver Actions A nuisance level threat from within would most likely begin with verbalizing of statements inappropriate for the workplace yet arguably ambiguous as threats of violence. The perceiver of the threat, typically a coworker already at odds with the one making the statement at issue, may be overreacting or misinterpreting what was heard. Also, if the perceiver is a corporate sentinel with a particular sensitivity to inappropriate comments, owing to primary duties associated with monitoring institutional compliance to anti-harassment or grievance resolution programs, the perceiver may also be discerning a level of nuanced hostility that the originator of the comment neither intended nor realized. Thus, a gauche rendering of stupid remarks may fall short of an actual threat. After all, as management authority Peter Drucker once observed, "The experience of the human race indicates strongly that the only person in abundant supply is the universal incompetent."[32] The threat perceiver acting in good faith and recognizing the potential for stupidity to find verbal expression or for misunderstandings to ensue, would be willing to let go the perceived slight, perhaps mentioning it casually to the originator at a time when both are relaxed. Indeed, if the target of the remarks is of a mind to brush off the matter, a corporate sentinel who was in earshot and poised to make more of the matter would be wise to avoid needless escalation and allow for matters to find quiet, interpersonal resolution at the lowest level.

Organizational Actions   Similarly, the organization rating the incident as nothing more than a nuisance may be willing to forgive an occasional faux pas, particularly if there is no adverse impact to others or to the workplace. At the same time, however, some ongoing monitoring is wise so as to ensure that an isolated occurrence does not become an adverse trend.

1: Escalating Irritation

Threat Perceiver Actions   As the threat evolves into an escalating irritation, the perceiver reports more of a targeted action that gives the perceiver reason for concern. Such action may take the form of angry outbursts, fist-shaking, or other belligerence directed at the perceiver. The genuinely concerned threat perceiver at this point sees the wisdom in reporting the circumstances and both seeking and following the counsel of management or of corporate sentinels who have responsibility for evaluating and defending against workplace violence.

Organizational Actions   Organizationally, management now takes a closer look to validate the incident reported and even communicates with the belligerent insider to establish clear boundaries of what is and is not acceptable conduct at work. In consultation with sentinels, such as trained security staff, management may also introduce some countermeasures, such as closer monitoring of the belligerent individual and advice to the threat perceiver about whom to call and what actions to take for personal protection. Alternatively, management may turn to other sentinels, such as employee relations staff to provide counseling resources to the belligerent individual, including coaching on modifying undesirable workplace behaviors and on handling stress and anger in more appropriate ways.

Scaling Note   At this point, a workplace with engaged employees and managers should derive the twin benefits of early warning and early intervention. Thus, if the majority of purported threats of violence rate between 0 and 1 on the threat scale, the institution addresses these as matters for timely resolution by frontline management. This rating again encourages resolving problems at the lowest level through open communication, without agonizing over perceived slights to the point of magnifying nuisances and irritations beyond reason or the capacity for the work team to address to businesslike resolution with minimal disruption to operations.

2: Chronic, Active Disruption

Threat Perceiver Actions   Threats of violence go beyond escalating irritation once threat perceivers have reason to develop concerns for their personal safety. No ambiguity remains at this point, and the belligerent insider may now have a reputation for expressing hostility and outbursts that upset the target or targets (usually the threat perceivers) and also interfere with the routine functioning of the place of business. Individuals demonstrate their appreciation that matters have reached this level on the threat scale by agreeing to make formal reports to authorities, as advised by the institution, and by taking seriously more specific advice to reduce their ongoing exposure, such as altering their patterns of contact or movement that bring them into contact with the belligerent individual, avoiding inflammatory remarks or retorts and taking de-escalation guidance to heart, maintaining confidentiality of any employer plans for containing the situation, and faithfully following all employer guidance on next steps.

Organizational Actions   The institution itself now takes the laboring oar in addressing the situation, including exploring all legal options. In some cases, this could even rise to the level of obtaining a restraining order on the part of the employer, so that the threat perceiving employee does not draw greater hostility by pursuing such an option directly. Meanwhile, the institution deploys multiple countermeasures at once to limit vulnerability of threat perceivers and any others who may be at risk, including office moves such as relocating individuals in apparent jeopardy, curbing and monitoring the belligerent individual's movements via available access control systems, and giving defensive briefings to additional threat perceivers voicing their concerns. Activating the functionality of always threat assessment team per institutional workplace violence policy is also likely to occur at this point, as is the establishment of monitoring points and consideration of disciplinary actions to use to remove threatening individuals from the workplace, possibly via suspensions or even paid administrative leave, depending on the particular circumstances.

3: Unacceptable, Proximate Harm

Threat Perceiver Actions   At this point, the internal threat assessment team has concluded that a belligerent insider really does pose a threat or the behavior of concern has escalated into physical confrontation or signs of a clear threat or impending attack. Threat perceivers demonstrate their understanding that the situation has reached this level by expeditiously relocating to a protected work space, if that option is available and directed, and by following advice from security sentinels or local police regarding precautions to take at home with family. Perceivers further do their part by testifying or giving depositions required of them to pursue legal action and even adopt lifestyle changes (such as altering commute routes and not going alone to parking garages late at night) if necessary.

Organizational Actions   The institution recognizes the seriousness of threats of violence, at this point, by making special accommodations for likely targets, including altering their work schedules to avoid exposure to possible attacks. In some cases, institutions may even deploy in-house or external protective resources to defend targets from attack in such volatile situations as administrative hearings or meetings where the belligerent individual's presence is required. They may even arrange surveillance of the antagonist to be able to ensure that the belligerent insider is not posing a threat to a targeted employee population. They will also be working closely with legal staff, police, and even prosecuting attorneys to explore legal remedies for the situation.

Scale for Exploiting Assets for Gain

0: Nuisance Level

Threat Perceiver Actions Nuisance-level threats include coworkers who are always seeking preferential treatment at another's expense, giving the impression that they are being mercenary or minimally collaborative unless forced. Threat perceivers recognize this level by sharing a view that such individuals are not team players and only out for themselves. As long as the sources of concern are performing their duties at some acceptable level, threat perceivers are likely to accept that the behavior at issue, although unappealing, falls within the range of normal variation that is suitable for ignoring or brushing off, in the hope that team dynamics may eventually influence migration to more collaborative behaviors.

Organizational Actions From the organization's perspective, nuisance behaviors such as these are of modest concern as long as they do not impede the flow of operations or radically interfere with the performance of others. Indeed, in the case of embezzlers and other insiders motivated by the desire to exploit access for gain, nuisance behaviors are almost a positive sign, since greater mischief is likely to come at the hands of devious insiders who mask their villainy under the guise of an engaging or neutral demeanor less likely to draw attention.

1: Escalating Irritation

Threat Perceiver Actions Escalating irritation arises when threat perceivers observe improprieties on the part of other employees but may yet feel reluctant to make an issue of incidents out of a lack of conclusive evidence or fear of being perceived as an informant. They may report suspicions informally, yet threat perceivers stop short of registering formal complaints or coming forward with testimony. They may underscore their concern, however, by asking for more controls over inventory, for example, so that at least the threat perceivers will not be blamed for losses caused by others. They may also be amenable to taking some steps to secure the institution's assets from internal losses and even to support internal investigations.

Organizational Actions To the institution getting wind of escalating irritation at internally caused losses, such notice represents an opportunity for stemming a tide that will no doubt result in more frequent and costly losses if left unchecked. The institution at this point assesses the problem and may set boundaries—for all involved in a function under scrutiny, if not for a specific individual suspected of being a problem. Thus, management may institute a change in cash handling procedures for all petty cash custodians rather than risk accusing one of embezzling in the absence of definitive proof. At the same time, introducing additional countermeasures such as spot checking balances and increasing the frequency of random audits could also serve the institution to keep losses in check.

Scaling Note At this point, a workplace with engaged employees and managers should find that minor insider exploitations will rate between 0 and 1 on the threat scale, and they will lend themselves to identification and elimination through transparency and application of management attention when they arise. However, the insiders aiming higher will avoid giving themselves away at the 0 to 1 level, to the extent that they can keep in harness their predatory impulses long enough to aim for greater returns.

2: Chronic, Active Disruption

Threat Perceiver Actions   Threat perceivers at this level approach the point of saying enough is enough. They may have witnessed repeated effects of an insider misappropriating funds or property to the point that they can no longer look the other way and that their inhibitions about being seen as an informant are overtaken by concern for the harm that the insider is causing to their team, institution, or even their job security. At this point, threat perceivers are ready to make formal reports to authorities and to forgo reservations about employer advice on how to react to the situation. One such situation, for example, could involve a lead employee in charge of ordering equipment whose pattern it is to order one more tool or appliance than necessary and to then take the extra item for personal use or to go through a charade of declaring it as surplus and later claiming it for himself.

Organizational Actions   At this point, it is doubtful that the danger is existential. However, it merits disciplinary action up to termination and may also be subject to legal remedy. This is where the institution activates multiple countermeasures at once, including discipline of the offender, deployment of controls and changes in procedures to make it impossible for the misappropriation to continue in its present form, and further monitoring and assignment of resources to evaluate how much has been lost and to plug the holes of vulnerabilities identified in the evaluation.

3: Unacceptable, Proximate Harm

Threat Perceiver Actions   Here the hostile insider has found expression of talent for self-enrichment by one or more serious breaches that threat perceivers recognize as wrong and distance themselves from to avoid disciplinary, legal, or reputational consequence. Even former confederates turn on ringleaders, in the hope of striking a plea agreement for lesser penalties in exchange for supplying evidence to capture the hostile insider. Such threat perceivers may themselves fear for their lives, requiring close protection at home and office, or even needing relocation to a position of safety that is out of the hostile insider's reach. Here, too, threat perceivers must be ready to adopt changes in lifestyle, including residences, patterns of movement, and even entering a witness protection program if the stakes are sufficiently high.

Organizational Actions   For its own part, the institution will have to make special arrangements to avoid major losses from this kind of hostile insider, including making special accommodations to protect or indemnify confederates who have turned on the insider in time to permit making a recovery of some or all assets in jeopardy. Additional arrangements may include use of special surveillance teams and collaboration with authorities to capture the predatory insider and freeze assets before the latter can move them beyond the reach of the institution or the law. Alternatively, extreme cases may leave the institution little choice but to attempt at least a partial recovery without involvement of government authorities, particularly if issues of reputational risk suggest the likelihood of an irretrievable loss of investor confidence and prospects for asset recovery hinge on coming to terms with the hostile insider directly or losing any chance of restitution.

Scaling Note   The more sophisticated the exploitive insider, the more likely that the institution will see no precursor warnings at the 0 to 2 levels before encountering this threat for the first time at the point of carrying out direct, proximate harm. However, having an active sensing network and capacity borne of the No Dark Corners innovations in transparency and employee engagement will increase the chance of the institution receiving some degree of warning that something is amiss before this insider has fully carried out an intended exploitation and escaped beyond the institution's grasp.

SPECIAL CASES

In the expansive galaxy of insiders who betray trust to the disadvantage of their fellows or their institution there shine too many star examples to track or enumerate. We thus confine ourselves to a sample pleiad to impart a sense of where these cases may fit on the insider threat scale and which No Dark Corners measures may avail in countering them.

Sympathizers

Sympathizers—whether adherents of a faith, political party, or personal cause ranging from animal rights to environmental defense—are insiders who would seldom present danger in or of themselves. Often lacking in maturity or in a surer sense of the world, sympathizers visibly allow their governing passions to overrule their judgment or obligations. Synonymous with useful idiots, a term popularly but unverifiably attributed to Lenin,[33] these individuals seldom verge beyond the nuisance level. However, because they make no secret of the zeal with which they champion the cause by which they navigate through life, sympathizers require little effort and few inducements for shrewd adversaries to manipulate them into serious betrayals or compromises. What may start as an innocuous inquiry about the sympathizer's availability to join an animal rights weekend rally, for example, could flourish into discussion of the sympathizer's duties at a bank that funds a hospital whose work includes animal research. Soon, the interlocutor has elicited details about the sympathizer's access to personal details of the bank's board of directors. Eventually, the sympathizer is persuaded to deliver those details to what he thinks are like-minded animal rights sympathizers who stated an intention of mailing a research study to each bank director along with a letter requesting that the recipient consider using the bank's influence to end animal experimentation. Only the sympathizer does not realize that he has played into the hands of an aggressive organization linked to using bombs and arson and by no means above using illegal tactics of intimidation to advance its cause, including targeting bank director residences and frightening their children with acts of violence.[34]

Even the most enlightened and nurturing employer possessed of the best features of a No Dark Corners workplace merits limited reach into a sympathizer's personal life to interfere with the latter's freedom of association. However, there is no obligation on the part of the institution to entrust sensitive information to employees who lack discretion or the capacity for separating their fiduciary duties from their ruling passions. Thus, defenders may wish to reserve sensitive information such as personal contact details of directors to the exclusive attention of proven employees who have demonstrated that they can be trusted. Alternatively, before entrusting sympathizers or other insufficiently vetted employees, defenders may consider testing them by releasing bait or outdated "sensitive" material to track whether the material surfaces where it does not belong. Maintaining open channels of communication and configuring work so as to limit opportunities for the sympathizer to obtain sole access to sensitive files will also avail. In this kind of case, it is likely that the sympathizer, being unaccustomed to operating clandestinely, may give him or herself away when trying to copy a list of director addresses and even confess to an apparent infraction in the service of what the sympathizer fervently believes is a higher cause. A good relationship with frontline management and team members would thus derive early warning from such an admission. This warning, in turn, would enable improving protection for targeted directors or even focusing other resources on lawful disruption of intimidation efforts and enlisting authorities in intervening in virulent, illegal attacks.

Lynch Mobs, Flash Mobs, and Overwhelming Crowds

Unexpected concentration of people in great numbers produces consequences akin to the sudden release of torrents of water into a dry lake. It can raise landlocked vessels, enabling them to rediscover mobility, as a Gandhi could animate multitudes into peaceful protest and irreversible victory. It can also drown passersby like a tsunami wave striking a shoreline after a catastrophic earthquake. When occurring within the confines of a space assumed to be accessible to persons who become insiders—at least for a time—such concentrations soon overtake traditional inhibitions and capacity for denying access or limiting the destructive potential of any lone individual. As a result, the overwhelming force of sheer numbers of people who may or may not qualify as insiders finds expression in such phenomena as lynch mobs in bygone days or, in the modern era, as flash mobs. Lynch mobs, however, followed a more gradual and visible arc, which gave astute authorities such as Texas Rangers the means to defeat them with economical application of resources. One former law enforcement figure noted that the Texas Rangers had struck upon the best technique for dealing with a mob:

> The Texas Ranger technique was to linger on the fringes of the disturbance, watching until they could identify the leaders, then work their way through the crowd to leaders and beat the hell out of them until, leaderless, the rioters became easy to disperse.[35]

Today's environment scarcely lends itself to resolution through such tactics. Although the lynch mob is an artifact of a more lawless past, the flash mob is organized not by a ringleader's polemic delivered before a public assembly but by telecommunications, social media, or viral e-mail or text messages. Springing forth in Manhattan circa 2003 as forms of performance art enlisting large numbers and tending to innocuous activities such as public pillow fights, flash mobs have since begun to descend into fights and vandalism among mostly youthful participants.[36] The more aggressive versions of this phenomenon have produced looting and serious property damage in cities from Philadelphia to London, leading the National Retail Federation in 2011 to discuss flash mobs in the context of multiple offender crimes targeting shopkeepers.[37] Flash mobs organized for robbery, or flash robs, leave retailers at a loss on how to defend their stores from being overrun by people entering as potential customers but plundering the shops after filling them beyond capacity with so many confederates that no store employee can reach let alone stop the mob from making off with goods or destroying displays and fixtures in the mob's wake.

The puzzle of how and whether flash mobs become insider threats and the extent to which they pose existential risk becomes a blueprint for addressing the dilemma of special cases or outliers that do not fit within the traditional purview of insider threat defense. First, the individuals constituting the mob hold no position of trust, hence no fiduciary duty to the institution. Thus they cannot be in a position to betray a trust if there is no trust in the first place. However, to the extent that mob participants are able to enter the premises the same way as legitimate customers and to the extent that these individuals belong to the same society populated by retailers and legitimate customers alike, the flash mob members do attain one valuable insider advantage: access. However, on an individual basis, these individuals themselves tend to occupy the lower rungs of the threat scale, ranging between nuisance to escalating irritation levels. Absent the power of the mob, they individually possess no more power than vandals or petty thieves—something the retail organization can readily handle through security measures, property insurance, or through a combination of the two that treats minor losses as a cost of doing business. As their number multiplies, however, the defender's capacity to absorb or prevent losses shrinks to the point of collapse and, in the worst case, to shuttering a business that has been plundered and then burned to the ground, leaving the minimally insured, struggling business owner bereft of a livelihood or the means to recover. Thus, a flash mob can become a devastating existential threat for a small retail business lacking the capital to rebuild or the capacity to offset losses from other income streams. For the larger institution, however, it is doubtful that the flash mob can produce more than episodic loss consistent with the nuisance or escalating irritation level. A long-term campaign of flash mob strikes targeting a particular institution could conceivably verge on the level of chronic, active disruption on the threat scale. At this point, it appears that as the flash mob increases its intensity of destructive potential its insider qualities diminish proportionately. When the mob's actions become indistinguishable from rioting and mayhem through large numbers of antagonists, access is no longer at issue, rendering moot the discussion of insider threat status. When the number of participants reaches riot threshold, access is gained by force and resulting confrontations take on an us-vs.-them character. In these circumstances, attackers take pains to victimize targets who patently differ from them in age or appearance, and being an insider becomes a liability because it opens one to attack by the mob.

Although a variety of measures may be available for defending against brutalization by flash mob, the more aggressive security options bear little connection to No Dark Corners strategies. Such defenses include using a security vestibule with double, interlocking doors designed to make it impossible for more than a set number of individuals to enter the premises at a time, which is also known as a man trap.[38] Adding protective lamination to display windows to make them shatter resistant and installing additional barriers or even an innovative intrusion deterrent[39] that can generate an irritating sound audible to youths but inaudible to the older adults constituting one's usual client base could all deter or limit damage. The principal drawback of such options is that they require budget or physical configurations that may not necessarily be available to the most frequently targeted organizations.

What No Dark Corners approaches do offer is an opportunity to gain early warning and attempt to anticipate flash mob attacks by taking advantage of the collaboration and creativity of an engaged workforce. If employees of the same generation as flash mob participants feel they have a stake in the health of the organization, for example, they can use social media themselves to monitor for signs of impending mob strikes. By extending transparency and collaboration among fellow shopkeepers in a given area and by reaching out to counterparts who have experienced flash mob attacks directly, defenders can also take a hand in their own protection by developing a checklist of indicators of an impending attack and corresponding actions to take. Defensive actions can include drills to enable locking down the store rapidly and ushering out customers from a back exit, doubly securing high-value items in locking containers within the locked store, and activating audible intrusion alarms as the mob approaches. Those willing to risk controversy in exchange for disrupting the portable devices that flash mobs rely on can even weigh the merits of interfering with wireless communications as a subway operator did to avoid a disruptive protest.[40] The wisdom of such communications interruption may be doubtful in the long run, as they appear equally likely to spawn subsequent, retaliatory actions that may prove more damaging than the initial event that was avoided.

Citizen Unrest and Uprising

Citizen unrest expressed as an insider threat bears many features of the flash mob. It is an insider threat only to the extent that citizens presumably share some common elements of constituency with the regime in power. Also, if the unrest is relatively infrequent, it shares the flash mob's tendency of seldom straying beyond the level of nuisance or escalating irritation on the threat scale. This kind of unrest or uprising is unlikely to start as an existential threat when it first arises. However, if unrest triggers overreaction through draconian measures, then overplaying the defender's hand may well accelerate the transformation of what began as a containable situation into an existential threat, as did the 2011 Arab Spring uprisings in Tunisia and Egypt but similar protests failed to do in Iran in 2009. Another difference is that citizen unrest and uprising aim at higher goals—regime change, for example—and target larger institutions—the state as opposed to a shopkeeper, for example. Nevertheless, in the twenty-first century, both flash mob and citizen unrest share common tools and tactics, including social networking media to coordinate deployments of multitudes of adherents and reliance on unexpected size and appearance of crowds to overwhelm opposition.

Eventually, organized and resolute defense prevails in most situations of civil unrest until and unless the defending force refuses to contain popular opposition or even breaks ranks and joins the uprising. Such was the case in 1991 with the last effort of hardliners to preserve the Soviet Union with tanks poised to overrun opposition of Boris Yeltsin's newly declared Russian republic in Moscow. Although superior in number and armament, Soviet soldiers refused to fire on the Russians and the day went to Yeltsin and Russia, sealing the collapse of the Soviet apparat.[41] By contrast, Iran's unrelenting suppression of 2009 protests, including use of deadly force on the streets and social media-blocking technology in the airwaves, robbed the uprising of its technological edge, rendering it a spent force before it progressed to win support of wider segments of the population. Indeed, as one analyst noted, when the Iranian regime called out the Islamic Revolutionary Guard, it was clear that the latter were not drawn from "the Twittering classes" and would remain loyal to the regime.[42]

No Dark Corners innovations have little to offer in stemming the tide of civil unrest, which has the potential to become an existential threat beyond the scope of defense against trust betrayers. Indeed, under some circumstances, if the target is an oppressive regime visiting hardship and privation upon its own citizens, it may be argued that it is the regime breaking faith with its citizens, hence betraying trust and itself becoming the threat from the inside. However, No Dark Corners approaches may offer to defenders the same kind of value in countering civil unrest that they do in countering flash mobs and other such crowds. They offer a starting point for gathering intelligence through transparency and making common cause with like-minded stakeholders in order to anticipate adverse events.

Sporting Event Mayhem

Athletic contests in large stadiums where the battle on the playing field inspires violent skirmishes or stampedes among spectators are insider threats only to the extent that participants share affiliation or pedigree with players or even with each other. Seldom do out-of-control sports fans turn out to be foreign dignitaries or first-time attendees of a given match. Instead, they are enthusiasts passionately supporting a team who find in a sporting venue an environment conducive to uninhibited expressions of team loyalty and equally expressive intolerance of opposing views. Recalling the crowd dynamics that play out to some extent with flash mobs and civil uprisings, obstreperous sports fans in a crowd may hover between the level of nuisance or escalating irritation. One difference, however, is that alcohol consumed before or during a game is more prevalent in this case, speeding the potential acceleration of a given threat into the level where unacceptable and proximate harm is likely to result. Although seldom an existential threat to teams or stadiums, mayhem associated with sporting events may prove fatal to those caught in its path.

Crowd control techniques—visible and active security presence, and rapid response to problems by friendly but firm authorities—can prevent sporting event hostility from escalating beyond the nuisance level.[43] Once people show signs of losing their individuality to the crowd or the introduction of drugs or alcohol produces a drinking-party atmosphere, the crowd is turning unruly and likely to become difficult if not impossible to control.[44]

The challenge of applying No Dark Corners techniques to a crowd in a sporting event is that work team collaboration developed over time cannot be infused on demand into large groups of people whose only unifying tendency may be in destroying with the impunity conferred by the mob. This is a far cry from the bond of team in a shared purpose to build or defend something of mutually recognized benefit or interest. There remains, however, an opportunity for deriving protective value from No Dark Corners strategies by widening the circle of those involved in otherwise unrelated aspects of the given sporting event. Instead of having an insular security staff concerned exclusively with protecting star athletes, for example, snack vendors, ticket takers, souvenir sales staff, event planners, fire marshals, local police, stadium managers, parking attendants, and security staff could all enter into a collaborative and mutually supporting network unified in a shared stake in a safe game with no harm to people or facilities. The net result is to extend the intelligence-gathering and protective cordons to watch and guide sports fans to event-free self-expression and confinement of conflict to the playing field.

Undermining Contemporaries

The peer who appears to be a supporter but repeatedly fails to deliver when relied upon presents a minor threat to the institution but an unacceptable one to the individual chronically victimized by such disappointments. What is a nuisance level threat to the organization may rise to so unacceptable a level for the victim as to cost an employer the services of a valued contributor who feels a career move is the only option for escaping from the toxic miasma surrounding the undermining contemporary. The latter is not an existential threat, but certainly an impediment to personal effectiveness and equanimity.

Some people visit on their friends or on people close to them the kinds of pettiness and perfidy that no enemy would tolerate. As one observer notes,

> People who lack self-confidence and are pessimistic about their own future may not support you . . . and they may suck every ounce of energy from you to fill their need to feel comfortable with themselves. Although these people deserve our compassion, spending time with them regularly is not at all healthy for us.[45]

On a personal level, such contemporaries become toxic friends, namely, consistent generators of adverse consequences, often by being excessively needy, negative, emotionally draining, controlling, gossiping, self-absorbed, or overly distracting.[46] However, the concern here is not so much with the toxic friends that bedevil one's personal life as those underminers on the job from whom there may be no ready escape.

Where can No Dark Corners offer value in dealing with the adverse effects of undermining contemporaries who become toxic friends? The same process that defenders use in vetting applicants before giving them tenure with the work team can assist individuals in avoiding the intrusion of underminers into their circle of trust. By taking time to let friendships evolve and by only gradually trusting a new friend after observing the individual in action in a variety of settings, one decreases the likelihood of entering into a toxic work friendship and also provides multiple early exit opportunities before the association advances to the point of an intimacy that can lead to compromise or undermining of one's effectiveness within the organization.

Prodigal Kin

If undermining contemporaries at least offer the benefit of limiting their reach to the workplace, prodigal kin have the potential to savage an individual's personal life to the point of turning that individual from an asset into a liability in the eyes of the institution. Wayward relatives categorized as prodigal kin may be spendthrifts whose impact is not only financial but whose chronic parasitic influence robs the targeted individual of the capacity to continue to perform on the job. To the institution, prodigal kin pose neither an existential threat nor much more than a nuisance. To their target, they offer many of the deleterious features of undermining contemporaries without the availability of boundaries for limiting their appearances and schemes to the workplace. Moreover, at first glance, the behavior of an insider afflicted by the machinations of prodigal kin may appear indistinguishable from that of a trust betrayer poised to turn on his or her employer.

The only proper involvement of the institution in addressing prodigal kin is either at the invitation of an employee seeking help or when the prodigal's actions directly impinge upon the institution. In the latter case, the prodigal family member who has made off with a corporate credit card entrusted to the care of the employee and then run up fraudulent charges for a skiing vacation at the institution's expense becomes no longer a forgivable, personal problem for the related employee to solve alone. Whether it is the employee who takes the lead in resolving the situation or the institution that steps in to recover the credit card and misspent funds, neither can afford to make a priority of rescuing the prodigal. Indeed, as one observer and counselor specializing in such cases found over time, rescuing does not help the prodigal because it insulates the individual from consequences, encouraging more future misadventures. Instead, the stance to adopt is for the related employee to be able to say,

> I am on your side always. But I won't apologize or make excuses for your behavior any more, nor will I make it easy for you to stay the same.[47]

In a No Dark Corners workplace, transparency and employee engagement combine to surface not so much the private details of prodigal kin experienced by a given employee but behavioral cues that suggest something is amiss. Then, whether at the behest of fellow team members or of a supervisor, the troubled employee finds the encouragement and support necessary to seek out timely assistance, typically through self-referral or, at times, directed referral to the institution's employee assistance program or counseling resources. For the institution, a situation such as this is a relief, compared to the alternative possibility that the troubled employee's behavior may show signs similar to that of a trust betrayer on the point of harming the employer for personal gain or other reasons. Instead of facing the twin burdens of impending loss or damage of assets and the likely loss of a productive employee, most defenders would prefer to discover that the problem is not with a treacherous insider but with an errant family member responsible for causing stress—a situation far more tractable for the institution than facing a direct insider threat.

Misguided Redeemers

Misguided redeemers are employees within the institution who are bent on adding value where it is not needed or where their perception of its worth is unshared by those competent to judge it. Although most misguided redeemers operate at the nuisance level, they can produce cascading, adverse impacts, particularly if their influence extends to major strategic decisions. Few cases better illustrate how misguided redeemers imperil the health and prospects of an institution more than the story of how IBM came to choose Microsoft to develop DOS (disk operating system) for the personal computer market.

Microsoft's rise as the leader in operating systems owes its opportunity in part to misguided redeemers who unintentionally created Microsoft's breakout opportunity by sabotaging themselves as a competitor who was IBM's first choice to do the work that transformed Microsoft into a meteoric success. An IBM team started out intending to give its business to Gary Kindall, founder of Digital Research and creator of the operating system known as CPM. Kindall, however, being relatively uninspired by the business aspects of his undertakings, placed little value on the IBM visit, departing the area and leaving his wife to meet with the IBM team. Dorothy Kindall, in her misguided thought to add value, refused to sign IBM's standard nondisclosure agreement. To make matters worse, she referred the IBM delegation to a corporate attorney who, in an even more misguided effort to add value, took great issue with the language of the nondisclosure agreement, effectively driving away the chance of a lifetime. Meanwhile, Bill Gates and the Microsoft team had accepted the terms of the nondisclosure on faith and demonstrated a willingness to work with IBM for what they perceived as an extraordinary opportunity. Gates rose to become the world's richest entrepreneur, whereas Kindall plummeted to obscurity.[48]

Misguided redeemers come in other forms, including the inept proposing ways to fix what needs no repair and, in a more insidious yet outwardly innocuous manifestation, the successful boss who cannot accept a subordinate's idea without altering it in some way. Called a variation on the need to win, this desire to add value stifles initiative and retards progress because once an executive offers even a 5% alteration of the suggestion, it becomes the executive's idea and the subordinate who proposed it loses 50% commitment to executing the idea that is no longer his or her own.[49]

Although the misguided redeemer also generally operates at the nuisance level, advancing to higher levels, particularly if the redeemer holds executive rank, is a very real possibility that can find its ultimate expression in missed opportunities or flawed strategic decisions, such as the Microsoft case highlighted. For the most part, it is only when a misguided redeemer approximates similar consequences that he or she becomes a harmful insider, albeit generally one who is also oblivious to the resulting damage or loss.

Where No Dark Corners approaches offer assistance in dealing with misguided redeemers is in sustaining enough transparency and shared responsibility among employees as stakeholders to enable them to recognize the phenomenon and to then alert someone in a position to take remedial action. This will likely mean enlisting an appropriate level of management or executive support to guide the misguided redeemer away from undermining behaviors while attempting to recover from any lost opportunities experienced in the interim.

FLEETING OR OCCASIONAL INSIDER THREATS— A NEBULOUS CATEGORY OF OTHERS

There are times and situations which produce shared trust and bonds that create an insider's team spirit where, under different circumstances, there would be no expectation of unity of effort or a clear way of distinguishing insider from outsider. Airline passengers illustrate both conditions. For the most part, airline passengers are strangers with only the most superficial connections to one another: a shared destination and capacity for paying for travel on the same conveyance. Few have loyalties to each other or to the particular air carrier transporting them on a given day. They do not know each other well enough to pretend to care about let alone trust one another. Thus, a passenger with hostile intent can hardly be considered a trust betrayer, having established no trust to violate. Consequently, it would appear that the terrorist infiltrating an airline cabin as a fellow passenger would be ranked among potentially lethal adversaries, yet still fall short of being regarded an insider threat. Then there is the case of United Flight 93 and a story of how passengers meeting all the foregoing criteria found a way to make common cause, resolved to resist 9/11 hijackers, and became a team of insiders sacrificing their lives to deny terrorist attackers an opportunity for greater carnage, resulting in Flight 93's crash into unoccupied ground in Pennsylvania instead of into a populated public building in Washington, DC.[50] Not until the passengers had used their mobile phones to gather information about other 9/11 air attacks and then surmised that they were in store for an identical fate did they unify as a team to die fighting. The terrorists they fought were already a team with a mission when boarding Flight 93. Was there an insider threat, if only for a time?

The case is perplexing. On the one hand, to the extent all passengers gain access to airport terminal and aircraft, they do become—at least temporarily—insiders by virtue of gaining entry to the interior of spaces which, if attacked from the outside, would be targets of an outsider threat. Having infiltrated past the usual defenses, then, terrorists such as those commandeering Flight 93 did take on some aspects of insiders. On the other hand, the rest of the passengers surely thought themselves no more insiders than outsiders as they were preparing to embark on a flight in innocent transit. At the point of departure, they had no bond of trust between each other, a condition equally extending to the terrorist hijackers who came on board in the guise of regular passengers. Yet, by the time the flight touched down away from its scheduled and also away from its commandeered destination, passengers other than terrorists had united, formed a bond and shared objective, and had in effect turned into insider threats jeopardizing the objectives of the terrorist hijackers. These circumstances permit variety in interpretation. Were there no insider threats, two different insider threats, or just a single insider threat? Any of these interpretations is arguable.

What about existential threats? That the hijackers and, later, the passengers mobilized into a counterattack all posed an existential threat for Flight 93 is undisputed. As the day's events bore out, no hijacked passengers or hijackers survived the transformation of passenger aircraft into guided missiles. However, if the hijackers did indeed pose a threat—regardless of whether insider or outsider, for the moment—they clearly aimed at accomplishing more than just taking the lives of their targets and passengers. Al Qaeda's objectives, to the extent explained in the course of analysis and reflection, were to "organize and conduct a complex international terrorist operation to inflict catastrophic harm."[51] Thus, the Flight 93 attack would appear to qualify for the highest level on the threat scale, that of unacceptable, proximate harm.

Our original definition of insider threat from Chapter 1, however, suggests that airline hijackers are not insiders any more than external computer hackers are. Both lack at least one key trait. Recalling that an insider threat is an individual and, more broadly, the danger posed by an individual who possesses legitimate access and occupies a position of trust in or with the infrastructure or institution being targeted, hijackers may gain legitimate access but hardly occupy a position of trust. Cyber hackers from the outside have neither. Consequently, when attempting to deploy insider threat defenses against such attackers, one must bear in mind that countermeasures optimized for defeating hostile insiders will hardly offer the same advantage against outsiders. Nevertheless, the institution's defenders may legitimately call into service the tools at hand, since the question of tool misapplication is moot if no other tools are available. Just because a screwdriver is unavailable for removing a bolt, it does not mean we cannot try using a pair of pliers to do the job in a pinch.

Where do No Dark Corners strategies offer value in cases such as United Flight 93, as defenders contend with an unscheduled change in flight path and hijackers taking the controls of the aircraft rather than just taking a single hostage and issuing a list of demands? Recall that until the events of 9/11 the standard security response was based on the historical expectation that hijacking was used either as a means of escape or political kidnapping.[52] Thus, the corresponding advice given to individuals concerned about airline hijacking tended to be to project calm, avoid confrontation or scrutiny, and await negotiations between terrorists and authorities to attain a nonviolent resolution— no matter how long it takes. In the case of Flight 93, along with the other 9/11 hijackings, this advice became instantly obsolete. However, Flight 93 passengers used their mobile phones and shared fresh information about the other 9/11 attacks to rapidly surmise that the situation had changed and that the old rules for responding to a hijacking were no longer in effect on this occasion. Through an open sharing of information and peer-level collaboration consistent with No Dark Corners, Flight 93's passengers accurately assessed the situation they found themselves in, weighed their options, and then acted on their best judgment without abdicating their power to airline sentinels, or authorities, or to some unseen deus ex machina as an alternative to taking responsibility for their own fate. The heroes of Flight 93 epitomized the best of No Dark Corners strategies in peer-level engagement.

EXTORTION AS ANOTHER INDIRECT THREAT

Extortion involves the removal or damage of assets through the application of force or intimidation.[53] It is not an insider threat per se, because the agent of extortion needs an insider to victimize in order to gain the desired assets or access to them. However, the institution may easily find itself facing the results of extortion if a trusted employee surprises coworkers, sentinels, and management alike by facilitating burglary, embezzlement, or sabotage.

What makes extortion give the appearance of an insider threat? The victim of extortion begins to display unaccountably odd behaviors that are consistent with the actions of a trust betrayer. Thus, as for the sympathizer or the employee abused by prodigal kin, the employee in the grip of extortion emits signals of being under the sway of forces potentially inimical to the institution. Properly interpreted and acted upon, these signals stimulate conversations among work team members and between employee and boss, with attending offers of assistance. Once again, the No Dark Corners environment of transparency and engagement increases the chances of detection and, with this, of timely intervention.

LESSONS OF ONE-OFF CASES

Cases that are not technically insider threats and thus appear to fall beyond the purview of insider threat defense may be safely set aside only by those with no stake in the institution's welfare. Otherwise, defenders must deal with the realization that cases perceived to be insider threats are real threats in the consequences they create. If a mechanism or channel exists to take such one-off cases off the plate of insider threat defense and spoon them onto a larger platter where specialized and mature defenses are already tailored for that particular threat and arrayed in a position to address it smartly, so much the better. However, many if not most organizations do not possess such an abundance of defensive resources at their instant disposal. It thus becomes necessary to extend those resources that have proven successful and have delivered value to the institution. Consequently, in a No Dark Corners environment where the engaged work team has become the first line of defense instead of the weakest link, the team may expect to extend the range of its finesse in safeguarding against hostile trust betrayers by applying existing protocols and team engagement to addressing other threats as they arise. Ultimately, the team will lose interest on whether a given antagonist is technically an insider. Instead, the dispositive issue will be whether that antagonist poses a threat to the institution where employees are not only wage earners but also stakeholders. If the team ethos makes reflexive the copilot level of exercising proprietary interest in the work and workplace, then the No Dark Corners team will deliver the benefit of early detection of anomalies that stand to pose an element of hostility or potential loss in the making. Then, in an environment supporting transparency and collaboration, team members detecting the anomaly reach out to their bosses and corporate sentinels as both sounding boards and for specialized expertise to assist with categorizing the anomaly on the threat scale as nuisance, escalating irritation, active disruption, or direct source of harm.

IMPLICATION OF CHANGING WORKPLACE
DYNAMICS FOR INSIDER THREATS

A defining point in distinguishing the hostile insider from insiders who are innocuous has traditionally been the former's propensity for trust betrayal. Betrayal, in turn, connotes violation of loyalties, suggesting a bond between employer and employee that need not be filial but must nonetheless exist in some elemental form to establish the preconditions for mutual trust. What if this bond ceased to exist or if it eroded to the point that assumed loyalties were no more than an illusion? The resulting condition would offer few assurances for the institution with critical assets to defend. Without shared bonds or perceptions of mutual loyalties, team members, sentinels, and managers might hesitate to answer the call to defend, particularly if the institution promoted no cohesion or benefits beyond a check for services rendered. Is this the workplace of the future? Analysts noting workforce evolution in developed countries from a now retiring industrial age to the new age of the knowledge worker began forecasting such changes for at least the preceding 20 years, beginning with the decline of traditional institutional employers and the rise of the knowledge worker. In order for the institution to defend against trust betrayal over time, it is important for it to function within the context of the modern workplace that is poised to become what one management authority labeled as the shamrock organization.[54] Subsequently, a separate observer has come to validate the characterization of the knowledge worker as holding true to predictions and poised to transform the way knowledge work is performed and its agents are treated. The organization ignoring these changing dynamics and expecting to mount a robust defense against hostile insiders deludes itself and may well breach its fiduciary duties by assuming that yesterday's assumptions about workforce loyalty and engagement will stand firm without special care to today's and tomorrow's vicissitudes.

THE SHAMROCK ORGANIZATION AS
INCUBATOR FOR NO DARK CORNERS

Peter Drucker and Charles Handy are different management authorities who recognized the same phenomenon: emergence of a knowledge society that has shifted the center of gravity to the knowledge worker, as the dominance of the industrial worker has faded along with the vanishing supremacy of the manufacturing age.[55] In Handy's construct, the impact of this change is a fundamental transformation of the institution into an organization assembled of three main parts, hence the shamrock.[56] One leaf of the shamrock consists of a small core of actual employees working directly for the institution, including essential workers and executives. Unlike the monolithic enterprise of years past, however, this core will be relatively small in number. Gone will be the multitudes of interchangeable minions and multilayered hierarchies of management. Indeed, the numbers of core employees will be so few that most will find themselves less in the position of workers climbing a ladder than prime contractors responsible for managing the delivery of a key product or service using knowledge workers who come from outside the institution as consultants or contractors. If the knowledge workers form this second leaf of the shamrock, what population remains to fill the third? These are the non-knowledge workers, including temporary and part-time workers and casual laborers who lack the cerebral capacity or specialized knowledge to occupy more than the bottom rung of any low-skilled labor pool.

What can they expect in terms of respective career arcs? The core employees can look forward to starting their careers later and ending them sooner. Their later start is necessary to obtain sufficient education and technical qualifications to be able to superintend the work of the knowledge workers under their oversight. The earlier end to careers will be a natural by-product of being overworked and handsomely compensated in the core business pressure cooker to the point of exhaustion. The third leaf of the shamrock, the flexible labor force, will have a hard lot more or less indistinguishable from what they have experienced through the ages. However, it is to the knowledge workers that Handy looks for piloting the kinds of sea change that affect not only the institution but how society will think about jobs and work in general. "Full-time work in organizations," he predicts, "will be a minority option," and "most people will find their place outside the organization, selling their time or their services into it, as self-employed, part-time, or temporary workers."[57] Knowledge workers will no longer think of themselves as having a single job and employer as having a portfolio of accounts that ebb and flow. This pattern will allow knowledge workers to take self-funded sabbaticals to raise children, pursue advanced degrees, or climb the world's tallest mountains in between stretches of intense work for multiple clients.

Within the shamrock framework, where the institution's core employees will be fewer and the organization will be smaller, flatter, and more selective about who becomes part of the core and how long he or she remains there,[58] it is only natural to wonder how and whether the institution will be able to command any loyalty from outsourced knowledge workers upon whom it relies more and more for performing critical functions. If working in the shamrock then threatens to dissolve traditional occupational loyalties, does this mean that the workplace of the future will increasingly find in every knowledge worker either a nascent trust betrayer at worst or, at best, an uncaring, fleeting insider with no stake in the institution's survival past payment of the last invoice for the last assignment?

Drucker's insight into managing the knowledge worker offers insight that dovetails well with key aspects of a No Dark Corners workplace. In Drucker's analysis, knowledge workers "see themselves as equal to those who retain their services as 'professionals' rather than as 'employees,' . . . [making] the knowledge society a society of seniors and juniors rather than of bosses and subordinates."[59] In this context, No Dark Corners anticipates precisely this kind of relationship through the copilot analogy where the core employee exercising prime contracting stewardship over a given function may serve as the institution's pilot. However, that pilot must of necessity treat outsourced knowledge workers, that is, copilots, respectfully out of recognition that the long flight to meet the organization's needs will require many pilots rotating into the cockpit and that a single master pilot will never be able to exercise total control over them all. Thus, copilot treatment in the form of one professional dealing with another will comport well with ambient conditions where knowledge workers think of themselves first as professionals whose principal loyalty is to their profession. As Drucker observed, knowledge workers "may have an attachment to an organization . . . but their primary allegiance is likely to be to their specialized branch of knowledge."[60] This new loyalty, in turn, serves the institution where the core employee overseeing the performance of the outsourced knowledge worker also possesses the same professional allegiance. Thus, the core employee who is an engineer treats the consulting engineers working for her on a peer level and, as one professional engineer to another, holds the consultants to the same high standard of performance as she holds herself in assuring not only the quality of work that both are delivering but in its safeguarding from denying the institution and the consulting engineer from pointing to a given job as a reference site or representative engagement.

At the same time, the outsourcing of certain kinds of knowledge work actually spares the institution from some of the forces that give rise to disaffected employees who are likely to grow into hostile insiders to varying degrees, although seldom into full-fledged saboteurs posing an existential threat. In the present as well as in the future shamrock organization, specialized knowledge that the institution needs only infrequently is best acquired from the outside than maintained from within. Why? Knowledge deteriorates quickly if not kept in constant use, hence the observation that "maintaining within the organization an activity that is used only intermittently guarantees incompetence."[61] An incompetent employee within the core organization is not only an unhappy employee but also an unpromotable one—particularly in a core institution that has grown flatter with fewer and fewer core employees. Leaving any employee to fester indefinitely in a position of incompetence with no realistic prospects for improvement or advancement fuels resentment that finds expression in any of the varieties of mischief catalogued above, including self-styled victims, deflectors, embezzlers, or worse. In this context, the organization is better served hiring outsourced specialists to perform a rare but complex task that they can be proud of and use as a reference with future clients than retaining a marginally effective insider whose ability to perform grows weaker over time along with diminishing bonds of loyalty to the employer whom the insider eventually blames for a stagnating career.

A FINAL CAUTION: INSTANT INTIMACY AND INSIDER THREATS

In a world where the rise of the knowledge worker presages fundamental change to the character and composition of the institution, with traditional loyalties migrating from employers to professions, it may appear likely that the workforce of tomorrow will become an amalgam of incompatible professionals briefly intersecting or colliding on their way to independent pursuits. Yet, all mortals need community and a chance to exchange ideas and to learn from dialogue and debate. As the number of fellow employees concentrated at the institution at any given time declines in the future, where will employees turn for business or social connections? One of the increasingly popular alternatives comes in the form of social networking sites. Although business networking sites such as LinkedIn may offer opportunities for reconnecting with colleagues and discovering new career opportunities, other sites such as Facebook go further in facilitating propagation of personal information and unguarded communications that may compromise participants. Opposing attorneys in child custody cases, for example, have taken to searching social networking sites for evidence that supports their client's case against a former spouse based on the latter's posted remarks and photographs or videos indicating irresponsibility or infidelity.[62] If adversarial lawyers can exploit such revelations, so can the institution's more virulent adversaries. Not only do such revelations open the discloser to extortion in flagrant cases, they also offer information that gives adversaries the means to influence or recruit the injudicious discloser who is too free with personal details.

Is the lonely employee searching or an online connection an animal lover? Then an animal rights extremist group may use the posting to manipulate this individual as in the case of the sympathizer noted earlier in this chapter. Does the employee favor a particular off-road track or camp site? Then a manipulative contractor can arrange to bump into this individual after business hours and, over a few beers at the camp fire, elicit confidential details to gain an advantage on a competitive bid. Worse still, if the employee making indelicate self-disclosures reveals a penchant for illicit tastes, an unscrupulous adversary can stage an entrapment involving a drug deal made to look on the point of police action, from which the adversary "saves" an insider—in exchange for a future favor that will be targeting the institution's assets.

Such compromises signal a larger issue: that of susceptibility of many people to instant intimacy at their own and at the institution's expense. In professional and personal relationships, as a journalist and long-term observer of the social scene concluded, "There is no such thing as instant intimacy."[63] Indeed, as a student of violent victimizations found in uncovering methods common for attackers when attempting to get close to their victims, this effort to establish instant intimacy presents in the form of forced teaming, a technique whereby the assailant creates a false bond with the victim by making common cause and saying "we" in referring to self and victim before launching attacks from rape to abduction.[64] To the defender, whether on a personal or professional level, attempts at instant intimacy should merit more suspicion than receptivity. The lesson to draw from No Dark Corners approaches to the background investigation and probation process applies equally in dealing with forced teaming or instant intimacy. Trust is earned and earning trust is something that takes time, hence traditions based in etiquette that reflect this observer's insight:

> Human nature does not change. It still takes a while to get to know and trust people, and the phony use of the manners of friendship by strangers and mere acquaintances only misleads people into thinking that instant intimacy is pleasant and safe.[65]

CONCLUSION

Existential insider threats being few and far between, the institution is more likely to experience more situations that do not fall within this category. In addition to rarely rising to the level of existential danger, these other threats may not even technically fit the definition of insider threat. Many loss-producing events may take on the appearance of the handiwork of a trust betrayer operating from within, only to unfold as non-insider attacks in the final analysis. Nevertheless, to those in the institution responsible for its defense, there may not be the luxury of caviling over strict definitions while leaving the organization to fend for itself when its insider threat defenses could instead be mobilized to offer positive value in countering any kind of attack.

Among the frequently occurring situations that defenders encounter as potential insider threats that present the capacity to become serious if not existential challenges, three common ones fall into the categories of cyber attacks, threats of violence, and exploitation of employer assets for gain. Most cyber attacks are not insider attacks, and the ones that are seldom attain the severity of posing a serious challenge to the institution's existence. Threats of violence are common internal events in the workplace, yet most of these incidents may be resolved well before causing significant impact, and their impact tends to be more harmful to individuals than to institutions. Exploitation of employer assets is a category encompassing near-limitless variation, with financial gain a common feature but by no means the only motivation for the trust betrayer harming an employer. One way for defenders to harness the unknown or perplexing aspects of these and related situations that do not call for the top priority commanded by existential insider threats is to array them along a threat scale.

The threat scale assists defenders in involving stakeholders with assessment of the relative severity of a suspected insider threat, ranging from the nuisance level to one of unacceptable, proximate harm, with two intermediate levels along the way. Unlike decisions about threats made from the comfortable distance and isolation of a disinterested party, the threat scale guides the perceiver of the threat and the affected organization in determinations of relative severity by walking representatives of each entity through what actions they are willing to take in reaction to the apparent threat. Properly applied, the threat scale drives home which actions are insupportable responses out of proportion to danger posed, demand on resources, and objectives sought.

A panoply of special cases that enters into popular categorization as insider threats—regardless of their actual merits—pose difficulties for the institution and, absent separate channels for addressing them, may leave the institution no alternative but to tap insider threat defenses to offer value in resolving these problems. Such cases call upon the institution to counter human naïveté or rascality, ranging respectively from easily manipulated sympathizers of causes to undermining contemporaries who cannot abide another's success no matter how much the institution benefits by it.

In all these cases, No Dark Corners approaches show promise by at least facilitating early detection of potential problems and timely engagement at the working level before situations get out of hand. Even the prospect of changing workplace dynamics, where traditional institutional loyalties appear poised to take a back seat to the knowledge worker's loyalty to a profession, remains congruent with those aspects of a No Dark Corners workplace where copilot relationships bridge the divide between the me boss—you worker bee mentality of another age. Finally, in an age of perhaps unwise instant intimacy, No Dark Corners' innovations in the arena of vetting and probationary cautions apply equally well in keeping at arm's length potential betrayers or villains who otherwise get too close too soon to their unsuspecting targets.

QUESTIONS FOR ONLINE OR CLASSROOM DISCUSSION

1. What would make a denial-of-service attack by external hackers or by a foreign government a possible insider threat?
2. If threats of workplace violence and violent attacks themselves may be tragic for victims but are seldom existential threats to the institution, under what circumstances might this change?
3. Of the various categories of nonexistential insider threat covered by the threat scale, why might embezzling be less frequently detected at the 0 or 1 level than at the higher levels?
4. How might an old-style martinet accustomed to micromanaging employees in a manufacturing environment end up causing knowledge worker consultants in information age workplace to either turn into insider threats or to become indifferent to the presence or activities of trust betrayers?

EXERCISES FOR GROUP PROJECTS

1. Using the threat scale, develop scenarios for categorizing cyber threats in a way similar to what was done above in the illustration for a case of threats of violence.
2. Using the threat scale, develop scenarios for categorizing exploitation for gain in a way similar to what was done above in the illustration for a case of threats of violence.

3. Are there any ethical concerns to using a No Dark Corners approach in, say, an environment where an oppressed people stage protests using the techniques of the flash mob in order to promote an uprising that is the only way for their voices to be heard by an autocratic and tyrannical regime? Are there practical impediments, regardless of any ethical concerns? Discuss.

4. Under what circumstances might the introduction of too many or too cumbersome security measures open the door to insider compromises?

ENDNOTES

1. N. Lewis, "Telepresence Challenges Medical Practice Models," *Information Week*, July 23, 2010. Retrieved August 18, 2011 from http://www.informationweek.com/news/healthcare/admin-systems/226200138.
2. R. Clutterbuck, *Kidnap and Ransom: The Response*, London: Faber and Faber, 1978, p. 89.
3. Revisit Chapter 6 and Table 6.1 for related detail on this theme.
4. E. Esen, *Workplace Violence Survey*, Alexandria, VA: Society for Human Resource Management, 2004, p. 2. Retrieved August 19, 2011 from http://www.shrm.org/Research/SurveyFindings/Documents/Workplace%20Violence%20Survey.pdf.
5. U.S. Postal Service Publication No. 45, *A Violence-Free Workplace*, Washington, DC: Government Printing Office, 1998, p. 2.
6. M. Harway, J. Sanchez, G. Seymour, and Y. Flores, *Intimate Partner Abuse and Relationship Violence*, Committee on Divisions and the American Psychological Association Relations (CODAPAR), American Psychological Association, June 24, 2002, p. 3. Retrieved August 19, 2011 from http://www.apa.org/pi/women/programs/violence/partner-violence.pdf.
7. Esen, p. 2.
8. Esen, p. viii offers that 9 out of 10 organizations have some workplace violence in place. This contrasts with SHRM's 1996 survey, which indicated that only about a third as many had such a policy in effect at the time.
9. M. Jickling, *The Enron Collapse: An Overview of Financial Issues*, Congressional Research Service Report RS21135, February 4, 2002. Retrieved August 20, 2011 from http://fpc.state.gov/documents/organization/8038.pdf.
10. P. Purpora, *Security and Loss Prevention*, 4th ed., Boston: Butterworth-Heinemann, 2002, p. 144.
11. R. Fischer, "Internal Theft Controls," in *Handbook of Loss Prevention and Crime Prevention, 4th Edition*, L. J. Fennelly, Ed., Boston: Elsevier Butterworth-Heinemann, 2004, p. 44.
12. Purpora, p. 135.
13. Fischer, p. 51.
14. R. S. Post and D. A. Schachtsiek, *Security Manager's Desk Reference*, Boston: Butterworth Publishers, 1986, p. 314.
15. Fischer, p. 48
16. Fischer, pp. 51–52.
17. Ibid., p. 52.

18. B. Beedle, "Employee Theft: How to Fight a Billion-Dollar Problem," *NPMA Journal* (National Property Management Association) 17(2) (2005): 22–24. Retrieved August 20, 2011 from http://www.npma.org/Archives/vol.17-2-Beedle.pdf.

19. Purpora, p. 149.

20. Purpora, p. 147.

21. Based on Fischer, p. 47.

22. N. Catrantzos, "Defending against the Threat of Insider Financial Crime," *Frontline Security*, Summer 2010, pp. 17–19. Retrieved July 4, 2011 from http://www.frontline-security.org/publications/10_SEC2_Money.php.

23. Based on Post and Schachtsiek, pp. 319–320.

24. B. Burnsed, "The Greatest Financial Scandals," *Bloomberg Business Week*, July 9, 2009. Retrieved August 20, 2011 from http://images.businessweek.com/ss/09/03/0311_madoff/index.htm.

25. The author is aware of precisely such a method of compensation that surfaced with the exposure of a bid-rigging scheme in a large institution. At such a point, the case could arguably merit moving into the category of embezzlement.

26. C. J. Sykes, *A Nation of Victims: The Decay of the American Character*, New York: St. Martin's Press, 1992, p. xii.

27. Ibid., p. 168.

28. P. F. Drucker, *Management: Tasks, Responsibilities, Practices*, New York: HarperBusiness, 1993, p. 233.

29. M. Goldsmith, *What Got You Here Won't Get You There*, New York: Hyperion, 2007, p. 218.

30. S. Bing, *Throwing the Elephant: Zen and the Art of Managing Up*, New York: HarperCollins, 2002, p. 83.

31. S. Adams, *Dilbert and the Way of the Weasel*, New York: HarperCollins, 2002, p. 11.

32. P. F. Drucker, *The Effective Executive*, New York: HarperBusiness, 1993, p. 18.

33. W. Safire, "Useful Idiots of the West," *New York Times*, April 12, 1987. Retrieved August 22, 2011 from http://www.nytimes.com/1987/04/12/magazine/on-language.html?pagewanted=1.

34. For details of such extremist tactics, see Anti-Defamation League, "Update: Animal Rights Extremists Target the University of California," in *Ecoterrorism: Extremism in the Animal Rights and Environmentalist Movements*, 2005. Retrieved August 22, 2011 from http://www.adl.org/learn/ext_us/ecoterrorism.asp?learn_cat=extremism&learn_subcat=extremism_in_america&xpicked=4&item=eco.

35. G. Gordon Liddy, *Will*, New York: St. Martin's Press, 1980, p. 272.

36. I. Urbina, "Mobs Are Born as Word Grows by Text Message," *New York Times*, March 24, 2010. Retrieved August 23, 2011 from http://www.nytimes.com/2010/03/25/us/25mobs.html.

37. National Retail Federation white paper, *Multiple Offender Crimes: Preparing for and Understanding the Impact of Their Tactics*, August 2011. Retrieved August 9, 2011 from http://www.nrf.com/modules.php?name=News&op=viewlive&sp_id=1167.

38. For details on man traps, see the British Security Industry Association's, *A Specifier's Guide to the Security Classification of Access Control Systems*, March 2011, p. 7 at http://www.bsia.co.uk/web_images//publications/form_132.pdf or a security hardware vendor's literature, Securitech, "Security Hardware Guide for Postal Facilities," n.d., p. 4, at http://www.securitech.com/Security%20Hardware%20Guide.PDF.

39. Such a device, the Mosquito, was invented in the United Kingdom. It emits a high frequency tone audible to 15–25-year-olds, which can be useful in keeping them from loitering in areas where legitimate users are older and unable to discern the tone. The author has witnessed a successful installation of such a device at an unattended facility formerly experiencing recurring vandalism by youthful offenders. Vendor information is available at http://www.movingsoundtech.com/.

40. B. Dickinson, "BART Shuts Down Cell Service to Stop Protests," *CNET News*, August 12, 2011. Retrieved August 23, 2011 from http://news.cnet.com/8301-1001_3-20091867-92/ this-day-in-tech-bart-shuts-down-cell-service-to-stop-protests/.

41. D. Sandford, "Moscow Coup 1991: With Boris Yeltsin on the Tank," *BBC News*, August 20, 2011. Retrieved August 23, 2011 from http://www.bbc.co.uk/news/world-europe-14589691.

42. G. Friedman, "The Iranian Election and the Revolution Test," *Stratfor*, June 22, 2009. Retrieved June 22, 2009 from http://www.stratfor.com/weekly/20090622_iranian_election_and_revolution_test.

43. P. E. Tarlow, *Event Risk Management and Safety*, New York: John Wiley and Sons, 2002, pp. 102–103.

44. Ibid., p. 100.

45. M. J. Clark, "Friends: Terrific or Toxic?" n.d., in *Integrated Leader*, p. 2. Retrieved August 23, 2011 from http://www.integratedleader.com/articles/FriendsTerrificToxic.pdf.

46. K. Treybig, "Friendship Gone Wrong," *Vertical Thought*, October–December 2006, p. 11. Retrieved August 23, 2011 from http://www.ucg.org/files/issues/pdf/vt06od.pdf.

47. J. Townsend, *Who's Pushing Your Buttons?*, Nashville, TN: Thomas Nelson, Inc., 2004, p. 109.

48. R. X. Cringely, *Triumph of the Nerds*, PBS Television Documentary, June 1996, transcript from Part II. Retrieved August 24, 2011 from http://www.pbs.org/nerds/part2.html.

49. M. Goldsmith, *What Got You Here Won't Get You There*, New York: Hyperion, 2007, pp. 48–49.

50. J. Wilgoren and E. Wong, "United 93: On Doomed Flight, Passengers Vowed to Perish Fighting," *New York Times*, September 13, 2001. Retrieved August 24, 2011 from http://www.nytimes.com/2001/09/13/us/after-attacks-united-flight-93-doomed-flight-passengers-vowed-perish-fighting.html?src=pm.

51. National Commission on Terrorist Attacks, *The 9/11 Commission Report: Final Report of the National Commission on Terrorist Attacks upon the United States*, New York: W. W. Norton, 2004, pp. 172–173.

52. R. Clutterbuck, *Kidnap, Hijack and Extortion: The Response*, London: Macmillan Press, 1987, pp. 19–21.

53. F. Bolz Jr., K. J. Dudonis, and D. P. Schulz, *The Counterterrorism Handbook*, Boca Raton, FL: CRC Press, 2002, p. 90.

54. This is the subject of most of Charles Handy's *Age of Unreason*, Boston: Harvard Business School Press, 1990.

55. P. F. Drucker, *Managing for the Future*, New York: Truman Talley Books, 1993.

56. Handy, p. 32.

57. Ibid., p. 48.

58. Ibid., p. 114.

59. P. F. Drucker, *Managing in the Next Society*, New York: Truman Talley Books, 2002, p. 254.

60. Ibid., p. 259.

61. Ibid., p. 274.

62. J. Ruzich, "What You Post Can Come Back to Haunt You: Attorneys in Divorce, Child Custody Cases Increasingly Searching Online for Evidence," *Chicago Tribune*, June 15, 2011. Retrieved August 25, 2011 from http://articles.chicagotribune.com/2011-06-15/news/ct-x-0615-divorce-facebook-20110615_1_divorce-social-networking-evidence-attorneys.

63. J. Martin, *Miss Manners' Guide to Excruciatingly Correct Behavior*, New York: W.W. Norton & Company, 2005, p. 107.

64. G. de Becker, *The Gift of Fear*, New York: Dell Publishing, 1998, p. 64.

65. J. Martin, *Miss Manners' Guide for the Turn of the Millennium*, New York: Fireside, 1990, p. 4.

CHAPTER 10

Consulting for No Dark Corners Implementation

Companies contract out work that their people either cannot do or will not do.

Gary L. McCullough
Vice President (retired)
Lockheed Martin Integrated Solutions

Let's look at these recurring problems and pre-solve them.
Anything we send to [bureaucratic channels] will be old enough to drive by the time we get it back.

Mark Sovern
Special Agent, Former Marine

When you're on a battlefield, you don't blow kisses.
We don't have to run to failure. We can stop and regroup.
You paint the corner you've been put into.

Mojgan (MJ) Hashemi
Professional Engineer and Security Systems Integrator

If enough people tell you that your thoroughbred is a mule, you should take a look at his ears.
They keep trying to make rocket science out of tic-tac-toe.

Derrek Jones
Security Manager and Certified Protection Professional

In the labyrinth of any problem that confronts us, we must select the most promising paths; if we attempt to follow all at once, we shall arrive nowhere. One of the deepest secrets of excellence is a discerning elimination.

Rex Stout
Author and mathematics prodigy

Everybody's ignorant—only on different subjects.

Will Rogers
Humorist and raconteur

INTRODUCTION

This chapter is about making it happen, whether as an internal agent of change tasked with a No Dark Corners implementation or as an outside consultant engaged to assist the institution with effecting desired improvement. Almost anyone can do it, but there are some preconditions. First, in addition to having relevant insight and expertise, it helps to know one's objectives and capacities well enough to be able to deliver value. Second, there must be an enabling professional context: an environment conducive to successful implementation. Accordingly, a key dilemma to resolve at the outset is to determine whether a No Dark Corners implementation is a project at whose helm an insider or an outsider will be most effective. What is the answer? As in most consulting endeavors, it depends.

THE INSIDE–OUTSIDE DILEMMA

Diagnosing, prescribing, and implementing a No Dark Corners program entirely from within, with no use of outside consultants or resources, appears attractive for a number of reasons. This approach ensures that the institution will be able to exert maximum control over the process, information flow, and principals involved, thereby reducing the potential for embarrassment in the event of failure or faux pas. Additionally, in-house resources offer ostensible economies, as employees are already being compensated at set levels and can theoretically be redirected to launch the program while attending to some, most, or all of their regular duties. Finally, since few sea changes take hold and produce lasting effects in any organization without internal buy-in of employees, having one's own people intimately involved with all aspects of the program increases the chance of such internal proprietary interest that would either be missing or waning if the program relied solely on outside consultants. After all, sooner or later, outside consultants must leave, and internal naysayers know better than anyone how to wait out the boss's good idea that no one will be around to champion once initial momentum has given way to institutional inertia.

There is, of course, a less encouraging series of attributes to expect from a program run exclusively by internal forces. First, the people tasked with effecting changes will invariably include staff intimately involved with operating systems currently in place. As a practical matter, even under the greatest encouragement with the most benign of executive sponsors, these people will find themselves in the organizationally untenable position of weathering implied criticism of their previous assumptions and efforts. The attending urge to defend a status quo in which they are vested will be overwhelmingly strong. Moreover, given that they are receiving no special compensation or advancement beyond the regular paycheck for their efforts, what do they have to lose from a failed effort? Failure's consequence will generally signal a return to the status quo, hence a return to comfort zones and processes already mastered by the very people who must otherwise stray from familiar shores to wade out to the uncertain waters of making changes that most will have never before attempted or witnessed in the workplace. Another drawback is that all insiders are known for their proven talents, and it will be no secret that they are as much novices in the new program as the people they are seeking to influence. Top management also faces a dilemma in having fewer incentive options when dealing exclusively with an insider implementation team. After all, if consultants deliver unsatisfactory results, they can be terminated or held to account before one's governing body. A simple, "Those guys let us down" absolves top management from much of the culpability for a flawed implementation or minor fiasco. "We'll never use them again" then lays the matter to rest. However, one cannot get rid of one's own employees the same way, nor reward them for an outstanding success the way one can pay a bonus to consultants or refer them to additional business within one's professional community. An even bigger drawback to relying too heavily on in-house resources, however, is the hurdle of hierarchy. In essence, if the senior-most insider leading the No Dark Corners implementation nevertheless ranks below recalcitrant executives or department heads, then the latter will chafe at and block any part of the undertaking to which they object, reasoning that if they outrank this program's leader, he or she will have no authority that they cannot negate with their own positional standing in the institutional hierarchy. No general takes orders from a captain or sergeant.

In this context, recourse to an outside consultant appears more attractive. Outside consultants can be chosen for their unbiased, task-specific expertise and allowed to concentrate exclusively on achieving defined objectives—unlike regular employees assigned the same work as a side job and expected to continue handling daily duties. Consultants can also be terminated for nonperformance or visibly expelled for any unanticipated consequences that embarrass top management. Moreover, if consultants possess more specialized expertise, their chance of success is greater and the time necessary to show results, shorter—making them ultimately more cost-effective if one weighs lost productive time and reputational risk associated with a failed program that diverts valued employees from the core business before the program falls of its own weight. Additionally, contrarians within the institution who would never accept new ideas from internal peers or rivals would be much more receptive to the same ideas coming from outside consultants speaking with the authority of expertise and with a breadth of knowledge beyond the single institution being served.

What might be the downside to exclusive reliance on outside consultants, however? First, there is substantial loss of buy-in by employees if excluded from contributing to the new program. Second, if a situation develops where all the work is at the hands of consultants, implementation will grow to depend exclusively on the consultants, resulting in a lengthening of the consulting engagement to the point where it may become prohibitively expensive and impossible to sustain. Another drawback is that any red team analysis uninformed by cooperative insiders will ring false and struggle for credibility below a superficial level. Finally, overreliance on consultants will deny the institution an opportunity to nurture internal champions necessary for delivering long-term results beyond the length of the consulting contract.

INSIDE–OUTSIDE ILLUSTRATION: SAME ADVICE, DIFFERENT RECEPTION

This is a true story with names of persons and institutions altered in the interest of discretion.

PROBLEM ONE

Joe was a senior consultant with Global Crisis Management. A financial powerhouse, International Banking and Investments (IBI), retained Joe through his firm to troubleshoot in the wake of a problem that had recently occurred at IBI's headquarters. During an electrical fire caused by utility crews beyond IBI's control outside of two downtown headquarters buildings, smoke from the fire engulfed the stairwell that IBI's employees used for emergency evacuation. Confusion made matters worse on some floors because IBI's public address system could not be heard over the voices of employees talking loudly as they were evacuating from positions of relative safety into stairwells where they started coughing and crying, struggling to see and sense their way out of the buildings. To make matters worse, some senior, revenue-generating employees involved in complex financial trades simply ignored evacuation orders and fire alarms, dismissing them as fire drills of secondary importance to attending to IBI's core business. IBI management's tasking to Joe: Develop brief policy guidance and some clear messages to communicate to employees what to do in similar emergencies in the future.

PROBLEM TWO

Two years after solving Problem One, Joe accepted employment as the middle manager in charge of an emergency management function for a public agency, District One (DO). Although DO did not experience the same kind of triggering event that led IBI to commission a policy and guidance effort to clarify to employees what to do in certain kind of emergencies, Joe noticed that such guidance was absent at DO and accordingly set out to fill this void by drafting a policy and related guidance for the agency. Drawing on what had conceived for IBI, Joe developed a draft policy that he vetted through institutional stakeholders from other departments and worked diligently for 6 weeks with a policy task force to present the policy in what was DO's standard format. This is where the similarity ends.

DIVERGENT OUTCOMES

IBI

The private sector agency, which at the time was paying $350 per hour for Joe's time, accepted most of Joe's work product as delivered. IBI staff working with Joe collaborated on some changes to tailor the final product more closely to IBI's particular needs. Joe incorporated their changes within a day and turned a finished product to IBI, after which the latter arranged for its chief executive to introduce the topic to all IBI employees in a brief video message that summarized the key points Joe had drafted for this purpose, explained the need for the policy, and summarized the basic guidance regarding whether to evacuate or shelter-in-place. The video and related guidance documents also emphasized, as Joe had underscored, that when an emergency befell the institution, everyone's job changed and the emergency job took precedence over all others. This language assisted executives who had experienced difficulty in explaining to senior revenue-generating employees why they simply could not go on trading while a fire or other emergency was in progress. *Time elapsed from start of engagement to finish*: 1 week.

DO

The public agency saw Joe as an internal middle manager without necessarily recognizing the value of the expertise he offered on the matter, since his contribution was expected as part of his regular compensation. Joe went through six presentations of his policy draft to an executive policy review committee whose members changed at least three times. Between presentations, different executives and committees suggested different changes to reflect the interests of their divisions and departments. At one point, the senior executive chairing the policy group, who was new to line management, confessed a discomfort with the policy or with why it should be codified in the absence of a problem that needed resolution. Ultimately, at that executive's and another's behest, Joe conducted a half-day emergency exercise for the benefit of executives new to the issue and interested in better understanding how the institution managed agency response to crisis. The policy, however, continued to receive additional input, and Joe continued to revise drafts. In the end, the policy underwent 22 overhauls. *Time elapsed from start of engagement to finish*: 20 months.

LESSONS

1. When IBI was paying Joe as an expert, its staff treated his products seriously and, remaining mindful that caviling and meetings came with cost, reduced such distractions to a minimum.
2. DO, by contrast, treated Joe's contributions and initiative in surfacing the same issue before any embarrassment or emergency as meriting importance in proportion to Joe's standing in the institutional hierarchy. Joe was in middle management. Therefore, what he had to offer was of inferior importance or priority to executive management.
3. Over the course of making changes and endless revisions, Joe noted that a rule of negotiation by Chester Karrass appeared to be in force at DO: Demands are infinite if their price is zero. By contrast, since IBI had to pay for Joe's services, it was more prepared to take them seriously and deal with his products expeditiously.
4. IBI had experienced an event that raised issues of reputational risk and highlighted the significance of what it commissioned Joe to produce. DO, by contrast, had not experienced the same kind of triggering event and did not appear prepared to appreciate the initiative involved in anticipating such an event for the good of the institution. As Joe mused later, IBI asked for a product, but DO did not. Thus, IBI placed itself in a position to request and benefit from consulting services that may have been premature in terms of the task-relevant maturity of counterpart executives at DO.

RECOMMENDED: OUTSIDE DIAGNOSIS, HYBRID PRESCRIPTIONS, INTERNAL IMPLEMENTATION

Under the circumstances, one approach to maximize the chances for a successful No Dark Corners program implementation would be to use external resources to analyze needs and identify the most promising paths for the institution in migrating in the direction of work-team engagement and copilot approaches to insider threat defense. Rare is the insider who can deliver an objective analysis of an organization's vulnerabilities without reflecting the bias of his or her own function and place in the hierarchy. Rarer still is the employer who will accept from an insider even the most objective diagnosis without assuming such bias—even when the insider has managed to suppress it. The old truism infecting every workplace continues to suggest that one cannot be a prophet in one's own land. Thus, an outsider may well be the best or only change agent able to initiate a program with diagnostic observations, which the wise sponsor will also exploit for assessing in-house staff as candidate champions of the program for the long term. What better opportunity for the external consultant to spot future internal champions than when working with them side by side in a red team undertaking to identify and shore up vulnerabilities? Besides, as one executive consultant noted in interacting with internal counterparts frustrated at trying to perform the same role, the in-house counterparts typically welcomed his arrival because, at the external consultant's level of compensation, it was much more likely that their bosses would listen to what the internal staff had been advising for years.[1] Although outside spectators may see most of the game, it takes players on the field to advance to the goal line. Accordingly, charting the course for the implementation should be a hybrid responsibility, involving consulting expertise on the one hand and in-house conversance with the intricacies of the organization on the other hand. This collaboration also sets the stage for a hand-off from consultant to internal forces for implementation and long-term program stewardship. Thus, this last and ongoing part should definitely remain under the lead of the institution's own people, who will have to maintain the positive pressure to get and sustain results so that the institution may reap the benefits of the new program.

INSTITUTIONAL INSERTION POINTS FOR A NO DARK CORNERS PROGRAM

There are three general situations that create conditions likely to lead an institution to consider implementing No Dark Corner strategies and, accordingly, seeking out internal or external assistance in tailoring such defenses to the workplace. These situations are cases of sudden impact response, postmortem redesign, and strategic anticipation. The first two are direct consequences of adverse events linked to trust betrayal. The last is leader-directed change arising from a vision that may be the result of learning from other institutions' debacles and not wishing to wait for one's own victimization or from a visionary leader's alacrity in adapting to changing threats without waiting to be told or attacked. Each of these situations demands different skill sets and mixes of internal and external staff. Each also comes with situation-driven constraints affecting the time and intensity of the consulting effort.

Sudden Impact Response

The institution finding itself in a situation requiring sudden impact response is in the throes of facing grave danger or potential ruin at the hands of a malicious insider. Such a condition is likely to combine known and unknown dangers, with executives of the institution at times conflicted over whether the situation is dire or exaggerated. A good example of a sudden impact response appears in Chapter 7, under the section "A Distress Call and Unpredicted Turn of Events."

Capabilities required for assisting with a sudden impact response are likely to be wide ranging and specialized to the point of being difficult to cover entirely with internal resources. In the example in Chapter 7, which epitomizes this category of engagement, the institution needed or appeared to need instant access to capabilities ranging from body guards to computer forensics experts, from surveillance teams to detectors of electronic spying devices. Few institutions have such resources on standby for immediate deployment. Moreover, few consultancies can afford to keep all these skills in-house or on retainer for mobilizing on demand. Consequently, a call to defend against so potentially complicated or pervasive an insider attack is best handled by an experienced security professional who either has the capacity and professional network to assemble the needed resources in time or by a counterpart professional in government service with access and authority to draw on similar resources from government agencies. A major challenge for the former is getting the right talent where needed at a cost that is not prohibitive. Often, the best subcontractors are few in number and, if already engaged at a far remove from where the crisis is unfolding, may simply not be able to drop work in progress at any cost. A major challenge for the latter, that is, government resources, is the jurisdictional hurdle compounded with questions of interagency conflicts and hierarchical coordination—all of which may become so time-consuming as to render assistance moot if the resources do not arrive in time to disrupt an attack in progress. Thus, the consultant responding to a situation such as this must be able to organize and deploy the right mix of talent to address the institution's threats, whether real or perceived. To give full value to the institution under siege, the consultant must also possess the wherewithal and integrity to demobilize expensive resources as they become unnecessary, as well as to actively assess and reassess conditions on the ground as the feared insider attack is being blunted or resolved as something other than an existential threat.

Timing for a sudden impact response is likely to involve the greatest urgency with corresponding demand for immediate results. This is no time for turning to dilettantes or rising stars who show promise but have yet to prove their mettle in a crisis. Consequently, the institution would do well to give significant weight to the consultant's prior similar engagements and strength of credible referrals in not only addressing crises of similar scope but in reputation for sound judgment and adaptability under fire.

Focus of a sudden impact response will be containment with parallel investigation. It will be to stop the bleeding before the institution's body breathes its last gasp while concurrently seeking to diagnose any less visible wounds as organizational tourniquets go into place. As the sudden impact response winds down, assuming a successful outcome, the consultant will likely offer recommendations for mitigation to prevent recurrence. These recommendations may find their way to executive ears made more receptive through the acuity that accompanies the adrenaline-stimulating forces of a crisis. However, at the conclusion of this kind of engagement, it is unlikely that either consultant or client will be able to stave off fatigue long enough to make the transition from a successfully averted crisis to a long-term program of remediation.

Postmortem Redesign

The institution facing a situation requiring postmortem redesign has either suffered a catastrophic loss caused by a hostile insider or attracted sufficient negative scrutiny to be placed under a mandate to produce radical changes in order to avoid such losses. An example might be the scandal involving a Los Angeles police anti-gang unit in which unit officers were exposed in the 1990s for widespread corruption and misconduct in their zeal to curb gang violence by means that apparently proved more expedient than legal. The commission analyzing the case concluded that officers of the unit engaged in misconduct that went undetected because

> . . . managers ignored warning signs and failed to provide the leadership, oversight, management, and supervision necessary to control this specialized unit. The ultimate result is a police corruption scandal of historic proportions. . . .[2]

Capabilities required for assisting with a postmortem redesign are an amalgam of analysis, facilitation, and report delivery. Since such undertakings invariably begin with announced concern over the institution's qualifications to perform one or more functions, it is a practical impossibility for an in-house defender to superintend the postmortem redesign without his or her conclusions being suspect. Thus, it is usually necessary for an outsider to be visibly overseeing this undertaking. If an outside consultant is unavailable for this role, then the institution must at least enlist the services of a respected manager untainted by the perceived sins of the function being redesigned. A major challenge for the individual leading this effort will be to sustain objectivity on the one hand while providing a forum for ideas, venting, and criticism on the other hand. At the same time, the redesign effort's leader must be able to filter suggestions and veiled orders through the gauze of reason, fairness, and feasibility. The client, either in the form of the institution or of its governing body, will reveal its top priority in this engagement by the extent to which it gravitates to an attorney or technical expert to lead the effort. If the choice is the technical expert, then the client places a higher value on instituting meaningful changes, confident that, in doing so, the changes will also satisfy political masters and deflate negative criticism. If, instead, the choice is an attorney or more lofty appointee whose name carries celebrity status but whose practical experience with the mechanics of shoring exposures to insider threats is modest or nonexistent, then the top priority is appeasing inquisitors and doing whatever it takes to silence vocal critics in the near term. An analog for this situation may be found in the experiences of Nobel laureate Richard Feynman, whose experience on the commission investigating the explosion of the *Challenger* space shuttle at times struck Dr. Feynman as designed more to go through the motions than the mechanics of a robust inquiry (as noted in Chapter 7 under the section "Risks in Failure Analysis and Problem Solving").

Timing for a postmortem redesign is likely to hinge on political considerations, specifically the degree of pressure that the institution is under to show results. In some cases, however, merely constituting a group and appointing a respected professional to lead the undertaking is enough to prevent artificial time constraints from impeding the undertaking. A credible leader will insist on taking enough time to qualify any principals who are to play a significant role in the process and will assume an active role in crafting a schedule of activities and milestones that offer value to the client and to the ultimate welfare of the institution. A major undertaking under intense political and media scrutiny could take a year or more to perform. Otherwise, the more or less garden variety assignment need not extend beyond 3 to 6 months.

Focus of a postmortem redesign will be building on whatever failure analysis has already begun and concentrating on preventing reoccurrence of vulnerabilities by retiring unsuccessful measures with novel approaches. Red team formation is unlikely because recent losses will be sources of fresh scar tissue offering ready examples of what can and did go wrong. Regardless of the client's stated or ulterior agenda, the consultant leading this undertaking is likely to have no recurring access to the institution as part of the post-mortem redesign engagement per se. Thus, the assignment's major deliverable will be a report of findings and recommendations, generally presented orally before an executive body and also containing greater detail in written form for a wider audience to examine at length and refer to in the future.

Strategic Anticipation

It takes no great exercise of vision or fortitude to launch some aspect of a No Dark Corners program when one is under siege, either through having to respond to a threat in progress or to respond to cries for change in the wake of insider damage that has already befallen the organization. Besides, siege-related engagements, as described above under sudden impact response and postmortem redesign, lend themselves to fast, tangible results within a framework of standard business metrics. In the case of sudden impact, the metric of program success is whether the consulting effort has managed to avert or contain losses. In the case of postmortems, the measure of success is the extent to which the program answers critics, satisfies mandates, or appeases irate stakeholders. All these metrics can and should be set forth at the outset, so that institutional client and service-providing consultant alike can gauge success and agree on program direction, milestones, and an end point. However, the entire undertaking becomes much more challenging—and potentially transformational—when a visionary from the institution is initiating it without doing so under the lash of necessity. Then the engagement becomes fundamentally different. It moves from addressing what and when to also considering why and how and what else needs to happen. This strategic anticipation effort gives No Dark Corners a chance not only to attack root causes of exposures to hostile insiders but also to reengineer work flow and rethink routine processes that no longer provide the benefits that once justified their adoption. Like serious strategic efforts in any institution, this challenges the status quo and requires an influential internal champion in order to gain traction with employees in the organization. Success in this kind of undertaking is a shared prize, an ensemble performance relying on a strong internal leader as champion, a mature consultant as program architect, and willing spirits among those in the workforce whose initial collaboration and long-term ownership of the No Dark Corners innovations are essential for demonstrating desired results. Strategic anticipation such as that required for this kind of undertaking is on a level with the return of a Steve Jobs to resuscitate Apple as flagging computer maker by entering and soon dominating the markets for personal music (via iPods and iTunes), then for smart phones (iPhones), and for tablet computers (iPads). A similar level of innovation within an industry is the kind of strategic transformation that led Cirque du Soleil to command high ticket prices, win accolades, and radically alter the tired, down-market circus tent at the edge of town into a high-end cultural entertainment by setting tradition on its head, removing animal acts that were the staple of old-style circus acts and also a source of great expense and liability.[3] In public institutions, this kind of strategic vision is what resulted in a naval officer's leadership of his crew to recognition for operating the best ship in the Navy[4] and what enabled a seasoned combat veteran assigned to a dispirited unit in Vietnam to transform it from a lackluster target of frequent mortar attacks aided by local villagers to a formidable team of warriors that went from being "hard up" to "hard core."[5]

Capabilities required for strategic anticipation of insider threats to the point of introducing the full array of No Dark Corners defenses include a capacity for developing and sustaining trust, first between the institutional leader championing the transformation and the consulting agent of change guiding the effort, and then between those two and the team members, corporate sentinels, and frontline leaders who must embrace the transformation in order for it to deliver lasting value. In the case of the consultant, the individual must bring to the undertaking a combination of intellect, subject matter expertise, and bottom-line talent for getting results. Moreover, the consultant must also possess capacities for being analytical and pragmatic, for being articulate and persuasive while also being objective, decisive yet approachable. In short, for the institution to derive maximum value from a consultant assisting with a No Dark Corners suite of lasting changes, it must engage a consultant who is adept and wise. The consultant must be able to work as a peer alongside the executive leader championing the transformation, thus being able to speak truth to power while at the same time offering insight that the executive and institution do not themselves possess in countering hostile insiders.

Timing for strategic anticipation is likely to be more drawn out than for the two other kinds of engagement, with ultimate schedule and milestones emerging as the product of iterative assessments of the institution's needs, current situation, desired end state, and options for arriving at the end state based on analytical reviews between executive sponsor and lead consultant. This feature alone will deter entry into the market by contractors seeking a quick profit in exchange for delivering doctrinaire assessments whose only tailoring to the institution consists of substituting the employer's name in every place where "Your Organization's Name Here" would appear in an otherwise generic deliverable.

Focus of an assignment geared to strategic anticipation will be broad in overall scope but more narrow in taking aim at key areas where early demonstration of success through one or more pilot programs can produce the kind of dividends that will build momentum in reaching a tipping point and in winning over in-house influencers necessary for the kind of transformation that signals a cultural change. Several deliverables could fit into the overall engagement, including formation and fielding of a red team to identify heretofore undiscovered exposures; overhaul of the hiring and probation systems to virtually close the door to infiltrators and limit chances of retaining future underperforming or undermining new hires; reconfiguration of work flow in at least one area involving critical assets to eliminate (or come substantially close to eliminating) opportunities for lone individuals to intentionally or inadvertently cause catastrophic damage; and reprogramming of at least one corporate sentinel function to integrate its staff more closely with core operations and turn its specialists from hated sentinels to valued partners and advisers in the eyes of work teams.

Application Opportunities for No Dark Corners Consulting

The ideal No Dark Corners engagement would be a strategic anticipation undertaking where the institution's sponsoring executive is a respected leader and visionary possessed of both hierarchical authority and grassroots credibility, with the tenacity to see the program through from inception to implementation and the talent to cultivate and inspire subordinate leaders with the same vision for transforming the workplace into one leaving trust betrayers nowhere to hide and few opportunities for mischief. The ideal consultant supporting this leader—whether the consultant is external or in-house—would be a seasoned professional with expertise in insider threat defense that the leader does not possess, yet also with a deep understanding of the worlds of line management and frontline employees and sentinels. Both individuals would complement one another yet by no means coincide in life experience. Both would either already have or develop a bond of trust enabling the uninhibited exchange of confidences and unpleasant findings calling for tough decisions, secure in their shared objective of having the No Dark Corners undertaking leave the institution better off than it was before the consulting engagement. Each of these principals would bring others into their circle as needed—and only when needed—with the sponsoring executive being the final arbiter of need and value. The consulting effort would focus on certain key areas and, as management authorities often advise,[6-8] create a pilot program to smooth out rough spots in implementation and demonstrate success before advancing to an enterprise-wide rollout.

The business of operating institutions, however, seldom presents conditions where ideal and organizational reality coincide. Thus, from the consultant's perspective, the institution may find itself at any number of junctures along its path to erecting insider defenses and consequently perceive itself to be in need of assistance in only one or more key areas. In this kind of situation, as one leader in technology consulting advised over the course of many assignments,

> If they didn't hire you, don't solve their problem. . . . You must never allow yourself to forget that consulting is the art of influencing people *at their request*. Among consultants, the most prevalent occupational disease is offering unsolicited "help." It's bad for your bankbook, and it doesn't work. In fact, it usually backfires.[9]

Key areas, then, where a consultant can look to add value for implementing a No Dark Corners strategy include

- Red team formation and facilitation to uncover vulnerabilities
- Redesign of background check and probation process to filter out infiltrators and future problem employees
- Redesign of corporate sentinel function(s) to reduce unnecessary burdens on and improve collaboration with core business
- Redesign of work protocols in critical areas to reduce or eliminate unattended individual access to critical assets
- Training of frontline supervisors on detection of deception, lawful disruption, and use of threat scale in managing cases of suspected insider threats
- Codesign of pilot programs to implement innovations into routine operations
- Operational audits to discern whether stated process improvements are actually operating as conceived and delivering anticipated results

WHERE TO BEGIN

The starting point for any of the foregoing or combination of the foregoing engagements comes at the intersection of consultant ability to offer value and institutional client (namely, the executive sponsor) acknowledgment of a need for change. Because the very nature of such engagements delves deeply into matters of trust and trust betrayal, it is impossible for the consultant to understand the institutional landscape fully without establishing a relationship of trust with the client. Coincidentally, it is the absence of trust that often closes the door on use of internal consultants, since any shortfalls in credibility of a given department also attach to the people in that particular department, making it improbable that an executive will turn to such insiders for consulting advice on sensitive matters.[10]

Given that little will be possible without giving attention to establishing trust, pick one issue. In other words, select one problem or predicament to solve and use this as a starting point for opening discussion on insider threat defense. As leading executive coach Marshall Goldsmith counseled, "Pick one issue that matters and attack it until it doesn't matter anymore.[11] Although the consultant need not pursue such an issue to resolution in advance of being retained to do so, this approach at least equips the consultant with a focus that is substantive rather than aspirational or theoretical, thus improving his or her ability to speak with credibility to the sponsoring executive or client. In the absence of one key issue, use a checklist for gauging current insider defenses to obtain a general indication of further avenues to explore.

CHECKLIST FOR GAUGING CURRENT INSIDER DEFENSES[12]

RATING SCALE

For each of these questions, rate your answer as High/hard, Medium, or Low/easy. Assign a score of 9 for High, 5 for Medium, and 1 for Low.

1. Thinking like an attacker, how difficult would it be for you to get the organization to hire someone who appears presentable, friendly, skillful, and has no identifiable history of criminal convictions or controversy? Assume an Internet search of social networking sites as something an employer will also check to uncover threatening activities.

2. Wander around physically and electronically (as via internal websites or network applications) through the organization. How difficult would it be for you to gain access to sensitive information that has nothing to do with your job, including the kind of detail that would help you pick a worthy target or help you determine how to destroy it?

3. How hard would it be for you to enter into or hide within an area where the most critical assets of the organization reside? Trying this after business hours or on a weekend, how hard is it to talk your way into high value or sensitive areas where you do not belong or do not have authorization to linger?

4. What is the extent to which you can expect team members at a critical area to spontaneously keep you out if you do not belong there or are not a member of that team?

5. How hard is it to get through your organization's probation period? (Consider asking around to see who can remember the last time someone was released from employment during the probationary period. If this is a routine occurrence, then the answer is High. If no one can remember the last time a new employee did not survive probation, the answer is Low.)

6. How much attention is paid to verifying identity for new hires? (Check this not by asking the department responsible for the checking but by

finding recently hired employees and asking how carefully their identification was examined. If the process was a token effort that defaulted to the most junior clerk available, it rates Low. If there was careful scrutiny, it is High.)

7. What is the likelihood that if someone sees you doing something suspicious, threatening, or entirely out of place for the area, that that person will approach you directly or report the matter so that there is immediate follow-up with you while you are still in the area?

Total your scores. If all are High, your total would be 70. If all Low, 7; and all Medium, 35.

Totals:

55–70	Strong. There may be room for fine-tuning, but your organization is more resistant to hostile insiders than most, with good opportunities to detect or defeat the threat.
39–54	Above average. You have some defenses in place but probably need to bolster the ones that afford exploitable vulnerabilities.
7–35	Going through the motions. Your defenses are untested or more aspirational than substantive.

If the consultant can demonstrate the capacity to offer value to the institution and to earn and maintain the trust of the institution's sponsoring executive, then it is important for the consultant to understand his or her role, to agree to objectives of the engagement and resources necessary to see it through, set forth clear metrics, and also agree to what value the engagement is to deliver in defending the institution against malicious insiders. Only afterward comes agreement on matters of fees and closure of assignment. Discussion of each of these topics follows.

Consultant's Role

One experienced executive coach and strategy expert defines a consultant as someone who provides expertise for a client for a particular issue,[13] whereas another emphasizes that a consultant is someone who influences people at their request.[14] In either case, both agree that a consultant is not an employee, nor the boss of the many employees in the institution who are vital to insider threat defense. At best, the consultant strives to be a trusted adviser capable of providing insight and delineating a path for the institution to follow, supplying perspective and expertise along the way to facilitate the journey. Such a consultant ultimately serves as a go-to person for the institution's executive sponsor in times of urgency as well as under routine conditions.[15] Since the consultant lacks the authority to issue orders, he or she cannot be effective if running roughshod over the workforce, even with the implied imprimatur of a sponsoring executive. Thus, it is necessary for the consultant to make independent observations and to use techniques of elicitation (described elsewhere in this book) to identify vulnerabilities to insider threats. In many ways, the consultant may simulate the institution's first personification of an infiltrator or theoretical trust betrayer. Thus, the consultant must be able to not only think like an adversary operating from within but must also be able to present a compelling logic for why a hostile insider could and would exploit vulnerabilities that the institution has heretofore failed to address. Finally, the consultant's role is to offer both rapid framing, namely, an ability to quickly summarize salient issues, and value generation, which in this case means offering options and insights otherwise unavailable to the client.[16] At no point, though, must the consultant forget the importance of being an invited collaborator, since, "If people don't want your help, you'll never succeed in helping them, no matter how smart or wonderful you are."[17]

Objectives and Resources

If the institutional client is approaching the consultant for an engagement whose sole objective is to shore up weaknesses in the hiring and probation process in order to bar entry to infiltrators or malefactors, then it would be questionable for the consultant to offer a voluminous series of objectives with corresponding demand for more resources on the part of both the institution and the consulting organization. However, setting out clear objectives is not exclusively the consultant's task. As two systems analysts revealed, an igloo, a Bavarian castle, and a space station can all be construed to satisfy the objective of creating a means for protecting a small group of human beings from the hostile elements of their environment.[18] However, depending on which solution is right for the circumstances, one may dismiss options as too costly, unsuitable, or altogether incongruous. Thus, it is important to deal with ambiguities at the outset so that one does not end up building a space station where an igloo will suffice, or vice versa. Bearing in mind that the overall objective is to improve the condition of the institution in terms of its resistance to insider threats, it is of prime importance for client and consultant to look at objectives as outcomes to be achieved—not mere efforts to attempt. As Drucker said, any institution is measured "by its contribution; everything else is effort rather than result."[19] As opening discussions about the engagement touch upon many areas, including schedules, methods, and resource demands, consultants should continue to focus on the desired contribution to be made: tying this contribution to how it improves the condition of the institution. Only after ambiguities have been resolved and objectives rendered simple and lucid should discussion proceed to resource commitments on the part of the institution as well as of the consultant. If the consultant is to develop a red team, for example, to see how robust the defenses of a critical operation are, then the consultant should articulate what outside contractors or subcontractors are required to perform what tasks as well as what in-house participants, by function, are necessary for informing the red team's activities. The advice of an educator holds as useful today as 40 years ago: state the objective in terms of the need it serves rather than the form it takes.[20]

Metrics

Some engagements come with embedded metrics. As one executive coach pointed out, "In one way or another, there's always a metric hovering over what we do."[21] The sudden impact response either works or becomes a cautionary tale in a future failure analysis. Similarly, the postmortem redesign either satisfies inquisitors and mandates, or falls short of the mark. The more sophisticated applications of No Dark Corners innovations, such as those embraced in strategic anticipation, may require months or even years to establish and operate before bearing fruit. How does one measure the effectiveness of the undertaking that enabled them, particularly if the consultant has departed by the time their full yield arrives? Under these circumstances, it is necessary for the consultant and client to agree on measures of progress or indicators that show positive movement along the intended path, even though arrival may be beyond line of sight. If the probationary process has been overhauled as part of a redesign of the background check and probation system, for example, indicators of useful progress could include significant decline in absenteeism and tardiness of employees in their first year on the job as well as fewer disciplinary actions for the same population. If the main purpose of the engagement has been redesign of work protocols in critical areas to reduce or eliminate unattended individual access to critical assets, one indicator of progress may be significant decline in accidents in those areas owing to copilot-style availability of fellow team members to catch and correct human error. By giving thought and weight to such metrics in advance, the consultant and client also expose the added value that No Dark Corners innovations offer to core business in terms of productivity and loss avoidance overall, not just in terms of insider threat defenses.

Value

Except in those cases where the engagement is confined to serving a narrow set of objectives in a short duration, such as in a sudden impact response, the consultant and client should aim to express value in terms of how the engagement will contribute to improving the institution in the long term. This is the place to incorporate positive byproducts of insider threat defenses noted above, such as gains to productivity, reduction in avoidable accidents, and even benefits in efficiency thanks to reduction of needless burdens formerly imposed by corporate sentinels. Moreover, it is critical to involve the executive sponsor when the consultant sets out to codify the value that the No Dark Corners engagement will deliver. Even in institutions that are not businesses, stakeholders may be substituted for customers in this observation:

> The starting point for management has to be what customers consider value. . . . What is value to the customer is always something quite different from what is value or quality to the supplier.[22]

FEES, COMPENSATION, AND EFFECTIVENESS

Until the foregoing matters are broached and brought to conceptual agreement between consultant and client, introducing price into the discussion is premature or even counterproductive. Behavioral economics indicates that matters of cost often range into the illogical for a number of reasons. For example, "instant gratification is more important than long-run profit maximization for many human beings. This means that, among other things, we demand much more to give up or sell an object than we would be willing to pay to acquire that object, and we tend to overestimate our chance of success in the short term, but underestimate our chance of failure over the long term."[23] Prematurely entering into discussions of compensation is likely to leave the sponsoring executive worrying about being overcharged and the consultant overselling potential results in an effort to maximize profit. Nevertheless, if neither has probed sufficiently into the engagement to ascertain what lasting value a No Dark Corners innovation can supply to the institution's long-term advantage, discussions of fees and price take center stage. Strategically, if the undertaking delivers lasting, substantive value, even an apparently high fee will appear inconsequential when measured against savings realized or losses averted. However, if both consultant and client preoccupy themselves with cost to the point of deliberating commodity pricing or paying on the basis of billable hours, then the fee structure will impose at least two barriers to success.

First, it will incentivize the consultant to maximize the number of billable hours, ultimately raising doubts in the mind of the sponsoring executive whether the billings translate into value. As one contrarian observer of this kind of practice noted, "A consultant is a person who takes your money and annoys your employees while tirelessly searching for the best way to extend the consulting contract."[24]

Second, this kind of engagement will put a premium on consuming productive hours, thereby not only encouraging the consultant to employ subcontractors to increase billings (usually at a lower rate of compensation than the prime consultant, thereby further maximizing profits), but also diverting valued employees from core duties by compelling their participation in meetings, focus groups, and interviews. As these meetings increase, so does frustration on the part of the best and brightest employees. Soon, the latter find relief of this burden by assigning surrogates who do not equal their principal in knowledge, insight, or authority within the institution, but who instead offer one common attribute: availability. The net result is that this pricing model leaves consultants inadvertently denying themselves access to the key sources of institutional memory and influence that will be vital to any successful program implementation. In the end, this situation at best leaves consultant and executive sponsor arriving at a conclusion to the engagement that is based mostly on running out of time and budget with a shared desire to disengage, regardless of whether the undertaking has achieved any successes. When this kind of pricing model dominates the deliberations about the undertaking, it is no wonder that consultants working in such an environment remind themselves that they are being paid by the hour, not by the solution.[25] Besides, as another management observer noted, "more money leads to greater spending," and "having more time means taking more time."[26] In effect, the wrong kind of pricing structure can result in squandering or misapplication of resources without a corresponding level of results to show for the expenditures.

Under the circumstances, one of the more effective ways of gearing compensation to results emerges in the way executive coach Marshall Goldsmith works: He only accepts his fee if the client is satisfied that the desired improvement has occurred. Goldsmith also commits to consuming as little of his executive sponsor's valuable time as possible. In practice, this arrangement means that Goldsmith may work a year on a particular engagement before receiving any payment. However, because he establishes clear, objective metrics, he manages to stay in business and in demand as a high-end executive coach.[27] Other executive consultants, such as Alan Weiss, whose practice runs on value-based pricing, avoid the pitfalls of a billable-hours engagement by setting fees based on value and establishing a payment schedule that also ties to performance measures mutually agreed to in advance with the client.

MAKING CHANGE HAPPEN

Even if one possesses the appropriate expertise, a visionary executive sponsor willing to work collaboratively on a No Dark Corners engagement, and an enabling context where employees are willing to try new approaches and abandon counterproductive patterns, success is by no means assured. All too often, executives hear positive feedback on their new initiatives, leading them to declare premature victory because, as some analysts have found, most leaders confuse compliance and commitment.[28] The consultant must effectively diagnose the situation, tailor No Dark Corners innovations to the organization, and establish a collaborative framework for moving forward by eventually ceding the helm to in-house champions. All this can appear to be in harness, yet the physician's eternal question may linger: How does one assure the patient will ingest the proper dosage of medicine over time? Two answers are pilot programs and exemplars.

Pilot Programs

Pilot programs represent a low-risk demonstration opportunity for putting a new idea to the test without insisting on concurrent overhaul of existing structures and protocols. To doubters of the innovation and to defenders of the status quo, the pilot program is what a test drive would be to a motorist sitting reluctantly or tentatively behind the wheel of a new car that is supposed to be safer, more powerful, more fuel-efficient, and more comfortable than a beloved but obsolescent sedan. It may be difficult or impossible to pry the sedan from the driver's clutches by reason alone, but a test drive that demonstrates all the improvements advertised makes more of a difference than argument alone. Moreover, to an innovator, the pilot program is an opportunity for validation—or for rude awakening. If it provides the anticipated benefits, the pilot is a validation that wins over the undecided and enough naysayers to turn the tide of seething opposition into at least neutrality if not guarded support. If the pilot is a fiasco, then at least it fails without visiting catastrophic consequences on the institution, allowing course corrections and adaptive improvements before causing system-wide catastrophes.

The other principal benefit of pilot programs is that they permit innovation to find its most receptive champions while bypassing internal saboteurs. Management icon Peter Drucker absorbed this phenomenon first-hand by seeing how a medical institution introduced physical therapy into a community filled with hostility to this innovation. Drucker observed that the innovators championing physical therapy "didn't even try to convert the non-believers," instead picking three institutions that were eager to explore the benefits and working exclusively with these three until the positive results attained were so incontrovertible as to attract converts and speak for themselves. This phenomenon led Drucker, years later, to counsel against trying to convert everyone right away and, instead, to rely on pilot programs to leapfrog over naysayers.[29]

Exemplars

Not only is it impractical to try to convert everyone right away, it would be prohibitively taxing of time and people to attempt to do so. Besides, outside of the realm of cults and massive gatherings under the auspices of a shared, emotional bond, attempts at mass conversion have only ephemeral longevity or inspire as much derision as support. For this reason, a skilled leader in helping institutions effect change observed,

> In organizational life, no one believes what they read or what they hear. They believe only what they see. If you want to change people's behavior, change the exemplar's behavior.[30]

Under the circumstances, one of the most important tasks of the consulting engagement remains to identify leaders who will embrace No Dark Corners innovations. Why? There are two reasons. These leaders, regardless of whether they are informal leaders without hierarchical authority or managers who also possess credibility and respect within the workforce, serve as (1) champions of innovation and as (2) role models whose actions are congruent with their verbalized support of a new program. This is also why the consultant cannot long fill the role of exemplar, since "sustained leadership usually means becoming an insider."[31]

ENGAGING 101: SOME FEATURES OF STARTING A NO DARK CORNERS ASSIGNMENT

If, as discussed above, one of the prerequisites to a successful No Dark Corners engagement is the establishment of a relationship of trust between consultant and executive sponsor, then the first step is a mating dance between the two. For the consultant, this means interacting directly with the sponsoring executive, which can be difficult if the latter has tasked intermediaries with making preliminary arrangements. Why is it important to interact directly with the executive sponsor? The reasons include:

- Both executive sponsor and consultant have equal power to initiate or cancel work. Intermediaries can generally say no, not yes. They do not have the authority to alter scope based on discussion with the consultant, as they must first consult their principal. The net result may be a waste of time for all concerned.
- Intermediaries impose filters and increase the chance of a misunderstanding that may predispose the undertaking to failure instead of success. They may have presold the executive to expect results that the consultant cannot deliver based on ambient conditions or to undermine the consultant's capacity by misjudging where the consultant can offer the greatest value.
- Intermediaries are likely to lack the breadth of perspective of the executive sponsor, which will limit their ability to agree to objectives, assign appropriate value to a successful engagement, and appreciate pitfalls and complexities of instituting major changes. Because intermediaries have lesser responsibilities and, at times, no line authority, they may not realize what parts of the proposed engagement represent the most value to the core business—something that the executive would recognize in an instant.
- Absent direct interaction between executive sponsor and consultant, the consultant will be unable to establish a peer-level relationship with the executive and will accordingly experience an uphill climb in attaining mutual trust and respect.
- Intermediaries will be unable to communicate the precise level of executive commitment, as they may be viewing the engagement as a necessary burden or, alternatively, be hoping that the executive will come to value a No Dark Corners transformation in time. Lackluster commitment on the part of the sponsoring executive will all but assure flawed implementation.
- Intermediaries are likely to activate bureaucratic organs and processes at the expense of momentum, preferring to limit risk rather than seize opportunities. (Compare the difference between how Microsoft chief executive Bill Gates and his counterpart from Digital Research reacted to the same, once-in-a-career opportunity from IBM in Chapter 9's discussion of misguided redeemers. Gates

dealt directly with the IBM visiting team and launched Microsoft to meteoric success. His counterpart made himself unavailable and left intermediaries to extinguish the opportunity of a lifetime.)

- Intermediaries will have different equities to protect, including some that the executive sponsor accords a lesser priority. An intermediary who came out of a corporate sentinel function, for example, will most likely hesitate to allow the engagement to touch upon that function in any way that may appear to cast criticism of its effectiveness, for fear that this criticism will attach to the intermediary and stymie future career advancement. The executive, by contrast, is likely to understand intuitively that the consultant is not there to point the accusing finger of blame but to abandon what is no longer working in favor of a better way of doing business. The executive is more likely to appreciate that innovation requires organized abandonment.[32]

What happens once the consultant makes positive contact with the sponsoring executive? As for any consulting engagement, the two qualify each other. The executive does this by inquiring into the consultant's representative engagements and credentials. At the same time, however, the consultant must determine whether the executive is one with whom he or she could work productively. They need not form a personal friendship that extends to the grave, but the two must be able to work on a collaborative level that rises above the mere vending of technical expertise in exchange for coin. Although other consulting may allow or work best in such a transactional model, insider threat defense that involves close examination of trust and trust betrayal cannot proceed effectively without free-flowing information and exchange of confidences at a level that can be embarrassing in the absence of mutual trust and respect. Besides, if there is no trust, there will be inadequate agreement on the value of the engagement which, in turn, will lead to caviling over expenses and deliverables, ultimately resulting in a receivables risk for the consultant.

QUALIFYING AN EXECUTIVE SPONSOR OR CLIENT

I think consulting falls into two categories. Consulting organizations fill two basic needs. Companies contract out work that their people either cannot do or will not do. When I was selling for my own company, I tried to fit every opportunity into one of these two categories. My experience was jobs that did not fit neatly into one of these categories never came to fruition. As a consultant, it's important to qualify each opportunity early because time is a very precious commodity. Clients can be interesting, jobs can be exciting, but you only get paid for the ones you close. You must quickly qualify each opportunity and avoid the ones YOU are not convinced you can execute.

Always work smarter not harder. At first contact, try to qualify each opportunity into one of the two above categories, and if there is any doubt in your mind, move on.

Gary L. McCullough[33]
Vice President (retired)
Lockheed Martin Integrated Solutions

What kind of consulting agreement is most conducive to a No Dark Corners undertaking? A letter proposal signed by both executive sponsor and consultant is the kind of arrangement that gets to the heart of the objectives and value of the undertaking with a minimum of bureaucratic diversion. Anything more complicated triggers a laying of hands on the part of corporate sentinels, including attorneys, whose role it is to insist on the infusion of impenetrable language that goes to great length to minimize liability with little regard for what value emerges. Why? Attorneys and contracting officers concentrate their offers of expertise in their areas of knowledge, and they have no substantive expertise to offer in that part of the undertaking that actually addresses insider threat defense. The difficulty with allowing their introduction into structuring the engagement is not that they offer no utility, but that they take on the character of intermediaries, with all of the attending limitations previously described.

A good engagement agreement should be in plain language that executive and consultant can both understand without the assistance of translators, and it should make crystal clear what is to be done, how it is to be measured, and what payment is to be made for what measurable results. It can be as simple as a single-page contract attached to a proposal. The proposal, however, is premature if it precedes a substantive and candid discussion between client and consultant.

SAMPLE SINGLE-PAGE ENGAGEMENT AGREEMENT

This agreement has been used by the author as the basis for arriving at a mutually acceptable agreement that both executive sponsor and consultant are willing to sign to guide their collaboration. Revision and level of formality are adjustable to suit the ambient milieu. It is a single page if in Arial Narrow, 12-pt font, with tight margins.

We are contracting for a service which I will supply you for a price agreed in advance. You will pay for my actual expenses, and I will keep expenses reasonable, supplying details and receipts. I will not manipulate the work to artificially extend this agreement to get more money out of you, and you will not nickel-and-dime me to avoid paying for my deliverables and expenses. I will keep your business confidential and agree not to disclose any of the proprietary data or trade secrets you reveal to me in order for me to get the job done. You will own the specific report, product, or deliverable I tailor for your needs. This does not mean you own all the intellectual capital or material I use to produce this deliverable. If I create something new or universal or otherwise capable of being re-created by me for another job, that material remains my own, as long as I do not reveal your affiliations, proprietary interests, or trade secrets in using this intellectual capital elsewhere.

I am not your employee, and you are not going to construe our agreement to include attendance or participation in staff meetings and other administrative activities which we have not established as being part of the deliverables. You will not micromanage me or interfere with my approach to handling the job, once we have agreed to that approach. I will either charge you for any make-work or non-deliverable requirements you impose or will terminate our relationship as an alternative to wasting our time. If I charge you, I will also add an administrative fee of 25% on top of the cost of meeting each additional requirement. The same additional fee applies to any payment which you take more than 30 calendar days to pay from the date of my invoice. For every additional 30 days' delay in payment, I will charge another 10%, and will terminate our relationship without submitting final deliverables if you are more than 90 days in arrears or otherwise present a receivables risk.

The specific budget and deadline for this assignment are as follows:

DELIVERABLE:
APPROACH: See proposal dated _____ (copy attached).
DEADLINE/MILESTONES:
FEE:
ESTIMATED EXPENSES:
RETAINER:

Any changes to the foregoing details are acceptable if we both agree to them in an e-mail exchange.

This is the sum total of our business relationship. If we agree to do more business in the future, we will either re-execute another agreement like this or create an amendment which cites the foregoing general terms and modifies the scope, deadline, and price to our mutual satisfaction. I will start work as soon as we have both signed this agreement and you have returned the signed agreement with your retainer. This agreement is valid for a period of 30 days from the date of origin. After that, I will assume that these arrangements will not work for you or your employer and will simply move on to other assignments, without disclosing any information you have supplied to date in confidence.

Agreed to by these parties:
_____, Consultant   _____, Client
Date Signed: _____   Date Signed: _____

DELIVERING 101: SOME WAYS OF NAVIGATING A NO DARK CORNERS ASSIGNMENT

The details of the particular engagement will vary according to client need. However, some ways the consultant goes about gathering data and meeting obligations will increase chances of developing useful information and improving chances of successful implementation. These include

- If what is in place is not working, try something else.[34] This dovetails with the notion of organized abandonment, which is often necessary but difficult for organizations to institute on their own.[35]
- Remain alert and receptive to uncovering simple solutions, since, "Any fool can find a complicated solution to any problem; genius lies in finding the simple solution."[36]
- Listen to unheeded, internal sages who often have insight and good ideas but "no one in charge has ever listened to them."[37]
- Look beyond the façade. In other words, make observations after hours, in field locations, and of forgotten operations to see how they run compared to how the rest of the organization operates or is supposed to operate.

- Talk to people who do not expect to be consulted or asked their opinion, as they may have more candid observations that are free of an agenda. Along these lines, be prepared by having a letter or e-mail of introduction from someone in authority or, better still, a telephone number or local area reference that employees may call to verify who you are and to clear them to communicate without restraint.

SAMPLE LETTER FROM CLIENT VOUCHING FOR CONSULTANT

There are many occasions when it behooves the No Dark Corners consultant to wander unimpeded through the workplace to make independent observations and to benefit from unguarded comments and insights of people working in a given area. One of the ways to facilitate such freedom of maneuver is to equip the consultant with a letter such as the following. Who writes the letter? The executive sponsor or, if possible, a local area manager who is even more familiar to the employees in the particular workplace. What does the consultant have to do in order to obtain such a letter? Ask, and supply a draft such as this.

[LETTERHEAD OF INSTITUTION]

Date:	XXXX
To:	Employees and all Persons Doing Business at [name of site]
From:	[Name of executive sponsor or local manager]
Subject:	Consultant Authorized to Observe Operations and Ask Questions

[Institution's name] has contracted with [Consultant] to study some of our operations with an eye to assessing how well we are doing and where we could improve. Most of the consultant's visible work will involve making observations on site and talking to people about how things work in their respective areas. Accordingly, you may see the individual identified below coming to your area as part of this work. Please assist this individual to the extent you can do so without neglecting any core duties. [Consultant's name] is authorized to make observations and ask questions, but will be careful not to waste anyone's time. This individual will carry and display one of our contractor badges. Identifying information and a badge photo appear below:

First Name, Last Name of Consultant

[COPY OF BADGE PHOTO]

If there are problems or questions concerning this individual, please contact [local manager acting as host] at 123 456-7899 or me at 123 789-4566 [Give out full numbers so people can dial from a mobile phone if necessary]. If neither of us is available, please call [number of any 24-hour operations center which also has this letter] at any hour and ask to be put in touch with _____.

This authorization automatically expires on [projected end date of consulting agreement] or upon completion of [Consultant's] work for us, whichever comes first.

[Signature block of sponsoring executive or local manager]

- Take reasonable notes. Consultants who just talk without taking notes frequently give the impression that either they have phenomenal recall or are going through the motions of seeking input with no intention other than taking a ready-made product and passing it off as a custom report. Reasonable notes show that one is paying attention and facilitate later review in case an epiphany was missed. Reasonable note-taking, however, also means not allowing this process to interfere with open dialogue. It also includes knowing when to close the notebook in order to listen intently.
- Ask, "What else?" after closing your notebook or whenever there is a possibility that an employee needs a slight nudge to encourage more candor.
- Look to see what is not there. Walk around, talk to people, and see the difference between what defenses the institution's management thinks are in place and how these defenses actually operate.
    - One way to highlight the uncovered discrepancies is to ask, "What's wrong with this picture?" Why is an area designated as critical and controlled by a card reader under view of a surveillance camera left casually propped open? Why are vendors allowed to wander unescorted in the vicinity of irreplaceable, high-value assets? Taking photographs of such examples of discrepancies between what should be happening and what is actually taking place help illustrate vulnerabilities in ways that will gain more attention when the time comes for corrective action.
    - Another way, which is a low-level form of red teaming, is to approach different departments or functions without revealing one's consulting engagement and to just ask for information to see how or whether sensitive details are easily compromised. Making telephone, e-mail, and even Freedom of Information Act inquiries is another technique for testing defenses and employee awareness.
    - Finally, using scenario questions to learn how people in the institution would respond to unusual events that might signal an insider about to strike can also avail. On a more time- and labor-intensive level, such a process can easily turn into a tabletop exercise. Sometimes, however, a simpler, one-on-one question-and-answer session may prove more illuminating for the consultant and instructive for the employee. Precisely such a technique has become the hallmark of Craig Fugate, Director of the Federal Emergency Management Agency, who developed the habit of using what-if questions to keep his staff on their toes and to establish a milieu of crisis anticipation.[38]

STEPS TO INTRODUCING NO DARK CORNERS IN THE WORKPLACE[39]

1. *Think like an attacker, not like a defender.* Develop scenarios to test how difficult it would be to penetrate the organization, instead of taking at face value what corporate sentinels tell you.
2. *Plan for copilots in every critical cabin.* Using the copilot metaphor and starting with critical areas, design them to operate with a level of transparency and mutual support that makes it virtually impossible for a single person to be running everything absolutely alone or without some level of coworker oversight. Make it a team effort, not an inquisition.

3. *Do not rely on lasers where you need flashlights.* Resist the temptation to rely exclusively on specialists or monitoring technologies for your defense, particularly if these sentinels communicate to the rest of the workforce, "Leave it to the specialists." The goal is engagement at the team level. Promote taking a proprietary interest in not only the job but in the team, so that teams become self-weeding, self-policing, and mutually supportive.

4. *Thank and follow up.* In those situations where team members report suspicious activities to a corporate sentinel, always begin by expressing thanks and then give some timely feedback, even if all you can say is that you looked into the matter and found it innocuous.

5. *Limit invasive controls to those that count.* Do not alienate employees by burdening them with so many controls that it restricts their ability to do productive work. If you weed out bad performers early and foster cohesive, self-policing teams, you should be able to trust people who have worked into positions of responsibility. Do not gratuitously annoy the people you depend on. Maintain a sense of balance and give due attention to the core business without attempting to make every employee a snoop or sentinel.

6. *Put cumbersome security procedures on trial for their life and abandon what is not working.* If your pre-employment background investigation program is not screening out weak or problem employees, overhaul it. If you cannot tell, start keeping track and gauging its results.

7. *Don't keep bad hires one minute past the time it takes to spot them, and use the probationary period as designed.* The point of probation is to avoid making bad things worse, to cut your losses before they become severe. The advantage to doing this when defending against potential infiltrators is that you eject them before they can mature their attack plans. When in doubt, release them from employment for any reason before probation is over.

8. *Use what you have.* Big organizations throw money at problems. Dynamic ones use focus. Focus attention on a problem and results will follow. Use government-sponsored programs such as ICE/IMAGE (Immigrations and Customs Enforcement's ICE Mutual Agreement for Employers). At the very least, make sure the organization follows its own security procedures. Often, there is a major disconnect between what is presumed or required to take place and what actually takes place.

FINDINGS 101: COMMON FINDINGS TO EXPECT IN A NO DARK CORNERS CONSULTING ENGAGEMENT

Every assignment is unique, as is every institution and the situation framing its No Dark Corners engagement. There are nonetheless a number of observations common to a variety of consulting assignments that the No Dark Corners undertaking may expose, including:

- A disconnect emerges between defensive procedures that executives or managers assume are in place to safeguard against insider mischief and the procedures actually followed in the field.

- • This frequently occurs through no particular act of malice and may be catalyzed by little more than convenience or inattention to vulnerabilities.
- • Illustrating such findings through "What is wrong with this picture?" depictions of the disconnect between perception and reality usually obtains appropriate management attention and remediation.

- • What happens during normal business hours at the headquarters may be a far cry from what happens on a different shift in the field. An institution may go to great lengths to organize work spaces at its headquarters so that virtually no one works alone or has opportunities for undetected mischief, yet these measures may be in place where they are easily deployed in administrative areas. Meanwhile, field facilities housing critical assets and operating equipment may be understaffed and ill defended because no one has thought to prioritize by criticality of assets and potentially devastating loss in such areas, and the relatively low visibility of some remote operations and their skeletal staffing after normal business hours may have failed to gain proper attention.
- • Corporate sentinels may be spending more time and energy finding reasons not to adopt new procedures than they would expend embracing them. Marginal background investigations that have become a token effort or formality, for example, will seldom be acknowledged as valueless by the department nominally managing them. Staging a pilot program at a facility or operating division where managers and sentinels are willing spirits and eager for better results will offer more value in winning over the naysayers in the long run than any charm offensive or sales campaign calculated to make converts of the avowed nonbelievers.
- • Some of the most virulent fault-finding under the guise of logic or business argument will come from functions fearing a loss of face or organizational influence, that is, concerns of turf. Nor will entering into a prolonged debate moderate criticism from these quarters, as "logic is not effective against passion."[40] Instead, using pilot programs and exemplars to advance the inoculation of the organization with innovations such as engagement at the team level with copilot work arrangements and changes in the vetting and probation systems will avail where argument alone robs the program of momentum.
- • An important supporter of the program will break ranks not so much out of logical or passionate opposition but as a reaction to that part of the program that stands in the way of expedience. Thus, the first time a new vetting and probation system stands in the way of a department head being able to hire an acquaintance or a reconfiguration of work in a critical operation affects his overtime budget or capital investment plan to redesign work space, yesterday's supporter will become today's antagonist. Dealing with the ramifications of a positive exemplar turned negative require the utmost of finesse on the part of the consultant and quiet leadership on the part of the executive sponsor, as only the latter's discreet or even overt intervention can prevent this situation from undermining progress of the engagement.

DISENGAGING 101: DRAWING THE ASSIGNMENT TO A CLOSE

An unsuccessful or marginal No Dark Corners undertaking will conclude without ceremony or hesitation; both executive sponsor and consultant will be eager to close the books and part for greener pastures in their particular areas of endeavor. A successful program, however, will bring with it a challenge less common in professional circles: parting gracefully without fraying the relationship of trust between executive sponsor and consultant. The executive sponsor who has derived demonstrable yield from the engagement may be tempted to bring the consultant into the organization as a direct employee, albeit a well-compensated one. After all, the consultant will have shown discretion and results—two highly coveted qualities in high demand. Alternatively, the executive may be tempted to extend the consulting engagement to derive extended benefit of these talents for the institution. By the same token, the like-minded consultant may be tempted to succumb to or even solicit such blandishments. In either case, such extensions would be a mistake. Why?

First, much of the success attributed to the consultant will hardly be reproducible by either a lone employee or by a consultant working out of his or her province. In reality, any success will be the outcome not only of consultant expertise and diligence, but also of executive support and the right mix of situational factors and employee receptivity indispensable for success yet never possible to predict with certainty. What is certain is that how the consultant was treated as an outside expert with ongoing support from the top of the institution would not be the same if that individual were to become an employee. At that point, gone are peer-level relationships, as the organization adjusts its receptivity to what the individual has to say or propose based on relative position within the institutional hierarchy. Moreover, political adversaries, who may have held themselves in check because of the temporary nature of the consulting engagement and because of the ongoing involvement of the executive sponsor for that duration, would hardly give the same support to a lower-ranking employee as they once did to an outside adviser to their executive. Additionally, the time that the executive spent supporting No Dark Corners innovations at the outset would no longer be available to invest in equal increments for a consultant-turned-employee. Nor would it likely be available for lesser engagements involving the same consultant assigned to assist in areas beyond his or her expertise. The net result would be loss of effectiveness and institutional impotence for the consultant, and frustration for the executive at not deriving assumed benefits of prolonging the engagement or the relationship.

Besides, if the consultant overstays his or her welcome, the extended presence is akin to affixing a crutch to the arm of a patient who should be walking unassisted by this point. It is therefore more important to the health of the institution, and to the credibility and repute of the consultant, for the consultant to organize a graceful disengagement, whose hallmarks include

- Identifying in-house champions of the program and training them to carry it on without the consultant.
- Creating a self-audit program to gauge progress over time, possibly offering to assist with an audit in 6 months to a year of program implementation, but aiming at building within the institution an internal capacity for performing this function.
- Leaving the door open to future consultation without a mercenary setting of hooks into the program such as introducing proprietary systems, or tools designed with planned obsolescence, that would compel the client to periodically return to the consultant. Such hooks eviscerate the goodwill developed in the course of the engagement and undermine the program of insider defenses by attaching it to perceived lapses in integrity demonstrated by the mercenary consultant.
- Requesting permission to use the institution as a reference site in seeking future business, or even obtaining referrals to a different institution's sponsoring executive for new business, or both.

The point, in the end, is that both institution and client are best served once both realize they must reach the point of being satisfied to stop.[41]

CONSULTANT FOUR-WORD MANTRAS FOR KEEPING THE ENGAGEMENT IN PERSPECTIVE

Mantra	Application
1. Up to a point.	Degree to which any argument can be accepted.
2. It's just a task.	. . . not a career. Don't make a task into your life's work.
3. Communicate with your silence.	A good thing to say when meetings are ranging beyond logic.
4. WAIT: Why am I talking?	A good thing to ask oneself when trapped in such meetings.
5. Reflect. Let it go.	Zen approach to dealing with bureaucratic irritations.
6. Relax. Start again tomorrow.	Alternative to the foregoing approach.
7. There are no shortcuts.	Remember when trying to implement change too rapidly.
8. Do your one thing.	A way to focus one's energy where most productive.
9. Do what you can.	Because you can't always do what you should.
10. I'll get over it.	For dealing with frustrations and irritating personalities.
11. Change where it counts.	Good for the individual as it is for the organization.
12. Put it in perspective.	A reminder to look at the bigger picture.
13. Always better, never best.	Waiting to be best means missing opportunities to improve.
14. More isn't always better.	A good thing to note, particularly about too many controls.
15. Strong personalities change things.	Why one should not always shrink from taking a stand.
16. Always have a plan.	As opposed to winging it.
17. Never argue with idiots.	People watching might be unable to tell the difference.
18. Don't pretend to know.	Admit areas of ignorance and no one dwells on them.
19. Stay focused. Shift gears.	If it isn't working, you don't have to grind to a halt.
20. Whose turn is it?	Give everyone a chance to talk.
21. Let's rejoin the team.	When people stray too much into individual preferences.
22. Just make it happen.	Agonizing is counterproductive. You must start sometime.
23. Eat what you kill.	Own the decision, own the outcome.
24. All choices have consequences.	Including the decision to avoid making a choice.
25. Improve conditions or leave.	Recognize when to go, even if it means turning down a job.

THE LASER AND THE FLASHLIGHT

Addressing the insider threat compels reconsidering traditional efforts to penetrate with the intensity and focus of a laser when institutions should instead be illuminating with a flashlight. No matter how deep the laser drills, it touches on only a fragment of the entire picture. Caught in the laser's beam, a clever insider can mask or explain away hostile activities with relative impunity. The same malicious insider, however, cannot deceive alert peers whose combined, wider gaze acts as a flashlight making enemy action visible before it is too late to intervene. The No Dark Corners approach redirects the laser of specialized monitoring of corporate sentinels working in secret because insider threat defense calls, instead, for a flashlight. Thus, a successful implementation offers the flashlight of open team and employee engagement as a means of implementing layered defenses, particularly on the front lines of detection and intervention, where critical operations take place.

CHECKING THE FLASHLIGHT'S BULB AND BATTERY

An institution may pride itself on a first-rate implementation of a cutting-edge No Dark Corners program. It may have summoned the best of internal and consultant talent, spearheaded a red team to uncover unseen vulnerabilities, addressed each vulnerability through a transformational overhaul of work flow and vetting systems, and taken its employees from weakest link to first line of defense against hostile insiders. It may have developed an operating environment where every employee and contractor acts like a stakeholder and, consequently, every stakeholder assumes the role of a copilot who is not about to let misdeed or folly steer the institution into a collision course. Yet the moment the organization becomes self-satisfied and loses its interest in periodic self-appraisal, it succumbs to new vulnerabilities at the hands of adversaries who can better adapt to change. The institution becomes one which, having substituted its laser for a flashlight, has forgotten to keep the flashlight in good repair, to test its beam, refresh its batteries, and assure that it continues to function. As a business analyst observed,

> The most robust organizations will not be those that simply have plans in place, but those that have continuous sensing and response capabilities.[42]

How does the institution guard against the perils of complacency? One way is to periodically commission a red team to reexamine institutional defenses against insider attack. The temptation will be to align with expedience and recommission the last red team for a perfunctory refresh of the previous red team effort. Alas, good defense is seldom convenient, and this is precisely the wrong course to take. Serious threats are adaptable threats, or as a scholarly observer pointed out,

> Intentional disruptions follow a different logic. Intentional disruptions constitute *adaptable threats* in which the perpetrators seek both to ensure success of the attack and to maximize the damage.[43]

Altering the composition of the red team takes a bold stroke on the part of the institution's sponsoring executive and chief advocate of the No Dark Corners program. Internally, the executive must cull red team participants to include representation of current expertise in the critical operations of the institution, while delicately passing over or even disinviting employees whose system knowledge is no longer as current as it once was or who may be out of touch with changing workplace dynamics. Thus, if a previous red team member was accustomed to dealing exclusively with a very large team of internal employees working primarily with manual systems and the organization has since infused automation into this work along with increasing reliance on specialty contractors working side by side with internal employees, the time may have arrived to include one of those contractors on the red team and an internal supervisor who is equally adept at the manual and automated system than rely too heavily on the previous red team member. Similarly, it may be advisable to either select another consultant to facilitate the red team's activities or, if using the same primary consultant who remains a trusted adviser and able facilitator, at least insist on new subconsultants or subcontractors to serve on the red team as simulators of today's and tomorrow's hostile insiders.

Another alternative for obtaining a fresh perspective is to resort to sister agencies or other counterparts within the same industry as sources to fill the pool of red team participants. However, obstacles come with such alternatives, the chief ones being objectivity and compromise. No counterpart can be entirely objective if linked to the institution in any kind of joint business relationship or, worse still, in a position of being subordinate to the institution or relying on its goodwill to advance its own agenda. As for compromise, no matter how collegial relations may be between counterpart organizations, there is always reluctance to parade one's flaws or Achilles' heel before contemporaries—which is precisely what a good red team will uncover. Additionally, although a consultant or contractor is readily constrained to sign confidentiality and nondisclosure agreements, requiring the same of counterparts may be perceived as either awkward or indelicate. Thus, on balance, using a consultant to organize and help staff the red team may be the more practical and less costly option in the long run.

CONCLUSION

In the average, vulnerable workplace, it is easier for a hostile insider to harm people and abuse assets than it is for defenders to thwart an attack. All a hostile insider needs are access to a worthy target, an open door, and a dark corner from which to strike. The adversary seeking to strike a devastating blow, as well as any number of petty scoundrels seeking to damage or exploit the organization to lesser ends, need look no further.

Any institution with critical assets numbers among the many worthy targets. The open door comes from a traditional culture presenting few restrictions to movement or assets in the average workplace. This openness flourishes because private and government agencies alike must answer to demanding stockholders, ratepayers, and various regulatory agencies, most of which insist on convenient access to voluminous information on the institution with little thought about the exposure this creates. Even when organizations have critical assets to protect, when it comes to their public customers, they cannot be perceived as having something to hide. In this environment, defenses against infiltrators or any type of insider threat require a cultural shift. The challenge is to close the door to infiltrators while leaving it open to legitimate workers and business.

Even if an infiltrator sets sights on a worthy target and exploits weak defenses, he or she still needs a dark corner free of oversight in order to gather pre-strike intelligence and then initiate an attack without risk of timely intervention and defeat. The best way to defeat such an attack is to remove the dark corners. For long-term, transformational change, the most promising approach appears to be one at whose helm resides a sponsoring executive from the institution, backed by a specialized consultant who can assist with diagnostic activities, red team formation and analysis, and crafting of a No Dark Corners program in collaboration with internal champions who will lead it and harvest the benefits of insider threat defense.

Modern society's penchant for relying on technology and corporate sentinels to solve problems can easily marginalize average employees, excluding them from their vital role in insider defense. Instead of treating such employees like the weakest link relegated to the sidelines, institutions should recognize them as the first line of defense, bringing them onto the front lines with a No Dark Corners approach. Consequently, in addressing the insider threat, we must reconsider our usual efforts to penetrate with the intensity and focus of a laser what we should instead be illuminating with a flashlight. The malicious insider who sidesteps the laser of overburdened corporate sentinels cannot deceive alert peers whose combined, wider gaze acts as a flashlight making enemy action visible before it is too late to intervene. Nor must this power to intervene be unexercised or allowed to grow dormant. It must be refreshed through periodic review and constant challenge, in order to anticipate changing and adaptive threats.

Despite much study and debate, the insider threat remains as alive as it remains statistically rare. Infiltrators continue to pose serious, existential risk, as they offer high yield in proportion to their expense, particularly when contrasted with the resources necessary to mount equally devastating frontal attacks. There are no easy answers. No Dark Corners shows promise, however, as an approach to close gaps in traditional defenses. By going beyond corporate sentinels to engage stakeholders in their own protection and by transforming the weakest links to the first line of defense, this approach offers the victory of ownership over surprise.

QUESTIONS FOR ONLINE OR CLASSROOM DISCUSSION

1. What kind of organization is more likely to be able to handle a No Dark Corners implementation exclusively with internal resources: a large institution or a small one?
2. Why is a sudden impact response likely to require outside resources and also be very expensive?
3. In which kind of insider threat situation is it most likely that the lion's share of the institution's needs will be answerable through the delivery of a comprehensive report? Why?
4. What advantages do pilot programs offer when attempting to institute changes along the lines of a No Dark Corners transformation?

EXERCISES FOR GROUP PROJECTS

1. Assume you were a department head of a corporate sentinel function whose budget or headcount might be adversely affected by a successful No Dark Corners implementation. What are some of the ways you could undermine the implementation without getting into trouble with its executive sponsor?
2. Assuming you were an intermediary, say a staff manager on rotation to serve as special assistant to the executive sponsor of a No Dark Corners consulting engagement. How might you unintentionally impede the undertaking?
3. Using the "Checklist for Gauging Current Insider Defenses," rate two different organizations. Now, looking at the similarity between some of their ratings and disparity between others, how do you account for the variation? Which of the two strikes you as more vulnerable to hostile insider action? Why?

4. Assume that the executive sponsor within your organization has a bond of mutual trust with a consultant who has an impressive reputation for integrity. What might still make this the wrong consultant for a No Dark Corners engagement, and what would be some key signs of this inappropriate fit?

ENDNOTES

1. A. Weiss, *Organizational Consulting: How to Be an Effective Internal Change Agent*, Hoboken, NJ: John Wiley & Sons, 2003, p. xiii.
2. R. Drooyan et al., *Report of the Rampart Independent Review Panel*, November 16, 2000, p. 1. Retrieved August 28, 2011, from http://www.ci.la.ca.us/oig/rirprpt.pdf.
3. W. C. Kim and R. A. Mauborgne, *Blue Ocean Strategies*, Boston: Harvard Business Press, 2005, pp. 12–15.
4. Captain D. M. Abrashoff, *It's Your Ship: Management Techniques from the Best Damn Ship in the Navy*, New York: Warner Business Books, 2002.
5. Colonel D. H. Hackworth, *Steel My Soldiers' Hearts*, New York: Touchstone, 2003.
6. J. M. Bryson, *Strategic Planning for Public and Nonprofit Organizations*, 3rd ed., San Francisco: Jossey-Bass, 2004, p. 260.
7. R. Townsend, *Up the Organization*, New York: Fawcett Crest, 1970, p. 37, although in the particular example Townsend cited he was particularly focusing on automation and advising the organization to never automate without a long enough period of dual operation.
8. P. F. Drucker, *Managing the Non-Profit Organization*, New York: HarperCollins, 1992, p. 128.
9. G. M. Weinberg, *Secrets of Consulting*, New York: Dorset House, 1985, p. 9.
10. N. Catrantzos, "Tackling the Insider Threat," *Connecting Research in Security to Practice*, Alexandria, VA: ASIS Foundation, 2010, p. 42. This content from *Tackling the Insider Threat* was used with the permission of the ASIS Foundation.
11. Weiss, *Organizational Consulting*, p. 4.
12. M. Goldsmith, *What Got You Here Won't Get You There: How Successful People Become Even More Successful*, New York: Hyperion, 2007, p. 192.
13. Weiss, *Organizational Consulting*, p. 3.
14. Weinberg, op. cit.
15. D. Maister, C. H. Green, and R. M. Galford, *The Trusted Advisor*, New York: The Free Press, 2000, p. 8.
16. A. Weiss, *Getting Started in Consulting*, 2nd ed., Hoboken, NJ: John Wiley & Sons, p. 8.
17. G. M. Weinberg, *Becoming a Technical Leader*, New York: Dorset House, 1986, p. 135.
18. D. C. Gause and G. M. Weinberg, *Exploring Requirements: Quality before Design*, New York: Dorset House, 1989, pp. 14–16.
19. P. F. Drucker, *Management: Tasks, Responsibilities, Practices*, New York: HarperBusiness, 1993, p. 86.
20. L. J. Peter, *The Peter Prescription*, New York: Bantam Books, 1972, p. 148.
21. M. Goldsmith, *Mojo: How to Get It, How to Keep It, How to Get It Back If You Lose It*, New York: Hyperion, 2009, p. 57.
22. P. F. Drucker, *The Essential Drucker*, New York: HarperCollins, 2001, p. 86.

23. J. T. Rosch, "Behavioral Economics: Observations regarding Issues That Lie Ahead," remarks of J. Thomas Rosch, Commissioner, Federal Trade Commission, before the Vienna Competition Conference, June 9, 2010. Retrieved August 31, 2011 from http://www.ftc.gov/speeches/rosch/100609viennaremarks.pdf.
24. S. Adams, *The Dilbert Principle*, New York: HarperBusiness, 1996, p. 151.
25. Weinberg, *Secrets of Consulting*. Weinberg uses this as his third law of consulting and means not in the sense of encouraging consultants to overcharge but in the sense that many organizations are more interested in going through the motions of having an outsider look at a problem area without actually wanting to accept a solution that would challenge the status quo.
26. F. Johansson, *The Medici Effect*, New York: Warner Business Books, 2002, p. 168.
27. M. Goldsmith, "Changing Leadership Behavior," in *The Art and Practice of Leadership Coaching*, H. Morgan, P. Harkins, and M. Goldsmith, Eds., Hoboken, NJ: John Wiley & Sons, 2005, pp. 56–57.
28. J. Leibner, G. Mader, and A. Weiss, *The Power of Strategic Commitment*, New York: AMACOM, p. 10.
29. P. F. Drucker, *Managing the Non-Profit Organization*, New York: HarperCollins, 1992, p. 128.
30. Weiss, *Organizational Consulting*, p. 15. Also, for a brief video discussion of this phenomenon in the context of a small group seminar, see Alan Weiss's discussion on changing behavior in this 2008 YouTube video clip: http://www.youtube.com/watch?v=sCAXtZ1QN_o.
31. J. Badaracco, *Leading Quietly*, Boston: Harvard Business School Press, 2002, p. 35.
32. Drucker, *Managing for the Future*, New York: Truman Talley Books 1992, p. 340.
33. Personal communication, March 1999.
34. D. Noone, *Creative Problem Solving*, Hauppauge, NY: Barron's, 1993 p. 115.
35. See note 30.
36. H. Holtz, *How to Succeed as an Independent Consultant*, 3rd ed., New York: John Wiley & Sons, 1993, p. 244.
37. Abrashoff, *It's Your Ship*, p. 44.
38. N. Catrantzos, 2010, p. 43. This content first developed for *Tackling the Insider Threat* was used with the permission of the ASIS Foundation. Subsequently, it has undergone minor revision.
39. A. Ripley, "In Case of Emergency: FEMA's New Administrator Has a Message for Americans: Get in Touch with Your Survival Instinct," *Atlantic Monthly*, September 2009. Retrieved July 13, 2011 from http://www.theatlantic.com/magazine/archive/2009/09/incase-of-emergency/7604/.
40. Holtz, p. 264.
41. L. J. Peter, p. 154.
42. N. Nohria, "The Organization: Survival of the Adaptive," *Harvard Business Review*, May 2006.
43. Y. Sheffi, *The Resilient Enterprise*, Cambridge, MA: MIT Press, 2007, p. 50.

CHAPTER **11**

Answer Guide

CHAPTER 1

QUESTIONS FOR ONLINE OR CLASSROOM DISCUSSION

1. If insider threats are indeed rare, and most people are not trust betrayers, how does this affect the ability to carry out research into hostile insiders?

    It limits selection of methodologies. For example, statistical analysis will likely be less fruitful than for a more commonly occurring event. In addition, this limits opportunities to examine trust betrayers closely, although individuals involved in performing damage assessments by debriefing traitors do have opportunities to see patterns emerging over time.

    How do you account for the claim that hostile insider action is comparatively rare?

    It could be that most people, most of the time, are "neither saving the world nor exploiting it."[1] This could also be a tribute to societal norms or legal penalties that make betrayal relatively unattractive for the vast majority of one's coworkers.

2. Why do you suppose that, as Band et al. assert, the majority of cyber insider attacks appear to be tracing to *former* insiders, that is, to employees or contractors who are no longer working at the targeted institution?

    The commoditization of information technology (IT) services has arguably resulted in lower wages and perceived status for IT workers who are, in perception or reality, underpaid as a class of knowledge workers. If their attending compensation and treatment reflects this diminished status, then one likely reason for slam-the-door attacks is revenge. The lack of access to or familiarity with a grievance system may also contribute to the perception that IT workers have no other means of redress other than to abuse their skills at their former employer's expense.

3. Identify three or more factors that affect the extent to which an act of trust betrayal may be more readily deterred or condoned based on ambient working conditions. What can a defender do about these conditions?

    - Uniformly poor or abusive treatment of employees without an effective ombudsman or grievance process tends to lead to a variety of minor and progressively greater betrayals, starting with petty theft. A defender can attempt to show the employer the wisdom and cost-effectiveness of instituting some redress procedures. Failing that, defenders can at least themselves become good listeners and be approachable, thereby increasing the likelihood that they will be the first to learn of possible abuses from an appreciative workforce.

- If organizational leaders are perceived to be abusive or hypocritical, this increases the likelihood that employees will condone petty theft and other minor hostilities as a kind of venting among coworkers. Defenders can do the same as for the preceding point.

- If supervisors and middle managers in effect condone minor betrayals and themselves carry out indiscretions as a form of informal compensation (I'm underpaid, so I can at least take some tools home), then any warnings and lectures they give regarding employer loyalty will fall on deaf ears. Defenders can begin with themselves and their work team, encouraging transparency and modeling the behaviors they would like to see permeate the workplace.

4. Taking into account the checkered trajectory of some IT ventures, ranging from Apple's failed Lisa handheld computer to Microsoft's problems with the Vista operating system and the much feared Y2K debacle that never quite unfolded at the turn of the last century, does the cyber community face unique challenges in credibility when casting the spotlight on the cyber-centric view of insider threats? Discuss.

   IT's command of an arcane discipline and vocabulary makes it easy to magnify how dire a given situation may appear, particularly if the work environment forces multiple departments into ruthless competition for scarce budgets and resources. The finesse is to avoid overplaying one's hand, whether this is in always having the most sophisticated PowerPoint presentations at budget meetings or making the most complicated case for resources that no one but the initiated can understand. Executives may not have fluent command of a discipline's argot, but they can readily spot exaggeration and one-sided arguments. They also have surprisingly strong recall when it comes to worst-case scenarios that never materialized, cost overruns, and schedule delays. One should be mindful of all of these factors before approaching the trough with an overembellished plea.

EXERCISES FOR GROUP PROJECTS

1. Review popular literature from the 1980s and explain what made 1985 the Year of the Spy. Now, retrieve a copy of Herbig's study of treason over time and draw out the similarities and differences between then and now in the individuals who are willing to commit treason against the United States. What, if anything, has changed? Does this affect the capability to defend against today's traitor? If so, how? If not, why not? Does the motivation to commit espionage have any impact on the ability of counterespionage officers to detect traitors?

   This item anticipates some of the discussion that will follow elsewhere in the book. One of the more telling differences, though, is that whereas yesterday's traitor was financially motivated, today's is increasingly influenced by divided loyalties. Ideological motivation is always more difficult to trace than financial motivation, since the traitor believing in a cause is willing to face personal hardship and will also not give away the telltale signs that accompany unexplained cash or blandishments.

2. Contrasting the 1980s with the present day, once more, how have advances in technology or changes in cultural norms affected the ease or difficulty of detecting a trust betrayer and intervening before this individual has an opportunity to carry out an attack?

On the one hand, the Internet has made it much easier to transmit large quantities of sensitive information without a complicated logistics network. On the other hand, detection technologies, including traffic analysis and sniffer programs, have also enabled defenders to monitor audit trails and trace suspicious activities. Moreover, search engines and fingertip, online resources now enable the average employee to perform his or her own due diligence when faced with an anomalous event that may signal nefarious activity. As the means of carrying out hostile activities remotely has advanced, so, too, has the means of discovery and intervention.

3. Identify a case of trust betrayal in your work environment, profession, or industry that led to significant changes in how one does business. Analyze this case individually and then as a group. To what extent were the changes beneficial? Did they meet their objective, or were they put in place as the result of overreaction? Were there any unintended consequences? Over time, is the affected institution better off for having instituted the changes? What alternatives might you propose as a team?

One commonly occurring corporate fixture is the genesis of an enterprise-wide ethics program when the institution has been caught in a scandal that causes reputational risk. The ethics program typically launches with a flourish and produces a spike in anonymous whistle-blowing. Over time, as the novelty wears off and external scrutiny also declines, the program undergoes staff reductions and transitions to a maintenance-level activity. This is not always bad, as there are invariably one or two overeager, overnight ethics specialists whose efforts to develop more internal business and to make themselves shine end up generating makework projects and loss of productive time that, if unchecked, can lose whatever dividends the ethics program once delivered.

CHAPTER 2

QUESTIONS FOR ONLINE OR CLASSROOM DISCUSSION

1. Identify at least two other ways of performing research on the insider threat that would not involve the Delphi method. Are there any attractive or limiting factors with these approaches?

One method would be a survey. It might be easier to administer and compile, making it more attractive, but whom would one survey? Trust betrayers? Not only are these people statistically uncommon, the nature of their offenses would make the credibility of their responses problematic. Another way would be a case study. This would allow looking at one particular event or trust betrayer and then trying to infer universally applicable insights. The case could be fascinating, but it could also risk the echo-chamber effect of loss of perspective through prolonged, narrow concentration on one individual or event.

2. What are some of the strengths and limitations of using technology to detect and deter insider attack? How would such methods work in your organization?

One of the most attractive features of technological monitoring is that this reduces the otherwise labor-intensive need to rely on people to monitor other people. The downside is that technology is seldom optimized to ascertain intent and tends to distinguish poorly between legitimate and nefarious actions. Besides, someone must oversee the implementation of the technology. In practice, the overseers are more sophisticated and comfortable with their systems than with understanding the people watched by them. This tends to open the door to designing systems that are optimized from the technician's view—which can be very user-hostile. Examples include needless proliferation and changing of increasingly complicated passwords that the user can neither recall nor recycle. As a result, a user who is otherwise conscientious about security may feel forced into a compromise by writing the password down and keeping this within easy reach, as an alternative to having to call customer support for a lengthy password reset process. Technology implementations seldom take sufficient account of unintended consequences or imposition of lost productive time, as Herley noted.

3. Identify at least three limitations of the average pre-employment background investigation, recalling your own for your present position, if possible.

For one, identity verification is often cursory and a perfunctory exercise conducted to satisfy legal, right-to-work requirements. More significantly, the entire process is often considered drudgery. Thus, by default, the background check is assigned to the junior-most clerk in the personnel or human resources function. Since most of the investigation itself tends to be contracted out, the process can easily become a form passing exercise with little attention paid to results. Some results, for example, include coded indicators of financial health, and interpreting these may be difficult for the clerk who is under pressure to expedite an already cumbersome recruitment process. Moreover, there is seldom an incentive but often a disincentive for slowing things down to take a closer look at the results of the background investigation or to ask for clarifying detail either from the applicant or from the firm conducting the investigation.

4. What makes an infiltrator a better choice for insertion into a target with the assignment to develop the means to carry out a fatal attack from within? Would a disgruntled career employee not be better suited to do this?

In theory, the career employee would have more knowledge and access. In practice, however, a disgruntled insider is already recalcitrant and would be resistant to control. Having a grudge to bear or axe to grind, the disgruntled insider takes the attack much more personally than an infiltrator. In the desire to settle old scores, the disgruntled employee is likely to develop a very idiosyncratic view of what is worth attacking and who should be on the top of the target list. An infiltrator, on the other hand, is likely to be more disciplined and responsive to direction by an organization that can also provide support and protection from discovery. Many disgruntled insiders are already mistrusted and kept at arm's length because of their chronically annoying behaviors. They would thus be more likely to give themselves away if they suddenly start to ingratiate themselves into a particular operation, whereas an infiltrator who is a newcomer can do the same without exciting remark.

5. How well does your probation system work for new employees? Compare your system with at least one other. Which is better? Why? What is the percentage of new hires released from employment during probation compared to that of those

retained after successfully completing the probationary period? Is either probation system actively used by hiring managers, or is its provision for release of underperforming new hires seldom exercised?

A good way to evaluate such probation systems is to talk to hiring managers and see whether they face tacit disincentives, such as losing a position if it goes too long unfilled. Also, how much of a burden is it for the hiring manager to replace an underperforming new hire? Is it a matter of going to the next most qualified applicant on the list, or does the employer force the manager to repost the job and go through another recruitment process from start to finish? Also, if managers are measured by how long they have unfilled vacancies, this could be a disincentive to taking full advantage of the probation system. If the policy says that a new hire may be released at any time for any reason during the probationary period but, in reality, efforts to get rid of such a new hire are questioned or hindered by the legal department, the recruiter, or an ethics office, then the value of the probationary period may be more aspirational than actual.

6. Does your organization operate under a situation where corporate sentinels may have power but lack status, whereas team members working on core business enjoy much greater status? If so, how does this affect the way that sentinels and team members get along with each other? Is there mutual respect or tension between the two camps? How can you tell?

One of the ways to tell is to look at compensation and reporting structure. An organization where people are underpaid and report to a function that occupies little weight in the organization may also have physical manifestations of this status in the form of distant and unattractive office space. Higher status brings better compensation, reporting to higher and more important parts of the organization, and access to better working conditions and resources, including bigger budgets. If the team members perceive themselves to be superior because of their status, they may flaunt this status and ignore rules and procedures generated by sentinels—unless their superiors insist otherwise. If the sentinels also recognize that the organization accords them lower status, they may seek to compensate for the apparent slight by lording over whatever power they have over team members who appear to be reaping more benefits than merit would give them. This means inattention to or "slow rolling" on urgent requests from team members or overattention to enforcement of the most minor rules, at the team members' expense.

EXERCISES FOR GROUP PROJECTS

1. Select an organization and then chart the process by which it recruits and hires new employees or otherwise grants liberal access to its facilities and operations. Examine that process and identify exploitable weaknesses. Using a red team approach, describe how you might exploit those weaknesses as an infiltrator and what defender actions or countermeasures would introduce obstacles to infiltration.

Do personal referrals carry extra weight for applicants? If so, all an infiltrator would have to do is arrange for a social introduction to someone who can make such a referral. One of the frequently underexamined weaknesses is the treatment of contractors and temporary employees. Often, there may be one set of stated rules that strictly prohibits unescorted access. However, in reality, the field practice may be to grant uninhibited access casually in the name of convenience. Indeed, it is worth looking closely to see how many of the stated due diligence processes give way to convenience, particularly if the first line of defense is a junior or overworked employee who just cannot watch or assess people who should be under the supervision of someone more senior or technically proficient in whatever a contractor is supposed to be doing for the employer.

2. Using open sources, identify an employer considered good to work for and another employer considered exceptionally difficult. Now look at their grievance processes and, to the extent that you can, the kind of people problems they have. What can you infer about which organization would be more vulnerable to an insider threat? Why?

   Hoovers, *Fortune, Harvard Business Review,* and Google searches can supply data on different businesses, including best employers in the eyes of employees. Media searches can highlight the worst employers. Also look for employers who figure prominently in hostile work environment lawsuits. Workers who are reasonably well treated and content, in an environment where they have the means to air their concerns and obtain redress for unfair treatment, will likely be more mutually supportive and interested in their employer's welfare as an extension of their own. Those working in an oppressive environment may care little for the employer's losses, or even contribute to them as a means of obtaining revenge for perceived wrongs. In the latter environment, it is less likely that employees not assigned sentinel duties will exercise much of a proprietary interest in reporting suspicious activity or in otherwise extending themselves more than they perceive their employer reciprocates on the job. High tardiness, absenteeism, and employee turnover rates may also signal that the workplace is poorly respected and ripe for any number of misdeeds, including slam-the-door insiders who cause damage or steal on the way out.

3. Identify a team environment for a pilot program and institute a No Dark Corners–style copilot approach to self-regulation as an alternative to invasive monitoring or overproliferation of rules. What kind of results would you expect? What did you experience?

   This could be a club, church group, or any community of interest. Trust is infectious and if introduced at the same time that invasive barriers to performance are lifted, the results can be encouraging. One of the things to watch for, though, is the Hawthorne effect, where subjects improve temporarily at the sign of any change that signals they are getting more attention and that someone cares after all.

CHAPTER 3

QUESTIONS FOR ONLINE OR CLASSROOM DISCUSSION

1. Looking at the drawing in Figure 3.1, adopt one of two positions and list actions on the part of corporate sentinels that would support your position.

   Position 1: The sentinel is erecting barriers to employees as they pursue core business.

   Every single block before the sentinel is, in the eyes of other employees, a makework activity or consumer of productive time that team members need for revenue-generating work or essential operations. Security rules can be seen as impeding productivity. Who needs them? Don't we all know and trust each other? As for audits, they always seem to arrive in the middle of a critical task when the team is short-handed and already overworked. Now productive work must take a back seat in order to go through what appears to be a pointless search for records and documentation to satisfy some martinet who wants to show the boss how smart the auditor is and how careless field people are by contrast. Similarly, passwords end up protecting very little when sentinels effectively guard the computer network more from users than from intruders. After all, the push to keep changing passwords just after one has become comfortable with them and the inability to reuse old favorites just ends up compelling team members to write down the passwords in discoverable locations, such as one's calendar. This exposure would not happen if team members were allowed to keep passwords indefinitely or until experiencing an event-driven need to change them (such as a fellow user with access to the same password being terminated). The rest of the blocks also can easily turn into symbols of a self-fueled bureaucracy that perpetuates rules and nuisances long after their reason for existence has been forgotten.

Position 2: The sentinel is removing these barriers to make employees more effective.

Security rules, if sensible and intelligently applied, can be seen as facilitating work rather than blocking it. Isn't it better to work in an area convenient to one's desk, for example, rather than having to go across town to a separate, secure building every time a team member wants to consult a sensitive, proprietary, or classified reference document? Audits can be shown to catch small irregularities in contracting or other processes in time to correct them before they result in work stoppage, liquidated damages, or subcontractor performance failures. Password changes can be simplified and consolidated through provisioning systems that allow linking different accounts to a master password or combination of authenticating mechanisms that only the individual team member can produce. These include using a combination of a social security number and security questions, or a biometric identifier (such as a thumbprint or hand-geometry scan) combined with one's unique badge or access card. Combining such things can be made to be not only easy for the end user but much more difficult for an adversary to simulate or counterfeit. All these blocks can be transformed from barrier wall to stepping stone in order to help advance rather than retard core business.

2. Now switch positions and make the opposite case.

See notes above.

3. If the drawing in the figure is insufficient to illustrate either case adequately, then what indicators would you develop and monitor to determine whether a corporate sentinel is impeding or facilitating operations?

Can the sentinel coherently articulate the reason for a given measure or hurdle? Does the sentinel realize the full extent of time, energy, and cost imposed and the tradeoff in lost productivity? If the case ultimately descends to rote sentinel insistence on following the rules and the vulnerability remains vague or unexplained, it is time to reexamine whether the imposed protections may not be defending against a threat that is no longer the same. On the other hand, if the vast majority of team members can readily adjust to minor intrusions of corporate sentinels under the banner of due diligence and only one or a handful of malcontents object vociferously, it may be wise to see if the objection is unrelated to the sentinel's issue but, instead, the foam of churned feelings from a chronic complainer.

4. What is the proper role of management in guiding the way sentinel and average employee interact with one another?

  The first thing management can do is abide by the same rules it is willing for sentinels to impose on the rest of the employees. By holding itself to a no-exceptions standard, management at once communicates an endorsement of the rules to the general employee population while also giving sentinels to understand that any excessively obstructive rules will impinge upon executives, not only on those who lack the authority to do something about measures that grow draconian out of all proportion to the object sought.

5. How should good-faith differences between employee and sentinel be resolved? By whom?

  This is a classic management problem lending itself to resolution by standard processes that a good organization should already have in place, including insistence on the differing parties first attempting to resolve the matter directly and professionally. Failing that, then either or both should avail themselves of the chain of command, with full disclosure and consultation of all stakeholders.

EXERCISES FOR GROUP PROJECTS

1. Select an organization (it need not be your own) where there are at least two well-run corporate sentinel functions that are generally accepted by employees and supported by management. Assume that your group is taking over both functions and that your task is to completely undermine them to the point of eroding all user support and voluntary compliance. To this end, what are at least three things you could do? How long would it be before you attained the desired effects?

  As Peter Drucker has observed, the spirit of the organization is created from the top, and if it decays it is because the top rots. Accordingly, a good place to begin the campaign of reversing sentinel credibility is by managing the sentinel function into the ground through common failures: micromanaging the staff, managing by fiat, ignoring staff insights, creating a dysfunctional management fad of the week culture, and even developing a quota for sentinels to meet in issuing violations, infraction notices, or negative findings against the general employee population. Next, end employee outreach and collaboration efforts. Compound this by insisting on physical insulation, that is, working in areas separated from core employees and functions via separate locked workspaces or, if possible, buildings that are in a separate campus. Results should begin to be visible within 30 days and could be devastating within 6 months to a year. Although such tactics would probably work for both organizations, it is possible to accelerate the process by identifying one or two signature collaborative successes of each sentinel function and turning them 180 degrees at the outset. Is the IT security function, for example, famous for making password protection easy and manageable? Then, overnight, with little notice or explanation, institute a complicated, user-hostile system requiring all users to create at least six different passwords for various applications and to change them every 30 days. To get the full benefit of this exercise, brainstorm not only acts of managerial malpractice but also develop a timeline for putting them into play.

2. Select a corporate sentinel function that is generally maligned or not respected within your organization or another. Assuming a timeline of 6–12 months, develop a turnaround strategy, assigning different tasks to group members with the intent of improving that sentinel function's effectiveness over time. Based on what you learned in this chapter and what the preceding exercise told you about what it takes to undermine a working sentinel function, what do you need to do in this case? What should you do first? Is this turnaround possible by working solely within the sentinel function's confines, or do you also need to go across organizational lines to attain the desired result? Elaborate. Conclude by giving a timeline of actions for your first 6 months of sentinel rehabilitation.

Often any organization may find that, over time, it has diverged from its original purpose or lost sight of it altogether. Begin by asking the raison d'etre of the sentinel organization. How do the jobs its people do translate into adding value to the institution served? Who decides this? Is the part of the core business that the sentinel organization reports to rating the sentinel group a valued and necessary part of the business or just a gesture at compliance to some imposed mandate? Although you can undermine a sentinel function thoroughly without much cross-organizational reach, fixing a dysfunctional one is altogether a different matter. You must develop an understanding of what the sentinel function is supposed to do and how this diverges from what it is doing. Some or even much of what it is doing may have thin or distant linkage to its reason for being there. Thus, part of the solution may well be to abandon counterproductive or makework activities, and it will take management imprimatur to make some changes. Other changes, such as abandoning the daily or weekly or monthly generating of audit trails that no one reviews may be possible to discontinue with minimal notice, advising only the few affected stakeholders. One method of tilting acquiescence in one's favor is to adopt a U.S. Navy–style preface, "unless otherwise directed." Thus, in cutting off a labor-intensive daily report on badge audit trails that goes to a wide audience but is neither read nor missed, begin with "unless otherwise directed, as of the first of next month we will no longer be issuing report X. This change will spare considerable demands on resources that we are in the process of redirecting to _____ where we have noticed recurring requests for additional assistance. If you still have a business need for the information from report X, rest assured we will still be able to accommodate you, although we may have to make other arrangements. Please call _____ at extension _____ for such arrangements." The timeline this time will be more difficult, because many of your actions may be contingent on user acceptance, management endorsement, and collaboration of stakeholders who may never before have been engaged in sentinel functions to the extent you would like to involve them.

3. Selecting an organization that appears to have too many sentinels concentrated at headquarters locations, can you develop an approach to embedding one corporate sentinel at each of multiple field sites where that one sentinel represents multiple sentinel functions and works in and with core business employees every day? Develop a pilot program to try this out. What dividends would you expect or be able to demonstrate to be able to make the case for trying this alternative approach? What resistance would you anticipate and from what organizations?

There are precedents for doing this, such as sending divisional HR representatives to major operating divisions of a given company, so that they can take on a position of one-stop shopping and serve as champion and accessible expert for the division served. The benefit to the sentinel function is almost immediate improvement of relationships with the field and a heightened sense of operational priorities to calibrate the sentinel's previous vision of what tasks are most important. At the same time, with an in-house advocate, both managers and rank-and-file employees begin to see the sentinel in a new light, developing peer-level relationships in the place of traditional antipathies. One selling point for a pilot program is to pick a division that leads the company in infractions and clashes with the sentinel function, promising improvement within 90–180 days. Measure before and then after the assignment of the embedded sentinel. Ideally, success will translate into a decline in measurable problems, with correspondingly fewer demands of executive time to mediate organizational clashes between line and sentinel functions. Resistance may come equally from the field and from the sentinels themselves, with the latter being more likely to surface because the pilot program would remove them from their comfort zones and established patterns.

CHAPTER 4

QUESTIONS FOR ONLINE OR CLASSROOM DISCUSSION

1. Identify a good leader and a bad one who held the same job at different times. What traits did they share? Where did they differ? How might the good leader have done a better job preventing or minimizing the damage of an insider threat?

    This could be anyone, a military officer or a business unit manager. They probably shared some basic level of technical qualification for the job, possibly including degrees or licenses in the same field. They probably mastered at least some of the same basics of survival in the institution, that is, how to get to work on time, whom not to offend, what basic deadlines to honor at all costs. Perhaps they diverged in their approach to treating people, with one being relatively the same accessible professional to all, whereas the other only "managed up," that is, only invested courtesy and attention to superiors, treating everyone else with scorn or inattention. Perhaps the bad leader took credit for others' accomplishments while pointing to scapegoats for failures. The good leader may have never felt the need to shanghai others' achievements and taken more than his or her share of the blame, less of the credit. Perhaps the good leader defended subordinates and felt obligated to smooth their path so that they could do productive work, whereas the bad leader delegated every burden to subordinates and took on more work than they could handle in order to scrape favor and look good to those in echelons above. The good leader would probably have inspired a certain loyalty, resulting in early warning of a possible insider threat if not direct suppression of that threat by loyal subordinates outraged at the betrayal. The bad leader, by contrast, could easily inspire even decent team members to look the other way in the case of an act of sabotage that they might not themselves perform but which they might feel the bad leader has brought upon himself or herself out of ineptitude or scorn for the people who do the productive work.

2. Can a good leader's example serve even in the leader's absence? How might that example affect a work team member rising to the position of copilot when no one else is around to take charge during a crisis?

   Many who find themselves in difficult circumstances recall a role model and ask themselves, "what would so-and-so have done?" Thus, the power of example can outlive the one who has supplied the example. On one level, such modeling behavior begins with absent parents. It may then be applied to teachers or respected peers. Attempting to replicate what a respected but absent role model would do is easier to simulate and follow than committing more than a few checklists to memory for use in a crisis.

3. Why might even a good leader fail to adequately defend against insider threats despite early detection of warning signs?

   No leader functions in a vacuum, but instead in the realm created by his or her manager. Competing priorities, a runaway bureaucracy that has taken a good idea and worked it into the ground—these are just some examples of why a defensive program that came off to a good start may falter.

4. Can you think of an example where a leader's poor resolution of a conflict between a corporate sentinel and a work team member may make matters worse? Discuss.

   One of the surest ways to frustrate both parties is to continually be seen as splitting the baby, that is, offering unsatisfying or counterproductive compromises that accomplish no useful end other than to demonstrate ostensible fairness to both parties by making them suffer equally. King Solomon's biblical offer to split a baby by sword so that both women claiming maternity could walk away with an equal portion epitomizes such a resolution—if carried out. In Solomon's case, using the avowed solution as a way of gauging which woman cared more about the child's life than about possession was an innovative way of sorting through conflicting information to arrive at truth. Many poor compromisers, however, would indeed split the baby, in the interest of fairness.

5. How can an informal leader with great credibility but relatively no formal authority on the job act to negate the impact of a trust betrayer?

   The leader could challenge the trust betrayer in front of the entire team, exposing the betrayal. Alternatively, the leader could use access to formal leaders to deliver a discreet warning that triggers increased scrutiny and ultimately catches the betrayer in the act.

EXERCISES FOR GROUP PROJECTS

1. From an executive perspective, develop a job description and interview questions for a hypothetical vacancy of a chief sentinel in your organization. Assign one group member to exemplify the ideal candidate and another to represent the worst possible choice. Interview each and then, on the basis of the interviews, establish rating criteria and, if necessary, revise your questions to home in on the desirable traits the process should identify. What has this process taught you?

   You eventually discover that an individual can come across well on paper and impressively in interviews yet still turn out to be the wrong person for the job. A look at research behind John Molloy's *Dress for Success, Live for Success* and related books suggests that actors and professional athletes enjoy a consistent edge in interviews because of natural or simulated poise. Attractive and tall people also have an advantage in such situations. The lessons to learn include finding ways to compensate for such phenomenon with more probing interview questions and better rating scales, as well as additional checks and balances. The best of the latter comes in the form of a well-designed new hire probation system.

2. Look at the career arc of the average employee who comes sailing into the institution without any adverse information in the background check or any difficulty in passing probation. At some point, though, this employee becomes jaded, dyspeptic, and begins to be seen as more a liability than an asset to the work team. What causes the transformation? Does it matter? What can or should the problem employee's boss do about the situation? What can or should team members do about it? Analyze options and make a clear recommendation of how to handle the individual, making any assumptions you like about information not given to you.

   Any number of life events can cause a good employee to sour. Peter Drucker has suggested that one of the factors may be the declining number of promotions available in institutions in this century when contrasted with the last. Life happens and some people advance over others, leaving occasional resentment in their wake. The why of what gives rise to malcontents may not matter so much, unless it reflects a systemic problem that leaders can address to mitigate organizational infection. The first thing bosses should do is talk to the problem employee before matters become worse. Too often, people at all levels of the institution ignore early signs of a problem in the hope that it will go away or on the pretext of minding their own business. Institutional well-being and productivity are everyone's business, however, and a display of legitimate concern is almost always possible to carry out in a way that is helpful or even welcome. Team members are on the front lines of detection, and their positive intervention can be much more helpful if it comes early. A leader's talk always has the implied possibility of disciplinary consequences. Not so for the same words from a peer. Depending on what scenario one chooses to play out, the matter can begin with a talk and end with a directed referral to an employee assistance program or with a corrective action plan where successful completion becomes the only way for the problem employee to stave off termination. If the case is severe and irremediable, it may also be an option to terminate the problem employee and absorb lawsuits and other threats as long as the toxic individual is removed and the workplace is insulated from this individual.

3. Chart a major issue affecting your industry or sector through the issue–attention cycle. Where in the cycle do you now find it, and where can you anticipate it going in its next evolution?

   A good place to look is legislation affecting an aspect of an industry or activity that may not be regulated and also not widely understood. After a major catastrophe, legislators react by proposing laws to foreclose the chances of recurrence—regardless of whether, in hindsight, those laws really supply the intended benefits. Sometimes it works, sometimes it does not. In Oakland, California, severe fires affected neighboring communities and reached the home of a state senator. Mutual aid brought a responding fire crew from a neighboring jurisdiction to the rescue. However, the crews hose did not fit on the nearest hydrant. As a result of this failure of interoperability, the senator's home burned down. What did the senator do? He sponsored legislation to mandate inter-operability across the board for responders in what ultimately became the State Emergency Management System (SEMS). Although SEMS could not directly force responders to use common terms and equipment, the law managed to gain force through control of reimbursement money from declared disasters. Thus, unless a given jurisdiction subscribed to SEMS, the state would withhold at least a portion of its disaster reimbursement money, thereby giving SEMS more weight.

CHAPTER 5

QUESTIONS FOR ONLINE OR CLASSROOM DISCUSSION

1. Thinking like an adversary, identify three exploitable vulnerabilities in your own organization's pre-employment background investigation process.

   Examples may include ability to present identification remotely without hav-ing it closely verified, as by sending in scanned documents that may be counter-feit. Another common example is the absence of a clearly articulated protocol for resolving discovered anomalies—other than succumbing to hiring manager pres-sure to move forward at all costs. What about consistency of application? Does the attention paid to the investigation's results vary depending on who happens to be handling the recruitment? Is one recruiter or forms clerk "easier," whereas another is seen as more of a stickler?

2. What is an example where a perfunctory escort may inadvertently give an out-sider a chance to penetrate defenses in a way that may mistake the consequence for the work of a hostile insider?

   One common example is token attention paid to outside custodial staff by a guard, secretary, or other escort who is trying to do too many things at once (such as carrying on telephone conversations, doing other work, or allowing oneself to be distracted while "watching" the janitor or maintenance crew). This inatten-tion allows the outsider to steal or copy confidential documents left exposed, to plant clandestine monitoring devices, or to even steal money from purses or wal-lets while the victim is attending a board meeting or otherwise engaged.

3. How would you distinguish between a good background investigation and one that is inadequate?

   First, look at the report of investigation and see if it is intelligible to the per-son or persons assigned to receive and act on the information contained therein. Next, look to see if adverse information is accurate and capable of being veri-fied. Consider also not just the investigation itself but the entire process in place, especially including the protocol for adjudicating adverse information in the best interests of the institution.

4. How would you distinguish a good provider of pre-employment background investigations?

   The best way is to conduct a competitive bid that includes a thorough check of references from prior similar engagements, a comprehensive litigation search to uncover performance shortfalls that have disadvantaged other employers using the given provider, and either pilot programs or running of some test cases to compare results for accuracy, timeliness, and completeness.

EXERCISES FOR GROUP PROJECTS

1. Compare and contrast background investigations from two very different environments. What are your two examples? What kinds of probes are unique to one organization that would not work for the other? Are depth and expense for one unsupportable for another? Why or why not? Can you craft a hybrid approach that would deliver a single background investigation that would serve the vast majority of the needs of both environments?

   Examples could be an intelligence agency and a private bank. The intelligence agency could include invasive probes, including lifestyle polygraphs and scenario/stress testing as a condition of employment. The bank, on the other hand, may only focus on indicators of financial irresponsibility—and may not even spend too much time or energy on that if the job in question involves cash handling where there are numerous checks and balances in addition to close supervision and daily audits. A highly competed position for the clandestine service of an intelligence agency is worth a lengthy and expensive vetting process because the cost of a mistake is high—penetration by an opposing service. But a bank teller position may be interchangeable and easy to replace with costs that can be managed to a minimal, acceptable level of loss through tight controls. Thus, the first may rely heavily on the background check, whereas the other treats it as a formality. If the relative value of the vetting process is this far apart, it is unlikely that a hybrid could be designed to serve both employers equally. However, a preliminary screening investigation for the intelligence agency to eliminate egregious applicants might be made to serve the bank as the sole background investigation for low-level employees.

2. Assume that you can design a work environment where no pre-employment background investigation is necessary. What would that environment be like? How would it operate in a way that compensates for the absence of vetting? What are some possible real-world applications where you could test such a design?

   Capitalizing on the foregoing bank example, some environments where pay is low and turnover high may get by with other screening tools and close probation in lieu of a thorough vetting process. In retail fast food restaurants, for example, many new hire–related problems are sidestepped through mandatory drug screening, since abusers tend to above average tardiness and absenteeism, making them undesirable employees. Moreover, in chains such as McDonald's, where the franchise owner is expected to spend a great deal of time in the store, careful attention to the cash register can be made to offset the usual problems associated with dishonest employees taking money or giving away food to cronies. Additionally, some of these retail environments include surveillance cameras where the employees may be uncertain about the level of off-site monitoring that takes place. Some private companies are intentionally guarded in revealing the full extent of their internal monitoring capabilities, at least partly to deter hostile action on the part of insiders who fear discovery or apprehension. Others possess extra capabilities that they use selectively and even make accessible to law enforcement under certain circumstances, such as Target Corporation's video forensics capacity. Try designing a business model that relies on a strong pre-employment background investigation program and then see if you can replace it with alternatives.

CHAPTER 6

QUESTIONS FOR ONLINE OR CLASSROOM DISCUSSION

1. Thinking like an adversary, where might you be most likely to give yourself away in an institution you were targeting?

   One area is any situation that deviates from formal ones for which you have rehearsed. If you are an infiltrator, you will have practiced responses for all possible questions in the job interview. But social situations are by their nature unscripted and require improvisation that may be challenging and where a slip is easy to make. Similarly, for a disgruntled insider, you may be ready for a formal disciplinary interview or investigation, but coworker banter or elicitation may coax unscripted reactions from you that give away your true intentions instead of the ones you wish to project. So, the social situation is one area where you may give yourself away. Another is an accident or unanticipated event that is neither at home or at work. Most of the mental rehearsals or scripting focus on deceptions where we spend most of our time. Consequently, little preparation goes into thinking through reaction to the rare or unexpected event. Thus, your hostilities or true character may come through to a complete stranger in a minor traffic accident. A third possibility is, after long involvement in a task or physical activity that produces fatigue and then unexpectedly thrusts you into a situation where exhaustion or illness leads you to lower your guard and make disclosures inconsistent with your cover story for what you are doing or where you are.

2. What are some outside resources you could tap to test the veracity of someone you suspect of being a trust betrayer?

   These will vary by organization and budget, but there are times when you can offer people the chance to clear themselves by taking a polygraph, or at least be prepared with an answer if they offer that option themselves. There are also specialists who will work as outsourced interviewers or who will analyze the content of statements and documentation to help you narrow down to manageable levels the number of people most likely to be behind a deception and the misdeed it is concealing. Although it is always useful to have a multidisciplinary team to assess threats and to use them enough so that they work well together, these teams also benefit from having access to specialty consultants who may possess expertise that only needs to be tapped occasionally, such as psychologists, handwriting analysts, or even forensic specialists who can enhance surveillance video to the point of being able to verify that the person who claimed to be somewhere was actually entering another of your facilities at the time in question.

3. What are some of the benefits you can derive from an open statement?

   First, you capture someone's own story without contamination by the interviewer, who is otherwise likely to interrupt within the first 8 seconds. Second, once started, the statement writes itself. This means you can ask people to write their statements on their own and turn them in later, so that they are not subject to contamination by comparing their stories while in the same room. Third, with techniques like scan, the structure of the narrative in the statement could help you quickly spot which statements are likely to be deceptive.

4. What makes the Wicklander–Zulawski (WZ) method potentially more conducive to a modern workplace than the Reid technique?

WZ does not use Reid's confrontational accusation approach, which many
unions, corporate employee relations representatives, labor attorneys, and even
managers would find draconian and inappropriate to use in their workplace.
WZ does present what sounds like a more socially acceptable rationale for having deceived the employer, but what counts most in the end is the admission of
deception and confession, not the reason given for the misconduct.

EXERCISES FOR GROUP PROJECTS

1. Pick an organization with a good mix of corporate sentinels, managers, and
access to outside resources. Now, to whom (by function) would you assign these
roles: interrogation, debriefing, interview, and elicitation? Explain why the people you have in mind would be better suited to one role than another because of
the function they currently perform. Are there people who could perform well in
more than one of those roles? Who and why?

Interrogation, if in the sense described in this chapter, may best be left to law
enforcement or authorities called in who have the capacity to arrest and confine a
deceiver guilty of a serious offense. Debriefing is something that may be handled
very well by a senior manager who possesses the right aptitude and can direct a
subordinate manager or staff member to go into a situation and come back with
particular information. A security representative may also be good at debriefing,
particularly if this person is a trained investigator. More likely, though, the latter
will be best suited to interviewing and the organization will already expect this
from that function. If there is no security or investigative arm, human resources
may have interviewers who are used to dealing with applicants but may or may
not be comfortable in other interview settings. A labor attorney who is also a
litigator may be an excellent interviewer. Supervisors and coworkers are in the
best position to elicit information because they have a reason for sustaining close
contact with the subject, whereas the sudden appearance of a corporate sentinel
or senior manager would put the subject on his or her guard, making elicitation
difficult.

2. What might be some good places to use for attempting to obtain information
from a subject you suspect of being deceptive?

If the setting is formal, as for an interview, it is usually a neutral location or
other private space under the interviewer's control. One popular theory is that
the location should be spartan in order to avoid giving the subject any distractions and to equally avoid polluting his answers with anything he sees in front
of him. However, if the setting is less formal and elicitation comes into play, it
may be more useful to choose a relaxing venue with a view but not too many
distractions. Some have found that walking alongside a subject through an arbor
or quiet setting encourages more free-flowing conversation and subsequent revelations than sitting across a desk on hard metal chairs.

3. What kind of documents could expose a hostile insider by indicating deception?

Double sets of identification in different names could expose an infiltrator.
Possessing diagrams or plans that the insider does not work with and has no
business reason to have in one's office could expose either an infiltrator or disgruntled employee planning an attack. Personal e-mail or blog postings stating

hostile intentions that run completely counter to what the insider is professing on the job could also be revealing. Evidence of involvement with a violent or extremist group or of undue interest in the exploits of such groups through collections of their guides and manifestos could also signal hostile intent that has otherwise been masked.

CHAPTER 7

QUESTIONS FOR ONLINE OR CLASSROOM DISCUSSION

1. Thinking like a sophisticated adversary who has caught wind of a possible investigation or sting involving authorities and closing in on the trust betrayer, how might you exploit the bias or biases of the authorities to your advantage?

    The approach most likely to benefit the trust betrayer in this position is to feign a change of heart and give the appearance of allowing oneself to be recruited as a double agent. Authorities with a prosecutorial or investigative bias will hesitate to miss an opportunity to improve their case for prosecution by having the insider now working for authorities to gather more evidence and expose confederates for a bigger case—even if the hostile insider is working alone. Additionally, the trust betrayer can use this offer of cooperation to bargain for leniency, a reduced sentence, or even immunity from prosecution, depending on the circumstances. Similarly, if facing an investigative bias, the offer to change sides presents authorities with investigative options they lacked going into the case, offering the potential of a case with improved yield and increased chance of successful conclusion. At the same time, playing to an intelligence bias supplies handlers with a nearly irresistible option to enlarge their involvement and expected yield, along with the career advancement attending such professional successes.

2. What is an example of a creative approach you can take to disrupt a hostile insider's attack without revealing your true agenda or exposing your work team to danger?

    One example from the arena of workplace violence has been used with great success. An obstreperous shareholder was looking to upset an upcoming board meeting and to embarrass the chief executive to the point of undermining the latter's ability to gain the votes necessary for a significant change in corporate direction. A fellow shareholder who got wind of this scheme alerted the executive who, in turn, sought the assistance of a specialty consultant. The consultant weighed the expense of maintaining close surveillance on the angry shareholder and of surrounding the chief executive with a protective detail. Not only were these options costly, but they themselves represented disruptions inconsistent with the open culture the executive had promoted throughout his professional career. Ultimately, the consultant collaborated with an associate who ran a travel agency to deliver a more low-key solution. Under the pretext of making a random call as part of a radio show contest, the consultant had an agent reach out to the irate shareholder and congratulate him on winning a prize: an all-expense-paid trip to a tourist attraction in the city adjoining the board meeting. Moreover, the "prize" included accommodations, meals, spending money, and the services of an on-call limousine. Also included were tickets to expensive evening dinner shows and first-class tours. The threatening shareholder was so taken with this apparent windfall, that he missed the shareholder's meeting. His on-call limousine driver was, in reality, a surveillance operative whose burden was eased because the angry shareholder was voluntarily communicating his precise whereabouts at all times in order to ensure that his chauffeur would be available. At the conclusion of the operation, the consultant acting as a staffer for the "contest" offered an additional bonus to the shareholder. He indicated that, as a prize winner, the shareholder now qualified for discount travel arrangements when next he planned to visit the same location. In fact, all that he would have to do would be to call the travel agency with a special code and the consultant would see that the travel agency would match or beat the best offer the angry shareholder could find—all the while embedding surveillance and disruptions to divert the shareholder from planned mischief.

3. What are some of the perils of asking team members to take the lead in using their wiles to disrupt the activities of a suspected insider threat?

   The principal challenge is to avoid having team members cross the line from lawful disruption to unlawful discrimination or harassment. Still, in extreme cases, if the risk is sufficiently high, top management may prefer to defend a civil lawsuit alleging discrimination to attempting to reconstitute operations after a catastrophic loss that could have been prevented. Other perils include the likelihood that at least some coworkers will lack subtlety in masking their intentions, thereby giving themselves away, whereas others may be so taken with the affront of trust betrayal as to be incapable of controlling their emotions to the point of keeping them in harness long enough to effect the disruption without triggering a premature attack or other negative reaction on the part of the hostile insider. By contrast, corporate sentinels and managers in the work team's chain of command may be sufficiently close to the problem to understand the situation yet also removed from the daily fray just enough to be able to retain more objectivity and discretion in parrying the insider's moves with lawful disruptions.

4. How can lawful disruption be useful in dealing with a volatile situation where tempers give signs of escalating into violence?

   This is where thought interruption comes into play. If one can change the subject long enough to get the volatile person or persons to redirect their thoughts and actions away from threatening words and behavior, the resulting change supplies a potential opportunity for de-escalation.

EXERCISES FOR GROUP PROJECTS

1. Identify a case where the presence of a hostile trust betrayer would leave your organization no choice but to bring in authorities to assist with the response. How do you meet your legal obligations while also defending the organization's equities, as the authorities present specialists that they propose to put in charge of managing a sting operation designed to catch the trust betrayer in the act of sabotage?

   The more serious the case, the more reputational risk it will pose and the more likely it will be to place top manager careers in jeopardy if mishandled. For this reason, it is important to assure that appropriate levels of informed, capable leadership from both the institution at risk and the authorities becoming involved meet to set forth objectives and rules of engagement. Involving the institution's legal counsel will assist with establishing the exact purview of the authorities engaged, but it then falls to management to guard against excesses on the part of either the institution's employees or the assigned staff representing the authorities. Regular management reviews and an agreed-upon timeline and clear threshold for the degree of exposure that the employer can sustain should also limit undue exposure of the organization to unintended consequences that harm the employer more than the authorities.

2. Under what circumstances might it be wiser for the institution to go it alone in disrupting an insider threat rather than involve authorities in a response? Offer a scenario to make the point.

If there is no legal requirement to involve authorities or if the authorities showing interest in the matter are known to be inept, corrupt, or so overmatched as to be capable of offering only impediments that increase exposure, it may be wiser to isolate the problem using only internal resources, retained consultants, or both. For example, a chief executive abducted in a foreign country and held for ransom in a country where ransom payments are illegal and authorities have been found in collusion with kidnappers or rival camps may be recovered through discreet negotiations and a ransom payment made in a neutral third country. Bringing authorities into the circle of trust with these arrangements, however, could needlessly risk the life of the abducted executive if the details reach a rival of the organization responsible for the kidnapping. Thus, in environments where one does not know whom to trust, circumspection and limited sharing are wisest.

3. At what point might it ever become acceptable to move from lawful disruption to disruption at any cost? Is this ever advisable? Debate the pros and cons.

In the case of an existential threat where, but for active intervention on the part of a defender, lives will clearly be taken or catastrophic forces unleashed, it may well become a matter of conscience whether to withdraw and wait for police or to take matters into one's own hands. Even if later exposed to censure or legal action, the defender who takes reasonable action to defend others under such conditions will normally make valid claim to extenuating and even exculpatory circumstances when judged by peers.

CHAPTER 8

QUESTIONS FOR ONLINE OR CLASSROOM DISCUSSION

1. When would a career employee who has turned criminal or mercenary be less of an existential insider threat than an infiltrator backed by a state-sponsored terrorist organization?

The infiltrator has the support and training of an organization with resources and focus. The organization selected the infiltrator, trained him, groomed him for the task of sabotage, and provides ongoing guidance and motivation, including whatever tangible and intangible rewards spur the infiltrator to necessary sacrifice. The organization also provides structure and discipline that are more likely to preclude casual mistakes on the part of the infiltrator that would give him away to alert defenders. Moreover, the state-sponsored organization has greater access to resources, including diplomatic pouches to use for smuggling weapons and currency into the country without fear of discovery. Finally, the state-sponsored antagonist need not worry about making the attack too extreme or destructive for fear of alienating local supporters on whom he relies for funding or other resources. By contrast, the careerist turned antagonist acts alone or with the weaker backing of a mercurial organization that supports her only so long as a payoff is in sight. The careerist has likely alienated fellow employees on the path to becoming untrustworthy. She lacks the discipline of a mature and focused organization directing her moves and thus is more likely to operate by trial and error. She is also more likely to be opinionated and unreceptive to advice on eluding discovery, even when good advice is proffered. Although possessed of some knowledge and access that may exceed that of an infiltrator, this careerist may lack the breadth and wherewithal that a professional organization of adversaries has at its disposal, such as the ability to design and place explosive charges or electronic eavesdropping devices where they can advance the attack. Surprised by alert defenders, the careerist is unlikely to be able to call on agents of her organization to suppress damning evidence, whereas the infiltrator's terrorist support cell has the will and capacity to stage accidents, assassinations, and decoying maneuvers to cover the infiltrator's tracks. Finally, the careerist has left a personal audit trail of residences, work history, medical records, and details of next of kin and other affiliations that leave a footprint for defenders to track and explore, making it very difficult for the careerist to conceal all telltale aspects of her trust betrayal once suspicion is aroused. On the other hand, the infiltrator possesses none of these encumbrances and has the backing to support creating a legend or cover story that will be difficult to refute and impossible to use against the infiltrator in any substantive probe.

2. Why is prevention of an existential attack more important to the institution than apprehension of the attacker, particularly if it is possible to catch the hostile insider in the act?

   Prevention accords primacy to safeguarding the institution's critical assets, including people. Apprehension may serve a greater societal good, but it nevertheless places these assets at some risk. Catching a malefactor in the act may appeal to prosecutors and police, but the desperate infiltrator may yet carry out some damage in a last-ditch effort to destroy an assigned target.

3. In the case described in "How One Event's Cascading Impact Ended a Line of Business," what differences in outcome might have arisen for Nokia and Ericsson if Phillips' plant in Albuquerque had been damaged by insider-triggered arson instead of a storm?

   In many ways Nokia would have still faced less existential risk than Ericsson, because Nokia had alternative suppliers and was better prepared for a supply chain interruption—regardless of the cause. However, a carefully organized arson attack could easily have incapacitated Phillips' plant more pervasively, making it impossible for Nokia to rely on that particular plant as an eventual source of chips for its cellular phones once the plant was back online and operating on extra shifts. Ericsson, on the other hand, would have experienced a shorter delay before realizing how dire the situation was for its cellular line of business. A more destructive arson attack could have conceivably propelled Ericsson to make an earlier entry into partnering relationships or cutting its losses by exiting the market if it could not find alternative suppliers.

4. What makes it wiser to begin security planning by asking what is critical instead of what is the threat?

Not all assets are the same, nor do they require comparable protection. Assets that are replaceable will not be so attractive to adversaries as will be assets whose damage can have cascading effects on the targeted institution. Additionally, no organization has unlimited protective resources. Thus, it is necessary to prioritize, and one manages this by first identifying what is critical and only afterwards turning to considerations of threat.

EXERCISES FOR GROUP PROJECTS

1. Identify a case not mentioned in this chapter where red teaming offered defensive value and, at the same time, possible embarrassment to the larger organization. Comment on what factors may undermine the red teaming effort or improve its traction within the organization.

   One series of examples comes from the exploits of Navy commander Richard Marcinko, the first commanding officer of the U.S. Navy's SEAL Team Six and subsequently the Naval Security Coordination Team OP-06D. The latter, better known informally as Red Cell, was at one point regarded as a premier identifier of vulnerabilities in security. Marcinko's exploits in Red Cell included breaching security of nuclear security installations and infiltrating sites otherwise considered impenetrable, including Air Force One. Marcinko ultimately ran afoul of his service and served time for fraud charges, which he claimed were retaliation for his infiltrations that embarrassed ranking military brass. One possibility is that Marcinko's aggressiveness in promoting his red team successes ended in elevating the red team over the organizations it existed to support, thereby losing their confidence in the process and setting up an adversarial relationship that no red team could win in the long run. Whether Marcinko overstepped his charter or simply triggered organizational antibodies as a result of his successes, the results were the same: a loss for both sides.

2. Under what circumstances could red teaming or other No Dark Corners approaches avail in a case such as the Barings collapse?

   It would be difficult to conceive of a situation where any approach would be able to compensate for a total failure in due diligence, as in the Barings debacle, since the institution was oblivious to the existential threat that Leeson had become with his high-risk trades that he was able to conceal from lack of oversight. If not left to his own devices, but instead brought into a transparent, team-centric environment, Leeson may have given himself away or at least benefitted from professional interactions that would have revealed to him that he was going over his head with his futures trading. Thus, some of the damage could arguably have been discovered sooner or contained before driving Barings to ruin. On balance, though, the absence of the most basic due diligence on the part of Barings pointed to systemic organizational weaknesses that would limit the effectiveness of the best red team or any other eleventh-hour threat defenses.

3. Why have decapitation attacks such as the two described here repeatedly failed, whereas other existential attacks with lesser objectives and fewer plotters succeeded?

   The reasons for this invite research and speculation. One possibility is that decapitation attacks such as those described have more moving parts and points of failure than an attack focused at an institution as a single target. With those

Managing the Insider Threat

points of failure come opportunities for mistakes, revelation, and even penetration by defenders. On the other hand, a single targeted institution can function as a closed system and, particularly if it is poorly defended, expose itself more openly to insider mischief than assassination targets whose movements and whereabouts are in a position to be better marked and secured.

4. Characterize the ideal red team and its opposite. Specifically, what attributes would virtually assure that a red team fails to add value in defending against an existential insider threat?

First, paying insufficient attention to the team's composition will greatly increase its chance of failure. Overstaffing it with people with a vested interest in defending the status quo but with little insight into how an adversary thinks or would strike would sharply limit its utility. So would convening red teams too frequently, as this would dispose managers to send not their best minds but their most expendable ones to the red team. Turning the team into a perfunctory organ of bureaucracy by ignoring its findings and disincentivizing participants from unearthing vulnerabilities would also guarantee that the effort would lose credibility and transform itself into a burden to be avoided rather than an opportunity to contribute to the institution's survival.

CHAPTER 9

QUESTIONS FOR ONLINE OR CLASSROOM DISCUSSION

1. What would make a denial-of-service attack by external hackers or by a foreign government a possible insider threat?

Unless an insider was actively engaged in enabling the attack from within the targeted institution, it would be difficult to justify categorizing this as an insider threat. However, if the ones carrying out the attack managed to elicit information from an unwitting sympathizer or if they planted misleading evidence in an attempt to implicate the institution's information technology professionals, the attack could take on the appearance of being an insider threat. Also, if the institution's best defenses were concentrated in a task force developed for dealing with insider threats and top management determined that these were the best people to combat the denial-of-service cyber attack, the technicalities involving whether it was or was not an insider threat would be moot for the defenders tasked with solving the problem.

2. If threats of workplace violence and violent attacks themselves may be tragic for victims but are seldom existential threats to the institution, under what circumstances might this change?

A threat of violence aimed at top management that succeeds in eliminating the leadership of the institution and also, say, the chief talent or source of innovation responsible for the institution's success or viability could spell ruin for the entire organization. Also, if the threat is carried out in such a way as to gain disproportionately significant media coverage that contributes to eroding stakeholder or investor confidence in the institution, the cascading impact of events triggered by a violent act could magnify reputational risk to the point of rendering the institution no longer viable in its current form. The impact of the Bhopal tragedy on Union Carbide—although not a case of violence—illustrates how avoidable fatalities can produce not only human tragedy but also lead to the demise of an institution.

3. Of the various categories of nonexistential insider threat covered by the threat scale, why might embezzling be less frequently detected at the 0 or 1 level than at the higher levels?

Embezzlers have higher aims, sophistication, and subject matter expertise than many other insiders—certainly more than those whose primary motivation is revenge. Embezzlers, in seeking to realize gain at the institution's expense, are more likely to plan more carefully and evaluate their options in order to maximize their returns. This means that they will be disinclined to risk capture or incarceration for petty rewards at the 0 or 1 level when they can face the same risks for much higher returns available at the higher levels on the threat scale.

4. How might an old-style martinet accustomed to micromanaging employees in a manufacturing environment end up causing knowledge worker consultants in information age workplace to either turn into insider threats or to become indifferent to the presence or activities of trust betrayers?

The old-style, dictatorial manager might have difficulty understanding that knowledge workers are best managed by being treated as professional peers rather than as order-takers. Not only will badly treated consultants lose any affinity they have for this manager and the organization, they will likely avoid any continuing contact or further work for them, thus having no incentive to care about the well-being of either manager or client organization. Additionally, the manager who does not recognize the difference between a knowledge worker and a worker on an assembly line will probably stray into the arena of co-employment, causing increases in labor disputes or liabilities for the institution. If the knowledge worker consultants are accustomed to being treated respectfully by their other clients and find this manager dismissive and insulting, they may even be induced to do inferior work or to stage a debacle after the consulting assignment is over, so as to embarrass the martinet or discredit him or her in the eyes of upper management. At worst, a knowledge worker feeling badly used by the micromanaging client may, in the heat of the moment or even in cold calculation, decide to exact revenge not only on the abusive manager but on the institution that spawned or enabled this individual to advance to a position of influence.

EXERCISES FOR GROUP PROJECTS

1. Using the threat scale, develop scenarios for categorizing cyber threats in a way similar to what was done above in the illustration for a case of threats of violence.

One cyber scenario could involve a denial-of-service attack while it is unfolding, where it remains unclear whether there is insider collusion enabling the attack to occur. Questions to help guide the response in the midst of the attending confusion and excitement could include:

- Is this a one-time event that we can put to rest rapidly and prevent from recurring, or is this something that is occurring with some frequency or escalation?
- Is the backup system in our business continuity plan available to be activated in a way that will give us an uninterrupted communications capability that can reduce the impact of this attack from unacceptable to more or less the nuisance level?

- Is this a problem that is containable without having to go to the point of having our attorneys look at it as a criminal or civil matter? If so, then it would appear to fit more appropriately into the 0 to 1 level.
- Does this problem rise to the level of requesting special contingency funds and outside resources to solve because it has overwhelmed us and looks as though it is getting worse? If so, this may be at the 3 level already.

2. Using the threat scale, develop scenarios for categorizing exploitation for gain in a way similar to what was done above in the illustration for a case of threats of violence.

   A good example here would be to use the threat scale to categorize the relative seriousness of the case of the credit union manager who was caught embezzling but was initially to be dismissed for an episodic misdeed before an adept investigator determined the problem was chronic and much more extensive—as described in Chapter 7 under Scenario 3: Disruption Taking an Unexpected Turn.

3. Are there any ethical concerns to using a No Dark Corners approach in, say, an environment where an oppressed people stage protests using the techniques of the flash mob in order to promote an uprising that is the only way for their voices to be heard by an autocratic and tyrannical regime? Are there practical impediments, regardless of any ethical concerns? Discuss.

   There are indeed ethical concerns—the same as for using any technique to ends opposite the ones it was designed to serve. There are practical impediments, chief of which is the incompatibility of the No Dark Corners strategy of copilot engagement at the team level with an autocratic environment where all decisions and power remain at the top. Without diffusion and a mutual stake in the health and survival of the organization, people on the front lines have no reason to extend themselves on the organization's behalf. Thus, in the environment described, employees on the front lines who would otherwise be supplying early warning intelligence would have no reason to do so. Indeed, an autocratic regime would likely discourage such intelligence, particularly if it communicated a picture inconsistent with the views or desires of the tyrant in power. Moreover, in such an environment, any display of initiative from the front lines would be more likely to raise eyebrows and invite derision or punishment, hence continuing incompatibility of some of the No Dark Corners basics with an environment fundamentally alien to collaboration.

4. Under what circumstances might the introduction of too many or too cumbersome security measures open the door to insider compromises?

   One of the best examples is what happens in a workplace when cyber sentinels insist on excessive frequency of password changes to decrease the chance of external cyber intrusion success through password compromise. As noted in Chapter 2 (endnote 12: C. Herley, "So Long, and No Thanks for the Externalities: The Rational Rejection of Security Advice by Users," *Proceedings of the New Security Paradigms Workshop*, Oxford, United Kingdom, September 8–11, 2009, pp. 1–12), there are times when well-intentioned rules create more problems than they solve. In this case, if the chief concerns are having someone from the outside come into possession of a password and also of having that password made difficult enough to defeat guessing and common password-generating programs, it may actually make more sense to require one password a year than several different passwords every 60–90 days. Why? An individual who can use a single password for a year on multiple accounts can be prevailed upon to make it difficult and to commit the password to memory—and nowhere else. The same person forced to do this multiple times in a year may feel no alternative but to write the password down because (a) the frequency of changing makes it difficult to retain in memory and (b) the requirement to use different passwords for different applications also makes an inordinate demand on memory. Add to this the common prohibition against recycling a previously used password, and the user now faces undue burdens and a practical requirement to record elsewhere a password that would otherwise be committed only to memory and thus be less susceptible to compromise—a lose–lose consequence of too much attention to the wrong kind of protection.

CHAPTER 10

QUESTIONS FOR ONLINE OR CLASSROOM DISCUSSION

1. What kind of organization is more likely to be able to handle a No Dark Corners implementation exclusively with internal resources: a large institution or a small one?

   A small one, particularly if it is already so small that copilot engagement is already vital to the way the organization does business. One finds such dynamics in family-operated businesses struggling to stay viable and in startup firms operating out of garages where everybody does every job or helps out where needed most. As the organizations become bigger, specialization sets in, as do silos and hierarchies, and bureaucratic obstacles to the collaboration of old—something No Dark Corners may help to resuscitate.

2. Why is a sudden impact response likely to require outside resources and also be very expensive?

   First, it requires outside resources because few institutions can afford to retain a standing army of specialists whose specialization they may never call upon in an entire career. Second, in order to deliver maximum value, the specialists must be experienced at the journeyman level or beyond, which means their services will not be available at discounted rates. Additionally, since a sudden impact response carries with it a sense of urgency, outside specialists used to this kind of response will be necessary, and they or their employers will charge a premium for expedited response—particularly if it is necessary to divert the specialists from other work that has already been contracted for so that they may instead be sent where more urgently needed.

3. In which kind of insider threat situation is it most likely that the lion's share of the institution's needs will be answerable through the delivery of a comprehensive report? Why?

   The postmortem redesign is this kind of situation because its key focus is typically the appeasement of a critical body demanding independent review and recommendations. This is also the kind of engagement where there may be emphasis on the report to the exclusion of attention on what is done to follow up on the report's suggestions, particularly if the only true objective is to satisfy critics with an independent review.

4. What advantages do pilot programs offer when attempting to institute changes along the lines of a No Dark Corners transformation?

Pilot programs provide hesitant members of the organization with a safe way to monitor implementation without having to gamble on success before seeing some positive results for themselves, thus increasing the chance of turning them into advocates for the program in the future. Pilot programs also offer program leaders an opportunity to bypass the most recalcitrant internal opponents by instead investing their energy in productive areas where they are welcome by willing collaborators instead of silent or vocal opponents.

EXERCISES FOR GROUP PROJECTS

1. Assume you were a department head of a corporate sentinel function whose budget or headcount might be adversely affected by a successful No Dark Corners implementation. What are some of the ways you could undermine the implementation without getting into trouble with its executive sponsor?
   - You could offer your own loyalists to serve as staff to help with the implementation, and have them clandestinely reporting to you, giving you advance notice of any missteps that you can then trumpet to executive management as worrisome failures.
   - You could use stall tactics to delay milestones and activities until obtaining enough verifiable indications that the program is going to extend beyond cost and budget, thereby giving you a business objection to raise when all programs are being reviewed.
   - You could engage upon a campaign of pestering disputation whereby you and your subordinates question every single recommendation or action, calling for additional meetings and clarification until you so burden the overall effort that all the busy champions start avoiding it because you have transformed their contributions into lost productive time.
2. Let us assume that you were an intermediary, say a staff manager on rotation to serve as special assistant to the executive sponsor of a No Dark Corners consulting engagement. How might you unintentionally impede the undertaking?
   - You might begin by trying to fit the engagement into your comfort zone, such as the construction contracts you were used to handling, thus insisting on statements of work, detailed schedules, inspectors, and a number of features that are incongruous for this particular effort.
   - You might show a tendency to deny the consultant access or reach into any institutional functions where you have no authority and are unable to open doors just by using your sponsoring executive's name, particularly with corporate sentinels, and especially if you are intimidated by previous experiences with their functions and functionaries.
   - You would most likely convey your personal sense of priorities rather than your executive's. Thus, what might be a big deal to you in your narrower area of authority may be inconsequential to your executive, yet you tell the consultant otherwise, as in resisting a change to how the probation system works for new hires because a senior labor attorney appears too formidable for you to want to challenge personally.
3. Using the "Checklist for Gauging Current Insider Defenses," rate two different organizations. Now, looking at the similarity between some of their ratings and

disparity between others, how do you account for the variation? Which of the two strikes you as more vulnerable to hostile insider action? Why?

This is where the results and attending discussion should speak for themselves.

4. Assume that the executive sponsor within your organization has a bond of mutual trust with a consultant who has an impressive reputation for integrity. What might still make this the wrong consultant for a No Dark Corners engagement, and what would be some key signs of this inappropriate fit?

Sometimes, trust alone is insufficient. The sponsoring executive may have a deep bond of trust with a retired mentor who consults from time to time and serves as an excellent sounding board on matters involving the core business. However, the mentor may be entirely innocent of insider threats, trust betrayal, and what it takes to change defenses that are no longer yielding the benefits that they were once assumed to provide. If the mentor does indeed possess advertised integrity, then he or she is likely to decline the No Dark Corners engagement on the grounds of it being beyond personal competence—a sure sign of a poor fit.

ENDNOTE

1. J. Badaracco, *Leading Quietly*, Boston: Harvard Business School Press, 2002, p. 3.

Appendix A: Three Rounds of Delphi Questions

The following materials were sent to Delphi respondents over the course of two months to solicit their thoughts as part of the insider threat study. An interval of at least two weeks separated each of the three rounds of Delphi questions.

A. DELPHI ROUND 1 QUESTIONS

1. What is an insider threat in your view? Are there different kinds of insider threat? Please elaborate.
2. What do you see or have you seen that is observable in insider tactics?

If it helps to think of specific cases, without revealing any confidential or sensitive details, please comment on these questions in relation to a significant case you have experienced:

3. What did the trust betrayer do and for what motives?
4. What caused the trust betrayer to be exposed?
5. What signs pointed the way to the exposure?

Any other comments or insights you would like to add.

B. DELPHI ROUND 2 QUESTIONS

Thank you for participating in this study, once again. This time, let me incorporate input that came out of the first round into the current round of questions. We begin with some common denominator observations for all of you to rate on a scale of 1–5, follow with six questions that encourage you to comment, and end with some scenario questions for your reaction.

Part I: Ratings

Please rate these questions according to whether you agree or disagree, so that I can tell whether I have captured ideas correctly from your previous input.

Observation/Statement	Your Rating (1–5)	Remarks (Optional)
A. Insider threats are people who possess legitimate access and occupy a position of trust in or with the organization that they are targeting.		
B. The hostile insider most dangerous to an organization is likely to display "beat the system" talk or behaviors.		
C. He or she is likely to be secretive.		
D. He or she is likely to demonstrate an excessively proprietary interest in the job, including working unpaid for long hours.		
E. He or she is likely to hoard or withhold information from others.		
F. He or she is likely to show signs of elitism, arrogance, or acting superior to others.		
G. He or she may display unexplained changes in personality, mood, or conduct.		
H. He or she may appear resentful, disgruntled, or antisocial.		
I. He or she is often the picture of the perfect employee.		
J. He or she gives the impression of wanting to get even.		
K. He or she is constantly seeking power.		
L. He or she uses words like "unfair" and "hostile workplace," particularly if a malicious whistle-blower.		
M. He or she exhibits a decline in job performance.		

Rating Scale: 1 = strongly disagree, 2 = disagree, 3 = neutral or no strong position, 4 = agree, 5 = strongly agree. Feel free to add comments, particularly if I have missed something.

Part II: Questions for Your Reaction and Comment

1. Some pattern analysis software (www.tagcrowd.com) identified **unexplained anger** as a common indicator that often surfaced in your collective descriptions of insider threats. Did I capture this correctly? In other words, does this make sense to you? Please comment.
2. Similarly, random audits or investigations based on reported suspicions, or even just as a matter of due diligence, appeared to emerge as a consistently mentioned countermeasure for stopping an insider threat before it is too late. Do you agree? Does this make sense to you? Please comment.

3. One of you pointed out that the more dangerous threats are either people who are suffering personal distress and seeking relief (like those responsible for workplace violence), or those who are more goal-oriented and seeking victory (like saboteurs). Do you agree? Please comment.

4. Another of you suggested that the most dangerous insiders generally fall into one of three categories: embezzler–thief, saboteur, and shooter. In this model, the embezzler–thief and saboteur are planners, while the shooter is more likely to erupt with "no coherent plan beyond buying large quantities of ammunition before the violent deed." Is it useful to think of insider threats by rating them High, Medium, or Low across these three dimensions? Do you agree? Please comment.

5. Who would you worry more about as a **threat to other people**: the insider who erupts or the insider who plans? Why?

6. Who would you worry more about as a **threat to the institution,** as someone who can take down the entire enterprise or organization: the insider who erupts or the insider who plans? Why?

Part III: Scenarios and Related Questions

Finally, look at two hypothetical insiders, Herman and Edna. They represent composites of your previous inputs and are chosen to represent potentially serious insider threats. You'll see a little information about them, followed by some questions.

Both Herman and Edna work for the same government agency, the state lottery commission of a northeastern state in the United States. This institution is co-located in a complex housing the offices of the governor and leaders of the state legislature, who participate actively in VIP events involving the lottery commission, particularly since it has become a reliable source of revenue to offset state fiscal pressures. You will find the descriptions of these employees incomplete, to leave room for your imagination and to reflect realistic information gaps that investigators and defenders face when initially encountering potential threats to their institutions.

Two Employees of State Lottery Commission

Herman	Edna
– 18-year employee of State Lottery Commission	– 18-year employee of State Lottery Commission
– Competent in his area but passed over for promotions for last 7 years	– Average worker but attendance and performance in decline during past 6 months
– Works uncompensated long hours and weekends	– Overheard complaining about being sued by former partner for unpaid child support
– Very jealous of his turf and prerogatives	
– Hoards information, likes to be sole expert in his area	– Changed work location after ridicule by two coworkers, one a former sexual partner who has since filed 3 grievances and 1 ADA complaint against her
– Bristles when questioned about his area, generally browbeats auditors with jargon and younger, timid supervisors into leaving him alone	
– Gives surface impression of ideal employee, but heard berating upper management in cafeteria and other informal settings	– Repeatedly asked supervisor for overtime opportunities in order to pay for her mother's dialysis treatments

Herman	Edna
– Rumored to have been involved somehow in involuntary transfer of one supervisor and in unexpected resignation of another because of allegations of discrimination that were not conclusively proven	– In last month, reported petty theft and vandalizing of her desk – Found her car "keyed" in employee parking lot before it was repossessed 2 weeks ago – Avoids her supervisor and no longer eats lunch in cafeteria – Is currently in process of having her wages garnished for unpaid child support as result of former domestic partner winning judgment against her in court

1. Which of these employees do you rate as potentially more dangerous to coworkers?
2. Which do you rate as a greater potential danger to the institution?
3. You just received a tip that one or both of these employees may be involved in some unauthorized activity that constitutes a threat to the State Lottery Commission or its staff. Who would you judge to be more likely to be involved in the following, Herman or Edna?

   A. An attack of workplace violence that targets the payroll manager, a supervisor, and two coworkers.

   B. A complex fraud scheme, undetected for years, that redirects a fraction of a penny spent on purchases of multiple lottery tickets. The funds go to an offshore bank account and, depending on the extent of the losses and negative press, the revelation could threaten the survival of the state's lottery system.

   C. Compromise of insider details of a VIP event to a group of extremists operating as a nonprofit corporation that has been suspected of planning to assassinate the governor as a political statement.

   D. Join an activist group through the Internet and, after being befriended by them at after-hours meetings and social events over a period of 18 months, offer to provide information that will allow insider access during an upcoming ribbon-cutting ceremony where the governor and several state government and business executives will be in attendance.

Comments on any or all of the above:

C. DELPHI ROUND 3 QUESTIONS

Thank you for your continued participation. Through your responses and comments, you have provided useful insights on indicators of insider threats, as well as ideas on how to stop them. You will find a one-page summary of highlights from the last round in Attachment 1. Some of you wanted to know how your answers corresponded with others, hence more detailed diagrams summarizing the findings in Attachment 2. Both attachments are purely optional, for perusal at your convenience.

   You have all been very gracious and generous with your replies, so I hope this final round will be less demanding and a little fun. Please respond in two weeks.

We now focus on countermeasures. There is only one rating question, and an opportunity to unleash your imagination in tackling one problem. Now, you are the opposition. Think like a terrorist for the rating question and your attending comments.

Your Task: Attack one of these critical infrastructure targets (your choice): water, electricity, or telecommunications utility. (Dr. Ted Lewis, author of *Critical Infrastructure Protection in Homeland Security* and one of my instructors, rates these as Tier 1 critical infrastructures because of their capacity for influencing cascading failures among the rest.)

Your Method: Infiltrate one of these infrastructure stewards (i.e., a public sector or private sector utility) or recruit an agent from within the utility to inflict maximum damage directly or by supplying invaluable information and access to your attack cell, which will do the dirty work.

Your Timing: 6 months–8 years. This is based on two things. One is the interval between attacks on the World Trade Center. Another is an al Qaeda operative quote by Richard Miniter in *Losing Bin Laden* (Washington, DC: Regnery Publishing, 2003, p. 95) which highlighted the willingness to lie in wait. Early in his training, an al Qaeda operative . . . recalls repeatedly chanting this Koranic verse: "I will be patient until patience is worn out from patience."

Rating Question

Please rate these countermeasures according to which you would consider the most challenging if planning to attack a critical infrastructure target from within. You will see the countermeasures described briefly below, with room for your ratings next to them.

Rating Scale: 1 = no obstacle, 2 = easily overcome, 3 = problem but surmountable with average planning and resources, 4 = significant hurdle but surmountable with considerable effort and resources, 5 = significant hurdle and possibly insurmountable.

Countermeasures

A. **Brother's Keeper** option that encourages coworkers to identify and act on suspicions of hostile or inexplicable insider activities. This could even be similar to acting on reasonable suspicion to report a substance abuse problem at work. RATING (1–5): _____

B. **No Dark Corners** option, or no alone zone, that configures work in a way that aims to reduce chances for a sole individual working in a sensitive area undetected, with either another trusted employee within line of sight or some form of remote surveillance or detection creating the possibility that someone may be watching. Some of you have seen this in the defense or nuclear security industry. RATING (1–5): _____

C. **Random Audits** option, which could be operational, process, financial audits or any combination that would potentially uncover evidence of hostile activity. RATING (1–5): _____

D. **Technology-Based Monitoring** option, which would involve automated controls and alarms that annunciate or terminate access and generate exception reports whenever an employee attempts to gain unauthorized access or exceeds a defined number of authorized queries and transactions in a sensitive area. RATING (1–5): _____

E. **Background Investigations or Updates** option, which involves screening of new hires and possible periodic update investigations of existing employees. RATING (1–5): _____

F. **Sting or Dangle Operations** option, which involves flushing out hostile insiders by pretext and could include luring a hostile insider to join what purports to be a terrorist organization that does not really exist or having a trusted insider exhibit behaviors that give the appearance of being an excellent recruitment target for you to cultivate, not realizing that this is a double agent. RATING (1–5): _____

G. **Other**: your own idea or ideas that do not fit into the options above and would rate at least a 4. RATING (1–5): _____

TASK: Which infrastructure did you select as your target (water, electricity, or telecommunications utility)? Why?

METHOD: Which method did you select (infiltrating with your own operative, or recruiting an agent already there)? Why? If you recruited someone already in place, what is the most you expect this person to do for you? COMMENTS on ratings, countermeasures, or your own thoughts about how you would conduct an attack and what would stop you.

Appendix B: Summary of Delphi Round 1 Findings Accompanying Round 2 Questions

THOUGHTS FROM DELPHI ROUND 1

For those of you able to review this information, here is some preliminary analysis of responses to the first round of questions in the Delphi survey on the insider threat. The next round will focus on telltale signs or indicators (aka traplines). The final round will focus on countermeasures (aka tripwires).

These were some of the more interesting insights that surfaced:

- Conversational spillage/inexplicably hostile behavior, own disclosure.
- "Beat the system" talk, behaviors; rumors and suspicions reported to management and then investigated; greatest loss from insider at highest level.
- Sick fun; frequent rotations, good auditing.
- Getting even a central theme.
- Reduce discoverability; decline in performance; visible antisocial behaviors. "Sudden" anomalies usually have precursors that supervisors don't act on.
- Persons who hate are usually outspoken about it.
- Unexplained changes of personality, mood, or conduct; unexplained money, family life, outside associates. Every advance in technology creates new vulnerabilities.
- Always exploits the organization's weakness. Deterred only by strong chance of discovery and swift punishment. Insider is never observed as a threat, employs secrecy, often the picture of the perfect employee. Whistle-blower.
- Self-aggrandizement. Ideology may play a lesser role in corporate cases but is primary in a terrorist scenario.
- Elitism or anger and aggression; considers others inferior. Expressed hate and anger. Secrecy, self-aggrandizement; growing hostility, unexplained anger.
- Constantly seeking power, dismissive of victim(s).
- For cases of violence, not sneaky but stewing in own myopic juices. Malicious whistle-blower slowly builds up a body of questionable documentation. A shooter acts alone and is looking for relief and can often be guileless. An internal saboteur is looking for victory and builds up to an attack.

In addition to looking for common themes and unique observations, I used a tool called Tag Crowd to make some patterns more visually obvious. This visual analysis of survey data is available at http://www.tagcrowd.com at no cost for individual and educational uses, thanks to Daniel Steinbock, a doctoral student at Stanford University. The output itself is called a text cloud, which is also referred to as a tag cloud. You will see two of these below.

Analysis

The first text cloud compilation and sorting of overall responses, highlights observations and themes common to the insider threat writ large, that is, the insider as an employee, often motivated by financial gain, operating in an organization, and subject to being given away by actions, audits, and behaviors.

The second text cloud, concentrating exclusively on the more telling remarks of respondents, begins to lend greater granularity to the first image. More indicators begin to surface, with the most telling summarized as unexplained anger, the two most prominent words in the text cloud. Other themes emerge as potentially revealing indicators, such as tendencies of self-aggrandizement and secrecy among hostile insiders, which offer possibilities for detection when tied to corresponding traits and behaviors. Interestingly, "whistle-blower" appears in both the more general text cloud and the more sharply focused one. Respondents with backgrounds in the worlds of corporate fraud investigations, intelligence, and clinical assessment of workplace violence threats independently converged on the notion that malicious whistle-blowers are beginning to emerge as nascent saboteurs. It is equally interesting to note that money and financial gain, which are prominent in Figure A.1, are absent from Figure A.2. One respondent indirectly offered the reason for this omission by noting that the most destructive damage is rarely driven purely by a desire for financial gain.

The foregoing use of text clouds fell short of supporting the investigator's preliminary sense of emerging distinctions in attempting to divide insider threats into overly restrictive and artificial categories. Consequently, the preliminary categorization effort postulating the existence of a spectrum of trust betrayers found insufficient traction to survive closer scrutiny. However, thanks to the text cloud analysis and the further, iterative study

FIGURE A.1   Text cloud showing frequency of words in summary of responses.

FIGURE A.2   Text cloud showing frequency of words appearing in subset of more interesting insights.

of responses that this analysis inspired, a dichotomy began to emerge and formulate the basis for Delphi Round 2 inquiries.

Specifically, is there value in broadly categorizing insider threats in terms of whether they plan their attacks? Evidence of planning corresponds to the insight of a behaviorist who noted that the saboteur's objective is seeking victory. By contrast, a dearth of planning that could instead present itself as an eruption corresponds to what the same respondent called the shooter's objective of seeking relief. Pursuing such a dichotomy further also offers value in that it creates nesting areas for the different types of cases already cited by the respondents while offering a simpler, more intuitive way of drawing distinctions and seeking corresponding behavioral signatures that could give away malicious insiders before they carry out their attacks. Thus, this new tentative categorization forms the basis not only for further questions but for formulation of two different kinds of insider threat scenario to now structure respondent thinking along common denominators without preordaining responses.

As Delphi Round 2 begins to sharpen the focus on traplines, that is, on the behavioral signatures and other indicators that will assist defenders in identifying hostile insiders, Table A.1 offers a framework for distinguishing the insider threats who can be fatal to an institution from those whose potential lethality is largely restricted to individuals.

TABLE A.1   Proposed Insider Threat Dichotomy

Those Who Plan	Those Who Erupt
More dangerous to institution	More dangerous to individual(s)
Seek victory	Seek relief
More meticulous, analytical, secretive, subtle, deceptive	Guileless, self-revealing
Target the institution	Target individual or individuals perceived to be causing them distress
Ideologically oriented or entirely mercenary	Victimized or self-described as victimized or wronged
Dismissive of victims, angry at them, acts superior to them	Dismissive of victims, angry at them, acts as if unfairly treated by them
Exploits organization's weaknesses	Exploits organizational weaknesses
Picture of the perfect employee	Declining performance
Self-aggrandizing, self-enriching, in control	Territorial, turf conscious, losing control
Getting even, disgruntled	Getting justice, disgruntled
Saboteur, Sleeper, Traitor	Desperate employee

Appendix C: Summary of Delphi Round 2 Findings Accompanying Round 3 Questions

HIGHLIGHTS OF DELPHI ROUND 2

Part I

	Disagree	Neutral	Agree	Strongly Agree	
A			58%	42%	Definition
B	17%	42%	33%	8%	Beat the system
C	8%	42%	17%	33%	Secretive
D	8%	17%	58%	17%	Owns the job
E		33%	33%	33%	Withholds info
F	8%	25%	25%	42%	Arrogant, elitist
G		25%	33%	42%	Unexplained changes
H		8%	67%	25%	Resentful
I	17%	42%	42%		"Perfect" employee
J	8%	50%	42%		Getting even
K	33%	42%		25%	Seeking power
L		42%	50%	8%	Says "unfair"
M	25%	42%	33%		Work declines

Part II

Most Useful Distinctions: unexplained anger as common indicator, random audits as strong countermeasure, and planner as insider most dangerous to institution.

Part III

Planner is more dangerous, more prone to complex fraud. But planner could also do more physical harm than insider who erupts. Also, planner may not be a joiner, hence not as likely to join a group or react well to handlers.

327

Overall

Some themes where there was strong convergence:

- Indicators of unexplained changes in behavior and in resentful or disgruntled presentation of the hostile insider.
- Secondary indicators of the hostile insider exercising overly proprietary interest in the job, expressing a perception of unfair treatment, and appearing arrogant or elitist.
- Random audit as a good, if not the best, countermeasure.
- The planner as the bigger threat to the institution, with some distinctions offered in remarks to the effect that a workplace violence attack, or rage killing, might constitute a personal tragedy for those victimized but was not an existential threat to the institution.

Other themes which showed early promise in surfacing useful distinctions for further probing ended up being dry holes. These include:

- The insider as one who withholds information. Respondents suggested that this might be true enough but was often difficult if not impossible to gauge until after the fact, hence of limited predictive value.
- Seeking power, being secretive, and exhibiting decline in performance also proved to be nonstarters. Clarifying comments explained that some of these traits were equally visible elsewhere, hence of limited value in trying to uncover hostile insiders. One respondent reasoned that ambitious competitors could easily seek power without becoming insider threats. Similarly, another respondent noted that, in his experience with traitors, once they had embarked upon a plan for stealing secrets to pass to a foreign power, they tended to level off in their outward ambitions and general performance. Evidently, this is to avoid inviting scrutiny while they concentrate their energies on their clandestine endeavors.
- Efforts at categorization, whether as an insider seeking victory versus relief, or as belonging to one of three classes [embezzler–thief, saboteur, or shooter (rage killer/workplace violence perpetrator)] also went nowhere. Parts of these were negated by the very respondents who first suggested them. Evidently, there is just too much variation in views and in real cases to permit ready categorization along these lines.

Appendix D: Delphi Expert Comments and Stories

Delphi respondents included a number of remarks and stories that went beyond their responses to specific questions. Select examples that illustrate or supplement other research findings appear below.

A. TRANSPARENCY: PUSHING OUT MANAGEMENT DATA

When they first started becoming available, and some time afterwards, management reports were pretty restricted. The idea was that it took a lot of work to produce them. They contained inside information that could be embarrassing to some people or could even increase liability if in the wrong hands. The trouble was that the reports only went to top managers, and any good top manager lacked the extra time necessary to break down the reports and study them at length to compare against employee and work unit performance. Sure, spot checks were possible. I tried those. But, they remained pretty much hit and miss. No one could spot check every operation, and it seemed unfair to single out only the ones within reach.

One day, I looked at a stack of attendance reports, budget variances, analysis of problems we had experienced with some expensive equipment, overtime statistics, and other such things that were piling up on my credenza. Realizing I would never have time to go through them all before my secretary ultimately filed or tossed them, I decided I either had to find a way for getting value out of them or taking my name off distribution. So, I broke them down and pushed them out to the frontline managers responsible for their various work units and teams. Guess what? They were the best people to get the reports. Why? Because they recognized every person and line item mentioned, knew instinctively what was working and what was out of line, and welcomed the chance to use them to keep score. It saved me a lot of work and put the right yardstick in the hands of the people who needed to measure in inches and feet every month the kinds of things I could only afford to look at in miles and on a quarterly basis. Besides, their own teams started looking forward to the details to know how well they did compared to another team at a different plant or compared to their own performance a year ago.

A great example was overtime. By parceling out OT reports to each manager and team, we saved $1.5 million the first year—just by looking through the eyes of the people closest to the affected areas. The same kind of cost savings occurred when we figured out how to do this with cellular telephone bills.

There is no substitute for displaying results for everyone to see. This is what makes metrics meaningful. Otherwise, employees treat what you are telling them like just an opinion.

B. TWO-PERSON RULE

It used to be called the two-man rule, or the two-person-integrity rule. According to one classified program's description of how this works, the rule is designed to bar access to a sensitive area or asset by any lone individual. Two authorized employees are considered present when they are physically in a position where they can positively identify use of unauthorized procedures in relation to the operation at hand. The two-person team must be knowledgeable of safety and security requirements, and both individuals must be present during any activity requiring access to sensitive areas or equipment. Each of the two is responsible for enforcing the two-person rule at all times while in the sensitive area where the rule applies.

C. A BUSINESS DECISION TO FAVOR INFILTRATORS

I would not target an insider already in place because the task of identifying an appropriate and vulnerable employee who could be recruited is too difficult, and failure would compromise my program.

One way to insulate the attack from compromise is to keep the infiltrator unaware of the ultimate objective. This could also help the infiltrator pass a background check, particularly if the details of the operation were spectacular enough to make him nervous, if he were aware of them. His time on the job would be spent figuring how to bypass technical countermeasures. He would act "normal," fit in, and be part of the team.

D. SMALL WORLD INSIDER CHALLENGES

Recruiting an agent is impossible in small town environments or small utilities where the locals all know each other intimately. In many ways, these environments create a degree of transparency that becomes lifelong and remains very insular. Outsiders spend years trying to achieve the same level of trust that is automatically conferred to Bobby Joe's grandson who is also the nephew of Rita Sue, the mayor's sister. In these places, infiltration is most effective via contractors.

Contract employees in place for extended periods of construction tend to be unescorted and gain unlimited access to critical areas because there is nobody to watch them. Companies often employ non-English–speaking workers who are faceless and interchangeable in their eyes, as long as they can meet the requirements of hard labor associated with construction work.

E. WHY NO "BROKEN WINDOWS" IN INFRASTRUCTURE DEFENSE

The reasons we have not extended these concepts from protecting communities to institutions and infrastructure are that we assume infrastructure is under private control. So, it becomes someone else's problem. Also, the traditional labor-management and public right-to-know pressures have dominated in the boardroom and in regulatory decision-making environments, thereby reducing the market for or receptivity to such concepts. Moreover, when there is success in altering the culture of these institutions, the victories tend to be attributed to and monopolized by the founder or chief executive. In reality, whether it is a teacher presiding in a classroom or a cop maintaining order on the streets of the precinct, or a Fortune 500 CEO bringing a company back from the brink of bankruptcy—no one does it alone. This achievement requires a sense of ownership on the part of all the people on the team. With it, amazing things happen. Without it, even mediocrity may remain out of reach.

Index

A

Accepted wisdom, 17–18, 156
Accepted wisdom, problems and limits of
   historical approaches
      on complications and cases, 7–8
      cyber-centric bias, limits of, 9
      on cyber insiders, 8
      existential threats, losing sight of, 8–9
      on hostile insiders, 5–6
      on motivations, 6
   implications, 9
   infiltrators, 4
   insider threat, 4
   overview of, 3
   terms of reference, 4–5
Accreditations, 79
Accusatory approaches, 98, 100–101
Active disruption, threat scale, 226, 231–232
   exploiting assets, 236
   organizational actions, 232
   threat perceiver actions, 231–232
   violence and, 234
Adaptable threats, 284
Adjudicative process, 82
   of adverse background checks, 90
   of adverse findings, 80–81
Adversary group, 143
Agents of change, *see* Corporate sentinels;
      Leaders and copilots
Aggregation of cases, 8
Agreement (sample), 276
All-Find investigations, 84–85
American airline security, 106
American traitors, 7
Arcane indicators, 75
Assets, exploitation of
   threat scale, 235–237
Attack
   anticipated yield of, 148
   desired, perceived effort for, 146–147
Attacker, perceived risk for, 147–148
Attacking, justification for, 148–149

Authorities, 140
   biases of, *see* Lawful disruption of insider
      threat
   collaboration with, 143–144

B

Background investigation
   adjudication of adverse findings, 80–81
   blurred accountability, 79
   case study
      all-find's approach, 84–85
      business outcome, 85–86
      pro-back approach, 85
      setting, 84
   credentials and credibility, 78–79
   defined, 75–76
   identity verification, 77
   nonemployee investigation, 86–87
   traditional process, 76–77
   transformational opportunities with No
      Dark Corners approach, 81–84
   trust betrayers, 78
   turnaround time, 77
Background updates, 68
Behavioral detection, 104–106; *see also*
      Deception and insider threat
Behavioral profiling, *see* Behavioral detection
Behaviors, characterization of, *see* Lawful
      disruption of insider threat
Betrayers, *see* Trust betrayal
Biases of authorities, *see* Lawful disruption of
      insider threat
Biometrics, 148
Business Executives for National Security
      (BENS), 191
Business networking sites
   intimacy and, 249–250

C

Canadian intelligence, 151
Capabilities
   postmortem redesign, 264

for strategic anticipation, 265–266
for sudden impact response, 263
Case study compilations and biographical
          narratives, 5, 6, 7
Catharsis, facilitating, 152
Citizen-soldiers, 8
Close probation, 28, 31
Collaboration, team members, 246
Commission on Critical Infrastructure
          Protection, 9, 179
Compensation, 271–272
Computer forensics expert, 41, 170
Computer industry and warning fatigue, 207
Concealment technique, 93
Consultants, 259
    role of, 269–270
Consultation, 82
Consultative escalation process, 83
Contamination threats, 144
Context-based anomaly detection, 119–120
Control Objectives for Information and related
          Technology (COBIT), 8
Conversation, 110–111
Copilot model, 26–29
    contrast with traditional strategy, 27–28
    new insider defenses
        close probation, 28
        team self-monitoring, 29
        transparency on job, 28–29
Copilots, 110; see also Leaders and copilots
Core employees, 247, 248–249
Corporate policy, 80
Corporate self-destruction, prevention of, 166
Corporate sentinels, 22, 23, 32, 281
    case study, 42–44
    cronyism/favor exchange, 45
    defined, 41
    dishonest employees, 47
    disruptions, 150–151
    expertise and alienation, 41–42
    guide to people security, 46
    human relationships, 46–47
    imperial overreach/power play, 44–45
    key activities for No Dark Corners, 39–40
    management responsibility in loss
          prevention, 47
    to other employees, 53
    outline of, 39
    perfunctory adaptation, 44
    personal safety and self-defence, 48
    pre-employment screening, 48
    procedural controls, 47–48
    security and civil rights, 51–52
    security practitioner for atisans, 53–55

sentinel alienation, 44
traditional role, 41
transformational role in No Dark Corners
          approach, 45–46
unfair labor practices, 50–51
workplace violence, 49–50
Cost–benefit analysis, 148
Counter-elicitation behaviors, 218, 224
Coworkers, 23, 49
Credentials
    and credibility, 78–79
    false, 31
Critical infrastructures, 179
Cronyism, 45
Cross-examination, 103; see also Deception
          and insider threat
Crowd, 238–240
    control techniques, 241
    in sporting event, 241
Crying wolf syndrome, 207
Curse of the indelicate obvious (in financial
          crimes), 121
Cyber attacks, 6
Cyber-centric bias, limits of, 9
Cyber insiders, 8
Cyber security specialists, 8

D
Dark Corners in workplace, 279–280
Debriefing, 109
Decapitation attacks through assassination,
          182–183
Deceiver's edge, 106–107
Deception
    detection
        interviewing to, 99–101
        representative methods for, 95
    from trust betrayers, 111–113
Deception and insider threat
    behavioral detection
        background, 104
        features, 105–106
        Israeli-style method (case study),
            104–105
        limitations, 106
    context-based anomaly detection, 119–120
    cross-examination
        background, 103
        features, 103
        limitations, 103
    deceiver's edge, 106–107
    deception detection
        interviewing to, 99–101
        representative methods for, 95

deception from trust betrayers, 111–113
detection dilemma, 118–119
disgruntled insiders, 116–118
in financial crimes, 121
inadequacy of defenses, 94
infiltrator's deception
  after probation, 115
  during probation period, 114, 115
  screening process, 112, 114
liars, 107
No Dark Corners applications, 107–111
  conversation, 110–111
  debriefing, 109
  elicitation, 111
  interrogation, 108–109
  interviewing, 110
polygraph examiners, 95–96
Reid technique
  background, 96
  features of, 97
  limitations, 97
role of deception, 93–94
  in scenarios, 128–129
sample scenarios, 122–128
scientific content analysis
  background, 101–102
  deception detection techniques,
    102–103
  features of, 102
  limitations, 102
in training environment, 121–122
WZ method
  background, 98
  features, 98
  limitations, 98–99
Deep smarts, 9
Defender-produced disruptions, 136
Defenders, 138, 142
  capacity of, 20–21
  dilemmas, 138–139
Defensible Space, 29, 30
Deflectors, 225
Delphi method, 17
Delphi research, 3, 9
Delphi research on insider threat
  accepted wisdom, 17–18
  alternative analysis
    infiltrator's challenges versus defender's
      capacity, 20–21
    infiltrator versus disgruntled careerist,
      18–20
    information gathering, 22–23
    standard screening process, 21–22
    vulnerabilities, exploitation of, 24

case study, 16–17
comparative study, 29–32
desired end-state facing infiltrator, 24–26
overview of, 15–16
trust and transparency, balancing, 26–29
  contrast with traditional strategy,
    27–28
  new insider defenses, 28–29
Delphi respondents, 18
Department of Homeland Security (DHS)
  existential threat defense with, 186–187
  protective security advisors, 188–191
Desired end-state facing infiltrator, 24–26
Detectives, 139, 140
DHS, see Department of Homeland Security
Disgruntled careerist, 18–20
Disgruntled insiders, 113
  deception of, 116–118
Dishonest employees, 47
Disruptions
  defender-produced, 136
  employer-induced, see Lawful disruption of
    insider threat
  at top, 165–167
Distress call and unpredicted turn of events,
    see Lawful disruption of insider
    threat
Domestic violence, 218
Draconian security measures, 24
Drucker, Peter, 57, 66, 168–169, 178, 247,
    273

E
Elicitation, 111, 128, 269
Embezzlers, 220
  and countermeasures, 221–222
Employee level in lawful disruption
    techniques, 149–152; see also Lawful
    disruption of insider threat
The enterprise-wide ethics program, 62
Epiphanies, 19
Equal opportunity, 52
Ericsson, Anders, 96, 181
Error reduction, 69
Escalating irritation, threat scale
  exploiting assets, 235
  organizational actions, 226, 231
  scaling note, 231
  threat perceiver actions, 226, 231
  violence and, 232–233
Escalation process, 83
Escorts, 87, 90
Espionage yielding decisive victory, 183
Executive attention, power of, 61–62

Exercises for group projects, 10, 32, 55, 71,
        91, 129, 172, 210, 286–287, 290–
        291, 293–294, 296–298, 299–301,
        302, 304–305, 306–307, 309–310,
        311–313, 314–315
Existential insider threat
    assistance with existential magnitude
            evaluation, 188
    case scenarios, 206
    dealing with infiltrators, 177
    decapitation attacks through assassination,
            182–183
    DHS protective security advisors, 188–191
    drawing from risk/vulnerability assessment
            team, 203–204
    duties for, 175–176
    espionage yielding decisive victory, 183
    existential threat defense with DHS,
            aligning, 186–187
    factors behind, 187–188
    homeland security, defining, 184–186
    kinds of, 178
    local task forces, 191–196
    overview of, 175
    people/property protection, 176–177
    priorities, 206–207
    red teaming
        defined, 196–197
        and nonexistential threats, 204–205
        value to counter, 201–203
    red team members
        from within, 203
        recruitment of, 197–201
    sabotage with cascading impacts, 178–180
        case study, 180–182
    software developer approach, 208
    spillover effects, 177–178
    threshold and accumulation, problems of,
            183–184
    in warning fatigue, 207–208
Existential magnitude evaluation, 188
Existential threats, 245
    defense with DHS, 186–187
Expertise and alienation, 41–42
Extortion, 51
    as indirect threat, 246

F
Failsafe, 83
Failure analysis/problem solving, risks in,
        144–146
Fair Credit Reporting Act, 22
False credentials, 31
Favor exchange, 45

Fees, 271–272
Feynman, Richard, 144–145, 264
Financial gain, 219–224
First-rate security practitioner, 54
Flash mob, 238–240
Focus
    of postmortem redesign, 264
    for strategic anticipation, 266
    of sudden impact response, 263
Foreign Corrupt Practices Act, 63
Frontal attacks, 3

G
Gates, Bill, 243
Gladwell, Malcolm, 96, 197
Government cyber/regulatory focus, 6
Grenade character, 154
Groupthink, 144

H
Handy, Charles, 247
Hijacking, 244–246
Hiring decisions for managers, 82–83
Hiring manager, 82, 110
Hoffman, Bruce, 175
Homeland security, defining, 184–186
Homeland Security Advisory System (HSAS),
        207
Hostile insider, 5–6, 112, 121, 146
    detection, 42
Human assaults on security, 46
Human behavior, 49
Human Intelligence (HUMINT) collection,
        99, 108
Human relationships, 46–47
Hybrid prescriptions, 261
Hypocrisy, 58

I
Identification and barrier systems, 48
Identity verification, 77, 90
Imperial overreach, 44–45
Impostors, 222–223
Indirect threat
    extortion as, 246
Individual motivations and psychosocial
        context, 5, 6
Infiltrators, 4, 19–20, 78, 146, 286
    case study, 128
    challenges of, and defender's capacity,
            20–21
    dealing with, 177
    deception of, 112, 114, 115; see also
            Deception and insider threat

versus disgruntled careerist, 18–20
  suspected, disrupting, 156–160
  traditional approach for, 20
Informal information, 49
Information processing, 63
Information Sharing and Analysis Center
    (ISAC), 198
Information technology (IT) network use
    violations, 5
In-house resources, 84
Inside attacker, 148
Insider defenses
  case study, 268–269
  close probation, 28
  team self-monitoring, 29
  transparency on job, 28–29
Insider exploitation opportunity, 43
Insider risk, unchecked, 204
Insider's guilt/justification for attacking,
    148–149
Insider threats, 4, 6; *see also* Deception and
    insider threat; Lawful disruption of
    insider threat
  changing workplace dynamics, 247
  crowds, 238–240
  defenses, 58–59
  early detection, 246
  flash mob, 238–240
  instant intimacy, 249–250
  lynch mob, 238–240
  misguided redeemers, 243–244
  prodigal kin, 242–243
  sporting event, 241
  sympathizers, 237–238
  systematic approach to, 226–227
  threat scale, *see* Threat scale
  undermining contemporary, 241–242
  of workplace violence, disrupting, 160–162
Insider threat study
  Delphi questions, 317–325, 327–331
Insouciant sentinel, 44
Institutional defenses, reexamining, 284
Institutional insertion points, *see* No Dark
    Corners implementation, consulting
    for
Institutional leaders, 144
Institutional legal counsel, 52
Institutions, 4, 41, 52
Intelligence/need-to-know bias, 141–143
Intelligence officers, 7
Intent, 51
Intentional disruptions, 284
Intermediaries, 274, 275
Internal implementation, 261

Internal talent, 197
International Banking and Investments (IBI),
    260
Interpersonal skills, 149
Interrogation, 111, 120
Intervention, 119
Interviewing process, 99–101, 110
Intimacy, instant, 249–250
Intimate partner abuse, 218
Investigative bias, 141
Investigatory inquiries, purpose of, 48
Israeli-style method (case study), 104–105

J
Jobs
  discrimination, 150
  threats to, 218–219
Judgment calls, 143, 146

K
Kidnapping, 51
Kindall, Dorothy, 243
Kindall, Gary, 243
Know-it-all character, 154
Knowledgeable escort, 87, 90
Knowledge worker, 247, 248

L
Labor force, 247, 248
Law enforcement officials, 52
Lawful disruption of insider threat
  behaviors, characterization of
    grenade, 154
    know-it-all, 154
    maybe person, 155
    no person, 155
    nothing person, 155
    sniper, 153
    tank, 153
    think-they-know-it-all, 154
    whiner, 156
    yes person, 155
  biases of authorities
    intelligence/need-to-know bias, 141–143
    investigative bias, 141
    prosecutorial bias, 139–140
  case study, 136–138
  collaboration with authorities, 143–144
  comparative observations, 167–168
  defender dilemmas, 138–139
  definition of lawful disruption, 135–136
  distress call and unpredicted turn of events,
      169–172
    actual outcomes, sequence of, 171

disruptions, 170
    online/classroom discussions, 172
    potential outcomes, 170
  by employee level, 149–152
    corporate sentinel disruptions, 150–151
    leader disruptions, 150
    team member disruptions, 152–153
  employer-induced disruptions
    anticipated yield of attack, 148
    insider's guilt/justification for attacking,
        148–149
    perceived effort for desired attack,
        146–147
    perceived risk for attacker, 147–148
  layered offense
    disruption at top, 165–167
    insider threat of workplace violence,
        disrupting, 160–162
    suspected infiltrator, disrupting,
        156–160
    unexpected development, 163–165
  practice, 168–169
  risks in failure analysis and problem
      solving, 144–146
Layered offense, see Lawful disruption of
    insider threat
Leader disruptions, 150
Leaders and copilots
  case study, 66–67
  concepts, 57
  failures of, 62–63
  insider threat defenses, 58–59
  issue-attention cycle
    alarmed discovery, 64
    awareness of difficulties, 64–65
    gradual decline of public interest, 65
    post-problem, 65
    pre-problem, 63–64
  journey of, 61
  leaders, role of, 59
  No Dark Corners strategy, 67–70
  overconfidence, effects of, 57–58
  power of executive attention, 61–62
  to sentinels, attitude of, 58–59
  understanding of institution, 59–60
Legal labor actions, 50
Liars, 107
Licenses, verification of, 78
Litigation search, 81
Local task forces, 191–196
Los Angeles County Sheriff's Department
    (LASD), 192
Loss prevention, management responsibility
    in, 47

Lying, 121
Lynch mob, 238–240

M
Malefactors, 109
Malicious compliance with work instructions,
    151
Malicious insider, 4, 5, 77
Management responsibility in loss prevention,
    47
Managers, hiring decisions for, 82–83
Marketplace espionage, 21
Maybe person, 155
McVeigh, Timothy, 182
Media, 7
Metrics, 270–271
Minor malcontents, 225
Miranda requirements, 52
Motivations, studies on, 6

N
National Institute for Occupational Safety and
    Health, 8
National Labor Relations, 52
National security information protection,
    141–142
Nepotists, 223–224
Nervousness masking, 107
New hire probation, 90
No Dark Corners approach, 29, 30, 31, 67–70,
    217, 220
  applications, 107–111; see also Deception
      and insider threat
  key activities for, 39–40
  transformational opportunities with, 81–84
  transformational role in, 45–46
No Dark Corners environment, 177
No Dark Corners implementation, consulting
    for
  assignment at end, 280–284
  case study, 259–261
  changes, 272–274
    exemplars, 273–274
    pilot programs, 273
  comments on, 257
  common findings, 280–281
  features of, 274–277
  fees/compensation and effectiveness,
      271–272
  hybrid prescriptions, 261
  inside-outside dilemma, 258–261
  institutional defenses, reexamining, 284
  institutional insertion points
    application opportunities, 266–267

postmortem redesign, 263–265
   strategic anticipation, 265–266
   sudden impact response, 262–263
intensity and focus of, 283–284
intentional disruptions, 284
internal implementation, 261
navigation of, 277–280
outside diagnosis, 261
starting point for, 267–271
   metrics, 270–271
   objectives and resources, 270
   role of consultant, 269–270
   value, 271
Nokia, 181
Non-accusatory technique, 98, 110
Nonemployee investigation, 86–87
Nonexistential threats, 204–205
Non-sentinel work team member, 60
No person (individual), 155
Nothing person, 155
Nuisance level, threat scale, 226, 230–231
   exploiting assets, 235
   organizational actions, 226, 231
   threat perceiver actions, 226, 230–231
   violence and, 232–233

O
Occupational Safety and Health
   Administration (OSHA), 176
Open statements, 102
Open work environments, 115
Organizational actions, threat scale
   chronic, active disruption, 226, 232
   escalating irritation, 226, 231
   nuisance level, 226, 231
   unacceptable, proximate harm, 226, 232
Outside consultants, 259
Overconfidence, effects of, 57–58

P
Patrol systems, 48
People/property protection, 176–177
People security, guide to, 46
Perfection, 61
Personal safety and self-defence, 48
Peters, Tom, 26
Physical confrontation, 218–219
Physical constraints, 52
Pilferers, 221
Police-centric membership, 191
Polygraph examiners, 95–96
Polygraph Protection Act, 96
Positive behaviors, 107
Postmortem redesign, 263–265

Power play, 44–45
Predictive profiling, *see* Behavioral detection
Pre-employment background investigation,
   69, 76
   case study, 84–86
Pre-employment screening, 48
Prioritization, 176, 206–207
Pro-Back investigations, 85
Problem solving, risks in, 144–146
Product contamination, 144
Pronouns in SCAN, 102
Prosecuting attorneys, 140
Prosecution, 138
Prosecutorial bias, 139–140
Protected labor actions, 50
Protective Security Advisors (PSA)
   incident management, 189
   information sharing, facilitating, 189–190
      during incidents, 190
      owner/operator requests, 190
      Regional Resilience Assessment Program
         (RRAP), 190
   infrastructure protection enhancement, 189
   role of, 189
Proximate harm, threat scale, 226, 232
   exploiting assets, 236–237
   organizational actions, 232
   threat perceiver actions, 232
   violence and, 234
Public interest, gradual decline of, 65

Q
Questions, 10, 32, 55, 71, 91, 129, 172, 209, 286
   for online/classroom discussion, 289–290,
      291–293, 294–296, 298–299, 301,
      303, 305–306, 307–309, 310–311,
      313–314

R
Random audits, 22
Rationalization, 98
Redeemers, misguided
   insider threats, 243–244
Red team formation, 264, 267
Red teaming, *see* Existential insider threat
Red team members, 197–201, 203
Regional intelligence personnel, 142
Regional Resilience Assessment Program
   (RRAP), 190
Reid technique, 95, 96–07; *see also* Deception
   and insider threat
Representative methods for deception
   detection, 95
Reputation, 184

Retaliation, 117
Risk assessment, 60
Risk/vulnerability assessment team, 203–204
Rotational assignments, 69–70

S
Sabotage with cascading impacts, 178–180,
        180–182
Sapir, Avinoam, 96
SCAN, *see* Scientific content analysis (SCAN)
School violence, 118, 119, 120
Scientific content analysis (SCAN), 101–103;
        see also Deception and insider threat
Searches, 52
Secondary security controls, 148
Security and civil rights, 51–52
Security design enhancements, 48
Security practitioner, 31
        for atisans, 53–55
Self-aggrandizement, 224–225
Self-monitoring team, 69
Self-quiz, 88–90
Self-styled victims, 224
Sentinel alienation, 44
Sentinel monitoring of employee performance, 68
Shamrock framework, institution, 247–249
Shunning, 151
Sniper, 153
Social engineering, 216
Social networking sites
        intimacy and, 249–250
Society for Human Resource Management,
        218–219
Software developer approach, 208
Software license agreements, 8
Spillover effects, 177–178
Sporting events, 241
Standard screening process, 21–22
Statutory violations, 51
Sudden impact response, 262–263
Sullivan, J., 192
Supervisory control and data acquisition
        (SCADA), 23
Surveillance, 50–51
Suspected infiltrator, disrupting, 156–160
Suspected insider threat, 152
Suspension, 166
Sympathizers, 237–238

T
Tank, 153
Team members, 149
        disruptions, 152–153
Team self-monitoring, 29

Telepresence technology, 217–218
Termination, 166
Terrorism Early Warning (TEW) Group, 192–195
Terrorist attack prevention, 4
Think-they-know-it-all, 154
Thought interruption technique, 136
Threat management program, 49
Threat perceiver actions, threat scale
        chronic, active disruption, 226, 231–232
        escalating irritation, 226, 231
        nuisance level, threat scale, 226, 230–231
        unacceptable, proximate harm, 226, 232
Threat scale, 226–237
        active disruption, 226, 231–232
        escalating irritation, 226, 231
        exploiting assets, 235–237
        illustration, 227–230
        nuisance level, 226, 230–231
        rating and level, 226, 230–232
        sympathizers, 237–238
        threats of violence, 232–234
Threats of violence, 218–219, 232–234
Threshold and accumulation, problems of,
        183–184
Timing
        for postmortem redesign, 264
        for strategic anticipation, 266
        for sudden impact response, 263
Tolerance, 184
Townsend, Robert, 46
Training investment, 108
Transparency
        on job, 28–29, 69
        and trust, 26–29
Transportation Security Administration (TSA),
        106
Trust, 220
        betrayal, 4, 6, 7, 21, 79, 93
        literature, 6
        and transparency, balancing, 26–29
Trust betrayer, 57, 64, 78, 147, 178
        deception from, 111–113
Turnaround time for background
        investigation, 77

U
Undercover investigations, 50
Unfair labor practices, 50–51
United Flight 93, 244–246

V
Vandalism, 4
Verbal threats, 218–219
Video surveillance, 51

Violence, threat scale, 232–234
Vulnerability
    assessment, 177
        team, 203–204
    exploitation of, 24

W
Warning fatigue, 207–208
Whiner, 156
Whistleblowers, 224–225
Wicklander–Zulawski (WZ) method, 98–99;
        see also Deception and insider threat
Willful ignorance, 83

Women and partner violence, 218
Workplace
    dynamics, changing, 247
    dysfunction, 146
    safety, 69
    violence, 49–50
        insider threat of, 160–162
Work verification, 69
WZ method, *see* Wicklander–Zulawski (WZ)
        method

Y
Yes person, 155